Contents

Active Reading

"[T]hey understood that the woman was troubled, and that what she was doing had nothing to do with sexual titillation; it was more of a cry for help."

2

The Reading-Writing Connection 15

3

Strategies for Conveying Ideas: *Narration* and *Description*   29

4

Strategies for Making a Point:
Example and *illustration*   69

5

Strategies for Clarifying Meaning: *Definition* and *Explanation*   109

6

Strategies for Sorting Ideas: *Classification* and *Division*   144

7

Strategies for Examining Two Subjects: *Comparison* and *contrast*   184

8

Strategies for Explaining How Things Work:
Process and *Directions*   223

9

Strategies for Analyzing Why Things Happen: *Cause* and *Effect* 254

10

Strategies for Influencing Others:
Argument and *Persuasion*   293

"The health and well-being of American citizens should not be placed in the hands of those who rely on biased rumors and media hype."

"[O]ur conviction is that birth and adoption are the purview of married heterosexual couples."

"I was shocked, truly shocked. But you know what? I also didn't care. Those two women did a helluva job of raising one fine man. A helluva job."

"At its most fundamental level, what we call 'creative violence'—head-bonking cartoons, bloody videogames, playground karate, toy guns—gives children a tool to master their rage."

"We are now a society in which the chief form of play for millions of young-sters is making large numbers of people die. Hurting and maiming others is the central fun activity in video games played so addictively by the young."

11

Combining Strategies: Further Readings   344

Appendix: WRITING WITH SOURCES   363

Thematic Contents

The Simon and Schuster

SHORT PROSE READER

Fifth Edition

ROBERT W. FUNK
Eastern Illinois University

SUSAN X DAY
University of Houston

LINDA S. COLEMAN
Eastern Illinois University

ELIZABETH McMAHAN
Illinois State University

Upper Saddle River, New Jersey 07458

Cataloging-in-Publication data available from the Library of Congress.

The Simon & Schuster short prose reader / [compiled by] Robert
W. Funk . . . [et al.]. —5th ed.
  p. cm.
  Includes bibliographical references and index.
  ISBN-13: 978-0-13-601455-3
  ISBN-10: 0-13-601455-0
  1. College readers.   2. English language—Rhetoric—Problems,
exercises, etc.   3. Report writing—Problems, exercises, etc.
I. Funk, Robert.   II. Title: Simon and Schuster short prose
reader.
  PE1417.S453 2008
  808'.0427—dc22

                                        2008004572

Editorial Director: Leah Jewell
Editor-in-Chief: Craig Campanella
Editorial Assistant: Tracy Clough
Marketing Director: Brandy Dawson
Marketing Manager: Lindsey Prudhomme
Text Permission Specialist: Jane Scelta
Senior Operations Supervisor:
  Sherry Lewis
Operations Specialist: Christina Amato
Project Manager: Maureen Benicasa
Director, Image Resource Center:
  Melinda Patelli

Manager, Cover Visual Research &
  Permissions: Karen Sanatar
Manager, Visual Research: Beth Brenzel
Image Researcher: Melinda Alexander
Full-Service Production
  and Composition: Pine Tree
  Composition
Full-Service Project Management:
  John Shannon
Printer/Binder: Courier Companies
Cover Printer: Courier Companies

Credits and acknowledgments borrowed from other sources and reproduced, with permission, in this textbook appear on appropriate page within text (or on pages 385–386).

Pearson Education Ltd., London
Pearson Education Singapore, Pte. Ltd
Pearson Education Canada, Inc.
Pearson Education-Japan
Pearson Education Australia PTY, Limited

Pearson Education North Asia Ltd, Hong Kong
Pearson Educación de Mexico, S.A. de C.V.
Pearson Education Malaysia, Pte. Ltd
Pearson Education Upper Saddle River,
  New Jersey

PEARSON
Prentice
Hall

10 9 8 7 6 5 4 3 2 1
ISBN-13: 978-0-13-601455-3
ISBN-10:   0-13-601455-0

Education and Learning

Language and Writing

Minority Perspectives

Gender

Human Behavior

Social Issues

Editing Skills:
Contents

Chapter 7 Strategies for Examining Two Subjects:
Comparison and *Contrast*

Twain, "Two Views of the Mississippi"	Quotation marks inside quotations
Britt, "Neat People vs. Sloppy People"	Using apostrophes
O'Shaughnessy, "A Whole New Ballgame"	Choosing *its* or *it's*
Seal, "The Trouble with Talent"	Using dashes

Chapter 8 Strategies for Explaining How Things Work:
Process and *Directions*

Fleischman, "Shopping Can Be a Challenge"	Using parentheses
Keillor, "How to Write a Personal Letter"	Using short sentences for emphasis
Nelson, "Making Fake Flakes"	Punctuating quotations

Chapter 9 Strategies for Analyzing Why Things Happen:
Cause and *Effect*

Ullman, "The Boss in the Machine"	Using commas
King, "Why We Crave Horror Movies"	Checking pronoun reference
Wong, "Fifth Chinese Daughter"	Using parallel structure
Critser, "Supersize Me"	Eliminating wordiness

Chapter 10 Strategies for Influencing Others:
Argument and *Persuasion*

Debate: Same-Sex Parents	Subject-verb agreement
Debate: Violent Media	Using questions
Perspectives on Immigration to the U.S.	Using colons

Preface

Good readers are usually good writers, and good writers are always good readers. Researchers tell us that reading and writing are complementary processes that involve the use of language to create meaning. This text is designed to reinforce this relationship and to encourage reading by students who want to improve their writing. The selections are short and lively, not too difficult, but rich enough to provide ideas for thought and discussion. The instructional apparatus accompanying each reading has two main goals:

1. to encourage students to use writing as a means of exploring the readings, and
2. to point out strategies used in the essays that students can employ in their own compositions.

The Simon and Schuster Short Prose Reader is a flexible resource. The numerous readings, activities, and writing topics give instructors the freedom to select from a broad range of assignments and approaches.

NEW TO THE FIFTH EDITION

Features new to this edition include the following:

- A comprehensive appendix on **Writing with Sources,** which includes a sample documented student essay and offers guidance for locating and evaluating secondary sources, incorporating paraphrases and quotations, avoiding plagiarism, and documenting sources using **MLA** style.
- Two sets of paired readings that **debate** the pros and cons of same-sex parenting and the influence of violent media (Chapter 10).
- A suite of articles and graphics that offer differing **Perspectives on Immigration to the United States** (Chapter 10).
- Chapter-opening **images** (photographs, advertisements, cartoons, diagrams) that introduce students to each rhetorical strategy and encourage them to make connections between the print and visual texts.
- A process selection that combines written text with **photographs** to illustrate the art of movie makeup (Chapter 8).
- Additional help in understanding and creating **tone** (Chapter 1 and throughout the book).
- Updated links to **Web sites** where students can find additional information about the readings and their authors.

- **Thirteen new readings,** including selections by Lilly Gonzalez, Franklin Zimring, Jeff Pearlman, John Leo, Robert Samuelson, Arnold Schwarzenegger, and Anna Quindlen, along with **four new student essays.** Many favorites by Russell Baker, Judith Cofer, Brent Staples, Gloria Naylor, Isaac Asimov, Judith Viorst, Suzanne Britt, Mark Twain, Wayson Choy, Stephen King, Jade Snow Wong, Garrison Keillor, and Langston Hughes have been held over from previous editions.

These additions strengthen the key features that have made the first four editions of *The Simon and Schuster Short Prose Reader* a popular and successful text.

THE READING SELECTIONS

The readings are brief, accessible, and easy to teach. They cover a wide range of topics and viewpoints to involve students with ideas and issues that relate to their own experience and also expand their understanding of people, places, and ideas. A special effort has been made to appeal to a cross section of students by including a number of works by women and writers from diverse cultural backgrounds. Many of the selections are standard pieces that have been used successfully in writing classes; others are new readings that have never been anthologized before.

ORGANIZATION

The readings are grouped according to their major pattern of organization and presented as strategies for approaching a given writing task. The introduction to each strategy explains the point, the principles, and the pitfalls of using this particular pattern. An Images and Ideas page begins each introduction with a relevant visual accompanied by questions that draw connections between the image and the chapter's rhetorical strategy. This opening material is followed by four published essays (seven in Chapter 10) and a student essay that further illustrate the strategy. Chapter 11 provides four additional essays that combine strategies in a variety of ways.

INSTRUCTIONAL FEATURES

Two **introductory chapters** present a concise explanation of the interrelated processes of reading and writing. Chapter 1 gives specific directions for learning how to become active readers, including a sample reading that has been annotated by an active reader. Chapter 2 describes the process of writing in response to reading. It includes a sample student essay and a brief reading to respond to and write about.

The **prereading apparatus** includes three instructional aids: (1) a brief thinking/writing activity (Preparing to Read) that gets students ready to read by evoking thoughts and feelings on the subject of the reading; (2) a short biographical headnote that provides a context for reading; and (3) a list of Terms to Recognize that defines potentially unfamiliar words in the selection.

The **postreading apparatus** includes a selection of activities that instructors can assign, as needed, to help students increase their skills in reading and writing:

1. *Responding to Reading*—a journal-writing or possible in-class assignment that asks students to record their reactions to an issue or idea in the selection they have just read. This brief activity promotes fluency and may be used as the basis for the essay assignments that follow.

2. *Considering Content*—a series of questions that assist students in becoming focused, attentive readers. Answering these questions assures basic comprehension.

3. *Considering Method*—several questions that help students to identify successful strategies in the reading and to examine rhetorical choices that the author made.

4. *Writing Step by Step*—a sequence of specific directions that guide students in writing a short essay imitating the reading's structure and purpose. This directed writing can be used to provide inexperienced writers with a successful composing experience.

5. *Other Writing Ideas*—additional writing assignments that relate to the rhetorical mode or subject matter of the reading. These assignments, which include a mix of personal and academic topics, focus on Collaborative Writing, Using the Internet, and Writing about Reading.

6. *Gaining Word Power*—an exercise that examines words and phrases from the reading selection and promotes active vocabulary building.

7. *Editing Skills*—an exercise that assists students in checking and improving the essay they have just written. Each editing section focuses on a different skill, one that pertains to some grammatical, mechanical, or rhetorical feature of the reading selection.

This extensive apparatus gives teachers and students a wide variety of choices for exploring the reading-writing connection.

OTHER FEATURES

To help instructors who want to correlate reading assignments or organize their courses according to issue-centered units, the **Thematic Contents** groups the reading selections according to several common themes. The text also includes a guide to **Editing Skills** and their locations within chapters. With these references, instructors can direct individual students to sections addressing their particular editing problems.

INSTRUCTIONAL SUPPLEMENTS

Instructors using the fifth edition of *The Simon and Schuster Short Prose Reader* will receive pedagogical advice and support from two new ancillaries:

- A thirty-two page **Teaching Guide**, bound directly into the back of the text, that contains directions for using the book, suggested teaching strategies, chapter previews, ideas for teaching the use of secondary sources, and advice and guidelines for teaching all or part of the course online.
- An online **Instructor's Web Site** that includes responses to all the postreading questions in the text, answers to the vocabulary and editing skills exercises, teaching tips and background information on the readings, guidance for implementing the writing assignments, and suggestions for making connections among the readings in the book.
- The online Web site also provides materials and advice for **Online Learning**, including digital copies of six pedagogical aids that appear with each reading in the textbook and suggestions for importing these features into online course management systems.

ACKNOWLEDGMENTS

We want to extend appreciation and thanks to the many people who have helped us in producing this book, especially our editors and the editorial staff at Prentice Hall: Leah Jewell, Craig Campanella, and Deborah Doyle. We are indebted to the students in our writing classes for field-testing the assignments and for providing us with inspiration and insights as well as sample essays. We are also grateful for the excellent ideas and suggestions provided by our reviewers: Shelly Beard, Owens State Community College; Constantina Michalos, Houston Baptist University; Joyce Stoffers, Southwestern Oklahoma State University; and Daniel Cano, Santa Monica College. And of course we must thank Bill, Brian, Casey, and Danny for their patience, support, and encouragement.

Robert Funk
Susan X Day
Linda S. Coleman
Elizabeth McMahan

CHAPTER 1

Active Reading

Most people who write well also read well—and vice versa. The two skills are so intertwined that they are often taught together, as we do in this textbook. Reading gives you not only information and amusement, but also a sense of how sentences work and how paragraphs are best organized. Most of the time, you get this sense without really paying attention: it just seeps into your mind with the rest of the material. In this textbook, we ask you to make the reading-writing connection more consciously than you may have done before. By looking carefully at good writing, you will better understand the content as well as the techniques the writers use. And by being aware of yourself as a reader, you will develop useful strategies for attracting and keeping the attention of your own readers.

LEARNING TO BE AN ACTIVE READER

Did you ever finish reading something, look up from the page, and realize that you didn't take in anything at all? That you passed your eyes over the print, but you might as well have stared out the window? At such times, you know that you have been an extremely passive reader. On the opposite end of the spectrum, you've probably had the experience of being swept away from reality while reading, so involved in the printed word that the rest of your world fades. Much of your college reading won't be able to carry you off that completely. By learning to be an **active reader,** though, you will be able to handle your reading assignments competently—remembering more and using what you have learned more effectively. The main idea is to stay involved with the reading through interaction—bringing mental and emotional energy to the task.

KEEPING A JOURNAL

One good way to become an interactive reader is to keep a journal about your reading. In a journal, you can experiment with ideas and express your responses with greater freedom than you can in formal writing assignments. Before each reading selection in most chapters of this book, we ask you a Preparing to Read question, which you may answer in your journal as well as in class discussions. This activity starts you thinking about the ideas you will find in the essay that follows. After each selection, we give you a Responding to Reading suggestion to consider in your journal, encouraging you to write about your personal reactions. You will see as this chapter goes along how your two journal entries fit into your role as an active reader.

PREVIEWING THE READING

If you're the type who simply plunges into a reading assignment, you're missing something. Study skills experts emphasize the value of previewing the reading, getting your mind ready for full comprehension. **Previewing** involves more than merely counting the number of pages you have to go: no one needs to remind you to do that! The trick is to develop a mental set that makes your brain most receptive to the material.

Title

Try stopping after you read the **title** and asking yourself what it suggests to you. The sample essay we use in this chapter is named "Handled with Care." Where have you heard such a phrase before? What image does it bring to your mind? The title often gives you a clue about what's ahead.

Author and Other Publication Facts

With some assignments, you will recognize the author's name. Bob Greene is the writer of "Handled with Care," and you may know that he was a longtime columnist for the *Chicago Tribune*. You may also know that his columns often comment on culture and politics and the connections between them. Again, the author's name provides clues about the essay that follows. You may know something about the time period when it was written (as you would if the byline reads "Mark Twain"). Similarly, if the byline reads "Dave Barry," you can expect something humorous about modern life.

Even when you don't recognize the author, you can take note of other publication facts. The date of publication, if you have it, gives you an idea of how current the information is. If the reading is reprinted, as the ones in this textbook are, consider where it originally appeared and whether that means anything to you. If an essay first showed up in *U.S. News and World Report,* you can assume it will have a conservative political slant; if it came from *The Nation,* it will probably have a liberal viewpoint. If it came from a city newspaper, like the *Chicago Tribune,* you can't be so sure about the political perspective, since most big newspapers attempt to cover the spectrum.

Visual Features and Supplements

Page through the reading, notice its design, and look at parts that stand out from the ordinary print, such as headnotes, headings, photos, diagrams, boxed material, summaries, and questions after the reading. Your textbooks, like most of the successful Web pages you visit, are specially designed to include lots of these helpful materials. Unfortunately, many students skip them, thinking they're not as important as the rest. Actually, they are there to focus attention on what *is* important in the reading. Or they may give you information that assists you in understanding the reading; for example, the headnote paragraphs before essays in this textbook give a little biographical information about the writer. The Terms to Recognize section lists some difficult words from the essay and their definitions, so you won't have to look them up in the dictionary right away. In this list, we provide only the definition that fits the way the term is used in the reading; the term probably has other meanings as well.

Some reading material doesn't include any obvious help. It's just straight print. But you can benefit from the only visual clue: paragraph indentations. Read the first sentence of each paragraph. This survey will probably give you ideas about the content and organization of the reading.

Responses and Predictions

"This preview stuff just slows me down," you may be thinking. "I don't have time for it." Let us assure you, the first stage does seem slow, but it makes later stages faster and more efficient. It also markedly increases your memory for what you read.

The main thing you're doing as you preview is responding to clues and making predictions about what the reading contains. It may seem like a guessing game, but actually you are clearing the brush from pathways in your brain, making the way easy for the information to get through. Through guessing what to expect, you are directing your attention, focusing on the material so that it won't be fighting through a tangle of thoughts about why you squabble with your roommate and what you'll have for lunch.

Instead, let your mind wander through the associations and experiences you already have with the material suggested by your preview. What people, events, and feelings in your own life did you stumble across in your preview? If you are from Chicago, you are able to visualize the setting of the essay and may even be able to predict Bob Greene's overall style. Or the title, "Handled with Care," may have reminded you of a delicate package that happened to reach you intact, miraculously, through the mail.

A FIRST READING

Now is the time to plunge in. Try to place yourself in a setting that aids concentration. This setting varies from person to person, and you probably know your ideal situation. You can't always get it, but at least don't undermine yourself by choosing a spot where you know you'll be distracted or where you know you'll be lulled to sleep. Sitting up at a table or desk is a good idea because the position suggests that you are going to work.

You'll need a pencil, pen, or pad of Post-its to read interactively. Make it a habit. Mark words and terms that you need to look up later. Write questions— or just question marks—in the margins near material you don't quite understand. Write your spontaneous responses *(Yes! No! Reminds me of Aunt Selma! What!? Prejudiced crap!)* in the margins. Underline sentences that you think may contain the main ideas and phrases that impress you with the way they are worded. We provide one reader's markings of "Handled with Care" in this chapter.

STAYING AWARE OF CONVENTIONS

Conventions are the traditional ways of doing things: for example, we have conventional ways of beginning and ending telephone conversations, and we expect everyone to follow them. If a friend closed a phone conversation by saying, "Pick me up at 9:15," and immediately hung up, you would think it strange not to have any of the usual sign-off words. The same type of expectation goes for writing **conventions,** some of which we outline here. Stories and poems don't have to follow these conventions, but nonfiction works like essays, textbooks, and manuals do. You can enhance your reading by looking for conventional features as you go along. They provide clues to the author's purpose and help to break down complicated readings into manageable chunks.

Subject

Each piece of writing is expected to deal with one subject or topic. This should be fairly clear to you near the beginning, perhaps even from the title ("Why We Crave Horror Movies," in Chap. 9, is about exactly that). Once you identify the subject, you can be pretty sure the whole reading will stay on that topic.

Main Idea or Thesis

We expect a reading not only to have a subject but also to say something *about* the subject. That is the **thesis** or main idea. Frequently, the main idea comes up early in the reading, clearly expressed in one sentence. At other times, you must put together the main point piece by piece as you read. It may finally be stated in a sentence at the end, or it may not be stated directly at all. As you read, underline sentences that seem to add to your understanding of the author's main point.

Supporting Material

Writers must prove their main points by providing convincing **supporting material.** This can be in the form of logical reasoning, emotional appeal, examples, evidence from experts, specific details, facts, and statistics. Different main points and different readers lend themselves to different types of supporting material; for example, your math textbook uses mostly logical reasoning and examples, while an essay about capital punishment might use all the forms we listed. While you read an assignment, ask yourself: *What forms of supporting material does this author use and are they appropriate for the intended audience?*

Patterns of Organization

The conventions of subject, thesis, and supporting material deal with the content of the reading. You also need to look at *how* the content is presented. After each selection in the following chapters, you will see questions called Considering Content and Considering Method. The method questions ask you to consider the techniques the author used to present material, including organization.

We organize the chapters in this book according to **patterns of development** that are the most conventional ways to organize writing: patterns such as comparison and contrast, cause and effect, and narration. Each chapter explains one basic pattern, though in practice, most authors combine several strategies to support and develop their central pattern. As you read an essay, notice how the writer uses patterns to arrange ideas.

Paragraphs

As a reader, you will also notice how writers package their meaning in units of thought called **paragraphs.** Paragraph indention usually signals the introduction of a new topic or a new aspect of a current topic. In other words, writers start new paragraphs to show that they are moving on to another topic or subtopic. Paragraphs in prose essays tend to be longer than paragraphs in newspapers and magazines, where journalists break their paragraphs frequently to make narrow columns of type easier to read.

Transitions

Another element of a writer's method involves how he or she makes connections between ideas. These connections are called **transitions.** A common place for a transition is between two paragraphs (at the end of one and/or at the beginning of the next one), where the author shows the logical relationship between them. Recognizing transitions helps you direct your thought process in the way the author wants you to. For example, a paragraph that begins "Furthermore, . . ." lets you know that you should expect material that adds to and agrees with the material before it. A paragraph that begins "On the other hand, . . ." lets you know that you should expect material that contradicts or shows the opposite of the material before it. By noticing transitions, you prepare the appropriate mindset for understanding what comes next.

A SAMPLE ESSAY

Handled with Care

∙∙∙

BOB GREENE

The day the lady took her clothes off on Michigan Avenue, people were leaving downtown as usual. The workday had come to an end; men and women were heading for bus and train stations, in a hurry to get home. 1

She walked south on Michigan; she was wearing a white robe, as if she had been to the beach. She was blond and in her thirties. As she passed the Radisson Hotel, Roosevelt Williams, a doorman, was opening the door of a cab for one of the hotel's guests. The woman did not really pause while she walked; she merely shrugged the robe off, and it fell to the sidewalk. She was wearing what appeared to be the bottom of a blue bikini bathing suit, although one woman who was directly next to her said it was just underwear. She wore nothing else. 2

Williams at first did not believe what he was seeing. If you hang around long enough, you will see everything: robberies, muggings, street fights, murders. But a naked woman on North Michigan Avenue? Williams had not seen that before and neither, apparently, had the other people on the street. 3

It was strange; her white robe lay on the sidewalk, and by all accounts she was smiling. But no one spoke to her. A report in the newspaper the next day quoted someone: "The cars were stopping, the people on the buses were staring, people were shouting, and people were taking pictures." But that is not what other people who were there that afternoon said. The atmosphere was not carnival-like, they said. Rather, they said, it was as if something very sad was taking place. It took only a moment for people to realize that this was not some stunt designed to promote a product 4 or a movie. Without anything telling them, they understood that the woman was troubled, and that what she was doing had nothing to do with sexual titillation; it was more of a cry for help.

The cry for help came in a way that such cries often come. The woman was violating one of the basic premises of the social fabric. She was doing something that is not done. She was not shooting anyone, or breaking a window, or shouting in anger. Rather, in a way that everyone understood, she was signaling that things were not right. 5

The line is so thin between matters being manageable and being out of hand. One day a person may be barely all right; the next the same person may have crossed over. Here is something from the author John Barth: 6

> She paused amid the kitchen to drink a glass of water; at that instant, losing a grip of fifty years, the next-room-ceiling plaster crashed. Or he merely sat in an empty study, in March-day glare, listening to the universe rustle in his head, when suddenly a five-foot shelf let go. For ages the fault creeps secret through the rock; in a second, ledge and railings, tourists and turbines all thunder over Niagara. Which snowflake triggers the avalanche? A house explodes; a star. In your spouse, so apparently resigned, murder twitches like a fetus. At some trifling new assessment, all the colonies rebel. 7

The woman continued to walk past Tribune Tower. People who saw her said that the look on her face was almost peaceful. She did not seem to think she was doing anything unusual; she was described as appearing "blissful." Whatever the reaction on the street was, she seemed calm, as if she believed herself to be in control. 8

She walked over the Michigan Avenue bridge. Again, people who were there report that no one harassed her; no one jeered at her or attempted to touch her. At some point on the bridge, she removed her bikini bottom. Now she was completely undressed, and still she walked. "It was as if people knew not to bother her," said one woman who was there. "To tell it, it sounds like something very lewd and sensational was going on. But it wasn't like that at all. It was as if people knew that something very . . . fragile . . . was taking place. I was impressed with the maturity with which people were handling it. No one spoke to her, but you could tell that they wished someone would help her." 9

Back in front of the Radisson, a police officer had picked up the woman's robe. He was on his portable radio, advising his colleagues that the woman was walking over the bridge. When the police caught up with the woman, she was just standing there, naked in downtown Chicago, still smiling. The first thing the police did was hand her some covering and ask her to put it on; the show was over. 10

People who were there said that there was no reaction from the peo- 11
ple who were watching. They said that the juvenile behavior you might
expect in such a situation just didn't happen. After all, when a man walks
out on a ledge in a suicide attempt, there are always people down below
who call for him to jump. But this day, by all accounts, nothing like that
took place. No one called for her to stay undressed; no one cursed the
police officers for stopping her. "It was as if everyone was relieved," said a
woman who saw it. "They were embarrassed by it; it made them feel bad.
They were glad that someone had stopped her. And she was still smiling.
She seemed to be off somewhere."

The police charged her with no crime; they took her to Read Mental 12
Health Center, where she was reported to have signed herself in voluntarily.
Within minutes things were back to as they always are on Michigan Avenue;
there was no reminder of the naked lady who had reminded people how
fragile is the everyday world in which we live.

MARKING THE TEXT

Here is an example of how a student reader marked the Bob Greene essay.

Handled with Care

Like a package with breakables in it

....

BOB GREENE

*—Emotion—
shock value!*

The day the lady took her clothes off on Michi- 1
gan Avenue, people were leaving downtown as
usual. The workday had come to an end; men and
women were heading for bus and train stations, in
a hurry to get home.

Time of day important?

She walked south on Michigan; she was wearing 2
a white robe, as if she had been to the beach. She
was blond and in her thirties. As she passed the
Radisson Hotel, Roosevelt Williams, a doorman,
was opening the door of a cab for one of the hotel's
guests. The woman did not really pause while she

Why?

walked; she merely shrugged the robe off, and it fell
to the sidewalk. She was wearing what appeared
to be the bottom of a blue bikini bathing suit,

What difference would that make?

although one woman who was directly next to her said it was just underwear. She wore nothing else.

Contrast with other outrageous events

Williams at first did not believe what he was seeing. If you hang around long enough, you will see everything: robberies, muggings, street fights, murders. But a naked woman on North Michigan Avenue? Williams had not seen that before and neither, apparently, had the other people on the street.

3

Subject—an unusual event 4

Papers were wrong—misreported the event!

It was strange; her white robe lay on the sidewalk, and by all accounts she was smiling. But no one spoke to her. A report in the newspaper the next day quoted someone: "The cars were stopping, the people on the buses were staring, people were shouting, and people were taking pictures." But that is not what other people who were there that afternoon said. The atmosphere was not carnival-like, they said. Rather, they said, it was as if something very sad was taking place. It took only a moment for people to realize that this was not some stunt designed to promote a product or a movie. Without anything telling them, they understood that the woman was troubled, and that what she was doing had nothing to do with sexual titillation; it was more of a cry for help.

Main point?

People had sympathy

Transition: expand on "cry for help"

The cry for help came in a way that such cries often come. The woman was violating one of the basic premises of the social fabric. [She was doing something that is not done. She was not shooting anyone, or breaking a window, or shouting in anger]. Rather, in a way that everyone understood, she was signaling that things were not right.

5

more overt "violations"?

Who is?

Supporting material from expert—more examples

The line is so thin between matters being manageable and being out of hand. One day a person may be barely all right; the next the same person may have crossed over. Here is something from the author John Barth:

Thesis? 6

She paused amid the kitchen to drink a glass of water; at that instant, losing a grip of fifty years, the next-room-ceiling plaster crashed. Or he merely sat in an empty study, in March-day

7

glare, listening to the universe rustle in his
head, when suddenly a five-foot shelf let go. For
ages the fault creeps secret through the rock; in
a second, ledge and railings, tourists and turbines
all thunder over Niagara. Which snowflake trig-
gers the avalanche? A house explodes; a star. In
your spouse, so apparently resigned, murder
twitches like a fetus. At some trifling new
assessment, all the colonies rebel.

| ?

| ?

The woman continued to walk past Tribune
Tower. People who saw her said that the look on
her face was almost peaceful. She did not seem to
think she was doing anything unusual; she was
described as appearing "blissful." Whatever the
reaction on the street was, she seemed calm, as if
she believed herself to be in control.

8

*Because she was
acting out her cry
for help?*

She walked over the Michigan Avenue bridge.
Again, people who were there report that no one
harassed her; no one jeered at her or attempted to
touch her. At some point on the bridge, she
removed her bikini bottom. Now she was completely undressed, and still she walked. "It was as if
people knew not to bother her," said one woman
who was there. "To tell it, it sounds like something
very lewd and sensational was going on. But it
wasn't like that at all. It was as if people knew that
something very . . . fragile . . . was taking place. I
was impressed with the maturity with which people
were handling it. No one spoke to her, but you
could tell that they wished someone would
      help her."

9

| Def. of maturity

Back in front of the Radisson, a police officer
had picked up the woman's robe. He was on his
portable radio, advising his colleagues that the
woman was walking over the bridge. When the
police caught up with the woman, she was just
standing there, naked in downtown Chicago, still
smiling. The first thing the police did was hand her
some covering and ask her to put it on; the show
was over.

10

| A quiet response!

People who were there said that there was no reaction from the people who were watching. They said
that the juvenile behavior you might expect in such
a situation just didn't happen. After all, when a
man walks out on a ledge in a suicide attempt,
there are always people down below who call for
him to jump. But this day, by all accounts, nothing
like that took place. No one called for her to stay
undressed; no one cursed the police officers for
stopping her. "It was as if everyone was relieved,"
said a woman who saw it. "They were embarrassed
by it; it made them feel bad. They were glad that
someone had stopped her. And she was still smiling. She seemed to be off somewhere."

Contrast with   11
what was expected

*People identified
with her? Feared
for her? for
themselves?*

The police charged her with no crime; they took
her to Read Mental Health Center, where she was
reported to have signed herself in voluntarily.
Within minutes things were back to as they always
are on Michigan Avenue; there was no reminder of
the naked lady who had reminded people how
fragile is the everyday world in which we live.

12

*Because?
Surprising? Main
point? See ¶ 6.*

CLARIFYING MEANING

Put yourself in the student reader's place to see what happens next after reading and marking the text.

Using the Dictionary

First, use a dictionary to look up terms and words you marked as unfamiliar
on the first reading. In this textbook, some will be defined just before the
selection. Be sure to look up even words you *think* you know but are a bit
fuzzy on. What exactly does *assessment* mean in paragraph 7? Though we
often use the word to mean *evaluation,* in this case it means *taxation,* which
makes more sense in the context.

You may use specialized dictionaries to look up unfamiliar references in
the selection. For example, Greene writes that John Barth is an author. If you
looked in a biographical or literary dictionary, you would find that Barth is
a contemporary author who sees the world as absurd, as making no real sense.
This detail helps you understand the quotation. Many writers make references

to names from mythology, philosophy, and literature that you will need to look up. The reference librarian will show you where the specialized dictionaries are kept in the library and which are online.

Reading Aloud

Return to the spots where you drew a question mark, and read those passages slowly aloud. Hearing your voice find the proper way to read a sentence may shed the necessary light on its meaning.

Discussing

Having a conversation about your reading will usually help you understand it. Another person who has read the same selection will probably have different reactions and may be able to clarify points that stumped you. Even someone who has not read the selection may be a good sounding board to discuss the ideas with.

Rereading

At some point, you will need to go back and reread the whole assignment, especially if you are going to be tested on it or intend to write a formal essay about it. With difficult material, the second read through will be more comfortable and will allow you to notice things you missed the first time.

MAKING INFERENCES AND ASSOCIATIONS

Bob Greene's essay is a good example of one that isn't completely spelled out for you. You have to make judgments about what he writes, inferences or conclusions about the meaning.

Reading between the Lines

You can train yourself to infer knowledge that lies below the surface meaning of the words. To *infer* means to arrive at an idea or a conclusion through reasoning. When you infer, you balance what the writer says with your own ideas and hunches about what is left unsaid. This process may sound difficult, but making **inferences** is a skill that can be learned.

Developing Inference Skills

Here are some suggestions for improving your ability to read between the lines:

  Read beyond the words. Fill in details and information to complete the writer's suggestions. Use the writer's hints to discover the meanings that often lie beneath the surface. But don't go too far: you should be able to point to words and phrases that support what you have inferred.

Question yourself as you read and after you finish. You might use questions like these: Why did the author include these details? What does this example mean? How am I supposed to react to this sentence?

Draw conclusions and speculate on outcomes. In reflecting on Bob Greene's essay, for example, you might ask yourself these questions: Is the article saying that people are more sensitive than we usually assume—or less sensitive? Is the message of the selection positive or negative? Would people have reacted differently if the woman had not been young, blonde, and attractive? What truths about our society does this incident suggest?

Make associations between the reading and your own experience. For instance: Have you ever witnessed a "cry for help"? Was it like the one Greene describes, or different? How did you and other people respond?

Your own observations and reflections add richness to the selection's meaning. Our Responding to Reading exercises will assist you in developing your personal reaction.

Responding to Tone

To get a complete understanding of an author's meaning, you need to pay attention to the **tone** of the writing. Tone means the attitude a writer conveys toward the topic and sometimes toward the readers. The language, sentence structure, and selection of details will tell you if the writer is serious or humorous, critical or sympathetic, friendly or hostile, passionate or indifferent, sarcastic or sincere—or any of numerous other attitudes. Most writing will appeal to your emotions in one way or another, and the author's feelings are likely to affect you the most.

WRITING TO UNDERSTAND AND RESPOND

If you write out your Responding to Reading assignment, you have already begun the interactive process that will set the selection firmly in your memory. Study skills experts point out that we have four modes of verbal communication: we listen, we read, we speak, and we write. Different people learn best through different modes, but college learning often emphasizes only the first two: listening to course lectures and reading textbooks. When you add the other two modes to your study habits, you more than double your learning potential. Speaking in class and discussing the material with friends and classmates are important. Writing about what you have heard and read is equally important. Here are some ways to write about a reading assignment:

1. Without looking at the reading, write a summary, 100 to 200 words long, of the selection. As you write, you will develop a sense of which parts of the selection are unclear in your mind. These will be the parts you find it hard to express. Compare your summary to the original, and revise your summary to make it as accurate as possible. This summary will be a fine study aid if you are going to be tested.

2. You can make another study aid by constructing an outline of the important points. This outline can be a simple list of key thoughts in the order they appeared in the essay, like this:

   A. A woman removed her clothes while walking down Michigan Avenue.

   B. The witnesses said the crowd reacted in a sad way, not in the excited, noisy way one might expect.

   C. The woman was crying out for help by violating conventional behavior.

   D. The episode reflected the thin line between ordinary and shocking events.

   E. The crowd identified with the woman instead of looking at her as a freak.

   F. After the woman was taken away, Michigan Avenue quickly went back to its usual state.

3. In your journal, write a letter to the author of your selection. What would you say to him or her if you could? Do you have any questions? These might be brought up in class discussion if you have them on hand.

4. You will also benefit from writing out answers to the Considering Content and Considering Method questions, which are designed to help you focus on meaning and technique.

The writing you have done so far will be of great help to you when you need to draft an assigned essay of your own based on your reading. This process is the subject of the next chapter.

WEB SITE

www.csbsju.edu/academicadvising/helplist.htm

Visit this site to gather additional strategies for effective reading and studying.

CHAPTER 2

The Reading-Writing Connection

The connections between reading and writing are strong: in both activities you use language to create meaning. In Chapter 1, you learned how writing can help you to understand and remember what you read; in this chapter, you will learn how reading and responding to essays can help you to improve your writing.

WRITING IN RESPONSE TO READING

The basic principle of this book is that reading and writing go together. Each chapter follows a four-part pattern that you will discover works well in many of your college classes: (1) read a selection, (2) examine the content, (3) analyze the techniques, and (4) write something of your own that relates to the reading.

When you read, you get ideas for your own writing. Reading can supply you with topics to write about and show you how to write about them. Even when you already have a topic, reading can help you to come up with material to develop that topic. Reading will also provide you with models to follow. By studying the strategies and techniques that professional writers use, you can learn methods and procedures for writing effectively on many different subjects and in many different writing situations.

BUILDING AN ESSAY

Writing an essay is a lot like building a house. A writer fits separate pieces of meaning together to make an understandable statement. If you want to write well, you need to learn the basic skills of constructing an essay.

Despite differences in education and personality, most writers follow a remarkably similar process of *prewriting, planning, writing, revising,* and *editing.* Whether building a single paragraph or a ten-page article, successful writers usually work through several stages, which go roughly like this:

1. Find a subject; gather information. (Prewriting)
2. Focus on a main idea; map out an approach. (Planning)
3. Prepare a rough draft. (Writing)
4. Rework and improve the draft. (Revising)
5. Correct errors. (Editing)

If you follow these operations, you will learn to write more productively and more easily. But keep in mind that this sequence is only a general guide. The steps often overlap and loop around. The important point to remember is that writing is done in stages; successful writers take the time to build their essays step by step and to polish and finish their work the way a good carpenter sands rough surfaces.

Source: © 1999 United Feature Syndicate, Inc.

Finding Ideas

One of the most difficult challenges of writing is coming up with a topic. Even when you are responding to a reading, you still have to decide what to say about it. In this textbook and in most classes, you will be given some direction toward a topic; the job from there on is up to you. Rather than wait for inspiration to strike, you can go after the ideas you need by doing some **prewriting.** Here are three methods that experienced writers use to generate material for writing.

1. **Freewriting.** Write without stopping for five or ten minutes. Don't pause to consider whether your ideas are any good or not; just get down as many thoughts as you can within the time limit. If you're freewriting on a computer, turn down the contrast to write without seeing the screen, or turn the monitor off. After the time is up, read through your freewriting and highlight anything that strikes you as interesting or important. Then do some more freewriting on one or two of these points. Here is an example of

freewriting done by student Tara Coburn in response to "Handled with Care," the article by Bob Greene that you read in Chapter 1:

> Basic themes of Greene's essay. People watched a break in normalcy with maturity, saw the fragility of life, a lesson with tones of sadness, embarrassment, sympathy, but then forgot it. Compared with the lesson of the fragility of life when the situation is personal. The reaction of the people on Michigan Avenue was formed by their detachment from the woman. If they'd known her, someone would have spoken to her, helped her, the world would not have gone back to normal, the incident would not have been forgotten. Their lesson was fleeting but when there is a tear in the social normalcy of your daily life and someone you love shows you the fragility of life, it is more real.

At this point, Tara stopped and looked at what she had written. She liked the idea that surfaced in the last sentence and decided that she had a topic she could develop into an essay. She put the freewriting aside for a while—to let the ideas work around in her mind before she moved on to the next stage in the process.

2. **Brainstorming.** As an alternative to freewriting, you can ask yourself a question and list as many answers as you can. For example: *What have I done that's unexpected or out of the ordinary?* or *When is it all right to get involved with someone in trouble?* Challenge yourself to make the list as long as you can. If necessary, ask yourself a new question: *When is it a bad idea to help someone in trouble?* In making this list you have already started writing. Think of it as a bank of raw material on which you can draw.

In order to develop ideas for her topic, Tara Coburn posed this question to herself: *When did the fabric of my life begin to tear?* And then she brainstormed a list of responses to that question:

> part of my world, my fabric, was belief in my dad
> thought he could do anything
> helped us build a snowman
> finished the ice cream
> fix anything
> even our cat brought him things
> build anything—bed, chairs, room
> not a book smart guy
> tear happened gradually

getting older, tired, looking older
can't fix everything—computer
as strong as everything seemed, it was fragile
not a cry for help, more a sign that he can't help
anymore
like the people on Mich. Ave., it's a sign it's my turn
to come forward

3. **Questioning.** Write a broad topic—such as *Helping People in Trouble*—at the top of a sheet of paper. Then write the headings *Who? What? When? Where? Why? How?* down the page. Fill in any thoughts about the topic that occur to you under these headings. If you can't think of anything for one heading, go to the next, but try to write something under each heading. The goal is to think creatively about the topic as you try to come up with material to use in writing.

Devising a Working Thesis

At this stage, you need to collect the ideas that you came up with in prewriting and organize them. One way to focus your material is to ask yourself, *What point do I want to make?* The answer to that question will lead you to your main idea, or working **thesis.** Once you decide what point you want to make, then you can go through your prewriting material and decide which details to use and which ones to toss.

As you learned in Chapter 1, a thesis says something *about* the subject of a reading. As a reader, your job is to discover the writer's thesis; as a writer, your job is to provide a clear thesis for your readers. Look at the difference between a **subject** and a thesis in these examples:

Subject: Helping strangers
Thesis: I think we are responsible for helping people in trouble.

Subject: Doing something socially unacceptable
Thesis: As soon as I got to college, I set out to prove that I was an adult and beyond the control of my parents.

Here is an example of the thesis statement that Tara Coburn devised from her freewriting and her brainstorming list:

When I saw that my dad's strength was limited, I began to realize that life was fragile and fleeting and that I would have to learn to be strong and do things for him and for myself.

You may change or refine your thesis as the paper develops, but having an idea of what you want to say makes the actual writing considerably easier.

Making a Plan

Having a plan to follow makes you less likely to wander from your main point. An outline of your major points will provide you with a framework for your first draft; it can help you shape and arrange your thoughts and keep you from making organizational missteps. There is no need for complete sentences or balanced headings in your outline. Just make a list of your main points in the order that you plan to cover them. The following brief plan is based on the thesis you just read:

SOMEONE TO HELP

1. Opening
     Yarn ankle bracelet—first clue that life is fragile
     My social fabric—my belief in my dad
2. Always thought Dad could do anything
     Helped us with the giant snow bunny
     Lifted its head—not as easy as it looked then
3. Dad always did the hard work
     Cranked the ice cream
     Even the cat came to him
     Built furniture, almost everything around me
4. Realized he was getting older
     Hair and beard turned white
     Couldn't fix the computer—but I could
     I became the fixer—my chance to grow stronger
5. Closing
     People on Michigan Ave—strangers didn't know what to do
     I love my dad—I can step forward to help him
     Helping makes me grow and become stronger

Composing a Draft

If you have an outline or plan to work from, you shouldn't have any trouble producing the first draft of your paper. Don't fret about trying to write a brilliant **introduction.** Skip it if you can't come up with anything inspired, and start right in on the first main point. You can always come back and add an introduction when you revise.

Some people write the first draft from start to finish without bothering to search for the best word or the right phrase. If that's your method, fine. But many successful writers stop to reread what they have written, especially when they get stuck; rereading helps them to regain momentum and bring back fluency. The main goal is to get your ideas down on paper in a reasonably complete draft. Then you are ready for the important next step: revising.

Improving the Draft

Set your first draft aside, at least overnight, so you can look at it in a new light. This process of looking at your draft *again* is called **revising,** and it literally means "re-seeing." In fact, you want to try to see your work now with different eyes—the eyes of a reader.

When revising your draft, concentrate on making major improvements in content and organization. Such improvements might include enlarging or narrowing the thesis, adding more examples or cutting irrelevant ones, and reorganizing points to improve logic or gain emphasis. Tackling the simple problems first may seem reasonable, but you will find that dealing with a major difficulty may eliminate some minor problems at the same time—or change the way you approach them. If you try to do the fine-tuning and polishing first, you may burn up valuable time and energy and never get around to the main problems.

Targeting the Readers

Most of the writing you do has an **audience**—the person or group of people who will read what you've written. Keeping these readers in mind will help you decide not only what to say but also how best to say it.

You already have considerable reader awareness: you would not write a letter applying for a job in the same way you write a thank-you note to dear Aunt Marie. But writing a class assignment presents a special problem in audience. You know you're writing for your instructor and perhaps other members of the class, but you also know that they are going to read your paper no matter what. In order to develop your writing abilities, you need to get beyond the captive, limited audience of an instructor and your classmates and learn how to write for readers who have different expectations and interests.

Although they often have specific, well-defined audiences, many successful writers still find it useful to imagine an audience that is reasonably informed and generally attentive, readers who will keep reading as long as the writing is interesting and worthwhile. For example, when we write the chapters of this book we think about the students who have been in our classes over the years. If you can picture such an audience, you'll have an easier time deciding what to revise and how to improve your paper. Having other people read your drafts and give you their reactions will also teach you a lot about the importance of audience.

Getting Feedback

Writers routinely seek the help of potential readers to find out what is working and what is not working in their drafts. Someone else can often see places where you *thought* you were being clear but were actually filling in details in your head, not on the page.

The ideal people to help you evaluate your first draft are the members of your own writing class. They will be familiar with the assignment and will understand why you are writing the paper and for whom. In many writing classes, students work together on their papers. Meeting in small groups, they read photocopies of each other's drafts and respond to them; sometimes they post their drafts on a class Web site or submit them electronically on a computer bulletin board. If your instructor doesn't set up a peer review system, try to get several readers' reactions to your drafts. You can meet together outside of class or use an Internet mailing list. Here are some questions to use in asking for feedback:

Have I made my thesis clear to the reader?

Does the introduction get the reader's attention?

Are there any points that the reader might not understand?

Do I need to give the reader more reasons and examples?

Have I shown the reader how every point relates to the thesis?

Does the conclusion tie everything together for the reader?

Polishing the Final Draft

When you are satisfied with the changes you've made to improve content and organization, you can move on to matters of spelling, word choice, punctuation, capitalization, and mechanics. This is the **editing** stage, and you cannot skip it. Readers become quickly annoyed by writing that is full of errors.

For Better or For Worse®   **by Lynn Johnston**

Here are some additional tips that will help you polish and correct your final draft:

1. Let your work sit for a day to clear your head and increase your chances of spotting errors.
2. Read your draft out loud, listening for anything that sounds unclear or incomplete or awkward.
3. Don't try to do everything at once; save time to take a break when you need one.
4. Slow down when you edit: look at each word and punctuation mark individually, and watch for mistakes that you know you usually make.
5. Ask a reliable reader to check over your draft one more time before you turn it in.

SAMPLE STUDENT ESSAY

The essay that follows was written by Tara Coburn, a first-year student at Eastern Illinois University. She was responding to some of the ideas expressed in "Handled with Care" by Bob Greene. The comments in the margin call your attention to important features of organization and development.

Someone to Help

When I was eight, I had a favorite red yarn ankle bracelet that I wore for an entire year. I tugged on it one day to show that it was strong enough to last another year, and it broke. It was a clue that the things we count on in life are fragile. In his essay "Handled with Care," Bob Greene describes how the sudden appearance of a naked woman on busy Michigan Avenue taught the people walking in the street a similar lesson—that "the line is so thin between matters being manageable and being out of hand." Part of my world—my "social fabric"— was based on my childhood belief that my father could do anything. When I began to see that my dad's strength was limited, his weakness reminded me that life is fragile and fleeting and that I would have to learn to be strong on my own.

As a child, no matter how big the problem, I always thought, "Dad can do it." One winter, the

Margin notes:

Introductory 1 paragraph: opens with a specific example, relating main idea to the reading and moving into the thesis.

Thesis: last sentence of first paragraph.

2

other neighborhood children and I had a grand plan to build a giant snow bunny. We somehow managed to lift the bottom and middle balls into place, but the head was far too heavy for us to boost up six feet onto a half-finished snow bunny. My very first thought was to ask my dad, and he tramped out into the snow to check the situation. At the time, he seemed to lob the snow bunny's head effortlessly into place, but thinking back I realize how heavy that big ball of snow must have been.

Dad was always the one we called on to do the hard work. When the homemade ice cream was getting to the final stages of freezing, we called Dad to kneel down and crank the final turns that no one else could manage. His reputation as a Mr. Fix–it was renowned, even to our cat, Mousie. When she had played too roughly with the mouse or snake from the backyard, she'd drop the dead animal at his feet with a look that said, "Daddy, I broke my toy. Will you make it play again?" My dad built much of the world I lived in, from the chairs in the living room to the bed I slept in. Being surrounded by things he built is probably the reason my ideas about him were so important to me.

The tears in my social fabric appeared gradually as I realized that my dad was getting older. When I came home from college for the first time, I noticed that his beard had started to turn from red to white; he was becoming an old man. Not only was his appearance changing, but the arrival of our household's first computer also revealed that my dad cannot fix everything. Now when he says to me, "The computer's little doodad is spinning and I can't make it stop!" his frustration is obvious. But his inability has given me the chance, for once, to be the fixer. I always relied on him, but as he gets older and I learn more, I can let him rely on me. The fragility I now see in my dad has given me the chance to be stronger.

First body paragraph begins with topic sentence and develops it with an extended example.

Second body paragraph begins with topic sentence and develops it with several examples. [3]

Paragraph ends by summing up the significance of the examples.

Third body paragraph begins with topic sentence and develops it with two specific examples [4]

End of paragraph sums up the point and connects it to the main thesis.

	The people on Michigan Avenue did not step	5

Conclusion returns to Greene's essay to make a point through contrast.

The people on Michigan Avenue did not step forward to help the naked woman. One passerby remarked, "No one spoke to her, but you could tell that they wished someone would help her." The crowd felt sorry for the woman, but they were strangers and didn't know how to respond. My dad's turn from strong to fragile was not a cry for help; it was just a sign that he cannot always help me as he once did. But because I know and love my father, I can step forward to help him. And by helping him I have grown strong and have learned to help myself.

Closing sentences reinforce the thesis.

RESOURCES FOR WRITERS ON THE INTERNET

You can find a lot of advice on the writing process at Web sites and online services. They vary widely in quality, presentation, and amount of detail. The following are some of the most helpful and usable:

- **http://web.uvic.ca/wguide/**
  The University of Victoria's Hypertext Writer's Guide will help you through the basics of the writing process and answer questions about essays, paragraphs, sentences, words, and documentation.
- **www.powa.org/my/**
  Paradigm Online Writing Assistant offers useful advice on writing various types of papers. It contains sections on discovery, organization, editing, and other topics.
- **http://owl.english.purdue.edu/owl**
  The Online Writing Lab (OWL) at Purdue University has printer-friendly handouts, interactive Power-Point presentations, and hypertext workshops about the process and mechanics of writing—one of the most extensive collections of advice about writing on the Web.

RESPONDING TO A READING

Now that you have seen samples of close reading and of writing in response to reading, it's time to try these skills yourself. Use the advice in Chapters 1 and 2 as you practice.

PREPARING TO READ

Are you a successful writer? Do you like to write? Did you have any experiences in English or other classes that affected your attitude toward writing? What were they?

· ·

Learning to Write

· ·

RUSSELL BAKER

The winner of a Pulitzer Prize for journalism, Russell Baker began his career as a writer for the Baltimore Sun *and moved to the* New York Times *in the 1950s, where he wrote the "Observer" column from 1962 to 1998. He hosted the* Masterpiece Theater *series on PBS from 1992 to 2004. Baker is known for his humorous observations of everyday life, but in this excerpt from his autobiography* Growing Up *(1982), his lighthearted tone gives way to a serious description of an important personal event.*

TERMS TO RECOGNIZE

notorious (*para. 1*)	known widely and usually unfavorably, disreputable
prim (*para. 1*)	formal and neat, lacking humor
listless (*para. 2*)	without energy, boring
ferocity (*para. 2*)	fierce intensity, savagery
irrepressible (*para. 2*)	impossible to control or hold back
essence (*para. 3*)	the most important ingredient or element, fundamental nature
antecedent (*para. 4*)	the word that a pronoun refers to
exotic (*para. 6*)	rare and unusual
reminiscence (*para. 8*)	a thing remembered, a memory
contempt (*para. 10*)	scorn, disrespect
ridicule (*para. 10*)	mockery, teasing
ecstasy (*para. 11*)	bliss, delight, joy

When our class was assigned to Mr. Fleagle for third-year English I anticipated another grim year in that dreariest of subjects. Mr. Fleagle was   1 notorious among City students for dullness and inability to inspire. He was said to be stuffy, dull, and hopelessly out of date. To me he looked to be sixty or seventy and prim to a fault. He wore primly severe eyeglasses, his wavy hair was primly cut and primly combed. He wore prim vested suits with neckties blocked primly against the collar buttons of his primly starched white shirts. He had a primly pointed jaw, a primly straight nose, and a prim manner of speaking that was so correct, so gentlemanly, that he seemed a comic antique.

I anticipated a listless, unfruitful year with Mr. Fleagle and for a long   2
time was not disappointed. We read *Macbeth*. Mr. Fleagle loved *Macbeth* and wanted us to love it too, but he lacked the gift of infecting others with his own passion. He tried to convey the murderous ferocity of Lady Macbeth one day by reading aloud the passage that concludes

> . . . I have given suck, and know
> How tender 'tis to love the babe that milks me.
> I would, while it was smiling in my face,
> Have plucked my nipple from his boneless gums. . . .

The idea of prim Mr. Fleagle plucking his nipple from boneless gums was too much for the class. We burst into gasps of irrepressible snickering. Mr. Fleagle stopped.

"There is nothing funny, boys, about giving suck to a babe. It is the—   3
the very essence of motherhood, don't you see."

He constantly sprinkled his sentences with "don't you see." It wasn't   4
a question but an exclamation of mild surprise at our ignorance. "Your pronoun needs an antecedent, don't you see," he would say, very primly. "The purpose of the Porter's scene, boys, is to provide comic relief from the horror, don't you see."

Later in the year we tackled the informal essay. "The essay, don't you   5
see, is the. . . ." My mind went numb. Of all forms of writing, none seemed so boring as the essay. Naturally we would have to write informal essays. Mr. Fleagle distributed a homework sheet offering us a choice of topics. None was quite so simpleminded as "What I Did on My Summer Vacation," but most seemed to be almost as dull. I took the list home and dawdled until the night before the essay was due. Sprawled on the sofa, I finally faced up to the grim task, took the list out of my notebook, and scanned it. The topic on which my eye stopped was "The Art of Eating Spaghetti."

This title produced an extraordinary sequence of mental images. Surg-   6
ing up out of the depths of memory came a vivid recollection of a night in

Belleville when all of us were seated around the supper table—Uncle Allen, my mother, Uncle Charlie, Doris, Uncle Hal—and Aunt Pat served spaghetti for supper. Spaghetti was an exotic treat in those days. Neither Doris nor I had ever eaten spaghetti, and none of the adults had enough experience to be good at it. All the good humor of Uncle Allen's house reawoke in my mind as I recalled the laughing arguments we had that night about the socially respectable method for moving spaghetti from plate to mouth.

Suddenly I wanted to write about that, about the warmth and good 7 feeling of it, but I wanted to put it down simply for my own joy, not for Mr. Fleagle. It was a moment I wanted to recapture and hold for myself. I wanted to relive the pleasure of an evening at New Street. To write it as I wanted, however, would violate all the rules of formal composition I'd learned in school, and Mr. Fleagle would surely give it a failing grade. Never mind. I would write something else for Mr. Fleagle after I had written this thing for myself.

When I finished it the night was half gone, and there was no time left 8 to compose a proper, respectable essay for Mr. Fleagle. There was no choice next morning but to turn in my private reminiscence of Belleville. Two days passed before Mr. Fleagle returned the graded papers, and he returned everyone's but mine. I was bracing myself for a command to report to Mr. Fleagle immediately after school for discipline when I saw him lift my paper from his desk and rap for the class's attention.

"Now, boys," he said, "I want to read you an essay. This is titled 'The 9 Art of Eating Spaghetti'. "

And he started to read. My words! He was reading *my words* out loud 10 to the entire class. What's more, the entire class was listening. Listening attentively. Then somebody laughed, then the entire class was laughing, and not in contempt and ridicule, but with openhearted enjoyment. Even Mr. Fleagle stopped two or three times to repress a small prim smile.

I did my best to avoid showing pleasure, but what I was feeling was 11 pure ecstasy at this startling demonstration that my words had the power to make people laugh. In the eleventh grade, at the eleventh hour as it were, I had discovered a calling. It was the happiest moment of my entire school career. When Mr. Fleagle finished he put the final seal on my happiness by saying, "Now that, boys, is an essay, don't you see. It's—don't you see—it's of the very essence of the essay, don't you see. Congratulations, Mr. Baker."

WEB SITE

www.albany.edu/writers-inst/olv6n2.html#baker
Read a transcript of a 1991 interview with Russell Baker, who talks about his life and his writing career.

SUGGESTIONS FOR WRITING

1. Baker's experience in eleventh-grade English changed the way he thought about himself. Have you ever had such an eye-opening experience—some event you really want to write about, some incident you want to "recapture and hold" for yourself? Write an essay in which you describe what happened.

2. Write an essay about the most important thing that happened to you in school. It could be either a positive or negative experience—one that taught you something about yourself or about school or about the subject you were studying.

3. USING THE INTERNET. Take a look at the list of common myths about writing at http://wire./rutgers.edu/i_myth.html. Then get together with a small group of classmates and talk about how each of you feels about writing. Compare notes on what you like and don't like about writing. Which of the ten myths do you still believe in? Discuss the kinds of writing that you have done, and tell each other about previous writing experiences. Then write an essay explaining your thoughts and feelings about writing. If you changed your attitude (as Baker did), tell about that change.

4. Write an essay describing your writing process: how you get started, how you go about getting ideas, what you like to write about, where you like to write, whether you like background music or need quiet, whether you make an outline or plunge right in, how long it takes to complete an assignment, whether you work in stages, how many drafts you write, whether you write by hand or use a computer, how much correcting and recopying you do, and so on. Think carefully about the way you write, and describe it in as much detail as you can. Conclude your essay by explaining what you think you could do to make your writing process more efficient.

Strategies for Conveying Ideas: *Narration* and *Description*

IMAGES AND IDEAS

Source: AP Wide World Photos

Source: Robert Funk

FOR DISCUSSION AND WRITING

Look at the two photographs reproduced here. First, give each one a title that you think expresses the mood or atmosphere of the picture. The title will probably be a general word or phrase that describes an emotion or state of mind.

Next, choose one of the pictures to write about. One purpose is to present a detailed description of the picture to someone who has never seen it. The description should carefully differentiate this photo from other ones like it— that is, if your readers were to look at five winter scenes, they could pick out this particular one. In your description, get across the feeling or state of mind you used in your title. Be sure to use words that are very specific and have strong associations. Your description should be at least one paragraph long.

Now consider changing your approach. Create a caption for the photograph. Write another paragraph telling a story of what events led to the scene or what led to the viewer's witnessing of the scene. Use your imagination to provide the details of the story.

He falls back upon the bed awkwardly. His stumps, unweighted by legs and feet, rise in the air, presenting themselves. I unwrap the bandages from the stumps, and begin to cut away the black scabs and the dead, glazed fat with scissors and forceps. A shard of white bone comes loose. I pick it away. I wash the wounds with disinfectant and redress the stumps.

—Richard Selzer, "The Discus Thrower"

That powerful paragraph, written by a surgeon good with words as well as with scalpels, combines description and narration. Dr. Selzer, narrating an experience in treating a terminally ill patient, uses description to make his account of this brief event vividly, compellingly real. Simply put, a narrative is a story; **narration** is the telling of a story. The preceding passage is taken from a longer narrative (with a beginning, a middle, and an end) that makes a point. As you can see, the strength of narrative and descriptive writing lies in the use of vivid language and in the selection of precise details.

THE POINT OF NARRATION AND DESCRIPTION

Although the selections in this chapter combine several writing strategies, they are primarily narratives that make a point using descriptive details to add clarity, liveliness, and interest. You will notice that most of the readings throughout this text use both narration and description to help them develop many different kinds of essays.

Using Narratives

Consider how often we use narrative in everyday speech. If you want to convince your daughter to avoid becoming pregnant as a teenager, you'll probably tell her the story of your high school friend who made that mistake and missed her chance to become the architect she always wanted to be. We tell stories because they are convincing—they have the ring of truth to them—and most people are able to learn from the experience of others. So, narrative is a good strategy to consider if you are writing to persuade, to make a point.

If you are going to write a narrative essay, be sure your story has a point. You wouldn't tell a joke without a punch line, and only mothers and close friends will hold still for stories without a purpose.

Much more frequently, you will use short narratives as part of a longer essay. Notice in your reading how often writers begin essays with a brief narrative to catch our interest and lead us into the topic. Once the writers have our attention, they may move to other strategies to develop their ideas and present the material, but a good story makes an effective lure.

Using Description

Essays of pure description are rare, but descriptive details provide one of the most common ways of adding interest and clarity to your writing. **Description** can put a picture in the minds of readers, helping them to see what you mean. Most writing would seem dull and lifeless without descriptive details, like this sentence:

> The firefighter rescued a child.

Although the action referred to is exciting, the sentence is blah. But add some descriptive details, and the sentence gains meaning and interest:

> The exhausted firefighter, a rookie on the force, staggered from the flames with the limp body of an unconscious child cradled in his arms.

You can, of course, include too much description. But use any details that come to you while writing your first draft. Then, when you revise, decide whether you've gone too far, and eliminate any that seem overdone or unnecessary. Of course, add more details if you think you have too few.

THE PRINCIPLES OF NARRATION AND DESCRIPTION

Good narrative and descriptive writing depends, as does most other writing, on making choices. In narratives, the main choices involve deciding which events to include and which ones to leave out. In descriptions, the choices involve selecting words that appeal to the senses—usually to sight, but also to touch, taste, hearing, and smell.

Organizing the Events

If you've ever listened to a boring storyteller, you know how important a concise and effective framework is to a narrative. Organizing a narrative seems easy because the story almost always proceeds in **chronological order** (according to the time in which events happened). But a poor storyteller (or a writer who fails to revise) will get things out of order and interrupt the tale with "Oh, I forgot to mention that Marvin got fired just before his cat got lost and his dog was run over." Or the storyteller will get hung up on a totally unimportant detail:

> The moment I saw him—I think it was at the senior prom—or was it at the homecoming dance—or it could have been the party at Yolanda's—oh, wait, I don't think it was at a party at all, it was at a football game—or no, a basketball game. . . .

even though the point of the story has nothing to do with where or when it happened.

Get your story straight in your mind before you begin, or else straighten it out when you revise. Eliminate any dull or unnecessary material, and then go to work on making it interesting.

Including Specific Details

All good writing is full of specific details, but a narrative will simply fall flat without them. Recall the paragraph we quoted by Dr. Richard Selzer. We could summarize that paragraph in a single sentence:

> After the patient fell back awkwardly in bed, I removed the bandages, cleaned, disinfected, and rebandaged the ends of his amputated legs.

What did we leave out? The details—in this case mostly descriptive details—and what a difference they make in allowing us to visualize the doctor's performance.

Selecting Descriptive Words

Effective description depends heavily on the use of specific details, but also crucial are the words you choose in presenting those details. Consider this sentence quoted from Dr. Selzer's paragraph:

> I unwrap the bandages from the stumps, and begin to cut away the black scabs and the dead, glazed fat with scissors and forceps.

Look at what happens when we substitute less specific, less descriptive words in that same sentence:

> I take the bandages off the amputated legs, and begin to remove the dead tissue with my instruments.

The meaning is the same, and most of us would probably have written it that way, but it's clear that the force of Dr. Selzer's sentence lies in his word choice: *unwrap, stumps, cut away, black scabs, glazed fat, scissors, forceps.*

Good description stems from close observation, paying close attention to the sights, sounds, textures, tastes, or smells around you. Then you must search for exactly the right words to convey what you experience to your readers. Try to think of words that go beyond the general to the specific:

GENERAL ◄————————————► **SPECIFIC**

a drink	a soft drink	a diet cola	a stale diet Coke
move	run	run fast	race headlong
weather	rain	cold rain	cold, blowing rain

You get the idea. As you read, be alert for words that convey **images,** that let you know how something looks or feels or moves or tastes or smells or sounds.

When you revise, try to replace the following useful but run-of-the-mill verbs with words that are more specific and more interesting:

is (are, was, were, etc.)	go	get	has
come	move	do	make

Notice the difference a livelier word choice makes:

O'Malley moved on to second base.
O'Malley slid into second base.

I'm going to do my homework.
I'm going to struggle with my homework.

Lapita made a chocolate mousse.
Lapita whipped up a luscious chocolate mousse.

Keep a vocabulary list and try to use the new words in speaking and writing. The theory is that if you use a word three times, it enters your vocabulary. Part of becoming a good writer (as well as a good speaker) depends on increasing the number of words you have at your command, so get to work on it.

THE PITFALLS OF NARRATION AND DESCRIPTION

The narratives included in this chapter, written by experienced authors, will not show you the many things that can go wrong in this kind of writing. Descriptions and narratives are among the easiest kinds of writing to do, but they are probably the most difficult to do well. You need to find someone who will read your draft, not only for enjoyment, but also with the promise of helping you improve it. It's always hard to see the flaws in our own writing. It's especially hard with narratives and descriptions. But you can do a good job if you are willing to work at it and can find a reliable person to help you in revising.

As you rewrite, ask yourself—and ask your helper to answer—the following questions:

1. Is the point of my narrative clear? It may not be stated directly, but readers should be able to see *why* I'm telling this story.
2. Are the events in order? Are there any gaps? Any backtracking?
3. Are there enough details to be clear and interesting?

4. Are there any unnecessary details that I should take out?
5. Do the descriptions provide an image (a picture, a sound, a smell, a taste, an atmosphere, an action)?

Respond to the questions as honestly as you can—and have your helper do the same. Then keep revising until you are both happy with the results.

WHAT TO LOOK FOR IN NARRATION AND DESCRIPTION

As you read the essays in this chapter, pay attention to these characteristics:

1. *Look at the way the essay is put together.* Probably the events are told chronologically, as they happened, but if not, try to figure out why the writer departed from the usual method of organization.
2. *Decide what point the narrative makes.* Its purpose may be simply to entertain the readers, but more often it will illustrate or make a point. Look for an underlying meaning that you discover as you think about the story and the author's reasons for telling it.
3. *Consider the elements of the narrative.* Think about why these particular events, people, and descriptions are included. If they are not crucial, try to decide what they add to the story and what would be lost if they were left out.
4. *Notice the descriptive details.* Underline any sentences or phrases that appeal to your senses or put a picture in your mind.
5. *Pick out good descriptive words.* Most of these you will already have underlined. Add them to your vocabulary list.

PREPARING TO READ

Have you ever been involved in a serious accident or caught in a burning building or been especially frightened by something? Describe how you felt at the time. Were you terrified—or did everything happen too fast? Record the thoughts and feelings you experienced once the incident was over.

···

Rain of Fire

···

EVAN THOMAS

Evan Thomas, a graduate of Harvard and the University of Virginia Law School, has been assistant managing editor of Newsweek *magazine since 1991 and the lead writer on many major news stories. His vivid reporting on the September 11th disaster helped win for* Newsweek *the National Magazine Award for General Excellence in 2002. The following selection appeared in* Newsweek *(Dec. 31, 2001/ Jan. 7, 2002) as Part IV of an extensive article entitled "The Day That Changed America." If you want to find out how Virginia DiChiara made it down those seventy-eight flights of stairs, read the whole gripping article.*

TERMS TO RECOGNIZE

moseying *(para. 1)*	moving slowly and aimlessly
translucent *(para. 4)*	clear, letting light through
prosaic *(para. 6)*	everyday, ordinary
suffused *(para.8)*	spread throughout
cacophony *(para. 8)*	harsh, nerve-jangling sound

A self-described workaholic, Virginia DiChiara was normally out of her house and on her way to work by 7 A.M. But the morning of September 11 was so brilliantly beautiful that DiChiara decided to dawdle. She let her two golden retrievers play in the yard, cooked herself some eggs, poured herself a cup of coffee. "I was just moseying along," she says. "I didn't feel like rushing." She left her Bloomfield, N.J., home at 7:40, a 40-minute delay that would end up saving her life.

It was a little after 8:40 when she entered the lobby of the North Tower of the World Trade Center. Together with a Cantor Fitzgerald co-worker, she rode the elevator up to the 78th floor, where she crossed a lobby to take a second elevator the rest of the way to her office on the 101st floor. The elevator door opened and she pressed the button for 101. It was 8:46 A.M.

As the elevator doors closed, Flight 11 plowed into the northern face of Tower I some 20 floors above. The elevator went black and "bounced around like a ball," DiChiara recalls. "I remember seeing two lines shooting around the top of the elevator"—electrical cables that had come loose and were spitting current—and "everybody started screaming." In front of her was a man named Roy Bell, who later said that the sound of impact was "deafening," like someone banging a 2-by-2-foot sheet of aluminum with a hammer "six inches from your head." The right wall of the elevator car crashed into Bell, breaking several of his fingers and flinging him to the left side. Miraculously, the elevator doors remained open about a foot. Within seconds, Bell "just sprinted" out of the elevator, he recalls. "Inside was not where you wanted to be." 3

DiChiara had crouched down behind Bell. She saw Bell go through, and thought, "I don't hear any screaming, so I know he's not on fire . . . I'm outta here." She decided to go for it. But as she gathered herself, huge blue flames—translucent teardrops of fire, a foot in diameter—began falling in a steady curtain. DiChiara dropped her bag, covered her face with her palms and squeezed through the door, her elbows pushing the black rubber guards on the elevator doors. Left behind was her Cantor co-worker. DiChiara never saw her again; at times she feels guilty that she made it out and her co-worker did not. 4

DiChiara was aflame when she emerged from the elevator. "I remember hearing my hair on fire," she says. (She later joked, "I must have put on some extra hair spray.") With her hands she tapped out the fire. "I got it out, I got it," she said to herself. Then, feeling something else, she looked back and saw flames rising from her shoulder. In that instant, she remembered the old lesson from grade school: stop, drop, and roll. She threw herself to the carpeted floor and rolled over and over, frantically patting out the flames. "I remember getting up and just looking at myself," she says. "'OK, everything's out.' And then sort of laughing, almost like a hysteria, like a little giggle, like, 'Oh my God, let me do it again just in case I missed it.' I was so scared, like there was an ember on my body that was still going to go up." 5

DiChiara crawled some 20 feet down the hallway and sat with her back propped against a wall. She was wearing a sleeveless cotton shirt that day, and her arms and hands were seared with third-degree burns. In shock, she did not feel the pain—yet. Improbably prosaic thoughts crossed her mind. In the briefcase she'd left on the elevator were some airplane tickets recently purchased for a vacation jaunt to the Florida Keys, as well as a wad of cash. Should she go back and retrieve it? "No," she thought to herself. "Just stay right where you are." 6

Then she spotted a co-worker, Ari Schonbrun, head of global   7
accounts receivable at Cantor. "Ari!" she called out. He turned around
and looked at her. "Virginia! Oh my God!" he said. "Ari, I'm badly
burned," Virginia told him. She was gradually realizing how grave her
condition truly was, and beginning to feel it as well. "I'm in so much
pain," she said. Schonbrun was horrified. "The skin was peeled off her
arms," he says. "You knew this woman was in trouble." DiChiara read his
expression. "I knew by the look on his face that I was bad," she says.
Schonbrun told her, "Virginia, take it easy. We're going to get help. Don't
worry. You're going to be fine." She begged, "Whatever you do, don't
leave me." Schonbrun reassured her, "I'm not going to leave you. I'll be
with you."

The hallways were smoky, suffused with the nauseating smell of   8
burned jet fuel, littered with debris, and completely dark save for some outdoor light filtering in from windows at the end of the hall. Schonbrun gently
guided DiChiara toward a small security office behind the elevator banks
where the lights still worked. About a dozen people were huddled there,
including two security guards. DiChiara lay down on the floor, on the verge
of passing out. A woman sitting nearby was crying. One of the security
guards was furiously dialing for help on the office phone but couldn't get
through. The other guard had a radio, but she was paralyzed, crying.
Schonbrun told her, "You've got to calm down. You've got to get on that
radio and get us help." The guard tried, but the only sound coming over the
radio was a cacophony of screams.

Singed by his narrow escape through the elevator doors, Bell had also   9
made it to the security office. His doctors would later tell him that the few
seconds between his exit and DiChiara's made the difference between his
second-degree and her third-degree burns. Suddenly, a man appeared saying that he was a fire warden. There was a stairwell in the middle of the
tower that they could use, he announced. Schonbrun leaned over DiChiara
and laid out the options: either they could wait for someone to rescue
them, or they could start heading down by foot.

For DiChiara, there was no choice. No way was she going to sit there   10
and wait. Gritting her teeth, she got up and headed for the stairwell.

RESPONDING TO READING

Everyone has seen on television the visual images of the horrific events of September 11, 2001. The previous selection recounts the experience of one
woman caught up in that tragedy. What did you get from the reading that you
did not get from seeing the visuals?

CONSIDERING CONTENT

1. Why was Virginia DiChiara late going to work on September 11, 2001? Was she a person who was often late?
2. How did she know her hair was on fire? How did she extinguish the flames on her clothing?
3. How did DiChiara discover how severe her burns were? Why do you suppose she did not immediately know how gravely she was injured?
4. What help did the survivors get from the security guard's radio?
5. Why did DiChiara decide to struggle down seventy-eight flights of stairs instead of waiting for rescue?
6. What does Thomas show us about her character, throughout the narrative, that aids her in making that life-saving decision?

CONSIDERING METHOD

1. How is this selection organized?
2. What is the author's purpose? Who is the intended **audience?**
3. At the end of paragraph 2, Thomas includes this small detail in a sentence all by itself: "It was 8:46 A.M." Why do you think he made that stylistic choice?
4. In paragraph 7, Thomas writes, "In shock, she did not feel the pain— yet." What does he achieve with the use of that dash?
5. How does the writer engage our emotions in this narrative?
6. The piece is packed with specific details. Point out three or four that you find particularly effective and explain why you think Thomas included them.
7. What makes the concluding paragraph effective?

WRITING STEP BY STEP

Think about a catastrophe that you witnessed or were involved in—a flood, a fire, an auto wreck, an earthquake, a tornado, or a hurricane. Jot down as many specific details as you can remember. Then write a short narrative describing the experience. Use "I" in referring to yourself and "we" if others join you in the action. Or, write about the experience of someone else caught up in a major ordeal, the way Evan Thomas writes about Virginia DiChiara's struggles in the previous essay. Collect material through interviewing the other person, with your narrative purposes in mind.

A. Begin, as Thomas does, with a brief explanation of how you got involved—what you were doing, who (if anyone) was with you, and what led up to the catastrophe.

B. Then recount the events from beginning to end. Before you begin, make a detailed list of everything that happened and all the specific details you can recall. Next, decide which actions to include and which to leave out.

C. You do not need a thesis statement in a personal narrative. Let your readers infer what your point is.

D. Include any interesting thoughts that went through your mind (as Thomas does in para. 6). Use quotation marks, since you are, in effect, quoting yourself. If other people are involved, quote directly anything memorable that they said.

E. Use plenty of description (like "lines shooting around the top of the elevator," "translucent teardrops of fire, a foot in diameter," "frantically patting out the flames"), as well as pertinent specific actions ("She let her two golden retrievers play in the yard, cooked herself some eggs, poured herself a cup of coffee," "One of the security guards was furiously dialing for help on the office phone but couldn't get through"). Put pictures in your readers' minds. Lively verbs help create striking images—*moseying, plowed, bounced, shooting, banging.*

F. Avoid telling your readers what to feel. Let them experience your emotions through your forceful recounting of the events.

G. Experiment with a couple of very short sentences for emphasis.

H. Write a concluding sentence or a short concluding paragraph that brings the account to a definite close. Don't let your narrative just trail off at the end.

OTHER WRITING IDEAS

1. In his account of the survivors trapped on the 78th floor, Evan Thomas shows them experiencing many varying emotions—fear, panic, hysteria, courage, self-discipline, determination, resolve. Think of a time when you felt one of these emotions and write a narrative account analyzing the experience. Describe where you were, what happened, and how you reacted. You might conclude by explaining how you feel about the occurrence now, as you reflect on it.

2. COLLABORATIVE WRITING. Write a narrative to support or disprove some familiar proverb or saying, such as "Home is where the heart is," "Crime doesn't pay," or "Virtue is its own reward." Get together with several classmates before you begin writing to help one another decide what saying would make a good choice and what story might provide convincing illustrations.

3. USING THE INTERNET. Visit the Chicago Historical Society's Web site on the Great Chicago Fire and read the narrative by Bessie Bradwell Helmer (www.chicagohs.org/fire/witnesses/bradwell.html). Using the information you've acquired, write a narrative recounting your imaginary escape from the Great Chicago Fire of 1871. Or, if you prefer, follow the progress of a single lucky person who fled the conflagration and survived. You can follow the chronology of Bessie Helmer's account, but try for the immediacy that Evan Thomas captures in his reporting of Virginia DiChiara's miraculous escape. Supply your own specific events, vivid descriptions, and action verbs.

4. WRITING ABOUT READING. Analyze the writing strategies used in Thomas's essay. Use the five questions on page 34 in the introduction of this chapter to guide you in your analysis.

GAINING WORD POWER

Thomas uses a number of precise descriptive word choices in this narrative. Several appear in the Terms to Recognize section preceding the selection. Here are some others:

DiChiara decided to *dawdle*. (para. 1)

Flight 11 *plowed* into the northern face of Tower I. (para. 3)

DiChiara was *aflame*. (para. 5)

Her arms and hands were *seared*. (para. 6)

One of the security guards was *furiously* dialing for help. (para. 8)

We repeat these sentences below, minus the italicized words. Fill in each blank with your own definition of the missing word.

DiChiara decided to _____.

Flight 11 _____ into the northern face of Tower I.

DiChiara was _____.

Her arms and hands were _____.

One of the security guards was _____ dialing for help.

What is lost or changed in the second set of sentences? Which sentences do you prefer?

EDITING SKILLS: SENTENCE COMBINING

Writing lots of short sentences with little variety produces a choppy effect that sounds a bit childish. In order to make your writing fluent, you need to take those choppy sentences and combine them into a single sophisticated one. It works like this:

> Choppy sentences:
> She had two golden retrievers.
> She let them play in the yard.
> She cooked herself some eggs.
> She poured herself a cup of coffee.

If you combine those sentences, you get one of Evan Thomas's well-crafted sentences:

> She let her two golden retrievers play in the yard, cooked herself some eggs, poured herself a cup of coffee.

Here is another example:

> Choppy sentences:
> She threw herself to the floor.
> The floor was carpeted.
> She rolled over and over.
> She was frantic.
> She patted out the flames.

Thomas wrote his sentence this way:

> She threw herself to the carpeted floor and rolled over and over, frantically patting out the flames.

EXERCISE

Now you try it. Here are some short sentences to combine into a single effective one. Begin the first one with *if.*

> You may like to travel.
> You may want to travel alone.

You are a woman.
I have some tips for you.
My friend is a woman.
She travels alone a lot.
She has given me good advice.

You may be on a train or plane.
You choose your departure times.
You choose your arrival times.
Check the time of your arrival at your destination.
Be sure your arrival will be during daylight hours.

The station or airport may be far from your hotel.
You need to find the best way to get there.
Taxis are expensive.

You should travel light.
You should take only two bags.
One bag should be on wheels.
You will probably have to carry your own luggage.

Now examine the narrative you just wrote. If you find limp or choppy sentences, combine them into pleasing ones.

WEB SITE

http://911digitalarchive.org/
Click on "Stories" to read compelling personal narratives written by people who were involved in the tragedy of September 11th.

PREPARING TO READ

Did you ever have an experience that changed the way you look at the world—perhaps while traveling, or getting to know a stranger, or suffering a serious illness, or being inspired by a teacher?

••

Jackie's Debut: A Unique Day

••

MIKE ROYKO

Born in Chicago, Mike Royko (1932–1997) attended Wright Junior College there. He wrote a syndicated column for the Chicago Tribune *and was awarded the Pulitzer Prize. His columns often ridiculed human greed, vanity, and stupidity. The piece reprinted here is perhaps not typical, since it focuses on an uplifting event—a step toward reversing the usual pattern of ignorant prejudice. It appeared in the* Chicago Daily News *on Wednesday, October 15, 1972, the day after Jackie Robinson died. If you enjoy this article about Jackie Robinson, you might want to read Robinson's autobiography,* I Never Had It Made.

TERMS TO RECOGNIZE

scalpers *(para. 3)*   people selling tickets at higher than regular prices
Ls *(para. 4)*   elevated trains
caromed *(para. 11)*   hit and bounced
chortling *(para. 12)*   chuckling and snorting with laughter

All that Saturday, the wise men of the neighborhood, who sat in chairs   1
on the sidewalk outside the tavern, had talked about what it would do to baseball. I hung around and listened because baseball was about the most important thing in the world, and if anything was going to ruin it, I was worried.

Most of the things they said, I didn't understand, although it   2
sounded terrible. But could one man bring such ruin? They said he could and would. And the next day he was going to be in Wrigley Field for the first time, on the same diamond as Hack, Nicholson, Cavarretta, Schmidt, Pafko, and all my other idols. I had to see Jackie Robinson, the man who was going to somehow wreck everything. So the next day, another kid and I started walking to the ballpark early.

We always walked to save the streetcar fare. It was five or six miles,   3
but I felt about baseball the way Abe Lincoln felt about education. Usually,

we could get there just at noon, find a seat in the grandstands, and watch some batting practice. But not that Sunday, May 18, 1947. By noon, Wrigley Field was almost filled. The crowd outside spilled off the sidewalk and into the streets. Scalpers were asking top dollar for box seats and getting it.

I had never seen anything like it. Not just the size, although it was a new record, more than 47,000. But this was 25 years ago, and in 1947 few blacks were seen in the Loop, much less up on the white North Side at a Cub game. That day, they came by the thousands, pouring off the north-bound Ls and out of their cars. They didn't wear baseball-game clothes. They had on church clothes and funeral clothes—suits, white shirts, ties, gleaming shoes, and straw hats. I've never seen so many straw hats. Big as it was, the crowd was orderly. Almost unnaturally so. People didn't jostle each other. 4

The whites tried to look as if nothing unusual was happening, while the blacks tried to look casual and dignified. So everybody looked slightly ill at ease. For most, it was probably the first time they had been that close to each other in such great numbers. 5

We managed to get in, scramble up a ramp, and find a place to stand behind the last row of grandstand seats. Then they shut the gates. No place remained to stand. 6

Robinson came up in the first inning. I remember the sound. It wasn't the shrill, teen-age cry you now hear, or an excited gut roar. They applauded, long, rolling applause. A tall middle-aged black man stood next to me, a smile of almost painful joy on his face, beating his palms together so hard they must have hurt. 7

When Robinson stepped into the batter's box, it was as if someone had flicked a switch. The place went silent. He swung at the first pitch and they erupted as if he had knocked it over the wall. But it was only a high foul that dropped into the box seats. I remember thinking it was strange that a foul could make that many people happy. When he struck out, the low moan was genuine. 8

I've forgotten most of the details of the game, other than that the Dodgers won and Robinson didn't get a hit or do anything special, although he was cheered on every swing and every routine play. But two things happened I'll never forget. Robinson played first, and early in the game a Cub star hit a grounder and it was a close play. Just before the Cub reached first, he swerved to his left. And as he got to the bag, he seemed to slam his foot down hard at Robinson's foot. It was obvious to everyone that he was trying to run into him or spike him. Robinson took the throw and got clear at the last instant. 9

I was shocked. That Cub, a home-town boy, was my biggest hero. It   10
was not only an unheroic stunt, but it seemed a rude thing to do in front of
people who would cheer for a foul ball. I didn't understand why he had
done it. It wasn't at all big league. I didn't know that while the white fans
were relatively polite, the Cubs and most other teams kept up a steady
stream of racial abuse from the dugout. I thought all they did down there
was talk about how good Wheaties are.

Later in the game, Robinson was up again and he hit another foul   11
ball. This time it came into the stands low and fast, in our direction. Somebody in the seats grabbed for it, but it caromed off his hand and kept coming. There was a flurry of arms as the ball kept bouncing, and suddenly it
was between me and my pal. We both grabbed. I had a baseball.

The two of us stood there examining it and chortling. A genuine   12
major-league baseball that had actually been gripped and thrown by a Cub
pitcher, hit by a Dodger batter. What a possession! Then I heard a voice
say: "Would you consider selling that?" It was the black man who had
applauded so fiercely. I mumbled something. I didn't want to sell it.

"I'll give you $10 for it," he said.   13

Ten dollars. I couldn't believe it. I didn't know what $10 could buy   14
because I'd never had that much money. But I knew that a lot of men in the
neighborhood considered $60 a week to be good pay. I handed it to him, and
he paid me with ten $1 bills. When I left the ballpark, with that much money
in my pocket, I was sure that Jackie Robinson wasn't bad for the game.

Since then, I've regretted a few times that I didn't keep the ball. Or that I   15
hadn't given it to him free. I didn't know, then, how hard he probably had to
work for that $10. But Tuesday I was glad I had sold it to him. And if that man
is still around, and has that baseball, I'm sure he thinks it was worth every cent.

RESPONDING TO READING

Read again Royko's last paragraph. Explain in your journal why he wishes,
as an adult, that he had given the baseball to the man who bought it from him.
Do you think you would feel the same way?

CONSIDERING CONTENT

1. What made the old men of the neighborhood say that Jackie Robinson would ruin the game of baseball?
2. How did young Royko and his friend get to Wrigley Field, and why
   did they choose that way to get there?

3. What does he mean when he says, "I felt about baseball the way Abe Lincoln felt about education" (para. 3)?
4. Why was he surprised to see so many black people at the game?
5. Why were the black people wearing their good clothes?
6. When the young narrator says, "It wasn't at all big league" (para. 10), what does he mean?

CONSIDERING METHOD

1. How does Royko get the readers' attention in the opening paragraph?
2. How does he let us know that the "wise men of the neighborhood" are not truly wise—that he is being sarcastic? What small detail in the sentence gives us the clue?
3. Why does Royko tell most of the narrative through the thoughts of himself as a young boy?
4. In paragraph 3, why does he give the exact date—Sunday, May 18, 1947?
5. When you think about all the details he could have included in describing the crowd at the baseball game, why do you think he chose to relate how the black people were dressed?
6. In paragraph 10, Royko tells us something he learned later in life. How does he handle this shift in time so that we scarcely notice it?
7. In paragraphs 12 and 13, why does Royko give us the exact words of the man who wants to buy the baseball?
8. Explain why the final paragraph makes a good conclusion.

WRITING STEP BY STEP

Using Mike Royko's column as an example, write a narrative essay about a childhood experience that suddenly let you see some less than admirable aspect of the adult world. Royko, after making it clear that he grew up in a white section of the city, lets us see how the vicious action of his former hero on the Cub team opened his eyes to racial prejudice.

Think of a similar experience in your own past that will allow you to show the unfairness of some human behavior or the pain caused by some human weakness. Perhaps you could tell about your accidental discovery of disloyalty or cheating by someone you admired and trusted. Or you could tell the story of the first time you observed adult violence or adult cruelty. Write this assignment as a cautionary tale for an audience of high school seniors.

A. Think about the story and the insight you gained from it. Write out the meaning of the incident as a thesis statement, but do not include it in the essay. Just keep it in mind as a guide in selecting details.

B. Jot down the events you want to cover, leaving lots of space between them. Next, go over the events, and fill in the spaces with all the details you can think of about each event. Then, go through the whole sheet again, and carefully decide just which events and which details you want to use in your narrative. Select only the most descriptive details that will allow your readers to experience the event as you did.

C. Use *I* in telling your story. Consider narrating it from the point of view of yourself as a child, as Royko does. Try to remember how you actually saw things when you were young and innocent and tell the story that way. See Royko's paragraphs 1, 10, and 14 for good examples.

D. Begin, as Royko does, by briefly setting the scene. Be sure to work in the time, either here or later (as Royko does in para. 3).

E. Don't give away the point of your story, but try to work in a teaser (or a *delay*) as he does in his opening. The men are talking about what "it" would do to baseball, but we readers have no clue what "it" means and read on to find out.

F. In your conclusion, try to let your readers understand what you learned from the incident, but don't tell them straight out. See Royko's last three paragraphs, in which he tells us how he felt as a child and how he feels now as a man—and both are positive feelings. He lets us see how wrong racial prejudice is and at the same time reminds us of how proud blacks could feel about Jackie Robinson's success.

G. If exactly what people say is important to the story, put the speech in direct quotations, as Royko does in paragraphs 12 and 13.

OTHER WRITING IDEAS

1. Did you ever do something quite wrong in response to peer pressure? Tell the story of how this happened and how you felt about it at the time—and how you feel about it now.

2. USING THE INTERNET. Enter the name of Ida Wells-Barnett or Wilma Rudolph into your search engine, and you will find the story of another African American who, like Jackie Robinson, led the way in the fight against racial segregation. After reading about one of these women, write a narrative for a group of middle school students telling the story of her stand against injustice.

3. COLLABORATIVE WRITING. With a group of classmates, have a brainstorming session in which you discuss difficult ethical and moral decisions each of you has faced and how you responded. For many, deciding whether to cheat, steal, or tattle creates their first moral crisis.

Then, tell the story of a tough decision you had to make and what happened as a result.

4. WRITING ABOUT READING. What difference does it make that the story is told by an adult looking back? Write an essay about the use of memory and point of view in this selection. Think of how you would tell a story from your childhood now, in contrast with how you would've told it at the time.

GAINING WORD POWER

Following is the vocabulary entry for the word *unique*, which appears in Mike Royko's title. It comes from the *Webster's New World Dictionary*, 3rd college edition, published by Simon & Schuster. Can you make sense of it?

> **u|nique** (yoo& nēk') *adj.* [[Fr < L *unicus*, single < ONE]] 1 one and only; sole [a *unique* specimen] 2 having no like or equal; unparalleled [a *unique* achievement] 3 highly unusual, extraordinary, rare, etc.: a common usage still objected to by some—**u|nique′ly** *adv.*—**u|nique′ness** *n.*

All dictionaries are unique, but here's how to read this entry from the *New World*.

1. The boldfaced word itself tells you how to spell it, and the thin line (between the *u* and the *n*) shows where it divides into syllables. Some dictionaries use centered dots instead.

2. The syllables inside the parentheses (some dictionaries use slash marks) let you know how to pronounce the word. If you don't understand the symbols, check inside the front or back cover or at the bottom of the page.

3. The boldfaced abbreviation tells you the part of speech. Notice that further down in the entry you'll see other forms of the same word that are different parts of speech (*uniquely* **adv.** and *uniqueness* **n.**). Sometimes those other parts of speech have different meanings listed.

4. Those weird notations inside the double brackets give the *etymology* of the word—that is, they tell us how it came into our language. The entry reads this way: "The word *unique* comes to us from the French, derived from the Latin *unicus*, meaning *single*, derived from *unus*, meaning *one*." Check the explanatory notes in your dictionary to learn how to figure out the etymologies.

5. Various meanings are numbered. Some dictionaries list the most common meaning first; others begin with the oldest meaning, which would often be the least common. So, again, check your dictionary's

explanatory notes. The *New World* lists meanings from oldest to newest.

6. All dictionaries give warnings about usage. If you look up the word *ain't*, you will find it labeled *slang* or *nonstandard*, perhaps even with a warning that some people have strong objections to it. In the entry for *unique*, the third meaning of "highly unusual, extraordinary, rare, etc." is followed by a caution that this is "a common usage still objected to by some." Those *some* often include English teachers, so avoid writing *most unique* or *quite unique* or *very unique*. Remember the etymology.

Now, to practice what you just learned, look up the word *debut* from Royko's title, and answer the following questions:

1. How many syllables does it have?
2. What different ways can it be correctly pronounced?
3. What parts of speech can it be?
4. What language did it come from?
5. What are two meanings of the word?
6. Are there any usage labels or warnings?

EDITING SKILLS: PUNCTUATING CONVERSATION

When adding conversation to your narrative, you know, of course, to use quotation marks around other people's words. But you also need to notice how other marks are used with those quotation marks. Look at the punctuation in these sentences from Royko's essay:

Then I heard a voice say: "Would you consider selling that?"
"I'll give you $10 for it," he said.

The words telling who is talking—called a tag—need to be separated from the quotation. When the tag comes *before* the quotation, you can use either a comma or a colon to separate. When the tag comes *after* the quoted words, use a comma.

Sometimes you may want to put the tag in the middle:

"I don't want to sell it," I mumbled; "it's mine!"
"Go away!" I yelled, "or I'll call a cop."
"I'm going home," I told Joe, "before I lose this ball."

If you start a new sentence after the tag, you need a semicolon or a period, just as you would in any other writing.

And don't stack up punctuation. If you use an exclamation mark or a question mark, omit the comma or period.

Notice that periods and commas go before the ending quotation marks. But with question marks (and exclamation marks), you have to decide whether the tag is a question (or an exclamation) or whether the quoted words are.

> "Oh, well," Jamal said, "it takes all kinds!"
> Can you believe Jamal said, "It takes all kinds"?

Finally, whenever you change speakers, begin a new paragraph.

As you read your way through the selections in this text, pay attention to the way quoted material is punctuated.

EXERCISE

Now, for practice, put the necessary punctuation in the following sentences:

> Oh, heaven help us Marvin exclaimed I forgot to do our income taxes
>
> We'd better get started on them fast then responded Rosa
>
> Marvin groaned You get the receipts together while I try to find the calculator
>
> How am I supposed to know where to find the receipts asked Rosa
>
> Surely roared Marvin you've been keeping them all together some place
>
> Rosa was silent during a long pause, then asked Was I supposed to
>
> Marvin slapped his palm against his forehead and yelled We're doomed
>
> Don't worry, honey soothed Rosa they never send you to Leavenworth on a first offense

Go back and look at the essay you just wrote: Did you punctuate the conversations accurately? Check all your quotations carefully, and make any necessary corrections.

🐦 WEB SITES

www.negroleaguebaseball.com/
The online home of Negro League history.
www.blackbaseball.com/
The Negro League's Web Site.

Both sites provide historical background and perspectives that relate to the topic of Royko's essay.

PREPARING TO READ

How do you picture a typical prison guard? Have your ideas been shaped
by movies and television? In your journal, write a brief description of how
you think a prison guard would look, talk, and act.

••

A Guard's First Night on the Job

••

WILLIAM RECKTENWALD

*William Recktenwald is a journalist who once served as a guard in a maximum
security prison in Pontiac, Illinois. The following firsthand account first appeared
in the* St. Louis Globe Democrat *in 1978.*

TERMS TO RECOGNIZE

orientation *(para. 1)*	an introduction to and explanation of an activity or a job
contraband *(para. 2)*	smuggled goods
cursory *(para. 2)*	hasty, not complete or thorough
apprehensive *(para. 9)*	worried, anxious, uneasy
virtually *(para. 9)*	for all practical purposes
ruckus *(para. 9)*	noisy disturbance
din *(para. 10)*	loud, continuous noise
equivalent *(para. 15)*	the equal of, the same as

When I arrived for my first shift, 3 to 11 P.M., I had not had a minute   1
of training except for a one-hour orientation lecture the previous day. I was
a "fish," a rookie guard, and very much out of my depth. A veteran officer
welcomed the "fish" and told us: "Remember, these guys don't have anything to do all day, 24 hours a day, but think of ways to make you mad. No
matter what happens, don't lose your cool. Don't lose your cool!"

I had been assigned to the segregation unit, containing 215 inmates   2
who are the most trouble. It was an assignment nobody wanted. To get
there, I passed through seven sets of bars. My uniform was my only ticket
through each of them. Even on my first day, I was not asked for any identification, searched, or sent through a metal detector. I could have been carrying weapons, drugs, or any other contraband. I couldn't believe this was

what's meant by a maximum-security institution. In the week I worked at Pontiac, I was subjected to only one check, and that one was cursory.

The segregation unit consists of five tiers, or galleries. Each is about 300 feet long and has 44 cells. The walkways are about 3 1/2 feet wide, with the cells on one side and a rail and cyclone fencing on the other. As I walked along one gallery, I noticed that my elbows could touch cell bars and fencing at the same time. That made me easy pickings for anybody reaching out of a cell.   3

The first thing they told me was that a guard must never go out on a gallery by himself. You've got no weapons with which to defend yourself, not even a radio to summon help. All you've got is the man with whom you're working. My partner that first night was Bill Hill, a soft-spoken six-year veteran who immediately told me to take the cigarettes out of my shirt pocket because the inmates would steal them. Same for my pen, he said—or "They'll grab it and stab you."   4

We were told to serve dinner on the third tier, and Hill quickly tried to fill me in on the facts of prison life. That's when I learned about cookies and the importance they have to the inmates. "They're going to try and grab them, they're going to try and steal them any way they can," he said. "Remember, you only have enough cookies for the gallery, and if you let them get away, you'll have to explain to the guys at the end why there weren't any for them."   5

Hill then checked out the meal, groaning when he saw the drippy ravioli and stewed tomatoes. "We're going to be wearing this," he remarked, before deciding to simply discard the tomatoes. We served nothing to drink. In my first six days at Pontiac, I never saw an inmate served a beverage.   6

Hill instructed me to put on plastic gloves before we served the meal. In view of the trash and waste through which we'd be wheeling the food cart, I thought he was joking. He wasn't. "Some inmates don't like white hands touching their food," he explained.   7

Everything went routinely as we served the first 20 cells, and I wasn't surprised when every inmate asked for extra cookies. Suddenly, a huge arm shot through the bars of one cell and began swinging a metal rod at Hill. As he ducked away, the inmate snared the cookie box. From the other side of the cart, I lunged to grab the cookies—and was grabbed in turn. A powerful hand from the cell behind me was pulling my arm. As I jerked away, objects began crashing about, and a metal can struck me in the back.   8

Until that moment I had been apprehensive. Now I was scared. The food cart virtually trapped me, blocking my retreat. Whirling around, I noticed that mirrors were being held out of every cell so the inmates could   9 watch the ruckus. I didn't realize the mirrors were plastic and became terrified that the inmates would start smashing them to cut me up.

The ordinary din of the cell house had turned into a deafening roar. For   10
the length of the tier, arms stretched into the walkway, making grabbing motions. Some of the inmates swung brooms about. "Let's get out of here— now!" Hill barked. Wheeling the food cart between us, we made a hasty retreat.

Downstairs, we reported what had happened. My heart was thumping,   11
my legs felt weak. Inside the plastic gloves, my hands were soaked with sweat. Yet the attack on us wasn't considered unusual by the other guards, especially in segregation. That was strictly routine, and we didn't even file a report.

What was more shocking was to be sent immediately back to the same   12
tier to pass out medication. But as I passed the cells from which we'd been attacked, the men in them simply requested their medicine. It was as if what had happened minutes before was already ancient history. From another cell, however, an inmate began raging at us. "Get my medication," he said. "Get it now, or I'm going to kill you." I was learning that whatever you're handing out, everybody wants it, and those who don't get it frequently respond by threatening to kill or maim you. Another fact of prison life.

Passing cell no. 632, I saw that a prisoner I had helped take to the   13
hospital before dinner was back in his cell. When we took him out, he had been disabled by mace and was very wobbly. Hill and I had been extremely gentle, handcuffing him carefully, then practically carrying him down the stairs. As we went by his cell this time, he tossed a cup of liquid on us.

Back downstairs, I learned I would be going back to that tier for a   14
third time, to finish serving dinner. This time, we planned to slip in the other side of the tier so we wouldn't have to pass the trouble cells. The plates were already prepared. "Just get in there and give them their food and get out," Hill said. I could see he was nervous, which made me even more so. "Don't stop for anything. If you get hit, just back off, 'cause if they snare you or hook you some way and get you against the bars, they'll hurt you real bad."

Everything went smoothly. Inmates in the three most troublesome   15
cells were not getting dinner, so they hurled some garbage at us. But that's something else I had learned; getting no worse than garbage thrown at you is the prison equivalent of everything going smoothly.

RESPONDING TO READING

Now that you have read the essay, write a paragraph in your journal describing what kind of person you think William Recktenwald is and how he responds to his new job. In another paragraph, note any ways in which he is different from your expectations of a typical prison guard.

CONSIDERING CONTENT

1. What was the only piece of advice the author got during his orientation as a rookie guard?
2. What can you tell about race relations in Pontiac prison? Are the guards white and the prisoners black?
3. What qualities would a prison guard need in order to work in the segregation unit?
4. Why is the width of the galleries an important detail?
5. What kind of weapons does a guard carry?
6. At the end of the essay, why are the guards not much bothered by having food thrown at them?

CONSIDERING METHOD

1. Why does the writer quote directly the "welcoming" advice given by the veteran police officer?
2. The descriptive details in paragraph 2 have no vivid appeal to the senses. Why, then, are they included?
3. Look at the action verbs in paragraph 8: *shot, ducked, snared, lunged,* and *jerked.* Why are they more effective than *came, moved, took, stepped forward,* and *pulled?* What added feeling do you get from Recktenwald's verbs? Find five more examples of verbs that you think add color and emotion.
4. In paragraphs 7 and 9, the writer uses short-short sentences: "He wasn't" and "Now I was scared." Why do you think he uses such short statements?
5. How is the essay organized?
6. What sentence serves as a thesis statement to tell readers what the essay is about?
7. What is the author's purpose?
8. Do you think the conclusion is effective? Can you explain why?

COMBINING STRATEGIES

Recktenwald employs several writing strategies in narrating the story of his first day on the job. He combines description, illustrations, and examples (see Chap. 4) with cause-and-effect analysis (see Chap. 9). Choose one description and one example, and explain how each appeals to your emotions and to your understanding of the situation the author faced.

WRITING STEP BY STEP

Did you ever hold a difficult job? If so, write an essay describing a bad day. Use specific details that will let your readers share your experience. Follow the form of "A Guard's First Night on the Job." If you don't have a job, describe a bad day at home or at school.

A. Begin by giving your readers a brief orientation—that is, explaining where you work, what you do, maybe what time you begin if you have a shift job.

B. At the end of your introduction, let your readers know that the essay will be about a bad day on the job. Your purpose may be to entertain, if you have some humorous incidents to relate, or you may write simply to inform your readers about how trying your job is, as William Recktenwald does. Or maybe you want to make the point that your line of work is pitifully underpaid for the stress it causes you.

C. Use the informal "you" to speak directly to your readers.

D. Think of one particularly troublesome detail of your job that bothers you repeatedly (like Recktenwald's problems with the cookies) and focus on that. Or jot down a number of incidents that drive you crazy and relate those in the order in which they typically occur.

E. Include specific details (like the cigarettes, pen, plastic gloves, plastic mirrors) as you describe incidents.

F. Use action verbs whenever possible (like Recktenwald's *shot, snared, lunged, grabbed, jerked, barked, hooked,* and *hurled*) to give your readers a picture of what happened.

G. If you include people, briefly identify them ("Bill Hill, a soft-spoken, six-year veteran").

H. Write a closing that reinforces how bad your day can be without actually saying so, as Recktenwald does when he concludes that merely having garbage thrown at him means his shift is "going smoothly."

OTHER WRITING IDEAS

1. Describe the most stressful vacation you ever took (or the most stressful picnic or wedding or trip to the zoo or any activity that you would expect to be pleasurable but wasn't).

2. COLLABORATIVE WRITING. Get together with classmates or friends and talk about the first time you became aware of racial prejudice—directed either toward yourself or toward someone else. Then decide what specific details to include, and write about the experience.

3. USING THE INTERNET. Write an essay about the day in the life of someone with an unusual job, like farrier, sommelier, concierge,

celebrity personal assistant, stunt person, forensic accountant, body double, animal psychologist, or hotwalker.

4. WRITING ABOUT READING. Writers use concrete descriptions and examples to make abstract feelings easier to understand. What feelings does Recktenwald convey with his use of descriptive details and specific events? Identify five or six and evaluate their effectiveness. What feelings did they suggest to you?

GAINING WORD POWER

Since our brief definitions are sometimes cursory, look up in a college-size dictionary the following words from the Terms to Recognize list. Then write a sentence using each word.

orientation   apprehensive   cursory
contraband   equivalent

EDITING SKILLS: COMMAS AFTER DEPENDENT ELEMENTS

Copy these sentences from the reading exactly. As you write, look for a pattern they all follow.

As he ducked away, the inmate snared the cookie box.

When we took him out, he had been disabled by mace and was very wobbly.

As we went by his cell this time, he tossed a cup of liquid on us.

Each of these sentences has two parts. Notice that the second part, after the comma, can stand alone as a sentence; it's called an **independent clause.** If you read the first part alone, it does not sound complete. The first part is called a **dependent clause** for this reason. When you write a sentence in which the *independent* part comes after a *dependent* part, you need to put in a comma to separate the two.

EXERCISE

Put commas in the following sentences:

While planning is important do not overschedule your time.

Since the best courses fill up early plan at least a term or two in advance.

If you cannot write well you will be at a disadvantage.

Now fill in the blanks to make complete sentences below:

Although studying is the major task of college life, _____

_____.

Because grades are important to some employers, _____

_____.

_____, Henry

went to the basketball game.

Next, write three sentences that follow this dependent-comma-independent pattern.

Finally, check your essay to be sure that you have included the commas in sentences like these.

WEB SITE

www.prisonexp.org/
The Stanford Prison Experiment gives details about the controversial simulation study of the psychology of imprisonment that was conducted at Stanford University in 1971.

PREPARING TO READ

Think of the last time you were personally, emotionally affected by something that happened outside your own country or community. What was the experience or news that touched you? How did you react? Do you know why this particular happening moved you emotionally?

••

Road Work

••

Staff Sergeant Jack Lewis

The following selection appeared in the anthology Operation Homecoming: Iraq, Afghanistan, and the Home Front, in the Words of U.S. Troops and Their Families *(2006). This collection of eyewitness accounts, private journals, short stories, letters, and other writings grew out of a series of workshops sponsored by the National Endowment for the Arts and conducted by a group of distinguished American writers.*

TERMS TO RECOGNIZE

monstrous *(para. 1)*	exceptionally large, enormous
hypnotically *(para. 8)*	in a sing-song, trancelike way
dervish *(para. 10)*	member of a Moslem sect that engages in a whirling dance to bring about a mystic trance
capered *(para. 15)*	leaped or jumped around
superficially *(para. 15)*	not seriously, on the surface
animated *(para.15)*	active, energized
sedate *(para. 30)*	administer a calming drug
Gauloise *(para. 33)*	a French brand of cigarette, made with dark tobacco from the Middle East
IEDs *(para. 37)*	improvised explosive devices

Iraqi civilians are not only caught in the crossfire when hostilities erupt between American troops and insurgents, they are the victims of military-related accidents as well. In February 2005, forty-one-year-old U. S. Army Reserve Staff Sergeant Jack Lewis witnessed the aftermath of a late-night crash involving a nineteen-ton Stryker armored vehicle (call sign "Rattlesnake Six-Seven") and a small car. While Lewis had seen shocking acts of violence and bloodshed during his deployment with Tactical Psychological Operations Detachment 1290, 1-25 SBCT (Stryker Brigade Combat Team), nothing had struck him as hard emotionally as the suffering caused by this collision.

—Editors, *Operation Homecoming*

I never heard the boom-CRUNCH, only imagined it later. There was strong braking, followed by a great deal of shouting. Our Stryker moaned through its monstrous air brakes and then bumped, heaved, and finally ground itself to a halt. 1

"Six-Seven's in the ditch!" 2

"Did they roll it?" 3

"No, they're up. I think they're disabled." 4

"Where's the colonel? Is the colonel's vehicle okay?" 5

The colonel's vehicle was okay. 6

The major said that we would need a combat lifesaver. It wasn't combat. There were no lives left to save. But I dug out the CLS bag, because you never know, do you? And walked across a pitch dark highway. 7

Somebody was wailing in Arabic, hypnotically, repetitiously. 8

A single car headlight was burning, a single shaft of light beaming across the road like an accusing finger. When tactical spotlights suddenly illuminated the little car, we found the source of the wailing. 9

He was an older man with a silver beard, a monumental, red-veined nose, and a big, thick wool overcoat. He was hopping like a dervish, bowing rapidly from the waist and throwing his arms to the sky, then to his knees, over and over again in a kind of elaborate dance of grief. 10

Down the road a hundred meters or so, Six-Seven's vehicle commander and air guards had dismounted and were standing around in the ditch. Nobody had started smoking yet. 11

I walked to the car with an Air Force sergeant and moved the older man aside as gently as possible. He was built like a blacksmith, powerful through the neck and shoulders. 12

It's hard to describe what we found in the car. It had been a young man, only moments earlier that night. A cop or a fireman or a soldier would have simply said, "It's a mess in there." I used to be a fireman. I'm a soldier now. It was as bad a mess as I've seen. 13

I'm not a medic. We didn't have one with us. It's still my responsibility to preserve life. So I squeezed into the crumpled passenger area, sat on the shattered glass, and tried to take the pulse from his passenger-side arm (nothing) and his neck (nothing). I thought about CPR, but only for a moment. His left arm was mostly torn off, and the left side of his head was flattened. 14

Up on the highway, CIs walked around, gave and took orders. By the   15
car, the victim's father still capered madly, throwing his arms around, crying
out to God or anyone. I asked him, in my own language, to come with me, to
calm down, to let me help him. I put my arm around him and guided the old
Arab to the road. I sat him on the cold ramp of our Stryker and tried to assess
his injuries. It seemed impossible that he could be only as superficially
scratched up as he appeared. His hand was injured, bruised or possibly broken, and he had a cut on his left ear. I wrapped a head bandage onto him and
tied it gently in back. It looked like a traditional headdress with a missing top.
Every few seconds he would get animated, and I would put my hand firmly on
his shoulder. He would not hold still long enough for me to splint his arm.

"Why can't he shut up?"   16

"You ever lose a kid?" This is a pointless question to ask a soldier   17
who's practically a kid himself.

We moved him into the Stryker, assuring him that no, we weren't   18
arresting him. But he didn't care. Whenever he started to calm down, he
would look toward the car and break into wails. I sat next to him, put my
arm around his shoulder, tried to keep him from jumping around enough to
hurt himself or a soldier. I held him tightly with my right arm. By the next
morning, my shoulder would be on fire.

Forty minutes later a medic arrived.   19

"What's his status, sergeant?"   20

"He has a cut on his left earlobe. I think his hand is broken." (I think   21
his heart is broken.)

"Roger. Okay, I got this."   22

"Thanks." (Bless you for what you do every day, doc.)   23

I got out of the way, letting the old guy go for the first time in almost   24
an hour. He started wailing again almost immediately. While the medic
worked on him, the colonel's interpreter came over and fired a few questions at the man. It sounded like an interrogation.

They had been on their way back to Sinjar, just a few miles away. The   25
younger man had been taking his father back from shopping. They were
minutes from home.

We didn't find any weapons in the car—either piece of it. There was   26
no propaganda, nor were there false IDs. If we had stopped these people at
a checkpoint, we would have thanked them and let them go on.

The young man had been a student. Engineering. With honors. Pride   27
of the family. What we like to think of as Iraq's future.

Finally, I had to ask, "What does he keep saying?"   28

The terp looked at me, disgusted, resigned, or maybe just plain tired.   29
"He says to kill him now."

The colonel came over and asked the medic if he could sedate the   30
man with morphine.

"No, sir. Morphine won't help."   31

"Well, can't you give him something to calm him down? I mean, this   32
is unacceptable."

I walked away and lit a Gauloise. A sergeant came up next to me,   33
smoking. I didn't say anything. After a few moments in the black quiet, I
overheard him say, "It wasn't anyone's fault. It was just an accident."

"I know." Inhale. Cherry glow. Long exhale. "Why we gotta drive in   34
blackout—here—I don't get."

"If Six-Seven had turned their lights on a couple of seconds earlier. . . ."   35

"Yeah. I know." And he went to help carry the young man's remains   36
into the sudden light show of ambulances and police jeeps, surrounded by
young Arabic men with steely eyes.

The supersized staff sergeant who mans the .50 cal on our truck   37
walked down the road to kick a little ass and get Six-Seven's recovery
progress back on track. Within a few minutes, they had it hooked up. It
would be two weeks before that Stryker would roll outside the wire again,
this in an environment where trucks totaled by IEDs are welded back
together and sent again into harm's way in mere hours.

I went and sat on the back gate of the Stryker. I felt the cold creep   38
into me.

The old man sat next to me, perhaps too tired to continue his tirade   39
against cruel Fate, careless Americans, war and its accidents.

I haven't lost a full-grown son, just a little daughter. A baby. And she   40
wasn't torn from me in a terror of rending steel, stamped out by a sudden monster roaring out of the night. She went so quietly that her passing never woke her
mother. I like to think she kissed her on the way out, on her way home.

But still, sitting on the steel tail of the monster that killed his son, I   41
think I knew exactly how one Iraqi man felt.

"Just kill me now."   42

We sat and looked straight into the lights.   43

RESPONDING TO READING

Where you surprised at the author's reactions to this event? What caused his
strong emotional response to the father's grief? How do you think you would
have reacted? Explain.

CONSIDERING CONTENT

1. Why do you think Sgt. Lewis wanted to tell this story? For whom was he writing? Do you think you're part of the audience Lewis had in mind?
2. What do you learn about the Iraqis? What is the point of saying they didn't have any weapons, propaganda, or false IDs (para. 26)?
3. Why does the author include the details about the young man who was killed? What does he mean when he says, "What we like to think of as Iraq's future" (para. 27)?
4. What do you discover about the author's personal life? How does this information shape your understanding of the story?
5. What kind of person is Sgt. Lewis? Do you think you would like to meet him?

CONSIDERING METHOD

1. Take note of the verbs that Lewis uses in the second sentence of the opening paragraph of his narrative: *moaned, bumped, heaved,* and *ground to a halt.* What sights and sounds do these verbs convey?
2. Why does the author enclose two comments in parentheses (paras. 21 and 23)?
3. What do you make of the comments of the others on the scene (the young soldier, the medic, the colonel, the staff sergeant)? How do their reactions and attitudes compare to Lewis's?
4. In what ways does the author use dialogue (or spoken conversation) to advance the narrative? Is it effective?
5. Reread paragraph 36 with attention to the descriptive language. Find another paragraph that uses vivid description and point out specific words that bring the scene to life.
6. Consider the last two lines in the narrative. How do they make you feel? Why do you think the author ended his narrative in this way?

WRITING STEP BY STEP

Write an essay in which you tell the story of how you helped another person and realized that you benefited as well. Brainstorm a list of situations and choose the best example to write about. Remember that your own story doesn't have to be solemn: it could be humorous, or you could have been unsuccessful in your efforts.

A. Set the stage for your story in the opening paragraph by describing where you were when you encountered the challenge, problem, disagreement, or conflict that you helped with.

B. Then briefly explain the events that gave rise to the situation, including just enough background details to let your readers understand how the trouble arose.

C. Next, describe the person (or people) you helped. Use concrete details, as Lewis does in telling us about the Iraqi father.

D. Identify other people who played a part in this story. Use dialogue, as Lewis does, to give your readers a sense of how these other people felt and reacted.

E. Explain what you did to help the person in trouble (as Lewis does in paras. 15 and 18).

F. Mention any obstacles or difficulties you encountered in trying to help out.

G. End on a note of reflection: explain how you felt about your actions and how you benefited from helping someone else. You could also conclude with a thesis statement about the value of helping others.

OTHER WRITING IDEAS

1. Narrate an event in which you hid your true feelings about what took place. Some possibilities: a going-away party for someone you disliked, a weekend trip you didn't want to take, an interview for a low-paying job, a blind date, a conversation in which you held a minority opinion, an ex-girl/boyfriend's wedding. Make it clear why you didn't show your true feelings and how you felt about keeping them hidden.

2. COLLABORATIVE WRITING. Discuss with a group of friends or classmates whether the old saying "There is no education like adversity" is true or not. After you decide how you feel about the matter, think of an incident that illustrates your belief, and use it to make your point in a narrative.

3. USING THE INTERNET. "Road Work" is included in the book *Operation Homecoming*, an anthology of eyewitness accounts, private journals, short stories, and other writings by American military personnel stationed in Iraq and Afghanistan. The National Endowment of the Arts (NEA) sponsored the project. Visit the NEA Web site at www.nea .gov/national/homecoming/index.html, and click on "Anthology submissions" to read other essays and stories written by troops about their wartime experiences. Choose one selection, and write a summary of what you read and explain how you reacted to the story.

4. WRITING ABOUT READING. Near the end of his essay Lewis says, "I think I knew exactly how one Iraqi man felt." Do you think he really

did? Write an essay explaining what Lewis meant by this comment and analyzing why he was able to empathize with the Iraqi father.

GAINING WORD POWER

Lewis uses several striking **similes** to enhance his descriptions:

a single shaft of light beaming across the road like an accusing finger
hopping like a dervish
built like a blacksmith

Similes use *like* or *as* to compare things that are usually not seen as similar. A simile catches the reader's attention by pointing out a resemblance that is surprising or imaginative.

EXERCISE

Come up with a simile to describe each of these scenes or qualities and use it in a sentence. If you can, add another sentence or two to extend and explain the comparison.

Example: a person's personality

My roommate is like an empty candy wrapper. At first you think he's full of personality, but then you find out there's nothing there.

1. The sound of a school cafeteria
2. People waiting in a long line at a supermarket or bank
3. The effect of eating a big meal
4. Driving in a heavy downpour
5. The feeling of meeting someone's parents for the first time

Now look through the essay you have just written, and see if you can improve the descriptions by adding a simile or two.

EDITING SKILLS: CHOOSING *THERE, THEIR,* OR *THEY'RE*

Words that sound alike, called **homophones,** can be treacherous. In speech, we don't think about which one to select, but in writing we have to make a choice. Because homophones are often common words, such as *there, their,* and *they're,* we can't avoid using them. And because the meanings are quite different, we really do have to get them right or our readers will be confused.

First, look at the use of the word *there* in these sentences from "Road Work":

There was strong braking, followed by a great deal of shouting.
There were no lives left to save.

In these sentences *there* is just a fill-in word; it doesn't have much meaning. We use *there* to begin sentences like these when we want to say that something or someone exists or existed. The same spelling goes for the use of the word to indicate a place:

It's a mess in *there*.

Now look at the use of *their* in these passages from the same essay:

They had been on *their* way back to Sinjar, just a few miles away.
If Six-Seven had turned *their* lights on a couple of seconds earlier . . .

The word *their* is a possessive, showing ownership or belonging. In the first example it refers to "they" (the Iraqi man and his son); in the second example, it refers to the men in "Six-Seven" (the armored vehicle).
Finally, take a look at this sentence:

No, *they're* up. I think *they're* disabled.

In these examples, *they're* sounds just like the others, but you can substitute the words *they are* for it. *They're* is a contraction, just like *don't* for *do not* and *she's* for *she is*. If you can substitute *they are*, you know you have the right word. If you can't, you need *there* or *their*.
All right, let's review:

There are numerous sound-alike words in English.

You have to know the differences in *their* meanings if you want to use them correctly.

They're often common words that we use a lot.

EXERCISE

Fill the blanks in the following sentences with *there*, *their*, or *they're*.

1. _____ are no solutions to this problem.
2. Your cousins have arrived, and _____ going to stay for dinner.
3. When George Eliot and Jane Austen wrote _____ great novels, _____ were few creative opportunities for women besides writing.
4. The team members should have known that _____ luck

wouldn't hold. But _____ definitely looking forward to next season.

5. Although it wasn't _____ fault, the twins are sure to get blamed, and _____ not happy about it.

Look over the essay you have just written to see if you used *there, their*, or *they're*. Did you choose the right one? Go over some past papers, too, to see how accurate you are in using these three homophones. Copy three to five sentences in which you use one, and justify your choice in each case. (For more about homophones, see Chapter 4, p. 94.)

WEB SITE

www.afsc.org/iraq/stories.htm
Maintained by the American Friends Service Committee, this site focuses on the civilian side of the war in Iraq by posting personal stories of Iraqis and Iraqi refugees.

STUDENT ESSAY USING DESCRIPTION AND NARRATION

Domestic Abuse

Kelly Berlin

Kelly Berlin grew up in a farming community in east central Illinois. She attended Eastern Illinois University, where she wrote this essay for her freshman composition class. At that time she was planning to major in business.

It was the summer of my freshman year, and I had been baby-sitting   1
my two-year-old niece, Briana, at my sister's house every weekday for the past couple of months. It was late in the afternoon on a Friday, so I couldn't wait for my sister Kim to come home from work. Since she was already a half an hour late, I decided to take a shower so I wouldn't be late for my date later that evening. I was in the bathroom blow-drying my hair when my sister and her boyfriend Scott came home.

My sister and Scott had been dating a couple of years, despite the   2
disapproval of my family. Scott, even though he had a child, was not a good "father figure" for my niece. Scott was a regular drinker and smoker, and his appearance did nothing for him. He was over six-feet tall with big, bulging muscles; he wore tight clothes; and he had long, shaggy hair. My sister, on the other hand, standing only five-feet-five-inches tall, was slender with long, curly brown hair and a beautiful white smile.

I finished blow-drying my hair and was going to ask my sister to take   3
me home, but I heard her and Scott fighting in the bedroom. I went into the living room to watch television with my niece and to keep her mind off the shouting. I started to become worried because the yelling became more intense. All of a sudden, I heard a loud noise—not a boom, but more like a crack, a board breaking. The shouting stopped.

"Briana, stay here!" I left my niece in the living room and ran into the   4
bedroom. "Scott, what in the hell did you do to her? Get away from her!" My sister was lying limp on her bed with her face down.

"It's none of your business. Get out of here," he yelled at me with a   5
fierce look in his eyes.

I was shaking but yelled back at him with just as much determination   6
and strength. "Bullshit, if it's not my business. She's my sister. Don't think I'm just going to sit here while you push her around!" I turned, looked at my sister, and asked gently, "Kim, are you all right?"

"Yeah," Kim told me in a shaky voice. "I'll be all right. But my legs   7
hurt because I hit the foot board when he pushed me down."

"Scott, leave NOW!" I said with all the authority I could manage.   8

"Shut up, Kelly. This isn't your house, and I'll leave whenever I please."   9

My sister pleaded with him. "Scott, please leave me alone. Just leave   10
me alone."

He stormed out of the bedroom and out of the house like a raging   11
bull. I helped my sister sit up and looked at her legs. She had two long, wide
bruises forming across her upper thighs from where they hit the foot board.
I told her to stay on her bed while I checked on Briana and called my mom
for help.

My mom arrived about ten minutes later, and I told her what had   12
happened. She was furious and was determined to do something about it.
We called the police to report the incident and file charges. When the police
arrived at the house, I described the scene and signed my name to the
papers to file charges. Then, they took photographs of my sister's bruises
and recorded her statement. But she wouldn't sign the papers. She had
decided not to press charges. Well, I was confused, but I thought I could
still press charges against him. I was wrong. I hadn't actually seen Scott
push my sister. I had only heard them fighting and had found her lying on
the bed. We tried to convince my sister to press charges against Scott, but
she refused. She believed that he'd just gotten carried away, that he wouldn't
do it again. We tried to make her realize that he could very well do it again,
but she wouldn't believe us.

As it turned out, my sister was mistaken. Scott continued to beat her   13
and control her life, and she continued to refuse to press charges. Finally,
she realized he was not going to stop, so she left Scott. At one time, she put
a restraining order on him, which kept him away temporarily. And fortunately, he lost his license due to DUIs, so he had no legal transportation to
get to her house. Now, the only time he harasses her is when he's high on
drugs. But as time and experience have taught my sister, she now calls the
police herself.

CONSIDERING CONTENT AND METHOD

1. Do you think the topic is well chosen? Is the focus narrow enough?
2. What descriptive details does the writer include? Do you think they
   are effective? If so, why? If not, why not?
3. Do you like Kelly's use of direct conversation in telling the story?
   What does it add to the account?
4. What is the point of this narrative essay? Does the writer state it
   directly or merely imply it? If it is stated directly, tell where.
5. What suggestions would you make to the author to improve this essay?

Strategies for Making a Point:
Example and *Illustration*

IMAGES AND IDEAS

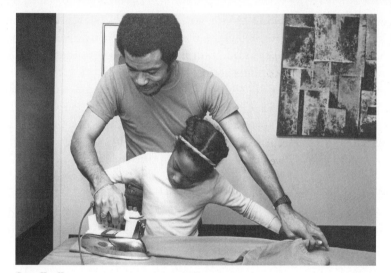

Source: Ken Karp

FOR DISCUSSION AND WRITING

What qualities of the father and daughter relationship are illustrated by this photograph? Make a list of three or four qualities that best define your relationship with one of your parents, and provide several examples of memories or experiences that illustrate each of those qualities. Then write a paragraph or two in which you describe the relationship with this parent, using the examples to make your description clear and convincing.

There's an old saying that a picture is worth a thousand words. It may be true. But we can't always communicate with pictures. Most of the time we have to convey our ideas with words—often with written words. You will find that your skills in describing and narrating can be put to good use in providing examples and illustrations to make a point.

Did you ever read a passage that seemed hard to get the meaning of—that remained fuzzy in your mind no matter how many times you plowed through it? Here's an example of the kind of writing we mean:

> A democratic plan of education includes more than the mere transmission of the social heritage and an attempt to reproduce existing institutions in a static form. The democratic school is also required to indoctrinate individuals with the democratic tradition which, in turn, is based on the agitative liberties of the individual and the needs of society.

If a person spoke those words to you, you could say, "What was that again?" or "Could you give me an example, please?" or "What do you mean by *agitative liberties?*" But you can't question the written page, so the meaning of whatever that writer had in mind is lost.

The difference between an **illustration** and an **example** is not clear cut. Some people use the terms to mean the same thing; some people use illustration to mean several short examples or a fairly long example, such as a brief narrative used within an essay. We don't think it makes a whole lot of difference what you call them—just be sure to use them.

THE POINT OF EXAMPLE AND ILLUSTRATION

Good writers use examples or illustrations to make their writing clear and to make it convincing. As a bonus, concrete examples make writing interesting.

Using Examples to Explain and Clarify

The paragraph about democratic education shows how vague writing is that uses only general statements. Here's another illustration to let you see how examples help in explaining ideas. We have deliberately taken the examples out of the following paragraph. See how much you can get out of it:

> You should define what you mean when any abstract, ambiguous, or controversial terms figure importantly in your writing. Serious miscommunications can occur when audience and writer do not share the same idea about what a word or phrase means, either *connotatively* or *denotatively*.

That's not too clear, is it? But read it now with the examples that were included in the original:

> You should define what you mean when any abstract, ambiguous, or controversial terms figure importantly in your writing. Serious miscommunications can occur when audience and writer do not share the same idea about what a word or phrase means, either *connotatively* (by its associations) or *denotatively* (by its direct meaning). Consider, for instance, the connotations of these words: *daddy, father, old man.* All denote *male parent,* but their understood meanings are quite different. Also, the phrase *good writing* seems clear, doesn't it? Yet three English teachers can argue endlessly about what constitutes good writing if teacher A thinks that good writing is honest, direct, and completely clear; if teacher B thinks that good writing is serious, formal, and absolutely correct; and if teacher C thinks that good writing is flashy, spirited, and highly entertaining.

A couple of the examples in that paragraph are definitions; the others explain the need for definitions. All the examples add clarity and meaning to the passage.

Using Examples and Illustrations to Convince

Examples and illustrations are essential in making a point—that is, as evidence to convince your readers that what you say is right. Take a look at this passage from an article about marriage laws and customs in the nineteenth century:

> Lawmakers passed a hodgepodge of bills setting the terms of the marriage contract. Before Americans could marry, they had to ask the government's permission. Thirty states prohibited people with physical or mental disabilities—epileptics or the "feebleminded, idiotic, imbecilic, or insane"—from marrying. (In many states, women over 45 were exempted from this rule.) Four states disqualified paupers or inmates in public institutions for the indigent. Washington and North Dakota didn't issue marriage licenses to people suffering from advanced tuberculosis. Most states banned interracial marriage; white citizens of Florida could not marry anyone of "one-eighth or more Negro blood." California's white residents couldn't legally marry "a Negro, mulatto, Mongolian, or member of the Malay race."

—*Wall Street Journal,* 25 Feb. 2004

The general claims in the first two sentences are backed up with a series of specific examples.

If you want to convince readers that they should run out and rent *Batman Forever*, you have to provide examples to explain why. You will need to discuss the thrill-packed plot, the wonderful gizmos and toys (including a Batmobile that climbs walls), the deadpan jokes, the uproarious physical humor of Jim Carrey, and Chris O'Donnell's spirited performance as Robin. The more illustrations of this sort you can provide, the more persuasive your essay will be.

THE PRINCIPLES OF EXAMPLE AND ILLUSTRATION

The success of a piece of writing often depends on how well you choose your supporting evidence.

Select Appropriate Examples

You must be sure, first of all, that the examples actually do illustrate the point you want to make. If, for instance, you are explaining how you feel about people who borrow a book and then write their own comments in the margins, be sure to focus on your feelings—of interest, outrage, violation, loss, or whatever you felt. Do not slide off the subject to discuss the interesting philosophy course you bought the book for and the time you accidentally left the book on a lunchroom counter and were quite sure you had lost it forever only to have the guy who sat behind you in class return it, saying he found it when he happened to stop in for a late lunch in the same greasy spoon that afternoon. When people do that sort of free associating in conversation, we tend to suffer through it, even as our eyes glaze over. But it will not do in writing.

Give Plenty of Examples

Keep in mind, though, that you need to supply enough examples to make your ideas clear and convincing. Say you want to persuade your readers that becoming a vegetarian is the key to a long life in a healthy body. If you offer only the single illustration of your uncle Seymour who never ate meat, never had a cold, always felt frisky, and ran in the Boston Marathon to celebrate his seventy-ninth birthday, you are not likely to sway many readers. They'll just think, "Well, wasn't he lucky?" You need either to dig up more examples—perhaps even some statistics about low-fat diets and heart disease—or else change your thesis to focus on Uncle Seymour's personal recipe for keeping fit. There's nothing wrong with using one long illustration, if that single illustration really does prove your point.

Include Specific Information

Finally, you need to develop your examples and illustrations with plenty of specific, graphic **details.** If you say that riding motorcycles is dangerous, you need to follow up with examples more specific than "Every year many people are injured in motorcycle accidents" and "The person on the motorcycle can't always tell what motorists are going to do." Instead, describe what happens when an automobile unexpectedly turns left in front of a motorcyclist traveling forty miles an hour. Mention the crushed noses, the dislocated limbs, the fractured femurs, the broken teeth, and the shattered skulls that such accidents cause. As a general rule, if you use an **abstract word,** like *dangerous,* follow it soon with a specific example, like "His splintered kneecap never did heal properly."

THE PITFALLS OF EXAMPLE AND ILLUSTRATION

If you are writing an essay developed almost entirely through the use of examples, you need to make sure those examples are connected smoothly when you furnish several in a row. Notice how the italicized **transitions** introduce the examples in this paragraph defining a psychological term:

> People who use reaction formation avoid facing an unpleasant truth by acting exactly opposite from the way they truly feel. *For example,* you may have known somebody who acts like the life of the party, always laughing and making jokes, but who you suspect is trying to fool everybody—including herself—into missing the fact that she is sad and lonely. *Another example* of reaction formation involves the person who goes overboard to be open-minded, insisting, "I'm not prejudiced! Why some of my best friends are _____!"

> —Ronald Adler and Neil Towne, "Defense Mechanisms"

Here are some other transitional expressions that you may find useful:

such as	that is	in the following way
namely	in this case	as an illustration
for instance	in addition	at the same time

It's quite possible to use too many transitions. Ask the friend or classmate who helps you edit your first draft to let you know if you've put in more than you need.

As you prepare to revise your essay, ask yourself (and your editorial helper) the following questions:

1. Does each of my examples really illustrate the point I'm trying to make?
2. Have I included enough examples to be convincing?
3. If I'm using a single illustration in some paragraphs, is that convincing?
4. Do any of my illustrations begin to prove the point and then stray from it?
5. Are any of my examples too short or my illustrations too long?
6. Have I used enough specific details?

WHAT TO LOOK FOR IN EXAMPLE AND ILLUSTRATION

As you study the essays in this chapter, focus on the way examples and illustrations are used.

1. In the paragraphs that have a **topic sentence** (the sentence that tells what the paragraph is about), look at the examples or illustrations and decide how convincing they are—that is, how well they explain, support, or enlarge on that idea.
2. Look for concrete, specific, sometimes visual details in the examples and illustrations themselves. Ask yourself what would be lost if these were omitted.
3. Underline the transitional terms used to introduce the examples and illustrations, and keep a list of them in your journal.

PREPARING TO READ

List three people, living or dead, that you consider heroes, and write a sentence explaining why you think each is a hero.

••

My Heroes

••

ELIZABETH BERG

Elizabeth Berg worked as a registered nurse for ten years before becoming a full-time writer, though she has written since she was a child. (She received her first rejection letter at age nine.) She has published a book a year since her first novel, Durable Goods, *in 1993, and many have become bestsellers.* Range of Motion *(1995) was made into a cable-TV movie with Rebecca deMornay in 2000. Berg's themes include the emotional effects of physical illness and "the power and salvation of female friendship." In 1999, Berg published a book of advice on the art and business of writing,* Escaping into the Open: The Art of Writing True.

TERMS TO RECOGNIZE

straight-laced *(para. 10)*	excessively strict
bowed *(para. 11)*	stooped or yielded in defeat
sophisticated *(para. 12)*	refined, worldly-wise
intent *(para. 12)*	firmly focused
luxuriating *(para. 13)*	basking, enjoying
relinquish *(para. 15)*	give up, let out of one's control
precipitated *(para. 16)*	caused

My eight-year-old daughter, Jenny, was given a school assignment not   1
too long ago to write about a hero. "So who did you pick?" I asked her. I
was imagining some possibilities: Rosa Parks, Christa McAuliffe, Sara Lee.
But Jenny answered, "Laura."

"Who?" I asked.   2

"Laura," she said again.   3

"You mean your friend from across the street?" I asked.   4

"Yeah!" she said.   5

I was a little mystified. "How come you picked her?" I asked.   6

"Because," Jenny answered in the ultrapatient voice of Instructor to the Hopeless, "she is my hero."

"Oh," I said. "I see."   7

I must confess that at first I was disappointed. I thought that if her   8 hero was only her friend, she had failed to appreciate the magnificent contributions that real heroes have made to the world. I thought I'd better go out that afternoon and buy some books about famous scientists, artists, athletes, world leaders. That would wise her up. Also, I'd have a look at what they were teaching in her school—didn't she have an appreciation for Martin Luther King?

But then I thought about who I would say my heroes are, and I real-   9 ized that if I told the truth, they wouldn't be famous, either. For although it is undeniable that there have been outstanding people in history who have set glorious examples and inspired me mightily, the people who inspire me most tend to be those who touch me personally, and in quiet ways.

For example, I had an eighth-grade English teacher named Mrs. Zinz.   10 She was demanding and rather straight-laced, I thought, but she taught us certain critical skills for reading and writing. She was concerned not only with what we learned but also with what we were becoming: She put a premium on honesty and tried to get us to understand why it was important. She insisted that we always do our best, and in her class, we almost always did. She told me that I was a terrific creative writer and encouraged my every effort.

As payment for all her good work, I, along with my evil best friend,   11 tortured her. We laughed at her in class, tried to pit our other teachers against her by telling them how unfairly she graded, and once, in a moment of extreme obnoxiousness, called her on the telephone over and over, only to hang up when she answered. Mrs. Zinz was no dummy. She knew who was calling her. In turn she called my mother, who insisted that I call Mrs. Zinz and apologize. With my face aflame, and between clenched teeth, I muttered a grossly insincere "Sorry." She accepted my apology warmly and with a style so graceful that I was infuriated all the more. And though I sulked every day in her class for the rest of the year, she never bowed by reacting to it. I got an A for the term. I moved soon after that and lost track of Mrs. Zinz. I never did apologize in any legitimate way to her. Ironically, she is still an inspiration to me, a lesson in how not to lower yourself to someone else's level, even when that person is doing everything she can to make you crazy. She is, in that way, a hero.

My grandfather, known to me as "Papa," was also a hero of mine.   12 For one thing, he made all of us grandchildren laugh all of the time. He told riddles that were viewed by us as the essence of sophisticated humor. When he greeted us, he shook our hands enthusiastically and at great length, shouting, "How do! How do!" We used to line up to sit on his lap and watch him pop his dentures in and out of his mouth, an astounding feat that thrilled and terrified us—especially before we realized that the teeth were false. He was unfailingly warm and kind and knew how to make a friend out of a stranger; he loved people. I saw him as a man who felt light inside, happy; and feeling that way is no small task in a world that often seems intent on taking back two for every one you get.

Then there is my mother-in-law, Sylvia, who at the age of retire-   13
ment went back to school to pursue a lifetime dream: getting a college diploma. She bumped her bifocals into microscopes, suffered verbal abuse at the hands of an insensitive computer instructor, got used to being the last one to finish every exam, and worried about homework on weekends when she could have been luxuriating in the fact that she had nothing to do. She says that she learned an awful lot, but if you ask me, it's she who did the teaching. I am honored that our family has her love of learning to inspire us.

Beyond that, there are people who are heroes to me because of what   14
they do: mail carriers, who, on days when I stay inside hiding from the cold or heat, subject themselves to hours of it; nurses, who care for those who can't care for themselves every second of every day. I admire stay-at-home mothers for their patience and their creativity in the face of almost no thanks or recognition, and working mothers for the way they juggle an awesome load of responsibilities.

There are people with chronic illness, for whom getting through each   15
day is heroic. There are people who have been married for sixty years, who have lessons to teach us all. There are those who are strong enough in heart and in spirit to speak up when something feels wrong to them, to go against the majority, and oftentimes to risk themselves for the sake of others. And then there are those whom I admire most of all: people who seem to have found the secret of calm and can relinquish the race for the pleasure of seeing what's around them, right here, right now.

I was thinking about all this when I saw Jenny and Laura come into   16
the house. I wanted to know a little more about what had precipitated Jenny's calling Laura a hero. Was it her sharing her brand-new toys? Being there to listen, to soothe, to make better a bad situation in the way that only good friends can? Well, as it happens, no. Jenny told me that Laura was her hero because Laura had saved her from drowning in a creek. *"What?"* I yelled.

Laura rolled her eyes. "Jenny, the water was only about an inch deep." 17 Jenny shrugged and said, "So? You still saved me."

Laura and I let pass a certain look between us. Then she and Jenny   18 went outside again to play.

If you're smart, I thought, you gratefully take your heroes where you   19 find them. As it happens, they are everywhere. So what if the water was only an inch deep? Someone was there, caring about Jenny and showing that she did, a safe hand stretched out to another who was in trouble. This seemed heroic indeed, and later that night when I was tucking her in, I told Jenny that I thought her choice was perfect. "I know," she yawned. "Good night."

RESPONDING TO READING

How did you define "hero" before reading Berg's essay? (For help, look at the examples you gave in Preparing to Read.) Did the Berg essay change your idea of what a hero is? Why or why not?

CONSIDERING CONTENT

1. Identify the three names Berg imagines as possible heroes for her daughter in paragraph 1. Why are these women heroes? Why does Berg include Sara Lee?

2. Berg's essay revolves around the understanding of the word *hero* by the daughter, which eventually expands the mother's thinking about the concept. What is the mother considering a *hero* at the beginning of the story? How does she expand on the concept by the end?

3. What kind of mother is Elizabeth Berg? List the details that back up your answer.

4. Why did the author and her friend torture Mrs. Zinz when they were in eighth grade?

5. "If you're smart, I thought, you gratefully take your heroes where you find them" (para. 19). What does this mean? Why is taking your heroes where you find them *smart*?

CONSIDERING METHOD

1. What are the three specific examples of heroes given by Berg? What do they have in common? What groups of people does Berg consider heroic?

2. This essay first appeared in *Parents* magazine in 1992. Name several of the statements and ideas that would appeal to the audience of this magazine.

3. Find instances where Berg uses direct quotations and dialog. Think about how these sections could be rephrased without direct quotations. What effect does using exact spoken words have?

4. What is Jenny's response to her mother's compliment in the end? What parent-child dynamics are underlined? Why do you think Berg closed this way, instead of with a restatement of her concept of heroism?

5. Would you recommend this essay to a good friend? Explain why or why not.

WRITING STEP BY STEP

A. Think of two to four people in your life whom you could consider *heroes*, using Berg's concept. These could be people from your school, your home town, your ethnic subculture, your family, or your social group.

B. Introduce your essay by naming some famous or highly recognized people that you consider heroes. You can include people who are highly recognized mostly within their own field—for instance, a chess player or computer programmer or fashion designer. These people should not be personal acquaintances of yours.

C. Write a transition paragraph that highlights the difference between famous heroes and everyday heroes. Explain what makes someone an everyday hero for you.

D. Develop a paragraph or two about each of the people who are your examples of everyday heroes. Be sure to provide vivid details. Leave no doubt about why you admire each one.

E. In this development, include at least one brief narrative, as Berg does for Mrs. Zinz, Papa, and Sylvia. Consider using direct quotations.

F. Close your essay with an incident or an episode rather than a summary or restatement.

OTHER WRITING IDEAS

1. Berg writes about getting "a lesson in how not to lower yourself to someone else's level" (para. 11). Write an essay on this topic, including examples of situations in which people either did lower themselves to someone else's level, or refused to do so. You might decide to give examples of both giving in and resisting.

2. COLLABORATIVE WRITING. Write a collaborative essay on the previous topic, with a team of three or four. Each person should contribute an example. Work as a group to put the examples into an

essay, organizing them to work smoothly together and adding an introduction and a conclusion.

3. USING THE INTERNET. In paragraph 10, Berg writes about an English teacher who "insisted that we always do our best, and in her class, we almost always did." Berg endorses the idea that people, even children, tend to rise to the expectations that others hold. Write an essay giving examples (or one long illustration) of this tendency. For inspiration, read the material on *self-fulfilling prophecy* at http://members .fortunecity.com/nadabs/prophecy.html.

4. WRITING ABOUT READING. What do you think of the author's concept of a hero? Do you agree with it? Are the examples convincing? Write an essay in which you analyze and evaluate the effectiveness of "My Heroes."

GAINING WORD POWER

Sometimes little words can mean a lot. What, for instance, does the word *wise* mean in this sentence?

That would wise her up.

Get together with several of your classmates and see how many other meanings of the word *wise* the group can come up with. Then look it up in a dictionary. Did you think of most of them? What are the differences among the words *wise, intelligent, smart,* and *brainy*?

Now, think about the word *set*. See how many sentences the group can write using *set* with a different meaning in each one. Do at least five. Then check the dictionary to see how many meanings there are. Surprising, isn't it, how much meaning can be packed into such a simple little word?

EDITING SKILLS: SEMICOLONS BETWEEN SENTENCES

If you tend to write mainly short, simple sentences, you may need to add some variety. If you have two sentences *that are closely related in meaning*, you can put them together—separated by a semicolon. For example,

He was unfailingly warm and kind and knew how to make a friend out of a stranger; he loved people.

Remember that the semicolon indicates a close relationship in meaning; it can't just go between any two sentences. Also, each of the sentences must be complete in most standard English writing for a semicolon to work between them. When you read older material, like novels by Jane Austen or Charles Dickens, you may see a fragment on one side of a semicolon and a complete sentence on the other, but that is not usually done these days.

EXERCISE

Dave Barry, a popular humorist, once described the new Jolly Green Giant this way: "He no longer looks like the 'Ho, Ho, Ho' guy; he now looks like Paul McCartney on steroids." Why do you think Barry chose a semicolon between his two sentences?

Go through the essay you just wrote to see whether you have any short, closely related sentences that come one right after the other. If so, try taking out the period, putting in a semicolon, and making the second sentence's capital letter lowercase.

A word of caution: Be sure to use a *semicolon* in joining sentences. A comma definitely will not do in most cases.

WEB SITE

www.modestyarbor.com/elizabethberg.html
Writers on Writing: the June 2002 interview with Elizabeth Berg.

PREPARING TO READ

Do you feel safe when you go out alone at night? Are there certain sections of town that you would refuse to enter alone after dark? Does the fear, or lack of fear, in any way relate to your gender, your age, or the color of your skin?

"Just Walk On By": A Black Man Ponders His Power to Alter Public Space

BRENT STAPLES

Born in 1951 in Chester, Pennsylvania, Brent Staples is a journalist who also holds a Ph.D. in psychology from the University of Chicago. His memoir, Parallel Time: Growing Up in Black and White *(1994), tells the story of his childhood in Chester, a mixed-race, economically declining town. He is currently on the editorial board of the* New York Times. *The selection reprinted here was first published in* Ms. *magazine in September 1986.*

TERMS TO RECOGNIZE

uninflammatory *(para. 1)*	not likely to cause violence or excitement
unwieldy *(para. 2)*	hard to manage or to deal with
indistinguishable *(para. 2)*	not clearly different from
elicit *(para. 3)*	draw forth
warrenlike *(para. 5)*	narrow and crowded like a rabbit hutch
bandolier *(para. 5)*	a belt holding bullets, draped across the chest
lethality *(para. 6)*	being lethal or deadly
bravado *(para. 6)*	pretended courage or false confidence
ad hoc *(para. 7)*	for this case only
labyrinthine *(para. 7)*	like the winding, confusing passages in a maze
berth *(para. 9)*	a safe distance
skittish *(para. 9)*	jumpy, easily frightened
constitutionals *(para. 10)*	walks to improve one's health

My first victim was a woman—white, well dressed, probably in her early 20s. I came upon her late one evening on a deserted street in Hyde Park, a relatively affluent neighborhood in an otherwise mean, impoverished section of Chicago. As I swung onto the avenue behind her, there seemed to be a discreet, uninflammatory distance between us. Not so. She cast back a worried glance. To her, the youngish black man—a broad six feet two inches with a beard and billowing hair, both hands shoved into the pockets of a bulky military jacket—seemed menacingly close. She picked up her pace and was soon running in earnest. Within seconds she disappeared into a cross street.

That was more than a decade ago. I was 22 years old, a graduate student newly arrived at the University of Chicago. It was in the echo of that terrified woman's footfalls that I first began to know the unwieldy inheritance I'd come into—the ability to alter public space in ugly ways. It was clear that she thought of herself as the quarry of a mugger, a rapist, or worse. Suffering a bout of insomnia, however, I was stalking sleep, not defenseless wayfarers. As a softy who is scarcely able to take a knife to a raw chicken—let alone hold one to a person's throat—I was surprised, embarrassed, and dismayed all at once. Her flight made me feel like an accomplice in tyranny. It also made it clear that I was indistinguishable from the muggers who occasionally seeped into the area from the surrounding ghetto. I soon gathered that being perceived as dangerous is a hazard in itself: Where fear and weapons meet—as they often do in urban America—there is always the possibility of death.

In that first year, my first away from my hometown, I was to become thoroughly familiar with the language of fear. At dark, shadowy intersections, I could cross in front of a car stopped at a traffic light and elicit the *thunk, thunk, thunk, thunk* of the driver—black, white, male, female—hammering down the door locks. On less traveled streets after dark, I grew accustomed to but never comfortable with people crossing to the other side of the street rather than pass me. Then there were the standard unpleasantries with policemen, doormen, bouncers, cabdrivers, and others whose business it is to screen out troublesome individuals *before* there is any nastiness.

I moved to New York nearly two years ago and I have remained an avid night walker. In central Manhattan, the near-constant crowd covers the tense one-on-one street encounters. Elsewhere, things can get very taut indeed.

After dark, on the warrenlike streets of Brooklyn where I live, I often see women who fear the worst from me. They seem to have set their faces on neutral, and with their purse straps strung across their chests bandolier-style, they forge ahead as though bracing themselves against being tackled.

I understand, of course, that the danger they perceive is not a hallucination. Women are particularly vulnerable to street violence, and young black males are drastically overrepresented among the perpetrators of that violence. Yet these truths are no solace against the alienation that comes of being ever the suspect, an entity with whom pedestrians avoid making eye contact.

It is not altogether clear to me how I reached the ripe old age of 22 without being conscious of the lethality nighttime pedestrians attributed to me. Perhaps it was because in Chester, Pa., the small, angry industrial town where I came of age in the 1960s, I was scarcely noticeable against a backdrop of gang warfare, street knifings, and murders. I grew up one of the good boys, had perhaps a half-dozen fistfights. In retrospect, my shyness of combat has clear sources. As a boy, I saw countless tough guys locked away; I have since buried several, too. They were babies, really—a teen-age cousin, a brother of 22, a childhood friend in his mid-20s—all gone down in episodes of bravado played out in the streets. I chose, perhaps unconsciously, to remain a shadow—timid, but a survivor.

The fearsomeness mistakenly attributed to me in public places often has a perilous flavor. The most frightening of these confusions occurred in the late 1970s and early 1980s, when I worked as a journalist in Chicago. One day, rushing into the office of a magazine I was writing for with a deadline story in hand, I was mistaken for a burglar. The office manager called security, and with the speed of an ad hoc posse, pursued me through the labyrinthine halls, nearly to my editor's door. I had no way of proving who I was. I could only move briskly toward the company of someone who knew me.

Relatively speaking, however, I never fared as badly as another black male journalist. He went to nearby Waukegan, Ill., a couple of summers ago to work on a story about a murderer who was born there. Mistaking the reporter for the killer, police officers hauled him from his car at gunpoint and but for his press credentials would probably have tried to book him. Such episodes are not uncommon. Black men trade tales like this all the time.

Over the years, I learned to smother the rage I felt at so often being mistaken for a criminal. Not to do so would surely have led to madness. I now take precautions to make myself less threatening. I move about with care, particularly late in the evening. I give a wide berth to nervous people on subway platforms during the wee hours. If I happen to be entering a building behind some people who appear skittish, I may walk by, letting them clear the lobby before I return, so as not to seem to be following them. I have been calm and extremely congenial on those rare occasions when I've been pulled over by the police.

And on late-evening constitutionals I employ what has proved to be an 10 excellent tension-reducing measure: I whistle melodies from Beethoven and Vivaldi and the more popular classical composers. Even steely New Yorkers hunching toward nighttime destinations seem to relax, and occasionally they even join in the tune. Virtually everybody seems to sense that a mugger wouldn't be warbling bright, sunny selections from Vivaldi's "Four Seasons." It is my equivalent of the cowbell that hikers wear when they are in bear country.

RESPONDING TO READING

Why don't we expect muggers to be whistling melodies from Beethoven and Vivaldi? In your journal write a brief explanation of the possible reasons.

CONSIDERING CONTENT

1. How does the author describe his physical appearance in the opening paragraph? What categories of readers would be drawn in by the opening paragraph?
2. Why does the woman take him for "a mugger, a rapist, or worse"?
3. What does the writer mean when he says "that being perceived as dangerous is a hazard in itself"? What illustrations does he offer to prove his point?
4. What kind of hometown background did Brent Staples have? What kind of person did he turn out to be?
5. At the end of paragraph 6, he speaks of three young men he was close to—"all gone down in episodes of bravado played out in the streets." Although he doesn't tell us how any of them died, can you guess? Give examples of the kind of "episodes of bravado" that may have cost them their lives.
6. How did Staples learn to deal with the problem of being a large, young African American man in the city?
7. Why would hikers in bear country wear cowbells? Explain how that wilderness situation is similar to Staples's urban situation.

CONSIDERING METHOD

1. Explain how the brief narrative in the opening paragraph catches our interest.
2. The thesis of this selection is implied, not directly stated. Write out in your own words a statement of the author's main point.

3. This essay first appeared in *Ms.* magazine, a publication that focuses on women's issues. What did the author probably assume about his audience? How did it affect his choice of examples?
4. How does description help to make Staples's illustrations interesting and convincing in paragraphs 1 and 5?
5. Using words that sound like the noise they describe is called **onomatopoeia** (for example, the *thunk, thunk, thunk, thunk* of the car door locks in para. 3). Explain why that word choice is effective. Can you think of other examples of words that sound like what they mean?
6. This essay is developed through example and illustration, yet Staples does not tell us how the three young men died (para. 6.) Why not?
7. Explain what makes the conclusion particularly satisfying.

WRITING STEP BY STEP

Stereotypes are oversimplified groupings of people by race, gender, politics, athletic ability, ethnic origin, and so on. Staples was stereotyped because he was a young black male, and as Staples says, "young black males are drastically overrepresented among the perpetrators of . . . violence." Although there is usually some grain of truth behind stereotypes, they tend to be negative and unfair. Women, for instance, are stereotyped as weak, passive, fickle, scatterbrained, and indecisive. Men, on the other hand, are supposed to be strong-minded and assertive, but dense and unfeeling. Stereotypes are unfair because they lump lots of people into a category whether or not the characteristics fit every individual.

A. Think of a stereotype that includes you. Choose one that you think is unfair to you; your essay will explain how you are different.
B. Begin, as Staples does, with a brief narrative, a story that illustrates how you *seem* to fit the type although you actually do not.
C. In the next paragraph, define the stereotype by giving examples of several characteristics people expect you to have—or not to have. For instance, if you are a male football player, people may take you for a clumsy hulk who can barely read and write.
D. Next, explain why people would tend to place you in this stereotype.
E. Then, explain why you don't fit the stereotype, and tell about some influence while you were growing up that helped you to avoid the typical pattern of behavior. Provide concrete examples, as Staples does in paragraph 6 when he tells about his childhood among the gangs in Chester, Pennsylvania.
F. In conclusion, explain how you felt about being stereotyped and how you have learned to cope with the mistaken views of people who took you for a different kind of person than you truly are.

OTHER WRITING IDEAS

1. Write the paper outlined in the previous section but instead illustrate how you are the perfect example of a stereotype. You may want to think of a positive stereotype—or else make your essay humorous.

2. COLLABORATIVE WRITING. With a small group of classmates discuss phobias, those irrational fears that most of us have—fears of spiders, of snakes, of high places, of flying, of closed spaces. Which ones do you have? Choose your worst or your most embarrassing phobia and tell in an essay how it limits your activities, how it makes you feel, how you think you got it, and what you do to control it. Or, choose one phobia from your group's collection and develop an essay of example together.

3. USING THE INTERNET. Use Internet sources to find out about treatments for phobias. Write an essay explaining two or three different ways that people can overcome these irrational fears.

4. WRITING ABOUT READING. In paragraph 5, the author says, "Women are particularly vulnerable to street violence, and young black men are drastically overrepresented among the perpetrators of that violence." Do you agree with this comment? Write a response to this idea.

GAINING WORD POWER

The following words appear in the reading but are not included in the Terms to Recognize. Look up each one in your dictionary and use it in a sentence of your own.

1. affluent (para. 1)
2. menacingly (para. 1)
3. dismayed (para. 2)
4. taut (para. 4)
5. vulnerable (para. 5)
6. solace (para. 5)
7. entity (para. 5)
8. attributed (para. 7)
9. precautions (para. 9)
10. congenial (para. 9)

EDITING SKILLS: COMMAS AROUND INTERRUPTERS

An **interrupter** is just what it sounds like—a word or group of words that interrupts or breaks into the flow of a sentence, like the italicized words do here:

I understand, *of course*, that the danger they perceive is not a hallucination.

You need a comma before and after the interrupter as a signal to your readers that the interrupter is an addition that can be removed without changing the meaning of the sentence. The first comma signals the start of the interruption; the second comma signals the end of the interruption. It would be quite misleading in that sentence, with its flow interrupted, to use only one comma. But if you move the *of course* to the beginning or to the end of the sentence so that it no longer interrupts the flow, then a single comma is fine:

Of course, I understand that the danger they perceive is not a hallucination.
I understand that the danger they perceive is not a hallucination, *of course*.

The principle remains the same, even when the interrupter is longer:

One day, *rushing into the office of a magazine I was writing for with a deadline story in hand*, I was mistaken for a burglar.

Remember: put commas *around* interrupters—one before and one after.

EXERCISE

We've omitted the commas from around the interrupters in the following sentences. Figure out where they belong, and put them back in.

1. Suffering a bout of insomnia however I was stalking sleep, not defenseless wayfarers.
2. After dark on the warrenlike streets of Brooklyn where I live I often see women who fear the worst from me.
3. I chose perhaps unconsciously to remain a shadow—timid, but a survivor.
4. The office manager called security and with the speed of an ad hoc posse pursued me through the labyrinthine halls, nearly to my editor's door.
5. Relatively speaking however I never fared as badly as another black male journalist.

Now check the essay you've just written to be sure that you have punctuated interrupters correctly.

❧ WEB SITE

www.pbs.org/blackpress/modern_journalist/staples.html
Video and audio clips of Brent Staples from the Public Broadcasting System.

PREPARING TO READ

Do men or women make better schoolteachers? Or does gender matter?
Does the age of the students make any difference?

●●●

One Man's Kids

●●●

DANIEL R. MEIER

*Daniel Meier received a master's degree from the Harvard Graduate School of
Education in 1984. He taught first grade at schools in Brookline and Boston, Massachusetts, before getting his Ph.D. at the University of California at Berkeley. He
now teaches early childhood education at San Francisco State University. His articles about teaching and his reviews of children's books have appeared in a number
of educational journals. The essay reprinted here appeared in 1987 in the "About
Men" series of the* New York Times Magazine.

TERMS TO RECOGNIZE

complying *(para. 4)*	agreeing to someone else's request or command
singular *(para. 5)*	exceptional, unusual, distinguished by superiority
consoling *(para. 6)*	offering comfort and advice
intellectual *(para. 7)*	guided chiefly by knowledge or reason rather than by emotion or experience
hilarity *(para. 7)*	spirited merriment, cheerfulness
complimentary *(para. 12)*	given free as a courtesy or a favor

I teach first graders. I live in a world of skinned knees, double-knotted 1
shoelaces, riddles that I've heard a dozen times, stale birthday cakes, hurt
feelings, wandering stories, and one lost shoe ("and if you don't find it my
mother'll kill me"). My work is dominated by 6-year-olds.

It's 10:45, the middle of snack, and I'm helping Emily open her milk 2
carton. She has already tried the other end without success, and now
there's so much paint and ink on the carton from her fingers that I'm not
sure she should drink it at all. But I open it. Then I turn to help Scott clean
up some milk he has just spilled onto Rebecca's whale crossword puzzle.

While I wipe my milk- and paint-covered hands, Jenny wants to 3
know if I've seen that funny book about penguins that I read in class. As I

hunt for it in a messy pile of books, Jason wants to know if there is a new seating arrangement for lunch tables. I find the book, turn to answer Jason, then face Maya, who is fast approaching with a new knock-knock joke. After what seems like the 10th "Who's there?" I laugh and Maya is pleased.

Then Andrew wants to know how to spell "flukes" for his crossword. 4 As I get to "u," I give a hand signal for Sarah to take away the snack. But just as Sarah is almost out the door, two children complain that "we haven't even had ours yet." I stop the snack mid-flight, complying with their request for graham crackers. I then return to Andrew, noticing that he has put "flu" for 9 Down, rather than 9 Across. It's now 10:50.

My work is not traditional male work. It's not a singular pursuit. 5 There is not a large pile of paper to get through or one deal to transact. I don't have one area of expertise or knowledge. I don't have the singular power over language of a lawyer, the physical force of a construction worker, the command over fellow workers of a surgeon, the wheeling and dealing transactions of a businessman. My energy is not spent in pursuing, climbing, achieving, conquering, or cornering some goal or object.

My energy is spent in encouraging, supporting, consoling, and prais- 6 ing my children. In teaching, the inner rewards come from without. On any given day, quite apart from teaching reading and spelling, I bandage a cut, dry a tear, erase a frown, tape a torn doll, and locate a long-lost boot. The day is really won through matters of the heart. As my students groan, laugh, shudder, cry, exult, and wonder, I do too. I have to be soft around the edges.

A few years ago, when I was interviewing for an elementary-school 7 teaching position, every principal told me with confidence that, as a male, I had an advantage over female applicants because of the lack of male teachers. But in the next breath, they asked with a hint of suspicion why I chose to work with young children. I told them that I wanted to observe and contribute to the intellectual growth of a maturing mind. What I really felt like saying, but didn't, was that I loved helping a child learn to write her name for the first time, finding someone a new friend, or sharing in the hilarity of reading about Winnie the Pooh getting so stuck in a hole that only his head and rear show.

I gave that answer to those principals, who were mostly male, 8 because I thought they wanted a "male" response. This meant talking about intellectual matters. If I had taken a different course and talked about my interest in helping children in their emotional development, it would have been seen as closer to a "female" answer. I even altered my language, not once mentioning the word "love" to describe what I do indeed love about teaching. My answer worked; every principal nodded approvingly.

Some of the principals also asked what I saw myself doing later in my 9 career. They wanted to know if I eventually wanted to go into educational administration. Becoming a dean of students or a principal has never been one of my goals, but they seemed to expect me, as a male, to want to climb higher on the career stepladder. So I mentioned that, at some point, I would be interested in working with teachers as a curriculum coordinator. Again, they nodded approvingly.

If those principals had been female instead of male, I wonder whether 10 their questions, and my answers, would have been different. My guess is that they would have been.

At other times, when I'm at a party or a dinner and tell someone 11 that I teach young children, I've found that men and women respond differently. Most men ask about the subjects I teach and the courses I took in my training. Then, unless they bring up an issue such as merit pay, the conversation stops. Most women, on the other hand, begin the conversation on a more immediate and personal level. They say things like "those kids must love having a male teacher" or "that age is just wonderful, you must love it." Then, more often than not, they'll talk about their own kids or ask me specific questions about what I do. We're then off and talking shop.

Possibly, men would have more to say to me, and I to them, if my 12 job had more of the trappings and benefits of more traditional male jobs. But my job has no bonuses or promotions. No complimentary box seats at the ball park. No cab fare home. No drinking buddies after work. No briefcase. No suit. (Ties get stuck in paint jars.) No power lunches. (I eat peanut butter and jelly, chips, milk, and cookies with the kids.) No taking clients out for cocktails. The only place I take my kids is to the playground.

Although I could have pursued a career in law or business, as several 13 of my friends did, I chose teaching instead. My job has benefits all its own. I'm able to bake cookies without getting them stuck together as they cool, buy cheap sewing materials, take out splinters, and search just the right trash cans for useful odds and ends. I'm sometimes called "Daddy" and even "Mommy" by my students, and if there's ever a lull in the conversation at a dinner party, I can always ask those assembled if they've heard the latest riddle about why the turkey crossed the road. (He thought he was a chicken.)

RESPONDING TO READING

What do you think about Meier's choice of career? Do you think it's reasonable and appropriate? Why or why not?

CONSIDERING CONTENT

1. Why did Meier write this essay? What point do you think he wanted to make?
2. Meier says, "My work is not traditional male work" (para. 5)? What does he mean by that statement? Do you agree?
3. What is a "singular pursuit"? Why does the author use that phrase to describe "male work"?
4. Why did the principals who interviewed Meier have "a hint of suspicion" about him (para. 7)?
5. What kind of answers did Meier give in his job interviews (para. 8)? What kind of answers did he avoid? Why didn't he mention the word "love"?
6. The author says that men and women respond differently to him when he talks about his job (para. 11). What are the differences?
7. How does Meier feel about his job? Do you think he is being defensive or apologetic about it?

CONSIDERING METHOD

1. In the first paragraph the author says, "My work is dominated by 6-year-olds." What examples does he give to explain and support this general statement?
2. Why does Meier open his essay the way he does? Why doesn't he state his thesis until paragraph 5?
3. Find the series of words that Meier uses to describe "male work" (end of para. 5) and the words he uses to describe what he does (beginning of para. 6). What is he saying about the difference between his work and "male work"?
4. What does the author mean when he says, "In teaching, the inner rewards come from without" (para. 6)? What examples does he give to make his meaning clear?
5. What is the effect of the series of phrases that begin with "No" in paragraph 12? Why are the positive comments in parentheses? Why is the last sentence in the paragraph not in parentheses?

WRITING STEP BY STEP

Think of a workplace that you know well—a place where you have a job now or had one in the past. If your primary work is being a student, then school is your workplace.

A. First identify and briefly explain your role at the workplace ("I am a cashier, salesperson, and general trouble shooter at Posh Pups, a pet grooming and pet supply store").

B. Then name three or four personal qualities that make for success in that job. ("To work at Posh Pups, you need to be loyal and good at math and to like people as much as you like animals.")

C. Think about the order in which you want to present these qualities. You might start with a less important quality and build up to the most important one. Or you may see that two of them are related and need to be placed in back-to-back paragraphs. Make a scratch outline to help you decide how to arrange your main points and examples.

D. For each quality you name, give at least one example of how it is important in the job. Think of a specific time when each quality was needed. Tell the story of how you or your co-workers showed a particular quality (or, unfortunately, showed a lack of it).

E. If an example is long and detailed, give it its own paragraph, as Meier does in paragraphs 2, 3, and 4 of his essay. If some of your examples are only a sentence or two, try to expand them with more details that will give your readers the sights, sounds, and feel of your work.

F. Close with a summarizing statement of how you feel about this job. Or offer a recommendation to anyone who might consider going into this line of work. Try to reinforce your thesis idea without simply repeating it.

G. When you revise, look at the transitions between your paragraphs. Try to fill in any gaps between your main points. Also check to see that you used transitions to lead into your examples. Ask your instructor or your classmates to help you improve the flow of your ideas.

OTHER WRITING IDEAS

1. Select one of the following general statements, or compose one of your own. Make it the central idea of an essay full of examples and illustrations. Draw examples from your reading, your conversation, your observations, and your own experience.

   a. Action heroes in the movies today are pretty much alike.

   b. Being a good parent is probably the hardest job there is.

    c. The stereotypical female (or male) is not easy to find in our society anymore.

    d. Being a teenager can be difficult (or easy or perplexing or a lot of fun).

    e. Jealousy is a destructive emotion.

2. COLLABORATIVE WRITING. Discuss with your classmates some superstitions that you or members of your family or community have held. Frequently, these superstitions have to do with success or bad luck in sports, performances, weather, or work. Do they have any validity? How did they develop? Write an essay of example about the role that superstition plays in your life or in the life of someone you know.

3. USING THE INTERNET. Search the Web for information about the workforce of grade school teachers today. Are there more men than there used to be? Can you find information about what discourages or attracts males to grade school teaching? Integrate information you find with information from Meier to write an essay giving examples of pluses and minuses for men considering the teaching field.

4. WRITING ABOUT READING. Write an essay in which you examine the *tone* of "One Man's Kids." How does the author's use of language and examples reflect his attitude toward his job?

GAINING WORD POWER

In paragraph 12 Meier uses the word *complimentary*. There is a word that's pronounced the same but has a different spelling and a different meaning— *complementary*. Do you know what each word means? English has many of these sound-alike words, and it's important to know the differences among them. They won't cause you any trouble in speaking, but they will change the meaning of your writing if you choose the wrong one.

    Here is a list of words from Meier's essay. Using your dictionary, find a sound-alike word for each item in the list and write down its meaning. Then use the word you found in a sentence.

fare	right	male
new	won	course
principal	seen	whether
through	two	hole

EDITING SKILLS: USING SUBORDINATION

Writers often combine two or more ideas in a sentence by using **subordination.** When one idea is subordinate to or dependent on another, it is less important. Take a look at these sentences from Meier's essay to see how the subordinate ideas are introduced by words that make them sound less important:

Although I could have pursued a career in law or business, I chose teaching instead.

Then, *unless* they bring up an issue such as merit pay, the conversation stops.

If I had taken a different course and talked about my interest in helping children in their emotional development, it would have been seen as close to a "female" answer.

As you can see, each of these sentences has two parts. Notice that the second part, after the comma, can stand alone as a sentence: that part is called **independent.** If you read the first part alone, it does not sound complete. The first part is called **dependent** for this reason. The opening words—*Although, unless,* and *If*—make the first statement of each sentence dependent. These words are called *subordinating conjunctions;* they indicate that the first idea is not as important as the rest of the sentence. (You will also notice that when the dependent part comes first, a comma separates it from the independent part.)

Subordinating conjunctions are familiar words; we use them a lot. Here are some of the most common ones: *since, because, if, even if, unless, although, even though, though, as long as, after, before, when, whenever, while, until,* and *wherever.* Skillful writers use subordination to give variety to their sentences and to keep readers' attention focused on the main ideas.

EXERCISE

Imitate the following sentences. Each one begins with a dependent statement followed by an independent one. You don't have to imitate each sentence exactly; just follow the dependent-independent pattern and use the same subordinating conjunction as the model sentence. Put in the commas, too.

Model: If we want clean air, then we will have to drive more fuel-efficient cars.

Imitation: If you like lasagna, then you should try the new Italian restaurant on Division Street.

1. While I was eating my lunch, a friend walked in.
2. Wherever I go in this city, I run into old friends.
3. Before you gather up your books, be sure your notes are complete.
4. Although Selma is a good athlete, she sometimes swears at the umpire.
5. Unless she sees the error of her ways, Selma may get tossed off the team.

Write at least one more imitation of each of the preceding sentences.

Go back to your example essay to see how many sentences like these you've written. What subordinating conjunctions did you use? Did you include the commas? Now combine some more of your sentences by using subordinating conjunctions and the dependent-independent pattern. If they sound sensible, keep them in your essay.

WEB SITES

http://userwww.sfsu.edu/~dmeier/welcome.htm
On Daniel Meier's home page you will find more information about his life, his research interests, and his teaching.
www.umaine.edu/eceol
The Early Childhood Education Online site provides a wealth of information about teaching young children.

PREPARING TO READ

What income do you think marks the federal poverty line for a couple? For a family of four? What is the minimum wage in your state these days? Write down your estimates before reading the next essay.

••

The Working Poor

••

TIM JONES

Tim Jones is a writer for the Chicago Tribune. *He has covered media topics including Oprah Winfrey's Texas trial for disparaging beef and Hormel Foods's efforts to stop the use of* Spam *as a word for unwanted e-mail. He often writes stories about areas where national economics and public media interconnect.*

TERMS TO RECOGNIZE

tapping *(para. 2)*   taking advantage or making use of

think tank *(para. 3)*   a group organized for the purpose of researching a problem

sparsely *(para. 6)*   thinly, lightly

severance *(para. 7)*   termination of employment

vise *(para. 14)*   clamping tool that holds material between two jaws

emphysema *(para. 14)*   a serious lung disease that makes breathing difficult

McArthur, Ohio. The food line begins to form during the sunrise   1
chill, more than two hours before the metal gates to the Care United Methodist Outreach pantry open. Hundreds of people like Theresa Ware arrive early because they fear the boxes of food stacked in neat rows will be gone by the time they push their rusty grocery carts to the head of the hours-long line. Ware keeps an eye on her watch because she can't afford to be late for work, not even if the reason is to pick up food. "This is a have-to case for us. It's humiliating," said Ware, 49, who makes $7.50 an hour working the afternoon shift at a nursing home. This recent visit was one of two food pantry stops she and her unemployed husband, Rocky, make every month. "We shouldn't have to do this," she said.

Theresa and Rocky Ware toil in the ranks of the working poor, a   2
growing category of millions of Americans who play by the rules of the
working world and still can't make ends meet. After tapping friends and
family, maxing out their credit cards, and sufficiently swallowing their
pride, at least 23 million Americans stood in food lines last year—many of
them the working poor, according to America's Second Harvest, the
Chicago-based hunger relief organization. The surge in food demand is
fueled by several forces—job losses, expired unemployment benefits, soaring health-care and housing costs, and the inability of many people to find
jobs that match the income and benefits of the jobs they lost.

The Center on Budget and Policy Priorities, a Washington think   3
tank, reported recently that 43 million people are living in low-income
working families with children. Other government data show the number
of people living below the official poverty line grew by more than 3.5 million from 2000 to 2002, to 34.6 million. And the U.S. Department of
Agriculture reported that the number of Americans who don't know
where their next meal will come from—categorized as "food insecure"—
jumped from 31 million to 35 million between 1999 and 2002. "The
reach of the economic slowdown has really pulled in a lot of folks who
never expected to be poor," said Stacy Dean, director of food stamp policy for the Center on Budget and Policy Priorities. "What you see now is
families turning to private relief for what often is a very small amount of
help."

"This is not just a function of unemployment. A larger percentage of   4
Americans are working poor, and the numbers have been growing for nine
years," said Robert Forney, CEO of America's Second Harvest. "This could
be the low-water mark for the economy, but for a whole lot of Americans—
40 million of them—the option of [earning] a living wage and benefits? Forget it."

Exploding Demand

Food pantry operators across the nation—urban, suburban and rural—   5
tell similar stories of exploding food demand from families, senior citizens, and the fastest-growing segment: the working poor. In southern
Ohio, where President Lyndon Johnson declared war on poverty 40 years
ago, cars will line roadsides for a half-mile or more waiting for the boxed
monthly buffet of dry milk, rice, cereal, canned fruit and vegetables,

instant mashed potatoes and, on good days, canned meat and chicken. "We're quickly seeing that communities that thought they were immune are now affected, whether urban or suburban," said Lisa Hamler-Podolski, executive director of the Ohio Association of Second Harvest Foodbanks. Rev. Walt Goble, who runs the Care United Methodist Outreach in McArthur, Ohio, a small and long-ago thriving village about 60 miles south of Columbus, said, "We're here from 11:30 to 4:00, or until we run out of food. Usually we run out."

Theresa and Rocky Ware have reluctantly joined the lines at food banks. Last year, in the sparsely populated, nine-county region of southeastern Ohio, 9.1 million pounds of food were handed out—that's up from 3.9 million pounds in 2000. In the past three years, the number of households served by food banks has more than tripled, according to Second Harvest of Southeast Ohio.   6

Although the national economy shows fitful statistical signs of recovery, the data do not take into account that declining numbers of employers offer health insurance and many new jobs pay the minimum wage, $5.15 an hour.   7

- Danny Palmer, who lives in the Ohio River village of Cheshire, lost his $20-an-hour welding job and now works at Wal-Mart for $5.95 an hour. Insurance coverage he got as part of a severance package from his former employer runs out next month. He has no health coverage with Wal-Mart.
- Melissa Barringer holds three part-time jobs to augment the income she and her husband, Brian, a laborer, earn to support themselves and their three teenage children. Last year, their combined income was $18,000. "We can't keep up," Melissa Barringer said as her children ate at a soup kitchen in Coolville, Ohio.
- Oscar Sanchez shows up every Thursday for bags of canned and dry goods at the Catholic Charities' Latin American Youth Center in Chicago's Pilsen neighborhood. Sanchez, 52, is a self-employed painter who lost his construction job three years ago. His hourly wage is $7. He has no health insurance.
- And in the St. Louis suburb of Ferguson, Mary Williams works as a temp and drives her 1983 Mercury Marquis to jobs that pay $7 to $8 an hour. The work is not steady. Neither she nor her son has health insurance.

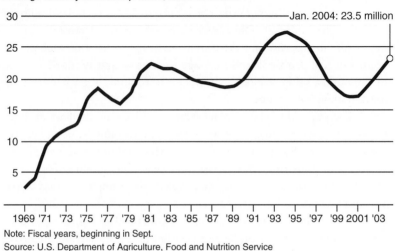

People seeking food assistance on the rise
Average monthly food stamp users; scale in millions

Jan. 2004: 23.5 million

Note: Fiscal years, beginning in Sept.
Source: U.S. Department of Agriculture, Food and Nutrition Service

All of them tell different stories but have one thing in common: They have jobs and are regulars at food pantries.

What the Numbers Miss

The plight of people like the Wares is not reflected in monthly unemployment figures. These Americans fly uneasily beneath the radar of the government's officially recognized economic distress status, the federal poverty line of $12,490 for a couple and $18,850 for a family of four. "The official economic numbers often lag behind the real story," said Gregory Acs, a senior research associate at the Urban Institute, a Washington-based research organization. 8

"Poverty numbers usually tell only part of the story. You can be technically not poor, but you still skip bills and go once or twice a week to the food pantry," Acs said, noting that upward adjustments in poverty levels do not account for all the financial pressures facing families. For example, the share of Americans under age 65 with employer-sponsored health insurance dropped from 70 percent in 1999 to 68 percent in 2002, according to the Urban Institute. Among low-income workers, the percentage dropped from 40 percent to 35 percent. 9

Some of those who are struggling visit Felipe Ayala, who has been running Chicago's Latin American Youth Center for 32 years. "We used to run out 10 of food at the end of the month. Now we can run out at the end of the first week," Ayala said. The increasing demand comes from people who are either out of work or, in the case of Oscar Sanchez, don't earn enough to provide a living for themselves. "It has gotten worse," Ayala said. "All the jobs are in the food industry or else they are in the suburbs. The lines here are always increasing."

Sanchez, who is divorced, said he goes every other Thursday to the base- 11 ment of the old school. People begin to file in at 9 A.M. and move from one metal folding chair to another before they can pick up white plastic food bags on which "Thank You" is printed in red letters. They wait patiently for their turn to get the food bags. "This is what keeps me going," said Sanchez, who has used the pantry for two years. As the weather warms up, Sanchez said, he is hopeful that there will be more work and steady work. He does not expect, however, to break his pattern of regularly visiting the pantry on 17th Street.

Nor is Mary Williams particularly hopeful. With three years of college 12 behind her, the 42-year-old former factory worker has not had health insurance since last summer. Williams makes about $400 a month and regularly visits a Salvation Army food pantry in St. Louis. Williams's battered car is starting to break down, and sometimes she has to drive up to an hour, one way, to get to work. "Most of the time it's a struggle," said Williams, a single parent. "And things aren't looking any better."

The pressure on working families has increased in the past few years as 13 many states have cut back Medicaid coverage in the face of their own budget troubles. Two recent reports show that as many as 1.6 million low-income people have lost publicly funded health coverage because of state budget cuts. In response, they cobble together an existence by skipping meals, borrowing from friends, moving in with family and cutting prescription pills in half or bypassing dosages altogether. Some ignore bills, which is one reason Ohio, for instance, a state hit hard by the recession, has the highest rate of loan foreclosures in the nation, according to the Mortgage Bankers Association.

Many are trapped in a bureaucratic vise: They make too much money 14 to qualify for Medicaid, the government's low-income health insurance program, yet too little to buy health coverage. Because they can't afford the property taxes, the Wares have turned their home over to their adult children, who pay the tax bill. Medical bills from Rocky's treatments for emphysema are mounting. "I get bills and I say to hell with it. They can come and throw me in jail," Theresa Ware said as she loaded food into the back seat of her truck.

RESPONDING TO READING

How accurate were your estimates of the poverty line and minimum wage? Did any of your ideas change from reading the facts and examples in the essay?

CONSIDERING CONTENT

1. Who are the working poor? What is the main point that Jones's article makes about them?

2. Give a few reasons for an "exploding food demand" at food banks in this country. Can you think of reasons that are not covered in the article?

3. Why does the researcher Gregory Acs say that "poverty numbers usually tell only part of the story" (para. 9)? What is the rest of the story?

4. How are health insurance and home ownership related to the topic of the working poor?

5. This article was published in 2004. Has the situation of the working poor changed since its publication? If you don't know, how could you find out?

6. Paragraph 3 mentions "private relief." What is that? What other kinds of relief for the poor exist?

CONSIDERING METHOD

1. What is Jones's attitude toward the working poor? How do you know? Choose a sentence and suggest how it would be rephrased by someone with the opposite attitude.

2. From many possible examples, the author chose four to present in paragraph 7. Why do you think he chose these four? What similarities and differences do you see among these four people?

3. The main topic of the article is put into words in paragraph 2. What is the purpose of paragraph 1?

4. Notice the lavish use of descriptive statistics in the article. Did you attempt to understand the numbers? Why or why not? Were they persuasive to you?

5. Did you spend any time looking at the graph from the USDA? Look at it again. What does it show? What conclusions can you draw from it? Take a survey among your classmates about who and who did not inspect this graph when reading the article. What conclusions can you draw from your survey?

6. If this article appeared in your local newspaper, would you read it? Why or why not? The actual article is twice as long as the part we reprint here. Would you read the whole thing if it were in front of you? Why or why not?

7. Jones uses two subheadings to break up the text and guide the reader's focus. Find two more places where subheadings would be suitable, and write them. Your instructor may have you work with two or three classmates.

COMBINING STRATEGIES

"The Working Poor" offers many examples of people who are working yet poor, the problems they encounter, and the solutions they find. The essay also discusses many of the causes and effects of the people's economic situation. List some of the causes and some of the effects mentioned in the article. List some other causes and effects that are not discussed in the article.

WRITING STEP BY STEP

A. Brainstorm with classmates about some way to get in trouble financially other than having a low-paying job. Some possibilities are using credit cards too much, buying a house that is too expensive, taking on expenses for others (like family members), having a high-priced hobby, making bad investments, gambling, leasing a vehicle with large payments, and sending children to costly schools.

B. Think of someone you know who has one of the problems you brainstormed. Freewrite for five minutes about the person and the problem. Choose three or four good examples of practices that have put the person into financial trouble.

C. Reread Jones's first paragraph. Write a paragraph to open your essay in which you present a verbal picture that illustrates the person and problem you will be writing about.

D. Develop a description of each example, devoting one or two paragraphs to each one. Be sure to use exact details. Use numbers like prices and percentages if possible.

E. Close with a look at the future. You can choose to suggest how the person might change in the future, or you can close more negatively and tell what will happen if the present course continues. (This second type of closing is what you see in the Jones essay.)

OTHER WRITING IDEAS

1. COLLABORATIVE WRITING. The Writing Step by Step essay focused on one person with a financial problem. Working with several other students, draft an article for your school newspaper which discusses one type of financial problem that college students might have. Provide several different examples, as Jones did in "The Working Poor." Solicit examples from other classmates and friends.

2. Instead of focusing on money difficulties, write an essay of example or illustration about another life problem that many people face.

3. USING THE INTERNET. Find information on one of the institutions mentioned in the Jones article: for instance, Second Harvest, the Center on Budget and Policy Priorities, the Urban Institute, Medicaid, the Mortgage Bankers Association, or the U. S. Department of Agriculture. Write an essay using examples to explain what the institution does, or focus on an interesting part of what it does.

4. WRITING ABOUT READING. Write an essay explaining *either* that Jones's article changed your view about the working poor *or* that Jones's article had little influence on your thinking.

GAINING WORD POWER

One elderly citizen referred to himself as "temporarily embarrassed" when he was broke. Brainstorm with classmates about some other euphemisms (mild terms substituted for harsh ones) for *poverty* and *poor*.

EDITING SKILLS: USING COMMAS IN SERIES

Notice where the commas are placed in the following examples containing items in series.

The surge in food demand is fueled by several forces—job losses, expired unemployment benefits, soaring health-care and housing costs, and the inability of many people to find jobs that match the income and benefits of the jobs they lost.

In southern Ohio, where President Lyndon Johnson declared war on poverty 40 years ago, cars will line roadsides for a half-mile or more waiting for the boxed monthly buffet of dry milk, rice, cereal, canned fruit and vegetables, instant mashed potatoes and, on good days, canned meat and chicken.

In response, they cobble together an existence by skipping meals, borrowing from friends, moving in with family and cutting prescription pills in half or bypassing dosages altogether.

The commas are necessary to let you know when one item ends and another begins. Try making sense of those words without the commas to see what an uphill task reading would be without commas:

The surge in food demand is fueled by several forces—job losses expired unemployment benefits soaring health-care and housing costs and the inability of many people to find jobs that match the income and benefits of the jobs they lost.

You can see that you have to read twice to figure out which groups of words go together. You might first read "job losses expired" and "unemployment benefits soaring," quite the opposite of the intended meaning.

Look at this sentence which includes a series:

After tapping friends and family, maxing out their credit cards and sufficiently swallowing their pride, at least 23 million Americans stood in food lines last year.

Jones doesn't use a comma before the *and* connecting the last item in a series (which is "sufficiently swallowing their pride"). This comma is optional in standard English usage. Jones could have written, correctly:

After tapping friends and family, maxing out their credit cards, and sufficiently swallowing their pride, at least 23 million Americans stood in food lines last year.

We like the comma before the conjunction *and*, ourselves. We think it makes the sentence easier to read on the first try. However, you will see educated writers like Jones leaving it out.

EXERCISE

Write a sentence describing a scene you know well or specially observe for this exercise. It could be your own room or a scene from nature or an event on the street. Try to string the descriptive details in a series using a model from Jones's article:

Cars will line roadsides for a half-mile or more waiting for the boxed monthly buffet of dry milk, rice, cereal, canned fruit and vegetables, instant mashed potatoes and, on good days, canned meat and chicken.

WEB SITES

www.epinet.org/content.cfm/issueguides_minwage_minwage
The Economic Policy Institute's guide to information on the minimum

wage includes facts, frequently asked questions, publications, tables, and charts.

www.dol.gov/esa/minwage/america.htm

On the Department of Labor's Web site on minimum wage you can find out the minimum wage in different states.

STUDENT ESSAY USING EXAMPLES

My Key Chain

David C. Lair

After his four-year stint in the army in the late-1990s, David Lair attended Eastern Illinois University, where he wrote this essay as a freshman. David was active in campus politics and planned to enroll in a pre-law program.

During my four years of army service, I led a very transient life. I   1
moved from Illinois to Missouri to California to Texas to Massachusetts to
Germany and back to Illinois again, never staying in one place for very
long. Consequently, I had to live a very sparse lifestyle with few possessions, and those that I did try to keep fared poorly through all my reloca-
tion. (In the army it is said that two or three moves have the same effect on
one's belongings as does a house fire). Therefore, when trying to think of a
possession that has been significant to me personally, my choices are nar-
rowed to only those items that I have been able to carry on my person. Of
these items, I believe that my key chain says more about myself and my life
than anything else does.

Upon entering the service I soon learned that my eventual duty sta-   2
tion, after I completed training at various posts in the states, would be
somewhere in Germany. At this time I bought a key chain decorated with
an Imperial Eagle and the inscription "Deutschland" (which means Germany); it also came equipped with a handy bottle opener. This key chain
was important because it came at a time when I was looking forward to
being stationed in Germany. My training was long and mentally arduous,
and the key chain served as a reminder of my goal. Whenever I felt discouraged, I pulled out my key chain and thought of traveling around Germany,
learning the language, meeting the people, and drinking the beer, which I
had heard great things about. I already had big plans for the bottle opener.

When I finally arrived in Germany, my outlook on life changed,   3
and so did the "function" of my key chain. Now I lived life for the present.
I traveled, learned the language, absorbed the culture, and sampled as
many brands of beer as I could find. Along with this transition, the duties of
my key chain became more based in the present. Now the keys on the chain
represented my "home" in the city of Fulda as I wandered around the conti-
nent; now the inscription "Deutschland" made sense to me linguistically;
and now the bottle opener was my most important tool. I will always look
back on this time as a very happy period in my life.

My tour in Germany ended last December, and I returned to the states   4
to begin my new life as a student. But the transition wasn't easy. I found that
my mind often dwelled on my former lifestyle; I also found myself missing
Germany. Once again, my key chain mirrored my state of mind. By this time
the metal around the opener was rusted, the "Deutschland" insignia was
scratched, and cracks had begun to form along the entire length of the
chain. I frequently looked at my beloved belonging and remembered the fun
I had had. As I sprung another cap from an imported beer, I realized that I
was now living in the past.

Recently, while opening a beer, my key chain broke in half. The stress   5
of opening all the beers finally drove the cracks completely through the key
chain. This development caused me to reflect on my present situation. I
decided that it was time to stop living in the past, and to start looking
toward my future once again

Over Christmas break my girlfriend and I will travel to Brazil to visit   6
her parents, who live in Rio de Janiero. I am very excited about the trip. I
am looking forward to exploring a new country once again and to meeting
new people. When she heard that my key chain had broken, my girlfriend
gave me a small present: a key chain with the Brazilian flag and the inscription "Brazil." Sure, there's no bottle opener, but we have "twist-tops" in
the United States anyway. Now I can once again take my key chain out of
my pocket and anticipate the future, while at the same time enjoying the
present.

CONSIDERING CONTENT AND METHOD

1. How important is the title? Is it too simple and direct? Would you suggest a more intriguing title?
2. What general claim is the author defending and developing in this
   essay? Does he support his claim adequately?
3. How does the key chain function as an example throughout the essay?
   What changes does the key chain undergo? What do these changes
   exemplify?
4. What details are most effective? Are there any points you would like
   to hear more about?
5. What do you think of the ending? How well does it sum up the
   whole essay? Could it be concluded in a different way?

Strategies for Clarifying Meaning: *Definition* and *Explanation*

IMAGES AND IDEAS

Source: Despair, Inc.

FOR DISCUSSION AND WRITING

What makes this poster funny? How does it contradict most of the clichéd or wise sayings you hear about beauty?

This poster is from a series called Demotivators. Explain the title of the series. Make up your own Demotivator poster, redefining an abstraction like love, honesty, perseverance, courage, hope, or independence. Write a paragraph explaining the caption and what kind of picture you would use.

"PowerTalk gives you a single mailbox icon for all incoming and outgoing mail—including fax, voice, electronic mail, and documents. Communication from online services and electronic mail from various sources are routed to your desktop mailbox when you install mail gateways supplied by the vendor," the manual for our new computer operating system cheerfully brags. Sounds great, but we have only the vaguest idea what PowerTalk *is!* How many of the terms in those two sentences would *you* need to have defined or explained? Moreover, how many terms would need definition and explanation for a reader in the 1970s?

THE POINT OF DEFINITION AND EXPLANATION

As suggested by the above quotation from the computer manual, the whole point of **definition** and explanation is to clarify things for people. Words are worse than unhelpful when they don't convey meaning but instead create confusion.

The special vocabulary of any group needs explanation when used to communicate with people outside that group. Some groups develop languages that are incredibly mysterious to outsiders. If you've ever been the outsider listening to a bunch of bridge players, computer gamers, or aerobic class addicts, you know the feeling of bafflement that grows quickly into boredom because you have no idea what they're discussing so enthusiastically. The same thing can happen when you read or write essays that don't define or explain as much material as necessary.

Some words can be defined briefly in parentheses, but complex ideas and terms need more than a phrase or sentence of explanation. In this chapter, you will read whole essays whose main purpose is to define and explain difficult or controversial concepts.

THE PRINCIPLES OF DEFINITION AND EXPLANATION

Definitions and explanations make use of a few basic techniques that can be found in almost all writing.

Descriptive Details

Can you imagine explaining anything without using descriptive details? "Why are you afraid you'll become a slave to your new silk shirt?" a friend might ask you. To explain, you would naturally give the details of caring for it: you must wash it in cold water by hand; then, instead of wringing it, you should wrap it in a clean towel to blot excess water; then it needs to hang dry on a padded hanger away from sun or electric light; when dry, it will be crinkled and must be ironed with a very cool iron; finally, on the day of wearing, it should be steamed while you shower and lightly re-ironed. In other words, you think you will be a servant to it.

Examples

Concepts are frequently defined or explained through examples. The classic Type A personality can be defined through examples of behavior: If Jake is Type A, he is extremely impatient in a long grocery line, he cannot find the time to go to a film starring his favorite actor, and he considers getting a promotion at work a life-or-death issue. He is likely to slam doors and throw books when angry.

In an essay in this chapter, Isaac Asimov uses himself and his garage mechanic as examples to show how subjective people's definitions of intelligence are.

Narration

Aesop's fables, which you probably remember from childhood, make use of narrative, or story, to explain a basic truth about humans. A "sour grapes" attitude is explained by the story of the fox who sees a bunch of delicious-looking grapes but can't reach them; the fox, therefore, comforts itself by deciding that they were probably sour anyway. A writer might define an abstract quality, such as heroism or courage, by telling a story with a hero who acts out the virtue.

In his essay in this chapter, Wayson Choy uses brief narratives to illustrate the "ugly, unjust" prejudice endured by his parents when they immigrated to British Columbia from China in 1918.

Comparison

Sometimes we define a word by emphasizing its likeness to something else. For example, we explain what a **fable** is by saying it's kind of a story. Writers use imaginative comparison to clarify meaning, too: "A true friend is a port in a storm" and "A true friend is as comfortable as an old shoe."

A comparison may be used for surprising effect. When the phrase "inner child" first became popular, it struck us as a remarkably apt description of the juvenile traits that lurk within every adult: fun-loving, self-centered, impulsive, dependent. These parts of our selves are easily comparable to children, and the phrase captures the idea well.

Contrast

Sometimes the best way to define something is to contrast it with something different. This technique can be quite simple: *dearth* is the opposite of *plenty*.

Or the definition can consist of a comparison spiked with a contrast. As our friend heard her five-year-old explain to her four-year-old, "Death is like going to Oklahoma, only longer."

In some cases, contrast is needed to correct a common misconception about a term. *Schizophrenia,* contrary to popular belief, does not involve having more than one personality. And being *educated,* according to Asimov's garage mechanic, doesn't mean being "smart."

THE PITFALLS OF DEFINITION AND EXPLANATION

When you write a definition or explanation, you risk making certain characteristic mistakes.

Missing Your Audience

Would you explain what a control key is to a computer whiz? We hope not. But if you were writing directions for a beginning word processing course, you'd be foolish *not* to define what a control key is. Analyzing your intended **audience** is important in all writing. If you misjudge what your audience needs to have defined or explained, you will either insult or confuse them.

Going in Circles

Some definitions are called circular because they don't go anywhere. They restate rather than explain. "A *smooth operator* is a person who functions without roughness," for example, tells you nothing. The second part of that definition only rewords the first part. The definition must lead somewhere, like this: "A *smooth operator* is a person who takes advantage of others by using charm and persuasion."

Abstraction

The previous circular definition also demonstrates the flaw of abstraction. It has no **concrete words** to hang onto. A high-flown sentence like "Our ideal leader is the hope of the future" provides no helpful terms about qualities we can actually identify.

Leaving Information Out

To say merely that a fable is a story doesn't get across the whole idea; it conveys only part of it: a fable has special features, like talking animals and a moral lesson. Incompleteness is a pitfall especially of short definitions, such as "Love is never having to say you're sorry." In this chapter, the essay "Mommy, What

Does 'Nigger' Mean?" shows that a sentence like "*Nigger* is a degrading label for an African American" is not a full definition.

Of course, an explanation is incomplete when your reader needs to ask for clarification. Sometimes it's hard to see the holes in what you have written yourself because you already know what you're trying to say. You need to enlist a good peer editor to point out whether you have omitted important information.

WHAT TO LOOK FOR IN DEFINITIONS AND EXPLANATIONS

Here are some guidelines to follow as you study the selections in this chapter.

1. *Focus on which term or concept is being defined or explained.* This focus will help you evaluate the essay's effectiveness.
2. *Identify the ways in which the writer develops the idea,* especially through the use of details, narration, example, comparison, and contrast.
3. *Figure out who the intended audience is.* Then think about how the essay would be different if written for a different audience. What definitions and explanations would be added or deleted?
4. *Ask yourself whether the definition or explanation is complete.* If it is not complete, does the writer tell you why?

PREPARING TO READ

What word could be used to label you? Consider even labels that you do not think accurate. Might someone call you a jock? a nerd? an egghead? a bimbo? a tramp? a hero? a male chauvinist? a rabid feminist? a spoiled brat? a bully? a heartbreaker?

••

"Mommy, What Does 'Nigger' Mean?"

••

GLORIA NAYLOR

Gloria Naylor came from a rural, working-class southern background and did not enter college until she was twenty-five, after working as a missionary and a telephone operator. Naylor graduated from Brooklyn College in 1981, and in 1983 she won the American Book Award for best first novel for The Women of Brewster Place. *In this excerpt from an article first published in the* New York Times *on February 20, 1986, Naylor discusses the ways a word's meaning changes according to the context in which it is used.*

TERMS TO RECOGNIZE

necrophiliac *(para. 1)*	someone sexually attracted to corpses
verified *(para. 1)*	proven true
gravitated *(para. 2)*	moved toward
mecca *(para. 2)*	a place regarded as the center of interest or activity
inflections *(para. 3)*	tones of voice
trifling *(para. 8)*	shallow, unimportant
connotation *(para. 9)*	the idea suggested by a word or phrase, in addition to its surface meaning
stratum *(para. 12)*	level
internalization *(para. 12)*	making other people's attitudes a part of your own way of thinking

I remember the first time I heard the word "nigger." In my third-grade 1
class, our math tests were being passed down the rows, and as I handed the
papers to a little boy in back of me, I remarked that once again he had
received a much lower mark than I did. He snatched his test from me and

spit out that word. Had he called me a nymphomaniac or a necrophiliac, I couldn't have been more puzzled. I didn't know what a nigger was, but I knew that whatever it meant, it was something he shouldn't have called me. This was verified when I raised my hand, and in a loud voice repeated what he had said and watched the teacher scold him for using a "bad" word. I was later to go home and ask the inevitable question that every black parent must face—"Mommy, what does 'nigger' mean?"

And what exactly did it mean? Thinking back, I realize that this could   2
not have been the first time the word was used in my presence. I was part of a large extended family that had migrated from the rural South after World War II and formed a close-knit network that gravitated around my maternal grandparents. Their ground-floor apartment in one of the buildings they owned in Harlem was a weekend mecca for my immediate family, along with countless aunts, uncles, and cousins who brought along assorted friends. It was a bustling and open house with assorted neighbors and tenants popping in and out to exchange bits of gossip, pick up an old quarrel, or referee the ongoing checkers game in which my grandmother cheated shamelessly. They were all there to let down their hair and put up their feet after a week of labor in the factories, laundries, and shipyards of New York.

Amid the clamor, which could reach deafening proportions—two or   3
three conversations going on simultaneously, punctuated by the sound of a baby's crying somewhere in the back rooms or out on the street—there was still a rigid set of rules about what was said and how. Older children were sent out of the living room when it was time to get into the juicy details about "you-know-who" up on the third floor who had gone and gotten herself "p-r-e-g-n-a-n-t!" But my parents, knowing that I could spell well beyond my years, always demanded that I follow the others out to play. Beyond sexual misconduct and death, everything else was considered harmless for our young ears. And so among the anecdotes of the triumphs and disappointments in the various workings of their lives, the word "nigger" was used in my presence, but it was set within contexts and inflections that caused it to register in my mind as something else.

In the singular, the word was always applied to a man who had distinguished himself in some situation that brought their approval for his   4
strength, intelligence, or drive:

"Did Johnny really do that?"   5

"I'm telling you, that nigger pulled in $6,000 of overtime last year.   6
Said he got enough for a down payment on a house."

When used with a possessive adjective by a woman—"my nigger"—it   7
became a term of endearment for husband or boyfriend. But it could be more than just a term applied to a man. In their mouths it became the pure

essence of manhood—a disembodied force that channeled their past history of struggle and present survival against the odds into a victorious statement of being: "Yeah, that old foreman found out quick enough—you don't mess with a nigger."

In the plural, it became a description of some group within the community that had overstepped the bounds of decency as my family defined it. Parents who neglected their children, a drunken couple who fought in public, people who simply refused to look for work, those with excessively dirty mouths or unkempt households were all "trifling niggers." This particular circle could forgive hard times, unemployment, the occasional bout of depression—they had gone through all of that themselves—but the unforgivable sin was lack of self-respect.   8

A woman could never be a "nigger" in the singular, with its connotation of confirming worth. The noun "girl" was its closest equivalent in that sense, but only when used in direct address and regardless of the gender doing the addressing. "Girl" was a token of respect for a woman. The one-syllable word was drawn out to sound like three in recognition of the extra ounce of wit, nerve, or daring that the woman had shown in the situation under discussion.   9

"G-i-r-l, stop. You mean you said that to his face?"   10

But if the word was used in a third-person reference or shortened so that it almost snapped out of the mouth, it always involved some element of communal disapproval. And age became an important factor in these exchanges. It was only between individuals of the same generation, or from an older person to a younger (but never the other way around), that "girl" would be considered a compliment.   11

I don't agree with the argument that use of the word "nigger" at this social stratum of the black community was an internalization of racism. The dynamics were the exact opposite: the people in my grandmother's living room took a word that whites used to signify worthlessness or degradation and rendered it impotent. Gathering there together, they transformed "nigger" to signify the varied and complex human beings they knew themselves to be. If the word was to disappear totally from the mouths of even the most liberal of white society, no one in that room was naïve enough to believe it would disappear from white minds. Meeting the word head-on, they proved it had absolutely nothing to do with the way they were determined to live their lives.   12

So there must have been dozens of times that the word "nigger" was spoken in front of me before I reached the third grade. But I didn't "hear" it until it was said by a small pair of lips that had already learned it could be a way to humiliate me. That was the word I went home and asked my mother   13 about. And since she knew that I had to grow up in America, she took me in her lap and explained.

RESPONDING TO READING

Do you agree that Naylor's relatives used the word *nigger* in a nonracist or counterracist way? Use your own reactions to the word to explain your answer.

CONSIDERING CONTENT

1. What are Naylor's background and social class? How do you know? Why are they significant to the main point of the essay?
2. Why was the child puzzled when the boy called her *nigger,* even though she had heard the word before?
3. List the definitions of the word *nigger* that were used in the author's grandparents' apartment.
4. Reread paragraph 12. How did the African American community's uses of *nigger* make it not racist, according to Naylor?
5. What does the last sentence suggest about the author's mother? What does it suggest about America?

CONSIDERING METHOD

1. What kind of a little third-grader was Gloria Naylor? Why do you think she presents her childhood self as no angel? What effect does this early presentation of self have on the reader?
2. Reread the description of the author's grandparents' apartment. List at least seven words or phrases that appeal to your senses.
3. How is paragraph 12 different from the rest of the essay? How does the appearance of the page prepare you for this difference?
4. The central part of the essay includes many direct quotations. Why do you think Naylor used people's exact words so often?
5. Does Naylor envision her audience as primarily black or primarily white or mixed? Explain.

WRITING STEP BY STEP

Following Gloria Naylor's essay as an example, write a paper discussing a term that has various—even contradictory—meanings, depending on con-text: who says it, when it is used, and whether it is applied to men or women, young or old, individual or group, for example. Like Naylor, you might think of a term, such as *wife, macho, liberal, success, feminist, jock,* or *marriage,* that holds more meaning than you once thought.

A. Before you start your essay, brainstorm and jot down the various ways you have heard your term used. Ask friends and classmates for help if you need it. Remember that your readers probably have their own definitions of the term.

B. See whether your definitions fall into groups. For example, can you separate the negative meanings from the positive ones? Or do different meanings belong to different social, racial, or ethnic groups? Try at least to decide on a reasonable order in which to present your definitions. For example, the most widely used meanings might come first, with rarer and rarer meanings following it until the last one is the rarest.

C. Begin your essay with a brief story, as Naylor does.

D. Launch into the body of your essay by looking back into your past. Write about how you used to think of the term, perhaps as a child.

E. Develop each meaning of the term with an explanation and examples of direct quotations using it. Keep looking at how Naylor develops her meanings.

F. Close the body of your essay with a speculation about why the term has such a variety of meanings. Look at Naylor's paragraph 12 for ideas about how to present your thoughts.

G. Use the last paragraph to reflect on the anecdote you used in the opening of your essay. This is how Naylor concludes her piece. Your discussion of the term has, by now, added a new dimension to the anecdote.

OTHER WRITING IDEAS

1. What is the first memory you have of someone saying something purposely to hurt you? Or a memory of your saying something purposely to hurt someone else? Write an essay about your own and others' response to the harsh words.

2. COLLABORATIVE WRITING. Think of a phrase or word that seems to be plain but is actually used to mean many different things; for example, "Just a minute," "Well," "I'm ready," and "I'll call you," are more slippery than they seem. A group of students in your class can have some fun discussing such sayings and developing ideas for a single report or individual essays.

3. USING THE INTERNET. Go to www.poynter.org; click on Diversity on the topic list; from the Diversity page, click on Diversity Tip Sheets. You will find a list of current articles about race. Locate one or two that concern the language used to describe race and write an essay about the complexities of labeling racial groups.

4. WRITING ABOUT READING. Naylor rejects the idea that use of the word *nigger* by African Americans indicates an "internalization of racism." Look at her essay again, and think about the ways her definition of the word *nigger* supports or weakens her position. Then write your own analysis of the issue, drawing on your experiences, observations, and reading.

GAINING WORD POWER

The following words appear in Gloria Naylor's essay. They have an ending, *-tion*, in common. This ending occurs frequently in our language, making nouns out of verbs: for example, the noun *conversation* comes from the verb *converse*, which means "to talk." Use your dictionary to find the verb behind each of the nouns in the following list, and give a brief definition of the verb. Begin each brief definition with the word *to*. The first one is done.

	Verb	**Definition**
connotation	connote	to imply or suggest
degradation		
description		
generation		
inflection		
internalization		
recognition		
situation		

Now see how it works the other way around. Here is a list of verbs that are used in Naylor's essay. Find the *-tion* noun that comes from each verb (some are obvious, but for others in the list you will need the dictionary). Be sure to copy the spelling of the noun exactly: sometimes the first part of the word will change. Then write a brief definition of the noun you have written. We did the first one for you.

	Noun	**Definition**
apply	application	a form to be filled out
consider		
determine		
explain		
gravitate		
humiliate		

Noun	Definition
migrate	
punctuate	
realize	
receive	
repeat	
transform	
verify	

EDITING SKILLS: HYPHENS

Consider the use of the hyphen—the short dash—in these phrases from Gloria Naylor's essay:

third-grade class	one-syllable word
close-knit network	third-person reference
ground-floor apartment	

The hyphenated adjectives, which modify the nouns that come after them, are called *temporary compounds*. They are compound because they consist of two words; they are temporary because the two words usually exist separately. They are hyphenated because they make up a unit that seems more like one adjective than two. Sometimes you need to hyphenate in order to make your meaning clear. Think about these examples:

an Italian art specialist	an Italian-art specialist
a small auto dealer	a small-auto dealer
comic book approach	a comic-book approach

In the second list, the hyphen shows which words go together—the specialist is not Italian, the dealer is not small, and the approach is not comic.

Sometimes, it is difficult to decide whether to hyphenate two words that frequently occur together (back-seat driver), whether to run them together as a compound word (backseat driver), or whether to leave them separate (back seat driver). There is not wide agreement even among professional writers about some of these blends. You will see "Thank you" and "Thank-you" about equally often. Your dictionary should be your guide to making the decision.

EXERCISE

Look up the following combinations to see whether words are hyphenated, compound, or separate. Write out the form your dictionary endorses.

back seat driver	open and shut case
happily married couple	least restrictive environment
girl friend problems	partway finished
back door business deals	part time worker
child like expression	better fitting word
an easy pick up	half baked plan

Look back on the essay you have just written. Did you use any compound words that needed hyphens? Did you leave out any hyphens? Check a dictionary or with your instructor before making any corrections.

WEB SITES

http://voices.cla.umn.edu/vg/Bios/entries/naylor_gloria.html
Voices from the Gap—a site maintained by the University of Minnesota—provides a biography and other information on Gloria Naylor.
www.salon.com/books/int/2007/04/25/asim/
Author and journalist Jabari Asim discusses the history and politics of the term "nigger" in this interview about his book *The N Word: Who Can Say It, Who Shouldn't, and Why* (2007).

PREPARING TO READ

If you took an intelligence test and scored low, how would you feel? What might you say that the test failed to measure about you?

••

What Is Intelligence, Anyway?

••

ISAAC ASIMOV

Isaac Asimov (1923–1992) was an American, born in Russia, who wrote more than 200 books, including children's stories, popular science, science fiction, fantasy, and scholarly science. With so many intellectual accomplishments, he was well qualified to wonder just what intelligence is—and is not.

TERMS TO RECOGNIZE

KP *(para. 1)*	kitchen patrol (working in the kitchen)
complacent *(para. 2)*	self-satisfied
bents *(para. 2)*	interests, tendencies
oracles *(para. 3)*	divine communications
devised *(para. 4)*	made up
foist *(para. 4)*	impose
arbiter *(para. 4)*	judge
indulgently *(para. 6)*	as if doing a favor
raucously *(para. 6)*	loudly, in a disorderly way
smugly *(para. 6)*	in a self-satisfied way

What is intelligence, anyway? When I was in the Army, I received a kind of aptitude test that all soldiers took and, against a normal of 100, scored 160. No one at the base had ever seen a figure like that, and for two hours they made a big fuss over me. (It didn't mean anything. The next day I was still a buck private with KP as my highest duty.)   1

All my life I've been registering scores like that, so that I have the complacent feeling that I'm highly intelligent, and I expect other people to think so, too. Actually, though, don't such scores simply mean that I am very good at answering the type of academic questions that are considered worthy of answers by the people who make up the intelligence tests—people with intellectual bents similar to mine?   2

For instance, I had an auto repairman once, who, on these intelligence tests, could not possibly have scored more than 80, by my estimate. I always took it for granted that I was far more intelligent than he was. Yet, when anything went wrong with my car, I hastened to him with it, watched him anxiously as he explored its vitals, and listened to his pronouncements as though they were divine oracles—and he always fixed my car.

Well then, suppose my auto repairman devised questions for an intelligence test. Or suppose a carpenter did, or a farmer, or, indeed, almost anyone but an academician. By every one of those tests, I'd prove myself a moron. And I'd *be* a moron, too. In a world where I could not use my academic training and my verbal talents but had to do something intricate or hard, working with my hands, I would do poorly. My intelligence, then, is not absolute but is a function of the society I live in and of the fact that a small subsection of that society has managed to foist itself on the rest as an arbiter of such matters.

Consider my auto repairman, again. He had a habit of telling me jokes whenever he saw me. One time he raised his head from under the automobile hood to say, "Doc, a deaf-and-dumb guy went into a hardware store to ask for some nails. He put two fingers together on the counter and made hammering motions with the other hand. The clerk brought him a hammer. He shook his head and pointed to the two fingers he was hammering. The clerk brought him nails. He picked out the sizes he wanted, and left. Well, doc, the next guy who came in was a blind man. He wanted scissors. How do you suppose he asked for them?"

Indulgently, I lifted my right hand and made scissoring motions with my first two fingers. Whereupon my auto repairman laughed raucously and said, "Why, you dumb jerk, he used his *voice* and asked for them." Then he said, smugly, "I've been trying that on all my customers today." "Did you catch many?" I asked. "Quite a few," he said, "but I knew for sure I'd catch *you*." "Why is that?" I asked. "Because you're so goddamned educated, doc, I *knew* you couldn't be very smart."

And I have an uneasy feeling he had something there.

RESPONDING TO READING

Do you think that people who are academically intelligent are often poor at nonacademic things? Why or why not?

CONSIDERING CONTENT

1. Why do you think that Asimov's high intelligence score "didn't mean anything" in the army?
2. What is the basic conflict discussed in this essay?
3. Why was the repairman sure he would catch "Doc" Asimov with the joke? Was the repairman stereotyping college professors?
4. What might be on an intelligence test written by auto mechanics? carpenters? farmers? parents of preschoolers? portrait painters? What point is Asimov making with this type of suggestion?
5. Which "small subsection" (para. 4) of society has set itself up as the definers of intelligence?
6. What do you think about Asimov's "uneasy feeling"? Do you think the mechanic "had something there"? Or do you think the nature of the joke would fool most people, intelligent or not?

CONSIDERING METHOD

1. Asimov's essay contains two anecdotes (look up the word *anecdote* if you have not already done so). How do the anecdotes help you understand the conflict the writer is discussing?
2. In a fitting reflection of the content of the essay, Asimov uses both highly academic words (*oracles*, *bents*, *arbiter*) and common, informal words. Point out some of the informal words.
3. Count the number of words in each of the six sentences that make up paragraph 4. Notice the variety in sentence length. This variation is a factor that makes writing lively instead of plodding. When you think your own writing sounds plodding, check to see whether you have a good range of sentence lengths. If they are too much alike, try to combine some of the shorter sentences into longer ones or divide long ones into shorter ones.
4. The last paragraph consists of only one sentence. What difference do you see between placing it in this position and simply adding it as a closing sentence to the preceding paragraph?
5. How do you think academics would respond to this essay? Was Asimov writing to them?

Combining Strategies

In this seven-paragraph essay exploring a definition, how many paragraphs are devoted to developing an example?

WRITING STEP BY STEP

Write an essay that investigates the meaning of an **abstract** term—an idea that cannot be directly observed, such as intelligence. You can use some of Asimov's techniques. We also suggest some other methods for developing an extended definition. Use any combination of techniques to develop your definition. To get your thinking started, consider these abstractions:

common sense	humility	educated
optimism	professionalism	cool
courage	resourcefulness	simplicity
generosity	street smart	beauty
laziness	foolish	stubbornness

Choose your own term, but be sure your choice is an abstraction (not something **concrete**, such as *submarine, pizza,* or *tennis*).

A. Begin with the question "What is _____, anyway?"
B. If you have an anecdote that will serve as an extended investigation of the term, include the story, as Asimov did.
C. Use examples of people you know who demonstrate the abstraction you are defining. Show how they behave or think, with specific details.
D. Use description. For example, an abstract feeling may have a counterpart in a certain type of landscape or weather that you could describe, such as "fluffy white clouds" to suggest peace and contentment or "loud thunder and hard-driving rain" to indicate anger.
E. Point out differences. A good definition will make clear the difference between the word you are explaining and other words with similar meanings. You might tell how feeling peaceful is different from feeling happy or calm.
F. Provide a contrast. We often explain words by clarifying what they are *not*. For example, you could point out that laziness does not merely include lying around doing nothing, which could be depression instead.
G. In your closing, let the reader know to what extent the abstraction is important in your own life.

OTHER WRITING IDEAS

1. Write an essay similar to Asimov's on questioning the usual definition of a term. Challenge the term's usefulness or its usual meaning or everyday misuse.

2. USING THE INTERNET. Make up a word for a concept or item that doesn't have a name, as far as you know. These new words, called *sniglets,* are sometimes collected in humorous books. Here are some examples:

BEAVO (n.): a pencil with teeth marks all over it.
FICTATE (v.): to inform a television or screen character of impending danger under the assumption that he or she can hear you.
OPUP (v.): to push one's glasses back up on the nose.

You may need to make up a related group of words and explain how you came up with them in order to write a whole essay. For example, you could make up several sniglets that describe your pet's behaviors. Find a Web site to spark your imagination.

3. COLLABORATIVE WRITING. Instead of presenting a unified definition of a concept, try to write an essay presenting all the different, even contradictory, meanings a certain term could have. For example, if you asked a group of people to explain what *sex appeal* means to them, you would probably get some widely varying answers. Work with a group of classmates to come up with meanings and to draft a group definition.

4. WRITING ABOUT READING. What's your response to Asimov's opening question: "What is intelligence, anyway?" Write an essay in which you define what intelligence means to you, both in yourself and in the people you know. Use the various methods of developing a definition that are discussed in the introduction to this chapter.

GAINING WORD POWER

Complete these sentences in a reasonable way, showing that you understand the vocabulary words included.

1. Troy indulgently promised to take Rachel _____
   _____.

2. Because he had a mechanical bent, Mark specialized in _____
   _____.

3. _____, the crowd cheered raucously.

4. Dr. Morse foisted his ideas on us when he _____
   _____.

5. By setting himself up as the arbiter of good taste in clothes, Sheldon
   _____.

EDITING SKILLS: USING THE RIGHT TENSE

One of the trickiest skills we learn as we grow up is using the correct tense for verbs. If you have ever learned a foreign language, you are fully aware of the complications of verb tense. In your native language, as you speak, you almost always choose the right tense, but in writing you can get in a snarl.

Asimov's essay shows a combination of tenses. For things that occur in the present or are true in the present, he uses plain old present tense: "I *have* the complacent feeling that I'*m* highly intelligent, and I *expect* other people to think so, too" (para. 2, italics added). For the story about the mechanic, which happened in the past, Asimov uses past tense: "Indulgently, I *lifted* my right hand and *made* scissoring motions with my first two fingers" (para. 6).

In telling stories, speakers and writers sometimes get confused as they go along, and they switch from past to present and back within the same anecdote. Haven't you heard someone tell a story this way:

> You know, if you wait too long, you have to go in person to deal with the licensing bureau. Well, yesterday I went to get my driver's license renewed. So I have to wait in line for an hour. I finally get to the front, and the guy tells me I should have brought my form that I got in the mail. So now I had to go home, and it took my whole lunch hour. When I get back, I tell the guy that if I starve to death, it's his fault. I hate these heartless bureaucracies.

The speaker gives you a sense of being there by switching to present tense, but in academic writing you usually stick to the past tense for events that took place in the past. If you're writing about what happened in a film or literary work, however, you can summarize plot in the present tense.

EXERCISE

The following paragraph mixes present and past tenses. Rewrite the paragraph, and put all the verbs into the present tense:

> *Spenser: For Hire* is based on the detective novels of Robert Parker and is several steps above the average television crime series. It is well acted and well worth watching. Robert Ulrich proved that he is an excellent actor in the part of the tough, well-read private investigator Spenser. He is believable when he fought the bad guys, and he was believable when he quotes Shakespeare. But when the script called for him to be cute and kittenish with his girlfriend, Susan, he is not believable. A cute Spenser was simply embarrassing. In the books, Spenser and Susan tease and traded playful insults, but they are not kittenish. The TV show needed to fix that part of their relationship.

Now look at the verb tenses in the essay you wrote in response to the Asimov article. Which tenses did you use? Are they consistent and logical? Check over your writing, and make any needed corrections in the verb tenses.

WEB SITE

www.thomasarmstrong.com/multiple_intelligences.htm
Describes alternate ways of thinking about intelligence.

PREPARING TO READ

Are you aware of having an ethnic heritage? Are you proud of your cultural roots? If so, why? If you don't know where your ancestors came from, do you feel somehow left out in today's multiethnic society? If so, how do you compensate for the lack?

••

I'm a Banana and Proud of It

••

WAYSON CHOY

Born in 1939 and raised in British Columbia, Wayson Choy is best known for his award-winning novel The Jade Peony, *in which he focuses on his cultural heritage in Vancouver's Chinatown during the first half of this century. A winner of the prestigious Governor General's Literary Award for Non-Fiction, he presently teaches English at Humber College in Toronto. This essay first appeared in the Facts and Arguments column of the* Toronto Globe and Mail.

TERMS TO RECOGNIZE

alien *(para. 2)*	a foreigner, an outsider
concubine *(para. 3)*	a woman belonging sexually to a man not her husband
Taoist *(para. 7)*	pertaining to a Chinese religion that teaches simplicity and selflessness
assimilation *(para. 12)*	cultural absorption of a minority into the main society
paradox *(para. 13)*	an apparent contradiction that turns out to be true

Because both my parents came from China, I took Chinese. But I   1
cannot read or write Chinese and barely speak it. I love my North American citizenship. I don't mind being called a "banana," yellow on the outside and white inside. I'm proud I'm a banana. After all, in Canada and the United States, native Indians are "apples" (red outside, white inside); blacks are "Oreo cookies" (black and white); and Chinese are "bananas." These metaphors assume, both rightly and wrongly, that the culture here has been primarily anglo-white. Cultural history made me a banana.

History: My father and mother arrived separately to the British   2
Columbia coast in the early part of the century. They came as unwanted

"aliens." Better to be an alien here than to be dead of starvation in China. But after the Chinese Exclusion laws were passed in North America (late 1800s, early 1900s), no Chinese immigrants were granted citizenship in either Canada or the United States.

Like those Old China village men from *Toi San* who, in the 1850s, laid   3
down cliff-edge train tracks through the Rockies and the Sierras, or like those first women who came as mail-order wives or concubines and who as bond-slaves were turned into cheaper laborers or even prostitutes—like many of those men and women, my father and mother survived ugly, unjust times. In 1918, two hours after he got off the boat from Hong Kong, my father was called "chink" and told to go back to China. "Chink" is a hateful racist term, stereotyping the shape of Asian eyes: "a chink in the armor," an undesirable slit. For the Elders, the past was humiliating. Eventually, the Second World War changed hostile attitudes toward the Chinese.

During the war, Chinese men volunteered and lost their lives as mem-   4
bers of the American and Canadian military. When hostilities ended, many more were proudly in uniform waiting to go overseas. Record Chinatown dollars were raised to buy War Bonds. After 1945, challenged by such money and ultimate sacrifices, the Exclusion laws in both Canada and the United States were revoked. Chinatown residents claimed their citizenship and sent for their families. By 1949, after the Communists took over China, those of us who arrived here as young children, or were born here, stayed. No longer "aliens," we became legal citizens of North America. Many of us also became "bananas."

Historically, "banana" is not a racist term. Although it clumsily   5
stereotypes many of the children and grandchildren of the Old Chinatowns, the term actually follows the old Chinese tendency to assign endearing nick-names to replace formal names, semicomic names to keep one humble. Thus, "banana" describes the generations who assimilated so well into North American life. In fact, our families encouraged members of my gener-ation in the 1950s and sixties to "get ahead," to get an English education, to get a job with good pay and prestige. "Don't work like me," Chinatown parents said. "Work in an office!" The *lao wahkiu* (the Chinatown old-timers) also warned, "Never forget—you still be Chinese!"

None of us ever forgot. The mirror never lied.   6

Many Chinatown teenagers felt we didn't quite belong in any one   7
world. We looked Chinese, but thought and behaved North American. Impatient Chinatown parents wanted the best of both worlds for us, but they bluntly labeled their children and grandchildren *"juk-sing"* or even *"mo no."* Not that we were totally "shallow bamboo butt-ends" or entirely "no

brain," but we had less and less understanding of Old China traditions, and less and less interest in their village histories. Father used to say we lacked Taoist ritual, Taoist manners. We were, he said, *"mo li."*

This was true. Chinatown's younger brains, like everyone else's of what-   8
ever race, were being colonized by "white bread" U.S. family television pro-grams. We began to feel Chinese home life was inferior. We co-operated with English-language magazines that showed us how to act and what to buy. Seductive Hollywood movies made some of us secretly weep that we did not have movie-star faces. American music made Chinese music sound like noise. By the 1970s and eighties, many of us had consciously or unconsciously dis-tanced ourselves from our Chinatown histories. We became bananas.

Finally, for me, in my 40s or 50s, with the death first of my mother,   9
then my father, I realized I did not belong anywhere unless I could under-stand the past. I needed to find the foundation of my Chinese-ness. I needed roots.

I spent my college holidays researching the past. I read Chinatown   10
oral histories, located documents, searched out early articles. Those early citizens came back to life for me. Their long toil and blood sacrifices, the proud record of their patient, legal challenges, gave us all our present rights as citizens. Canadian and American Chinatowns set aside their family tongue differences and encouraged each other to fight injustice. There were no borders. "After all," they affirmed, *"Daaih ga tohng yahn. . . .* We are all Chinese!"

In my book, *The Jade Peony,* I tried to re-create this past, to explore the   11
beginnings of the conflicts trapped within myself, the struggle between being Chinese and being North American. I discovered a truth: These "between world" struggles are universal. In every human being, there is "the Other"—something that makes each of us feel how different we are from everyone else, even family members. Yet, ironically, we are all the same, wanting the same security and happiness. I know this now.

I think the early Chinese pioneers actually started "going bananas"   12
from the moment they first settled upon the West Coast. They had no choice. They adapted. They initiated assimilation. If they had not, they and their family would have starved to death. I might even suggest that all sur-viving Chinatown citizens eventually became bananas. Only some, of course, were more ripe than others.

That's why I'm proudly a banana: I accept the paradox of being both   13
Chinese and not Chinese. Now at last, whenever I look in the mirror or hear ghost voices shouting, "You still Chinese!", I smile. I know another truth: In immigrant North America, we are all Chinese.

RESPONDING TO READING

Do you understand why Choy is proud to be a banana? In the last sentence, he says "In immigrant North America, we are all Chinese." How do you interpret this comment? Do you think it applies to you?

CONSIDERING CONTENT

1. What does Choy mean when he says he is a "banana"?
2. Why does he think "banana" is not a racist term? Do you agree? What about "apples" and "Oreos" and "white bread"?
3. What were the Chinese Exclusion laws and why were they eventually repealed?
4. What is the origin of the offensive term "chink"?
5. Why did Chinese parents want their children to get "English" educations?
6. What do you think is the main idea of this essay? Where is the thesis stated?

CONSIDERING METHOD

1. How do the first two introductory paragraphs prepare the readers for the rest of the essay?
2. In paragraph 1, Choy uses the phrase "both rightly and wrongly" to explain the metaphors underlying the terms *bananas, apples,* and *Oreos.* Explain how these words can be both right and wrong at the same time.
3. Choy uses a number of short-short sentences: "I'm proud I'm a banana" (para. 1), "They came as unwanted 'aliens'" (para. 2), "None of us ever forgot. The mirror never lied" (para. 6), "We became bananas" (para. 8), "I needed roots" (para. 9), "I know this now" (para. 11), "They had no choice. They adapted. They initiated assimilation" (para. 12). What does he achieve with this rhetorical technique?
4. Why is the phrase "going bananas" in quotation marks in paragraph 12?
5. How do the last three sentences serve to reinforce the theme and also to unify the essay?
6. Do you think you are part of the intended audience for this essay? Why or why not?

WRITING STEP BY STEP

In his essay, Wayson Choy focuses his essay on defining a word. For your essay, think of some words or expressions that need defining because they are misleading, unclear, or too indirect—and define them accurately. You might choose words used in TV commercials, personal ads, real estate descriptions, fast-food restaurants, or menu language. You can focus on a single expression (like "family values") or a group of related terms (like the names for sandwiches or sizes of soft drinks or the names of real estate subdivisions or the language of the funeral business).

A. Begin by telling how the word or name came to your attention.

B. Offer the accurate or dictionary meaning.

C. Then explain what the advertiser, salespeople, or promoters of the terminology want it to mean.

D. As you explain the true meaning, explain why the contrived expression was chosen. If the word or name caught on with the public, such as "lite" or "share" (for "tell" or "discuss") or "senior citizen," speculate as to why it became so popular.

E. Conclude by calling for action from your readers—perhaps urging them to protest this obvious attempt to manipulate the public through the misuse of language.

OTHER WRITING IDEAS

1. What is the difference between a "nerd" and a "geek"? Write an essay in which you define each of these terms and explain the distinctions between them. In addition to consulting reference books, ask a variety of people what they think the difference is. For help in setting up an essay that compares and contrasts, consult the introduction to Chapter 7, pp. 184–89.

2. COLLABORATIVE WRITING. With a group of three or four classmates, interview several international students on your campus, and ask for examples of expressions (such as "cramp my style" or "hit the hay") that surprised or confused them. How did they find out what the expressions really meant? Write up the results of your interviews.

3. USING THE INTERNET. At www.crede.berkeley.edu, you will find the Web site for the Center for Research on Education, Diversity, and Excellence. This organization explores how schools can work best in our multiethnic society. Click on "Five Standards" and you will see how CREDE defines effective pedagogy. Write an essay, based on these definitions, about how your own schooling has succeeded and failed in effectiveness.

4. WRITING ABOUT READING. Do you agree with Choy that "In every human being, there is 'the Other'—something that makes each of us

feel how different we are from everyone else, even family members" (para. 11)? For Choy, that "something" was being Chinese in a "white bread" culture. What in your experience makes you feel like "the Other"?

GAINING WORD POWER

Wayson Choy uses a number of *-ly* adverbs in his essay: *barely, primarily, separately, eventually, proudly, clumsily, actually, bluntly, totally, entirely, secretly, consciously or unconsciously, ironically, actually, eventually, proudly.* If you look carefully at how these words are used, you will notice that they occur in a number of different places in the sentence. Adverbs are often movable; you can put them at the beginning of the sentence or at the end, before the verb or after—in any number of spots.

Go back to Choy's essay and find six of the *-ly* words just listed above. Rewrite two or three of these sentences to illustrate how the *-ly* adverb can be used in several different places. Here's an example:

Choy's sentence: I might even suggest that all surviving Chinatown citizens *eventually* became bananas.

Rewrites: I might even suggest that *eventually* all surviving Chinatown citizens became bananas.

I might even suggest that all surviving Chinatown citizens became bananas *eventually*.

Now use five of the *-ly* adverbs in sentences of your own. Experiment with several different versions to see where the adverb can be placed.

EDITING SKILLS: CAPITALIZATION

Choy's essay illustrates many of the conventions for using capital letters in English. The author, of course, capitalizes the first word in every sentence. He also capitalizes the pronoun *I* every time he uses it. Here are some of the other capitalization rules he follows:

1. *Capitalize the names of nationalities, races, tribes, and languages:* Chinese, North American, Canadian, English, American.
2. *Capitalize the names of political, ethnic, and religious groups:* Communists, Old China traditions, Taoist.
3. *Capitalize brand names of products:* Oreos.
4. *Capitalize names of geographical locations such as cities, states, countries, and regions:* China, B.C., North America, Chinatown, U.S., West Coast.

5. *Capitalize the first and last words and all other words in titles, except articles, prepositions, and coordinating conjunctions* (a, an, the, in, into, at, to, by, and, but, or, nor, for, but, so, etc.): *The Jade Peony*.
6. *Capitalize the names of important government documents:* Chinese Exclusion laws, War Bonds.

Look over the essay you have just written, and check your use of capital letters. A college dictionary will give you a list of capitalization rules along with examples. Entries for specific words will also tell you when to use capitals.

EXERCISE

Supply capital letters where needed in the following sentences:

1. For years women lobbied in washington, d. c., for passage of the equal rights amendment.
2. At present, mexican americans are the fastest-growing minority in the united states.
3. The asian american population is growing rapidly, too, especially in california.
4. People of the muslim faith, adherents of islam, are also a fast-growing group in large cities like chicago and new york.
5. Our book club is reading ann tyler's dinner at the homesick restaurant.

WEB SITE

www.ryerson.ca/library/events/asian_heritage/choy.htm
The Asian heritage site for Ryerson Universiy in Toronto includes information about Wayson Choy's life and works.

PREPARING TO READ

Make a list of the subgroups you belong to within the diverse American population. Consider your geographical roots, your language, hobbies, interests, major, and job choice, for example. Are there prejudices against any of the subgroups you belong to? Is the language or jargon shared by the group part of that prejudice?

••

Viva Spanglish!

••

LILLY GONZALEZ

Lilly Gonzalez is a young writer who graduated from the Medill School of Journalism at Northwestern University in Evanston, Illinois. While in school, Gonzalez was president of Alianza, Northwestern's largest Hispanic/Latino organization. She was the author of a popular column in the Daily Northwestern, *where she once caused a controversy when she defined the term "booty call" and defended carefree sex.*

TERMS TO RECOGNIZE

phonetics *(para. 1)*	the sounds of speech and their combination to create meaning
inevitable *(para. 4)*	impossible to avoid
sellout *(para. 4)*	a person who has betrayed a cause or principle
implicit *(para. 6)*	understood without direct expression
embrace *(para. 6)*	to take up eagerly

It was 1985 and I was in a pre-kindergarten class at Palmer Elementary in the small South Texas town of Pharr. My teacher, Mrs. Herrera, thought I didn't know any English, and I had no plans to let her know I did (thanks to my eldest sister, who had made sure I knew English before I entered school). All the other kids in my class spoke only Spanish; I didn't want to be the conceited one who spoke in English. Then one day Mrs. Herrera stumped me with a question I couldn't answer in Spanish. I was forced to say it in English—and just like that, my secret was out. When my Spanish-speaking mother wanted to know why I had refused to speak English in school, I was stumped again. The Spanish word for "embarrassed"

1

(*avergonzada*) wouldn't come to me, so I tried a translation based on phonetics and told her I had been too *embarazada*. I thought she'd understand
my little Spanglish invention, but she just burst out laughing. I, her four-
year-old daughter, had just told her I was too pregnant to speak English.

And that was my first experience with Spanglish, a hybrid of English   2
and Spanish used by U.S. Latinos who live between two coexisting worlds
(Mexican Americans, for example). It wouldn't be the last time Spanglish
backfired on me. In fact, every time I'm surrounded by native Spanish
speakers, I pray that my Spanglish doesn't intrude into the conversation.
But it usually does, and the Spanish pros either smile at me with a pitying
look that says I've lost touch with my heritage or glare critically at me as if
I've just raped their language.

Strangers usually give me the pity smile. At Mexican restaurants, if my   3
server is Latino and my Spanish sounds less than perfect, I'm rewarded with
it. God forbid I should ask for *el menú de lonche* (Spanglish for "lunch menu")
instead of the proper *menú de almuerzo*. I encountered the pity smile when I
met my boyfriend's mother for the first time. She speaks flawless Spanish,
so naturally I was terrified. Around my third Spanish sentence, my Spanglish
popped out. "*Nunca hay donde parquear* (There's never anywhere to park)," I
said, wincing as soon as I had said that last word. *Parquear* is Spanglish for
the Spanish *estacionar*. She gave me the pity smile.

Those who know me better give me the critical glare. I hate the criti-   4
cal glare. Every time my family heads to Mexico to visit relatives, I dread the
inevitable. I'll be talking with my cousins and my Spanglish will trickle into
my otherwise fluent Spanish. They'll call me *pocha,* which means "sellout."
In my Spanish literature classes at Northwestern University, near Chicago,
there's added pressure to speak perfect Spanish. Professors jeer when I
speak up in class and Spanglish flows out of my mouth.

Don't they understand that Spanglish is my native tongue? I grew up   5
on the Texas-Mexico border with both Spanish and English, and my Spanglish is the product of that. I spoke Spanish with my parents, Spanglish with
my siblings and friends, and English with everyone else. My thoughts are in
Spanglish.

I left Texas to go to Northwestern in 1998, but every time I hear   6
Spanglish, I feel I'm home again. There's no better icebreaker than discovering that you and a stranger both speak it. It carries an implicit understanding of each other's background (immigrant parents, bilingual environment)
and plight (trying to make it in a country where Latinos are still a minority).
Suddenly, you're amigos, and you're dancing effortlessly between the two
languages. At Latino nightclubs, Spanglish wins me friends in the ladies'

room. Wherever the employees are Spanglish-speaking Latinos, it gets me perks. And at Northwestern, it has given me my best friends. I was in a dorm hallway my freshman year when I heard them speaking Spanglish, and I impulsively poked my head in their room and joined their conversation. They didn't mind—Spanglish speakers embrace other Spanglish speakers. It's an unwritten law.

And that's why I refuse to give it up, despite the pity smile and the critical glare. I've had a lifetime love affair with Spanglish, *embarazada* or not.   7

RESPONDING TO READING

What is your usual reaction when you hear foreign languages used in your community? Do you think that this reading will change the way you react to hearing other people around you speaking a language you don't know? Why or why not?

CONSIDERING CONTENT

1. Why were both Spanish and English spoken in Mrs. Herrera's prekindergarten?
2. Where in the essay is the direct definition of Spanglish? What is the definition? How are Spanglish words formed?
3. Why would the writer's cousins call her a sellout for using Spanglish?
4. Gonzalez writes, "My thoughts are in Spanglish." Why is it important what language your thoughts are in? If you have acquired a second language, have you ever found yourself thinking in it? What did it mean, if you did?
5. What do speakers of Spanglish have in common other than a shared vocabulary?

CONSIDERING METHOD

1. What does the title mean? How do you know? Why is it a good title for the essay?
2. What would the essay lose if it began without the opening anecdote?
3. Gonzalez explains three different reactions to her Spanglish. What method does she use to develop these explanations?
4. How would you describe Gonzalez's style—that is, the individuality of her expression? Point out some words and phrases that manifest her style. If you particularly like or dislike this style, explain why.
5. How did the writer help non-Spanish speakers understand the Spanish words in the essay?

6. Reread the opening and closing of the essay. How are they unified?
7. What are the two negative reactions Gonzalez notes in Spanish speakers when she uses Spanglish? What is the difference between these two reactions? What is the positive reaction she finds?

WRITING STEP BY STEP

In Preparing to Read, you listed the subgroups to which you belong. In this essay, you will write about one of these subgroups, how people in it are identifiable, and how people react to the subgroup. Choose a subgroup whose members can identify each other fairly easily; for example, fans of a certain kind of music, marathon runners, video game addicts, oil company wives, children of public school teachers, and film buffs.

1. Begin with an anecdote, as Gonzalez did. Use a story that introduces the subgroup in some naturally occurring setting. This should be one or two paragraphs long.
2. Next, provide a direct definition of the subgroup in one paragraph. Explain what the people in it have in common.
3. Think of two or three different reactions that others have when they realize you are a member of this subgroup. If you can, think of both negative and positive reactions, as Gonzalez did. Consider how people within the group and those outside it might react. Then explain each one of these reactions in a paragraph of its own.
4. Close with your ideas about whether your affiliation with this subgroup will be "a lifetime love affair" or not.
5. If possible, unify your closing with your opening through repetition of words or through direct reference to the anecdote you began with.
6. Give your essay a title that comes from the slang, jargon, dress, knowledge base, or behavior of the subgroup.

OTHER WRITING IDEAS

1. Gonzalez writes about how her Spanglish sometimes embarrasses or unnerves her. Write an essay about a habit, behavior, or trait you have that sometimes embarrasses you. Explain why.
2. COLLABORATIVE WRITING. Get together with three or four other students who have seen the film *Spanglish* (or rent it for this writing project). Discuss ideas the movie brings up about assimilation and about retaining native culture. As a group or individually, write an essay explaining two or three issues facing people as they integrate into a new culture.

3. USING THE INTERNET. Do Spanish-speaking children who attend bilingual preschools and elementary schools in the United States become fluent English speakers and readers? Use the Internet to find the results of research studies on this question. Explain your findings in an editorial for your city's newspaper.

4. WRITING ABOUT READING. Gonzalez says that Spanish speakers have both negative and positive reactions when she uses Spanglish. Write an essay in which you identify those reactions and explain, as best you can, why people have them.

GAINING WORD POWER

English is probably the biggest borrower of words from other countries, with over 120 different languages recorded as sources of today's vocabulary. New terms from other countries are called *loan words* or *borrowings,* though they quickly become integrated into the rest of our speech as legitimate English words. What reference books could you use to find the foreign origins of the following words? Write down the word and its origin.

assassin	barbecue
bazaar	chipmunk
jaguar	saga
slogan	tattoo
tea	voodoo

EDITING SKILLS: USING COORDINATION

Experienced writers vary their sentence types and lengths to make their writing more interesting. Writing that contains sentences all of the same type and length is boring to read, whether or not the reader understands why. Even Ernest Hemingway, who was noted for his lean, simple sentences, often put two or more together to make longer ones, as Gonzalez does in the following examples:

My teacher, Mrs. Herrera, thought I didn't know any English, and I had no plans to let her know I did.

The Spanish word for "embarrassed" (avergonzada) wouldn't come to me, so I tried a translation based on phonetics.

I thought she'd understand my little Spanglish invention, but she just burst out laughing.

The examples are called *compound* sentences because they are made up from two complete sentences. These are the sentences that are put together:

> My teacher, Mrs. Herrera, thought I didn't know any English.
> I had no plans to let her know I did.

> The Spanish word for "embarrassed" (avergonzada) wouldn't come to me.
> I tried a translation based on phonetics.

> I thought she'd understand my little Spanglish invention.
> She just burst out laughing.

To make short sentences into one longer sentence, you splice them together with coordinating conjunctions. There are only seven of them: *and, but, for, or, nor, yet, so*. Put a comma after each short sentence you are combining, but put a period at the very end. If you are dissatisfied with your writing because it sounds choppy, this method will help you achieve longer sentences.

EXERCISE

Using a comma and a suitable coordinating conjunction, combine the following pairs of sentences into compound sentences.

1. Many people take four or more years of Spanish in school.
   They still can't carry on an ordinary conversation in Spanish.
2. School courses often emphasize the grammar of a language.
   Teachers grade students on how correctly they read and write.
3. Reading and writing are important skills.
   They are not necessary to everyday chat.
4. A conversation-only class aims to help people speak Spanish in real-life situations.
   This skill is crucial to mastery of the language.
5. Only practicing out loud can improve conversational skills.
   Students in a conversation class are required to speak in Spanish, no matter how awkwardly.

WEB SITE

www.newsweek.com/id/60271
This article about Spanglish includes an interview with Ilan Stavans, the author of *Spanglish: The Making of a New American Language* (2003).

STUDENT ESSAY USING DEFINITION

Nothing to Be Scared Of

Kerri Mauger

Before entering Eastern Illinois University, Kerri Mauger attended high school in the south suburbs of Chicago. She wrote this essay for her first-year composition class. Kerri later transferred to a college near her hometown, where she planned to major in special education.

Early on the day of my eleventh birthday, my sister and I were downstairs watching TV. My mom came down and told us she wanted to talk to us in my room. We followed her upstairs, where she told us to lie on the floor. She said that there was a man outside with a gun and we had to hide so he would not come and get us. I was really scared and confused, and we stayed in my room for two hours in almost complete silence. When my father got home, he called the hospital, and I saw my mother taken away by force. My birthday party was canceled, and I was crushed.   1

For most of my life, I remember my mother being in and out of hospitals. No one was sure what was wrong with her, and it took many years to put a label on her condition. My mother was finally diagnosed with schizophrenia. It also took me a long time to understand my mother's illness. My dad was very secretive about her. I think he wanted to protect my sister and me, but in the long run ignorance hurt us even more.   2

Schizophrenia is a disabling brain disorder that affects about one percent of Americans. It strikes men and women equally and occurs at similar rates in all cultures and races. At times the symptoms don't appear connected to a severe mental illness, and people with schizophrenia look merely withdrawn and depressed. That's how our mother often seemed to us, especially at first—as if she no longer enjoyed her family or her life.   3

But schizophrenics usually decline over time, displaying more serious, more obvious symptoms. These include hallucinations, delusions, and problems with speech and movement. Schizophrenics have a hard time distinguishing between what is real and what is imagined. They also have trouble managing emotions, thinking clearly, and dealing with other people. They cannot always tell what other people's words and actions mean, so they often respond strangely and inappropriately.   4

People who have never encountered someone with schizophrenia may feel uneasy and even frightened by the bizarre and socially unacceptable behavior. My mother may sit and listen to the voices she hears all day long,   5 ignoring everything else. She explains that they are communicating with her through telepathy. She replies to these voices and denies that there is anything wrong with her. Some schizophrenics shout angrily at people on the street, believing that they have been insulted or threatened when they have not.

There is no cure for schizophrenia. Medication may help some people   6
with the symptoms, but no drug has helped my mother yet. Psychotherapy can also assist schizophrenics in controlling their thoughts and behavior, and many people with the disorder are able to lead rewarding and meaningful lives.

Along with drugs and therapy, family understanding can help. The   7
person suffering from schizophrenia needs sympathy, compassion, and respect. It is best to stay calm and nonjudgmental. Getting excited or starting to argue with the person can worsen an episode. Schizophrenia is not the person's moral fault or rational choice. It is sometimes easier to laugh at something we fear and do not understand. But ignorance about something like schizophrenia can be hurtful. I love my mother dearly and after many years of being afraid and uninformed, I can finally say I am not scared of her at all. She still is not a "normal" mother, but I know the facts and can deal with whatever comes my way.

CONSIDERING CONTENT AND METHOD

1. Why does the author begin with the incident about her birthday party?
2. Did you follow the explanation of *schizophrenia*? Do you understand the term better now that you've read this essay? Are there any questions about the disease that the author does not answer?
3. How effective are the personal examples and observations that the author includes in paragraphs 2, 3, 5, and 7?
4. How does the conclusion echo the beginning?
5. What is the point of this essay? How is that point clarified in the closing?

Strategies for Sorting Ideas:
Classification and *Division*

Food Guide Pyramid
A Guide to Daily Food Choices

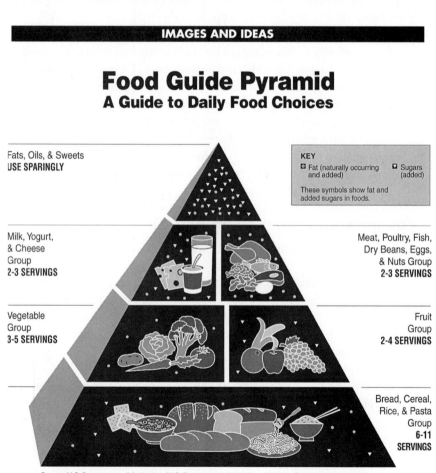

Fats, Oils, & Sweets
USE SPARINGLY

KEY
◻ Fat (naturally occurring and added)   ▨ Sugars (added)
These symbols show fat and added sugars in foods.

Milk, Yogurt, & Cheese Group
2-3 SERVINGS

Meat, Poultry, Fish, Dry Beans, Eggs, & Nuts Group
2-3 SERVINGS

Vegetable Group
3-5 SERVINGS

Fruit Group
2-4 SERVINGS

Bread, Cereal, Rice, & Pasta Group
6-11 SERVINGS

Source: U.S. Department of Agriculture/U.S. Department of Health and Human Services

FOR DISCUSSION AND WRITING

What is the point of this method of classifying foods? How many categories are there, and why are they arranged in a pyramid?

In a paragraph or two, classify the foods you eat and those you avoid. Put them in categories and label them; include specific foods in each category. Can you arrange them in a pyramid? If you want, you might make a humorous classification, such as foods you would eat all day long, foods you eat because they're cheap, foods that taste awful but are good for you.

The next time you get ready to do your laundry, look on the back of the detergent box. There you will see directions for sorting your clothes according to the temperature of the water that you should use. The directions may read something like this:

FOR BEST CLEANING RESULTS

Sort and select temperature and begin filling washer with water.

Hot	Warm	Cold
White cottons	Bright colors	Dark colors
Colorfast pastels	Permanent press	Colors that could bleed
Diapers	Knits	Delicates
Heavily soiled items		Stains like blood and chocolate

Do you follow a procedure like this when you do your laundry? Why do you suppose the detergent makers put directions such as these on the back of the box?

THE POINT OF CLASSIFICATION AND DIVISION

As the preceding laundry example shows, separating and arranging things helps us to accomplish tasks more efficiently and more effectively. This process of "sorting things out" also helps us to clarify our thinking and understand our feelings.

Many writing tasks lend themselves to grouping information into categories. For example, you might write a paper for psychology class on the various ways people cope with the death of a loved one. For a course in economics you might write about the three basic types of unemployment (*frictional*, *structural*, and *cyclical*). This approach—called **classification** and **division**—enables you to present a body of information in an orderly way.

Dividing and classifying also forces you to think clearly about your topic. By breaking a subject down into its distinct parts, or categories, you can look at it more closely and decide what you want to say about each part. For example, if you are writing an essay on effective teaching styles, you might begin by dividing the teachers you have had into the "good" ones and the "bad" ones. Then you could break those broad categories down further into more precise ones: teachers who held your interest, teachers who knew their subjects, teachers who made you do busy work, and so forth. As you develop each category, you have to think about the qualities that impressed you, and this thought process leads you to a better understanding of the topic you are writing about. You may end up writing only about the good teachers, but dividing and classifying the examples will help you to organize your thinking.

THE PRINCIPLES OF CLASSIFICATION AND DIVISION

Most things can be classified or divided in more than one way, depending on the reason for grouping the items. In the laundry example, for instance, you are told to sort the clothes according to the temperature of the water. Putting bright colors with knits doesn't make any sense if you don't know the reason—or basis—for the category: *items to be washed in cold water.* When you divide and classify a topic, be sure to have a sound basis for formulating your categories. The following suggestions will help you develop a useful system of classification.

Give a Purpose to Your Classification

Merely putting facts or ideas into different groups isn't necessarily meaningful. Consider these sentences that classify for no apparent reason:

1. There are five kinds of friends in most of our lives.
2. People deal with their spare money in four basic ways.

How could you give a **purpose** to these ideas? You would have to add a *reason* or declare a *point* for the categories. Here are some revisions that give purpose to these two classifications:

1. a. There are five kinds of friends in most of our lives, and each kind is important in its own way.
   b. Most of us have five kinds of friends, and each one drives us crazy in a special way.
2. a. People deal with their spare money in four ways that reflect their overall attitudes toward life.
   b. People deal with their spare money in four ways, only one of which is truly constructive.

Establish a Clear Basis for Your Classification

If you are going to classify items or ideas, you have to decide which organizing principle you want to use to form your groups. For example, if you are classifying friends, you could group them according to how close you are to them, as Judith Viorst does in her essay in this chapter. Or you could group them according to other principles: how long you have known them, what you have in common with them, or how much time you spend with the people in each group. The important thing is to choose a workable principle and stick with it.

Make Your Groups Parallel and Equal

In a classification essay, you usually announce the groups or classes in the introduction: several ways to handle criticism, four kinds of friends, three types of stress, three levels of intelligence, and so forth. You then devote one section to each group of your classification. A section can be one paragraph or several, but the sections for the major categories should be about equal in length. In a classification essay about friendship, for instance, if you cover "childhood pals" in 150 words, then you should use approximately the same number of words for each of the other kinds of friends.

Experienced writers also present each section in a similar way. For example, in this chapter psychologist David Elkind classifies the three basic types of stress that young people experience. He labels each one with a letter, describes it, and gives examples. He follows the same order—label, description, examples—in covering each type. He also mentions the same two conditions when explaining each type: whether it's foreseeable and whether it's avoidable. This parallel development helps the reader to recognize the similarities and identify the distinctions among the types.

THE PITFALLS OF CLASSIFICATION AND DIVISION

The following advice will help you to avoid some of the problems that writers sometimes encounter in developing an essay of classification.

1. *Know the difference between useful and useless ways of classifying.* Sorting your clothes by brand name probably won't help you get the best cleaning results when doing the laundry. And dividing teachers into those who wear glasses and those who don't is not a very useful way to organize a paper on effective teaching styles. But classifying teachers into those who lecture, those who use a question-discussion format, and those who run small-group workshops might be significant, mainly because such groupings would allow you to discuss the teachers' philosophies, their attitudes toward students, and their effectiveness in the classroom.

2. *Be sure your classification covers everything you claim it covers.* If, for instance, you know some teachers who sometimes lecture and sometimes use small groups, you can't pretend these people don't exist just to make your classification tidy. At least mention exceptions, even if you don't give them as much space as the major categories.

3. *Don't let the basis of division shift.* If you can see a problem with the following classification system, you already understand this warning:

TYPES OF TEACHERS

   A. Teachers who lecture
   B. Teachers who lead discussions
   C. Teachers who have a sense of humor
   D. Teachers who run workshops
   E. Teachers who never hold office hours

Notice that three types of teachers (a, b, and d) are grouped according to the way they run their classes, but two types (c and e) are defined by some other standard. You can see the confusion these shifting groups cause: Can teachers who lecture have a sense of humor? Don't those who use workshops also hold office hours?

4. *Be sure your groups are parallel or equal in rank.* The following classification illustrates a problem in rank:

KINDS OF POPULAR MUSIC

   A. Easy listening
   B. Country and western
   C. Rock 'n' roll
   D. Ice-T

Although Ice-T does represent a type of popular music distinct from easy listening, country, and rock, the category is not parallel with the others— it is far too small. It should be "rap" or "hip hop," with Ice-T used as an example.

5. *Avoid stereotypes.* When you write about types of behavior or put people into groups, you run the risk of oversimplifying the material. The best way to avoid this problem is to use plenty of specific examples. You can also point out exceptions and describe variations; such honesty shows that you have been thinking carefully about the topic.

WHAT TO LOOK FOR IN A CLASSIFICATION

As you read the essays in this chapter, pay attention to these points:

1. *Figure out what the author is classifying.* Then identify the basis for making up the groups and the purpose of the classification.
2. *Look for the specific groups or classes* into which the author has sorted the material. Jot down a brief list of the major categories just to see if you can keep track of them.
3. *Ask yourself if the groups are clearly defined.* Do they shift? Do they cover what they claim to cover? Are they parallel?
4. *Be alert for stereotypes.* How does the author handle exceptions and variations?
5. *Identify the audience.* How do you know who the intended readers are?

PREPARING TO READ

List five or ten of the people you call "friends." Are they all friends to an equal degree? Do you have a flexible meaning for the word *friend*?

••

Friends, Good Friends— and Such Good Friends

••

JUDITH VIORST

A popular humorist who writes essays and light verse for many well-known magazines, Judith Viorst was born in Newark, New Jersey, in 1931 and attended Rutgers University. She has written numerous children's books, including the enduring favorite Alexander and the Terrible, Horrible, No Good, Very Bad Day *(1972), as well as several books for adults, including* Imperfect Control *(1998) and* Suddenly 60: And Other Shocks of Late-Life *(2000). The following selection appeared in her regular column in* Redbook *magazine in 1977.*

TERMS TO RECOGNIZE

ardor *(para. 1)*	enthusiasm, intensity
nonchalant *(para. 2)*	indifferent, offhand
Tuesday-doubles *(para. 7)*	tennis played by four people, in pairs, on Tuesdays
sibling rivalry *(para. 11)*	competition among children for parental favor
dormant *(para. 13)*	sleeping, inactive
revived *(para. 13)*	brought back to life
calibrated *(para. 21)*	adjusted, determined

Women are friends, I once would have said, when they totally love   1
and support and trust each other, and bare to each other the secrets of
their souls, and run—no questions asked—to help each other, and tell harsh
truths to each other (no, you can't wear that dress unless you lose ten
pounds first) when harsh truths must be told. Women are friends, I once
would have said, when they share the same affection for Ingmar Bergman,
plus train rides, cats, warm rain, charades, Camus, and hate with equal
ardor Newark and Brussels sprouts and Lawrence Welk and camping.

In other words, I once would have said that a friend is a friend all the   2
way, but now I believe that's a narrow point of view. For the friendships I
have and the friendships I see are conducted at many levels of intensity,
serve many different functions, meet different needs and range from those
as all-the-way as the friendship of the soul sisters mentioned above to that
of the most nonchalant and casual playmates.

Consider these varieties of friendship: 3

1. Convenience friends. These are the women with whom, if our paths   4
weren't crossing all the time, we'd have no particular reason to be friends: a
next-door neighbor, a woman in our car pool, the mother of one of our children's closest friends or maybe some mommy with whom we serve juice and
cookies each week at the Glenwood Co-op Nursery.

Convenience friends are convenient indeed. They'll lend us their cups   5
and silverware for a party. They'll drive our kids to soccer when we're sick.
They'll take us to pick up our car when we need a lift to the garage. They'll
even take our cats when we go on vacation. As we will for them. But we
don't, with convenience friends, ever come too close or tell too much; we
maintain our public face and emotional distance. "Which means," says
Elaine, "that I'll talk about being overweight but not about being depressed.
Which means I'll admit being mad but not blind with rage. Which means
that I might say that we're pinched this month but never that I'm worried
sick over money." But which doesn't mean that there isn't sufficient value to
be found in these friendships of mutual aid, in convenience friends.

2. Special-interest friends. These friendships aren't intimate, and they   6
needn't involve kids or silverware or cats. Their value lies in some interest
jointly shared. And so we may have an office friend or a yoga friend or a
tennis friend or a friend from the Women's Democratic Club.

"I've got one woman friend," says Joyce, "who likes, as I do, to take   7
psychology courses. Which makes it nice for me—and nice for her. It's fun to
go with someone you know and it's fun to discuss what you've learned, driving back from the classes." And for the most part, she says, that's all they
discuss. "I'd say that what we're doing is *doing* together, not *being* together,"
Suzanne says of her Tuesday-doubles friends. "It's mainly a tennis relationship, but we play together well. And I guess we all need to have a couple of
playmates." I agree.

My playmate is a shopping friend, a woman of marvelous taste, a   8
woman who knows exactly *where* to buy *what*, and furthermore is a woman
who always knows beyond a doubt what one ought to be buying. I don't have
the time to keep up with what's new in eyeshadow, hemlines and shoes and
whether the smock look is in or finished already. But since (oh, shame!) I care

a lot about eyeshadow, hemlines and shoes, and since I don't *want* to wear smocks if the smock look is finished, I'm very glad to have a shopping friend.

3. Historical friends. We all have a friend who knew us when . . .   9
maybe way back in Miss Meltzer's second grade, when our family lived in that three-room flat in Brooklyn, when our dad was out of work for seven months, when our brother Allie got in that fight where they had to call the police, when our sister married the endodontist from Yonkers, and when, the morning after we lost our virginity, she was the first, the only, friend we told.

The years have gone by and we've gone separate ways and we've little   10
in common now, but we're still an intimate part of each other's past. And so whenever we go to Detroit we always go to visit this friend of our girl-hood. Who knows how we looked before our teeth were straightened. Who knows how we talked before our voice got unBrooklyned. Who knows what we ate before we learned about artichokes. And who, by her presence, puts us in touch with an earlier part of ourself, a part of ourself it's important never to lose.

"What this friend means to me and what I mean to her," says Grace,   11
"is having a sister without sibling rivalry. We know the texture of each other's lives. She remembers my grandmother's cabbage soup. I remember the way her uncle played the piano. There's simply no other friend who remembers those things."

4. Crossroads friends. Like historical friends, our crossroads friends   12
are important for *what was*—for the friendship we shared at a crucial, now past, time of life. A time, perhaps, when we roomed in college together; or worked as eager young singles in the Big City together; or went together, as my friend Elizabeth and I did, through pregnancy, birth and that scary first year of new motherhood. Crossroads friends forge powerful links, links strong enough to endure with not much more contact than once-a-year let-ters at Christmas. And out of respect for those crossroads years, for those dramas and dreams we once shared, we will always be friends.

5. Cross-generational friends. Historical friends and crossroads   13
friends seem to maintain a special kind of intimacy—dormant but always ready to be revived—and though we may rarely meet, whenever we do con-nect, it's personal and intense. Another kind of intimacy exists in the friend-ships that form across generations in what one woman calls her daughter-mother and her mother-daughter relationships. Evelyn's friend is her mother's age—"but I share so much more than I ever could with my mother"—a woman she talks to of music, of books, and of life. "What I get from her is the benefit of her experience. What she gets—and enjoys—from me is a youthful perspective. It's a pleasure for both of us."

I have in my own life a precious friend, a woman of 65 who has lived   14
very hard, who is wise, who listens well; who has been where I am and can
help me understand it; and who represents not only an ultimate ideal
mother to me but also the person I'd like to be when I grow up.

In our daughter role we tend to do more than our share of self-revelation;   15
in our mother role we tend to receive what's revealed. It's another kind of
pleasure—playing a wise mother to a questing younger person. It's another
very lovely kind of friendship.

6. Part-of-a-couple friends. Some of the women we call our friends   16
we never see alone—we see them as part of a couple at couples' parties. And
though we share interests in many things and respect each other's views, we
aren't moved to deepen the relationship. Whatever the reason, a lack of
time or—and this is more likely—a lack of chemistry, our friendship remains
in the context of a group. But the fact that our feeling on seeing each other
is always, "I'm *so* glad she's here" and the fact that we spend half the
evening talking together says that this too, in its way, counts as a friendship.

(Other part-of-a-couple friends are the friends that came with the   17
marriage, and some of these are friends we could live without. But sometimes, alas, she married our husband's best friend; and sometimes, alas, she
is our husband's best friend. And so we find ourself dealing with her, some-
what against our will, in a spirit of what I'll call *reluctant* friendship.)

7. Men who are friends. I wanted to write just of women friends, but   18
the women I've talked to won't let me—they say I must mention man-woman
friendships too. For these friendships can be just as close and as dear as
those that we form with women. Listen to Lucy's description of one such
friendship: "We've found we have things to talk about that are different from
what he talks about with my husband and different from what I talk about
with his wife. So sometimes we call on the phone or meet for lunch. There
are similar intellectual interests—we always pass on to each other the books
that we love—but there's also something tender and caring too."

In a couple of crises, Lucy says, "he offered himself, for talking and   19
for helping. And when someone died in his family he wanted me there. The
sexual, flirty part of our friendship is very small, but *some*—just enough to
make it fun and different." She thinks—and I agree—that the sexual part,
though small, is always *some*, is always there when a man and a woman are
friends.

It's only in the past few years that I've made friends with men, in the   20
sense of a friendship that's *mine*, not just part of two couples. And achieving with them the ease and the trust I've found with women friends has
value indeed. Under the dryer at home last week, putting on mascara and

rouge, I comfortably sat and talked with a fellow named Peter. Peter, I finally decided, could handle the shock of me minus mascara under the dryer. Because we care for each other. Because we're friends.

8. There are medium friends, and pretty good friends, and very good   21 friends indeed, and these friendships are defined by their level of intimacy. And what we'll reveal at each of these levels of intimacy is calibrated with care. We might tell a medium friend, for example, that yesterday we had a fight with our husband. And we might tell a pretty good friend that this fight with our husband made us so mad that we slept on the couch. And we might tell a very good friend that the reason we got so mad in that fight that we slept on the couch had something to do with that girl who works in his office. But it's only to our very best friends that we're willing to tell all, to tell what's going on with that girl in his office.

The best of friends, I still believe, totally love and support and trust   22 each other, and bare to each other the secrets of their souls, and run—no questions asked—to help each other, and tell harsh truths to each other when they must be told. But we needn't agree about everything (only 12-year-old girl friends agree about *everything*) to tolerate each other's point of view. To accept without judgment. To give and to take without ever keeping score. And to *be* there, as I am for them and as they are for me, to comfort our sorrows, to celebrate our joys.

RESPONDING TO READING

How many different kinds of friends do you have? How would you categorize the friends you listed in Preparing to Read? Would Viorst's categories work for you? Would you have to create any new ones?

CONSIDERING CONTENT

1. What ideas is Viorst giving up, according to the beginning of the essay? Why does she begin with what she no longer believes?
2. Make a list of the different kinds of friends discussed in the essay. Which kind is the exception from the others?
3. What kind of person is the author of this essay? What kind of life does she lead? Look at paragraphs 4, 5, and 11 for evidence. How might the writer's life situation limit her audience? Did you feel included?
4. What are the functions friends perform, according to the essay? Are there underlying similarities among most of the types?
5. Why do you think the women Viorst interviewed insisted that she discuss man–woman friendships?

CONSIDERING METHOD

1. How do you know when Viorst is beginning a section about a new type of friend? What other method might she use to signal such a shift?

2. What is the relationship between the opening of the essay and the closing?

3. What do the direct quotations do for the essay? Are they from famous people? Think of at least two reasons why they are included.

4. In paragraph 7, you can see the repetition of similar sentence openings. What words are repeated? Find another example of repetition of phrases or structures. What purpose does this repetition serve?

COMBINING STRATEGIES

Look at the ways Judith Viorst develops her explanations for each type of friend. She uses narration, definition, example, comparison and contrast, and cause-and-effect reasoning. Identify instances of at least three of these methods.

WRITING STEP BY STEP

Using Viorst's essay for inspiration, write an essay that classifies several different types of romantic relationships.

A. Brainstorm, with help from friends or classmates if you want it, for ideas about the various couples and kinds of romance you see around you. Jot down everything mentioned, even if it sounds silly or overlapping—you can sort it out later.

B. Choose three to six types to discuss in your essay. When the types seem closely related, you might combine several different ones from your brainstorming notes to make up one type.

C. Make up a label for each type, as Viorst does in "Friends, Good Friends—and Such Good Friends."

D. Develop a section explaining each type. Use examples of people who show each type of romantic attachment if you can—either people you know personally or public figures most of your readers will be able to identify. Interview your friends, as Viorst did, and use direct quotations from your interviews.

E. Be sure to show how the types are similar and different from each other by using comparisons and contrasts as you go along. Look at paragraphs 13 and 21 of Viorst's essay for samples of how to do this.

F. Use signals to show when you are shifting from one type to the next. You could use numbers and/or labels. Or you could use transitional words, like "The second type or style of romance is . . . ."

G. Write an introduction that discusses a misperception (of your own or of others) about romantic relationships. See Viorst's introduction for a model.

H. Close your essay with a statement that draws all the kinds of romance together, telling what they have in common. Alternatively, you may want to close, as Viorst does, by commenting on what you wrote in the introduction.

OTHER WRITING IDEAS

1. There are probably as many kinds of people you dislike as people you like. Write an essay categorizing the types that drive you crazy.

2. COLLABORATIVE WRITING. Judith Viorst wrote another essay in which she classifies the lies we tell. For example, she discusses lies that spare others' feelings, lies that save our own pride, and so on. Get together with a group of classmates to think of your own categories and examples of lies and liars. Have each person in the group list as many types and illustrations as he or she can; compare and discuss your lists. Then write your own essay on this topic.

3. USING THE INTERNET. Classify the variations of a single emotion: anxiety, nervousness, anger, pleasure, embarrassment, confidence, excitement, or pride, for example. Use the search term "emotional literacy" to find Web sites that might help you explore the topic. Remember to acknowledge your sources in your essay.

4. WRITING ABOUT READING. Viorst says that "the sexual part, though small, is always *some*, is always there when a man and a woman are friends." Do you agree? What do you think about friends of the other sex? Are cross-sex friendships different in quality from same-sex friendships? Would you try to restrict your sweetheart in his or her opposite-sex friendships?

GAINING WORD POWER

The following partial sentences include slightly different forms of the preceding Terms to Recognize. Complete each sentence in a reasonable way that shows you understand the word used. Use your dictionary to be sure you grasp the meaning.

1. Elena is an ardent hockey fan, but _____

_____.

2. Stanley did not understand the fine calibrations of politeness: he often

_____.

3. After _____, Jean's social life went into a period of dormancy.

4. The writer's nonchalance about spelling was clear when _____

_____.

EDITING SKILLS: USING PRONOUNS CONSISTENTLY

When Judith Viorst writes about her own experiences and ideas, she uses the pronouns *I* or *we* to identify herself:

> The friendships *I* have and the friendships *I* see are conducted at many levels of intensity.

> *We* all have a friend who knew *us* when . . . .

When she writes as someone addressing an audience directly, she uses the pronoun *you*:

> [N]o, *you* can't wear that dress unless *you* lose ten pounds first.

And when she writes about a person or persons, she identifies them first and then uses *he, she,* or *they* to refer to them:

> Convenience friends are convenient indeed. *They*'ll lend us *their* cups and silverware for a party.

> Evelyn's friend is *her* mother's age, . . . a woman *she* talks to of music, of books, and of life.

As you see, pronouns refer to three different "persons." Each person expresses a different point of view:

Person	Singular	Plural
First person (the person writing):	I, me, my, mine	we, us, our, ours
Second person (the person written to):	you, your, yours	you, your, yours
Third person (the person written about):	he, him, his, she her, hers, it, its	they, them, their, theirs

Writers often shift from one person to another, especially between first and third, as Judith Viorst does in her essay. But these shifts must be clear and logical. An unnecessary shift can distract or confuse a reader:

> Shift: If a student wants to succeed in graduate school, you have to know the rules of the game.

The sentence is about *a student,* so it's in third person; *you* is a second person pronoun.

> No shift: If a student wants to succeed in graduate school, he or she has to know the rules of the game.

> No shift: If students want to succeed in graduate school, they have to know the rules of the game.

EXERCISE

Rewrite the following paragraph, making the point of view consistently *third person* (people/they). You may have to change some verbs to fit with the pronouns you changed.

> Most people are interested in music, either as a spectator or as performers. You can enjoy music by watching MTV or attending concerts. We can also enjoy playing CDs and listening to music on the radio. Other people want to make their own music. If we are really serious about playing an instrument or singing, we can take lessons and join a band or choir. You might prefer, however, to play for your own enjoyment or to entertain your friends and family at parties. A person has many chances to express his love of music.

WEB SITE

www.bookpage.com/0711bp/judith_viorst.html
This site offers an interview with Judith Viorst about her popular children's books.

PREPARING TO READ

Are you an ex-smoker or do you know someone who is? How would you describe the attitudes of former smokers toward their past behavior and toward those who continue to smoke?

••

Confessions of an Ex-Smoker

••

FRANKLIN E. ZIMRING

Former smoker Frank Zimring is the William G. Simon Professor of Law and Wolfen Distinguished Scholar at the University of California at Berkeley, where he specializes in criminal justice and family law. Professor Zimring has also done professional consulting on public policy issues, such as drugs and smoking. For example, he currently serves as the principal investigator for the Center on Culture, Immigration, and Youth Violence Prevention. His most recent book, The Great American Crime Decline: Studies in Crime and Public Policy, *was published in 2006. The following, a more personal essay, first appeared in* Newsweek.

TERMS TO RECOGNIZE

watershed *(para. 1)*	critical turning point
cessation *(para. 1)*	stopping, ending
zealot *(para. 1)*	person with intense drive, fanatic
degenerates *(para. 2)*	social misfits
recidivist *(para.3)*	repeater, backslider
anecdotal *(para. 4)*	casual observation
vitriolic *(para. 4)*	harsh, blistering
unmitigated *(para. 6)*	undiminished, absolute
proselytizing *(para. 7)*	attempting to convince, convert
predestination *(para. 7)*	foreordained
excoriate *(para. 10)*	harshly criticize

Americans can be divided into three groups—smokers, nonsmokers, and that expanding pack of us who have quit. Those who have never smoked don't know what they're missing, but former smokers, ex-smokers, reformed

1

smokers can never forget. We are veterans of a personal war, linked by that watershed experience of ceasing to smoke and by the temptation to have just one more cigarette. For almost all of us ex-smokers, smoking continues to play an important part in our lives. And now that it is being restricted in restaurants around the country and will be banned in almost all indoor public places in New York State, it is vital that everyone understand the different emotional states cessation of smoking can cause. I have observed four of them; and in the interest of science I have classified them as those of the zealot, the evangelist, the elect, and the serene. Each day, each category gains new recruits.

Not all antitobacco zealots are former smokers, but a substantial number of fire-and-brimstone opponents do come from the ranks of the reformed. Zealots believe that those who continue to smoke are degenerates who deserve scorn not pity and the penalties that will deter offensive behavior in public as well. Relations between these people and those who continue to smoke are strained.

One explanation for the zealot's fervor in seeking to outlaw tobacco consumption is his own tenuous hold on abstaining from smoking. But I think part of the emotional force arises from sheer envy as he watches and identifies with each lung-filling puff. By making smoking in public a crime, the zealot seeks reassurance that he will not revert to bad habits; give him strong social penalties, and he won't become a recidivist.

No systematic survey has been done yet, but anecdotal evidence suggests that a disproportionate number of doctors who have quit smoking can be found among the fanatics. Just as the most enthusiastic revolutionary tends to make the most enthusiastic counterrevolutionary, many of today's vitriolic zealots include those who had been deeply committed to tobacco habits.

By contrast, the antismoking evangelist does not condemn smokers. Unlike the zealot, he regards smoking as an easily curable condition, as a social disease, and not a sin. The evangelist spends an enormous amount of time seeking and preaching to the unconverted. He argues that kicking the habit is not *that* difficult. After all, *he* did it; moreover, as he describes it, the benefits of quitting are beyond measure and the disadvantages are nil.

The hallmark of the evangelist is his insistence that he never misses tobacco. Though he is less hostile to smokers than the zealot, he is resented more. Friends and loved ones who have been the targets of his preachments frequently greet the resumption of smoking by the evangelist as an occasion for unmitigated glee.

Among former smokers, the distinctions between the evangelist and the elect are much the same as the differences between proselytizing and nonproselytizing religious sects. While the evangelists preach the ease and desirability of abstinence, the elect do not attempt to convert their friends. They think that virtue is its own reward and subscribe to the Puritan theory of predestination. Since they have proved themselves capable of abstaining from tobacco, they are therefore different from friends and relatives who continue to smoke. They feel superior, secure that their salvation was foreordained. These ex-smokers rarely give personal testimony on their conversion. They rarely speak about their tobacco habits, while evangelists talk about little else. Of course, active smokers find such blue-nosed behavior far less offensive than that of the evangelist or the zealot, yet they resent the elect simply because they are smug. Their air of self-satisfaction rarely escapes the notice of those lighting up. For active smokers, life with a member of the ex-smoking elect is less stormy than with a zealot or evangelist, but it is subtly oppressive nonetheless.

8   I have labeled my final category of former smokers the serene. This classification is meant to encourage those who find the other psychic styles of ex-smokers disagreeable. Serenity is quieter than zealotry and evangelism, and those who qualify are not as self-righteous as the elect. The serene ex-smoker accepts himself and also accepts those around him who continue to smoke. This kind of serenity does not come easily nor does it seem to be an immediate option for those who have stopped. Rather it is a goal, an end stage in a process of development during which some former smokers progress through one or more of the less-than-positive psychological points en route. For former smokers, serenity is thus a positive possibility that exists at the end of the rainbow. But all former smokers cannot reach that promised land.

9   What is it that permits some former smokers to become serene? I think the key is self-acceptance and gratitude. The fully mature former smoker knows he has the soul of an addict and is grateful for the knowledge. He doesn't regret that he quit smoking, nor any of his previous adventures with tobacco. As a former smoker, he is grateful for the experience and memory of craving a cigarette.

10   Serenity comes from accepting the lessons of one's life. And ex-smokers who have reached this point in their world view have much to be grateful for. They have learned about the potential and limits of change. In becoming the right kind of former smoker, they developed a healthy sense of self. This former smoker, for one, believes that it is better to crave (one hopes only occasionally) and not to smoke than never to have craved at all. And by accepting that fact, the reformed smoker does not need to excoriate, envy, or disassociate himself from those who continue to smoke.

RESPONDING TO READING

Would you add any types of ex-smokers to Zimring's list? What names would you give to each type?

CONSIDERING CONTENT

1. Reread the introduction. What does it reveal about Zimring's attitude toward smoking in general and former smokers more specifically? Find several words, phrases, or sentences that support your answer.
2. Name the four categories of ex-smokers and briefly define the behavior and goal of each group. Do you recognize these groups among the people you know?
3. Return to each category and closely examine what Zimring believes are the motives behind each group's behavior.
4. What is Zimring's attitude toward each group of ex-smokers? Find specific sentences or phrases that support your answer. You might begin by discussing the term he has selected for each category.
5. What is Zimring's purpose for writing this essay? Does he succeed?

CONSIDERING METHOD

1. Review the way Zimring orders the types of ex-smokers, and explain the effects of his choosing this sequence.
2. Reread Zimring's second sentence. Why does he say "former smokers, ex-smokers, reformed smokers" when these three groups are essentially the same?
3. In addition to his selection of key terms (*zealot* and *evangelist,* for example), Zimring uses a number of other religious comparisons or concepts to convey his attitudes and ideas. Find several examples and analyze Zimring's motives for this approach to his topic. Paragraph 7 might be a good place to begin.
4. Zimring uses other analogies and comparisons, as well. In the introduction, for example, where he wishes to communicate the intense challenges smokers face when they quit, he likens former smokers to "veterans of a personal war." Locate three more comparisons and describe Zimring's purpose for choosing each.
5. In paragraph 10, Zimring says, "This former smoker, for one, believes that it is better to crave (one hopes only occasionally) and not to smoke than never to have craved at all." What common phrase is Zimring echoing here and why might he have chosen to do this?

WRITING STEP BY STEP

When faced with a challenge or a problem, we can respond in one of several ways, so we often find ourselves brainstorming to discover solutions and then considering the strengths and weaknesses of each approach. We ponder, for example, the problem of how to make housemates or family members share cleaning duties, the challenge of how to make scarce money go further, or the problem of how to break unwelcome news to someone. Choose a problem that could be solved in one of several ways, and write an essay using Zimring's approach to quitting smoking as a model of classification.

A. Identify three or four solutions to the problem. On a piece of scratch paper or on your computer screen, brainstorm for a few minutes, jotting down ideas about each solution. If you need help, ask your classmates for ideas about your topic.

B. Decide on a reasonable order to present your solutions—from weakest to strongest (or vice versa), from your first hunch to your last solution, from the worst solution to the best, or along any range that seems reasonable.

C. Choose an attitude to take toward the topic, one that suits your purpose and your audience. This will determine the tone of your writing. In choosing an attitude, you might also consider the severity of the problem—a serious discussion of approaches to bad hair days could provide a humorous mismatch, for example. Franklin Zimring, in a similar way, chose a light tone to discuss a serious topic. However, a match between the topic and the tone is the usual expectation, and you should feel free to align them if you want: a humorous tone for a light topic, and a serious tone for a weighty topic.

D. Begin the essay with an introduction to the problem and the types of solutions you will suggest. As Zimring does, try to reveal your tone in the way you outline the problem and frame the solutions.

E. Write a one- or two-paragraph discussion of your first solution. Begin with a description of the approach.

F. Give the strength of the solution and provide an example of how it is (or would be) used.

G. Follow the strengths by discussing the weaknesses of the approach along with an example of its failings. You can use the same example for both strengths and weaknesses, or if you prefer, you can use different examples to show positive and negative elements.

H. Follow steps E, F, and G for the next two or three approaches you identified in the brainstorming stage.

I. In your closing paragraph, you might follow Zimring's model and write about why one response is better than all the others. On the other hand, you might explain why no solution is perfect.

OTHER WRITING IDEAS

1. Choose either a school setting or a workplace you know well, and write about the different approaches people take toward their work. Consider using specific people you know or have read about as examples of the approaches. Be sure to give enough examples and details for your reader to get a clear picture.

2. COLLABORATIVE WRITING. Working with a group of classmates, think of a quality that many people have but that they use in different ways— for example, power, beauty, charm, intelligence, or wealth. Develop an essay that explains three or four approaches to possessing this quality. Choose only one quality and explain three or four displays of it: "Some people use their power for good causes, some for control over others, and some to amass even more power." Consider evaluating each approach or explaining why people differ along these lines.

3. USING THE INTERNET. Identify another bad habit, such as gambling, that large numbers of people are forced to give up. Research the approaches offered on the Internet for ending the habit, and classify these into three or four categories of solutions. Write an essay based on your conclusion.

4. WRITING ABOUT READING. The author offers four types of ex-smokers. Write an essay about types of smokers. What makes them different from one another? Different motives or habits? Different ways of handling attitudes toward them?

GAINING WORD POWER

Zimring uses four key terms in his essay: zealot, evangelist, the elect, and the serene. Use a thesaurus to identify at least two **synonyms** for each of these words (*fanatic* for *zealot,* for example). Review "Confessions of an Ex-Smoker" and find one sample sentence for each of the key terms. Now rewrite those sentences using the synonyms. Write briefly about the effects of these changes on the tone of the sentences.

EDITING SKILLS: AVOIDING SEXIST LANGUAGE

In paragraph 3, Franklin Zimring writes, "One explanation for the *zealot's* fervor in seeking to outlaw tobacco consumption is *his* own tenuous hold on abstaining from smoking" (our italics). When this article first appeared in 1987,

it was generally more acceptable to use masculine pronouns to refer to virtually all living beings as if they were male. These days, however, you need to avoid
using masculine pronouns to refer to people of both sexes. If Zimring wrote
an article for *Newsweek* today, he probably would not write, "The hallmark of
the *evangelist* is *his* insistence that *he* never misses tobacco" (para. 6). More likely
he would cast that sentence in the plural this way: "The hallmark of *evangelists*
is *their* insistence that *they* never miss tobacco." Both sexes are included in all
plural pronouns. People don't think either male or female when they read *we,
us, our, you, your, they, them, their, ourselves, yourselves, themselves*. So, if you simply
write in the plural, the problem disappears.

Occasionally you can revise a sentence to eliminate the pronoun, like
this:

> (sexist) A tennis player must practice daily to stay at the top of *his* form.
> (revised) A tennis player must practice daily to stay in top form.

Or if you find yourself once in a while needing to write a singular sentence
for some good reason, it's quite all right to use both male and female pronouns, like this:

> Everyone on board must wear a lifejacket for *his or her* own safety.

Just don't do it this way too often, or your writing will get annoyingly
cluttered.

EXERCISE

1. Because your readers may be bothered by **sexist language**, you
   should write in the plural most of the time. For practice, find and
   revise other examples of sexist language in Zimring's essay.
2. Now go back over the essay you just wrote and check the personal
   pronouns. Did you use any (such as *he, his, him* or *she, her, hers*) that
   unfairly or inaccurately exclude the other sex? Make any necessary
   changes—such as using *he or her* or rewriting in the plural to allow *they,
   their,* or *them*.

WEB SITE

http://www.lungusa.org/site/pp.asp?c=dvLUK9O0E&b=22931

Visit the American Lung Association's Smoking Cessation Support site for
further information on the benefits and challenges of quitting smoking.

PREPARING TO READ

How can you tell when someone has good self-esteem? How do people with good self-esteem handle life's problems?

···

Types of Stress for Young People

···

DAVID ELKIND

David Elkind is a psychologist who specializes in child development and has written influential books on the subject. In this reading from his book All Grown Up and No Place to Go *(1988), he describes three kinds of situations that we all face but that are especially stressful for teenagers.*

TERMS TO RECOGNIZE

expenditure *(para. 3)*	cost
potential *(para. 4, 12)*	possible
foreseeable *(para. 4)*	seen ahead of time
transient *(para. 7)*	temporary, passing away with time
jeopardize *(para. 7)*	threaten
incorporates *(para. 10)*	combines
inevitable *(para. 12)*	certain to happen
introverted *(para. 14)*	withdrawn, not sociable
extroverted *(para. 14)*	outgoing
bouts *(para. 15)*	short periods

Most situations that produce psychological stress involve some sort   1
of conflict between self and society. So long as we satisfy a social demand
at the expense of a personal need, or vice versa, the social or personal
demand for action is a psychological stress. If, for example, we stay home
from work because of a personal problem, we create a new demand (for an
explanation, for made-up time) at our place of work. On the other hand, if
we devote too much time to the demands of work, we create new demands
on the part of family. If we don't manage our energy budgets well, we create
more stress than is necessary.

The major task of psychological stress management is to find ways to   2
balance and coordinate the demands that come from within with those that

come from without. This is where a healthy sense of self and identity comes in. An integrated sense of identity . . . means bringing together into a working whole a set of attitudes, values, and habits that can serve both self and society. The attainment of such a sense of identity is accompanied by a feeling of self-esteem, of liking and respecting oneself and being liked and respected by others.

More than anything else, the attainment of a healthy sense of identity   3 and a feeling of self-esteem gives young people a perspective, a way of looking at themselves and others, which enables them to manage the majority of stress situations. Young people with high self-esteem look at situations from a single perspective that includes both themselves and others. They look at situations from the standpoint of what it means to their self-respect and to the respect others have for them. This integrated perspective enables them to manage the major types of stress efficiently and with a minimum expenditure of energy and personal distress.

The Three Stress Situations

There are three major types of stress situations that all of us encounter. One   4 of these occurs when the potential stress is both foreseeable and avoidable. This is a *Type A* stress situation. If we are thinking about going on a roller coaster or seeing a horror movie, the stress is both foreseeable and avoidable. We may choose to expose ourselves to the stress if we find such controlled danger situations exciting or stimulating. Likewise if we know that a particular neighborhood or park is dangerous at night, the danger is both foreseeable and avoidable, and we do avoid it, unless we are looking for trouble.

The situation becomes more complicated when the foreseeable and   5 avoidable danger is one for which there is much social approval and support, even though it entails much personal risk. Becoming a soldier in times of war is an example of this more complicated Type A danger. The young person who enlists wins social approval at the risk of personal harm. On the other hand, the young person who refuses to become a soldier protects himself or herself from danger at the cost of social disapproval.

Teenagers are often caught in this more difficult type of situation. If   6 the peer group uses alcohol or drugs, for example, there is considerable pressure on the young person to participate. But such participation often puts teenagers at risk with parents and teachers, and also with respect to themselves. They may not like the image of themselves as drinkers or drug abusers. It is at this point that a sense of identity and a positive feeling of self-esteem stand the teenager in good stead.

A young person with a healthy sense of identity will weigh the danger   7
to his or her hard-won feeling of self-esteem against the feelings associated
with the loss of peer approval. When the teenager looks at the situation
from this perspective, the choice is easy to make. By weighing the labori-
ously arrived-at feeling of self-esteem against the momentary approval of a
transient peer group, the teenager with an integrated sense of self is able to
avoid potentially stressful situations. It should be said, too, that the young
person's ability to foresee and avoid is both an intellectual and an emotional achievement. The teenager must be able to foresee events . . . but
also to place sufficient value upon his or her self-esteem and self-respect to
avoid situations that would jeopardize these feelings.

A second type of stress situation involves those demands which are   8
neither foreseeable nor avoidable. These are *Type B* stress situations. Accidents are of this type, as when a youngster is hit by a baseball while watching a game, or when a teenager who happens to be at a place in school
when a fight breaks out gets hurt even though he was not involved. The sudden, unexpected death of a loved one is another example of a stress that is
both unforeseeable and unavoidable. Divorce of parents is unthinkable for
many teenagers and therefore also unforeseeable and unavoidable.

Type B stress situations make the greatest demands upon young peo-   9
ple. . . . With this type of stress teenagers have to deal with the attitudes of
their friends and teachers at the same time that they are struggling with
their own feelings. Such stress situations put demands upon young people
both from within and from without. A youngster who has been handi-
capped by an accident, like the teenager who has to deal with divorce, has
to adjust to new ways of relating to others as well as new ways of thinking
about himself or herself.

Again, the young person with a strong sense of identity and a feeling   10
of self-esteem has the best chance of managing these stress situations as
well as they can be managed. In the case of divorce, for example, the
teenager who incorporates other people's perspectives with his or her own
is able to deal with the situation better than other teenagers who lack this
perspective. For example, one young man, who went on to win honors at an
Ivy League school, told his father when he and the mother divorced, "You
are entitled to live your own life and to find happiness too."

This integrated perspective also helps young people deal with the   11
death of a loved one. If it was an elderly grandparent who had been suffering great pain, the young person can see that from the perspective of the
grandparent, dying may have been preferable to living a life of agony with
no hope of recovery. As one teenager told me with regard to his grandfather

who had just died, "He was in such pain, he was so doped up he couldn't really recognize me. I loved him so much I just couldn't stand to see him that way." By enabling the young person to see death from the perspective of others, including that of the person who is dying, the young person is able to mourn the loss but also to get on with life.

The third type of stress situation is one in which the potential stress is   12
foreseeable but not avoidable. This is a *Type C* stress situation. A teenager who has stayed out later than he or she was supposed to foresees an unavoidable storm at home. Likewise, exams are foreseeable but unavoidable stress situations. Being required to spend time with relatives one does not like is another stress situation that the teenager can foresee but not avoid. These are but a few examples of situations the teenager might wish to avoid but must learn to accept as inevitable.

To young people who have attained a solid sense of self and identity,   13
foreseeable and unavoidable stress situations are manageable, again, because of self-esteem and the integrated perspective. They look at the situation from the perspective of themselves as well as that of the other people involved and try to prepare accordingly. They may decide, as one young man of my acquaintance did, that "with my folks, honesty is the best policy. I get into less trouble if I tell the truth than if I make up stories." In the case of visiting relatives they do not like, integrated teenagers see it from the perspective of what it means to others, such as their parents. And with respect to stress situations like exams, because they want to maintain their self-esteem, they prepare for the exam so that they will make a good showing for themselves as well as for others.

It is important to say, too, that integrated teenagers come in any and   14
all personality types. Some are introverted and shy, others are extroverted and fun-loving. Some are preoccupied with intellectual concerns, others primarily with matters of the heart. Despite this diversity, they all share the prime characteristics of the integrated teenager: a set of attitudes, values, and habits that enable the young person to serve self and society, and a strong sense of self-esteem.

To be sure, life is complex and varied. Even the most integrated   15
teenager, of whatever personality type, may occasionally be so overwhelmed by stress that he or she loses the integrated perspective and suffers bouts of low self-esteem. We need to remember that teenagers are new at the game of stress management and have just acquired the skills they need for this purpose. Nonetheless, the general principle holds true. The more integrated the teenager is with respect to self and identity, the better prepared he or she is to manage the basic stress situations.

RESPONDING TO READING

Identify a source of stress in your own life and see whether you can classify it as Type A, Type B, or Type C. Write in your journal about the stress and whether self-esteem contributes to how you handle it.

CONSIDERING CONTENT

1. According to Elkind, what overall conflict causes most situations of stress?
2. Which type of stress does Elkind think is most difficult for teens? Why is this type the worst?
3. Elkind concentrates on how a teenager with good self-esteem would deal with stressful situations. How would a teen with low self-esteem deal with some of these situations?
4. What is an "integrated perspective" (paras. 3, 11, 13, and 15)? Give an example. Can you think of a synonym for the term?
5. In paragraph 7, Elkind writes, the "young person's ability to foresee and avoid is both an intellectual and an emotional achievement." Explain this statement.

CONSIDERING METHOD

1. How many times does Elkind repeat his main point? Why might a writer repeat the main point several times?
2. Divide the fifteen paragraphs into five main sections. What label could you put on each section?
3. How does Elkind let you know what to expect when you are reading his essay?
4. How do you know when a new paragraph takes up a new type of stress situation?
5. How does Elkind clarify what each type of stress situation is like?
6. Is Elkind writing *to* teenagers or *about* them? How do you know?

WRITING STEP BY STEP

Using Elkind's classification of types of stress as a model, write an essay in which you investigate types of social pressure in your world. Think about the influences that cause you to think and behave the way you do. Consider which influences you resist and which you accept.

A. Identify two to four types of social pressure you see at work in your environment.

B. Think of some general strength that people could develop that would help them deal with these types of social pressure. Discuss what you mean by this strength in the introduction to the essay.

C. Write a paragraph briefly presenting the types of social pressure you intend to discuss.

D. Explain each type of social pressure in its own section of the paper. Use examples and details to clarify what you mean.

E. For each type, include an explanation of how the basic strength you discussed early in the essay would apply to this type of social pressure.

F. Put in some kind of transitional material or signal when you switch from one type to another. See the editing section at the end of this selection for help.

G. Point out some circumstances in which the basic strength might fail to help a person deal with social pressure.

H. In your closing (one or two sentences), reaffirm the general principle you have developed.

OTHER WRITING IDEAS

1. Classify and explain the types of stress that distinguish a certain period of life other than the teenage years. For example, think about the first year of college, marriage, parenthood, or retirement.

2. USING THE INTERNET. Write an article for incoming freshmen alerting them to the types of stress typically experienced by college students. Offer your readers ideas and resources for handling these pressures. You can find information at Web sites dealing with stress management and reduction, such as http://stress.about.com/mbody.htm

3. COLLABORATIVE WRITING. Consider the types of stresses that seem to be assigned by sex. What are the types of stress usually felt most by women? What types of stress are felt most by men? Get together in a mixed-sex group to brainstorm for ideas. Write on either sex but not both.

4. WRITING ABOUT READING. Give examples of each type of stress from your own or your friends' lives. Explain what role self-esteem plays in handling these instances of stress.

GAINING WORD POWER

Elkind's essay on stress uses several words and their opposites, their **antonyms**, such as *extroverted* and *introverted*, *inevitable* and *avoidable*, *foreseeable* and *unforeseeable*. Use your dictionary or a dictionary of synonyms and antonyms to find the opposites of the following words from the reading. Be sure to choose opposites that are the same part of speech; in the three preceding examples, all the words can be used as adjectives. You may need to use two or three words instead of one. Your dictionary will help you determine parts of speech.

transient   jeopardize
expenditure   potential
incorporate

EDITING SKILLS: TRANSITIONS

Good writers use **transitions**—words and phrases that help connect ideas—to show how one sentence is related, logically, to the sentence before it. Look at these examples from the Elkind essay.

> On the other hand, the young person who refuses to become a soldier protects himself or herself from danger at the cost of social disapproval. [*On the other hand* is a transitional phrase indicating that a contrast is about to be made.]

> It should be said, too, that the young person's ability to foresee and avoid is both an intellectual and an emotional achievement. [The word *too* indicates that this sentence adds material consistent with the sentence before it.]

> Again, the young person with a strong sense of identity and a feeling of self-esteem has the best chance of managing these stress situations as well as they can be managed. [The word *again* lets you know that this sentence repeats something said earlier.]

Notice that the transitional words are separated from the main sentence with commas.

EXERCISE

Find at least two other sentences in the Elkind essay that include transitional words, and copy them exactly.

Now check your own essay to see whether you can provide more transitional "glue" to hold your thoughts together. Transitions can show several types of movement:

Addition: also, too, moreover, next, furthermore, again

Exemplification: for example, that is, for instance

Emphasis: especially, in fact, primarily, most importantly
Contrast: but, on the other hand, nevertheless, however
Comparison: likewise, similarly, also, too
Qualification: admittedly, of course, granted that
Causation: so, consequently, therefore, as a result
Conclusion: finally, in conclusion, in short, at last

Add at least one transitional word or phrase to your own essay.

WEB SITE

www.cio.com/article/29797
An article by David Elkind about the effects of technology on children.

PREPARING TO READ

Have you ever seen *The George Lopez Show* on television? How about *Greetings from Tucson, The Brothers Garcia, An American Family,* or *Taina*? If so, what do you think of these shows? If not, why do you suppose you haven't seen them?

· ·

The Latino Show

· ·

JULEYKA LANTIGUA

A journalist, writer and editor, Juleyka Lantigua earned a B.A. in Spanish Literature and Government from Skidmore College and an M.A. in journalism from Boston University. She has taken a variety of roles in magazine and book publishing, including managing editorships at Urban Latino, XXL, *and* Giant *magazines. She has also taught writing and journalism at various institutions, including LaGuardia Community College and the Frederick Douglass Creative Arts Center in New York. A nationally syndicated columnist with* The Progressive Media Project *since 1999, Lantigua has written on the environment, women's rights, health, immigration, education and politics. Her fiction and essays have been included in several anthologies. The following essay appeared in* The Progressive *in February 2003.*

TERMS TO RECOGNIZE

virtual *(para. 6)*	existing in effect only, not recognized or acknowledged
patriarch *(para. 7)*	male leader of a family, clan, or tribe
formulaic *(para. 12)*	based on an established model or approach
caliber *(para. 13)*	a level of excellence or importance, quality
amalgamation *(para. 14)*	mixture of various elements
ethnic *(paras. 14, 18)*	relating to people who share common and distinctive racial, national, and cultural heritage
generic *(para. 15)*	standing for a whole group, general, common
discernible *(para. 17)*	able to be seen or recognized, observable
suffice *(para. 18)*	meet the needs, be enough

Lately, Latinos are everywhere on television. We're behind the anchor desk of the local news. We appear on prime time shows as guests or supporting cast members. Some of us have even landed lead roles on network   1 sitcoms and dramas. And more of us are behind the cameras, at the writing desks, and in production meetings.

We're more visible not because TV executives value us as viewers but because they want to mine our purchasing power. Without offering an actual definition of this group, Nielsen Media Research estimates that there are almost nine million "Hispanic American TV households," a number that has grown by 19 percent in the last five years.

When we talk about the Latino television audience, we're talking about one of two broad groups of viewers: (a) those whose ancestors are from Latin America, Spain, the Spanish-speaking Caribbean, Mexico, or native Mexicans in the Southwest and West Coast territories that were gobbled up by the United States; and (b) those who themselves arrived from one of these countries in the last two decades (like me). This second group probably comprises the 4.5 million Latino households Nielsen qualifies as Spanish-dominant, meaning that only or mostly Spanish is spoken at home.

What networks and advertisers don't realize yet is that those in group "a" differ considerably from those in group "b." Latinos whose families have been here for generations, like millions of Mexican Americans, make up a type of mainstream Latino America, rooted in their heritage but living according to contemporary U.S. culture. Comedian and sitcom star George Lopez put it succinctly: "I'm just an American guy who happens to be of Mexican descent." Lopez, whose show was the most-watched program in its time slot with twelve million viewers through October 30, echoes the sentiment of millions of Latinos whose identities are American first, of Latino descent second. Many in this category are English-dominant or monolingual, having grown up in households where everyone spoke English.

Those in group "b" tend to have a split focus between their new lives in the States and their former or ongoing lives back in their home countries. They are also still experiencing the challenges of becoming fully integrated into American society. Group "b" has not attained the consumer power of group "a."

One obvious result is that the leading Spanish networks, Univision and Telemundo, have a tight hold on Spanish-dominant viewers. Another is the virtual Mexican Americanization of sitcoms, dramas, and commercials on the English networks. And no wonder: Mexican Americans and recently arrived Mexicans constitute a majority of the U.S. Latino population, 58.5 percent, or 20.6 million, according to the Census.

The proof is in the programming. Flipping channels during prime time might go something like this: First, there's *The George Lopez Show* (ABC), a comedy about a Mexican American airplane parts factory manager in Los Angeles. He is married to a Cuban American, and they have two children. Then, you get to *Greetings from Tucson* (WB), a comedy about a Mexican

American married to an Irish American—a household navigating three cultures. On PBS, you can find *An American Family,* a drama about a Mexican American patriarch trying to hold his family together. And finally, *The Brothers Garcia* (Nickelodeon's number-one live-action series), a sitcom about a Mexican American family trying to survive the pitfalls of raising their three kids through childhood and adolescence.

Admittedly, I have enjoyed watching some of these shows, and the writing can be inspired, funny, and original. But I have not connected with *any* enough to bring me back week after week.   8

What's missing from the shows I mentioned is a sense of belonging here *and* somewhere else, having a place to yearn for *and* memories that propel you toward your new life. That sort of immigrant motif could fuel a dramatic series about a different kind of Latino experience in the United States. But a show based on the immigrant experience may never happen, since Latinos are so determined to prove that we belong here as much as the next American.   9

George Lopez told hispaniconline.com, "They wanted to make me an immigrant of some sort. I'd rather get out of the business completely if that's what I have to do." I don't think Lopez, or any other Latino who feels like him, has an obligation to play up his immigrant heritage. He is simply demanding that he be placed in the rightful category of American of Latino descent. I respect that, but this category is not the same as Latino immigrant living in America. That's a political distinction Latino leaders are afraid to make, but it's real. And it ought to be reflected on TV.   10

Here's an idea: Create a Latino version of *Friends* where each of the amigos represents one of the larger groups of Latinos. The casting call for the twenty- and thirty-something roles might read something like this: Seeking a fifth-generation professional Chicana from L.A. who struggles to be independent from, and loyal to, her protective family; a Colombian college student activist who immigrated here as a teen and wants the U.S. to stop funding his country's civil war; an artistic Nuyorican from the Bronx (à la Jennifer Lopez) who dreams of making it big while staying true to her roots; a ninth-generation Tejana technology wiz navigating the social mores of dating outside her culture; and a Dominican law student from Washington Heights who immigrated with her parents as an infant and dreams of returning to become her country's first woman president.   11

This approach may be formulaic, but it addresses two key concepts that programmers and advertisers have not fully grasped.   12

First, the Latino audience, much like the general audience, is broken into age segments; no single show will do. There are the kids who watch   13

The Brothers Garcia and *Taina,* Nickelodeon's quirky sitcom about a Puerto Rican high school student who dreams of becoming an entertainer. Their middle-age parents might cozy up to *The George Lopez Show* and *American Family.* And increasingly, there are the twenty-five-to-forty-year-olds who have the lion's share of the spending. We are the folks who wrote letters to Showtime when they threatened to cancel *Resurrection Boulevard.* We're the ones who get hooked on shows like *Frasier, Seinfeld,* and *Friends.* And that is the caliber of show we expect from Latino programs.

Second, we need a show to counter "the generically Latino" charac- 14 ter. Defined by an absolute lack of ethnic identity, these supporting characters have brief exchanges with the white or black lead cast members, rarely finding themselves the protagonists of an episode or even of a storyline. *That '70s Show* is the biggest offender in this category. Barely out of his teens, the generically Latino, heavily accented, and over-the-top post-pubescent character "Fez" is a slimy amalgamation of every woman's nightmarish Latin lover. He orbits around the white cast and waits to deliver, or be the recipient of, a punch line.

On shows like *Law & Order* and *The Practice,* the generic Latino is usu- 15 ally a male criminal of varying ages and degrees of guilt or his helpless mother/sister/wife/ girlfriend who is shocked by the news of his arrest and who stands by his side no matter what. To the producers' credit, these characters don't always have accents, but they are still instantly recognizable by their surnames.

There are exceptions to the forgettable generic Latino. Esai Morales's 16 character on *NYPD Blue* does have storylines written for him, and he often appears in meaningful scenes. Or take nurse Carla Espinosa on the surprise hit *Scrubs.* Played by Judy Reyes, nurse Espinosa has worked for everything she's ever accomplished. She has a preoccupation with her family—namely, her needy mother. And she's in a committed relationship for which she has also worked very hard. Nurse Espinosa is the sole accent-free Latina I tune in to every week, even when it's a rerun. Of all the characters on all the shows, she is most like me and my Latina friends.

The other end of the spectrum has the character of Lucia Rojas-Klein 17 on *Good Morning, Miami,* a sitcom about the team that produces a morning TV show. The drama queen Cuban American co-host who wears daringly unprofessional outfits to work and whose occasional line is barely discernible because of her belabored accent is exactly the kind of walking stereotype non-Latinos learn to love on fluffy television programs. Another show, *CSI: Miami,* has no clearly identifiable Latino characters despite being set in one of the most Latino cities in the United States.

For the record, I don't believe Latino actors should be limited to   18
Latino roles. Benjamin Bratt's portrayal of Detective Curtis on *Law & Order*
and countless other performers have proven that over and over. But I am
saying that Latino characters and programs need to be more developed so
that a mere Spanish surname does not suffice to fill the ethnic quota.

RESPONDING TO READING

Before reading this essay, had you thought about whether or not Latinos are
fairly and adequately represented on TV? Did Lantigua convince you that
they are not? Can you think of other examples of shows or characters? Do
you think you would be interested in watching any of the shows she describes
(if you don't already)?

CONSIDERING CONTENT

1. What major division does Lantigua find in the Latino television audi-
    ence (para. 3)? How do the two groups differ from each other?
2. Why are the English networks dominated by Mexican American
    shows? What is missing from these shows, in the author's opinion?
3. Lantigua says that "a show based on the immigrant experience may
    never happen" (para. 9). Why not?
4. What is wrong with "the generically Latino" character (para. 14)?
5. Why does the author like nurse Espinosa on *Scrubs*? Why does she not
    like the character played by Lucia Roja-Klein on *Good Morning, Miami*?

CONSIDERING METHOD

1. What evidence is there that Lantigua is writing to Latino readers?
    What other audiences does she also hope to reach?
2. The author first divides the Latino audience in paragraph 3. What
    further division does she make later in the article? What is the point
    of this second division?
3. How many examples does the author use in her classification? What
    purpose do they serve?
4. Find three uses of statistics in the article. What points do they make?
5. What is the purpose of describing a Latino version of *Friends* (para.
    11)? Is it an effective technique?

WRITING STEP BY STEP

Write an essay that classifies the way that a specific group of people are presented on TV. You can choose an ethnic or racial group, as Juleyka Lantigua
does, or you can look at a different classification: children, athletes, married

couples, doctors, gay people, police, teachers, and so forth. You might want to narrow your topic by focusing on a particular type of show—for example, how parents are portrayed in situation comedies, or how politicians are presented in dramatic shows.

A. Begin by making a list of titles, characters, and other details for the group you have chosen. Ask friends and classmates to help you brainstorm examples; consult *TV Guide* or some other publications about television to gather specific material.

B. Divide the examples into at least three categories that illustrate the way TV shows draw on popular images and **stereotypes**.

C. Reread Lantigua's opening paragraphs. Write an opening for your own essay in which you explain a misconception or distinction that television producers and writers don't seem to recognize. Explain why they are wrong. Or write an opening that gives your overall evaluation of the way your target group is portrayed.

D. Introduce your categories by identifying the basis for your division and classification. Then name and briefly summarize your categories.

E. Choose an especially useful example to explain each category. In each case, examine the image or stereotype in some detail. You will probably need to explain your examples; your readers may not immediately see the distinctions you are making and may not be familiar with the shows.

F. Write a closing that refers to the points you made in your introduction (step C). Like Lantigua, you might suggest what changes could be made in the way this group is presented.

OTHER WRITING IDEAS

1. Using the directions in the Writing Step by Step assignment, write an essay that classifies stereotypes—ethnic or otherwise—that are used in popular magazine advertisements.

2. COLLABORATIVE WRITING. Get together with a group of classmates to discuss how each of you views your roots. Then write an essay that classifies people according to their attitudes toward their own backgrounds—ethnic, religious, cultural, racial, or class roots. For example, in what ways do people who come from a particular economic class relate to their past? What stances do people raised in a specific faith take toward religion in later life?

3. USING THE INTERNET. Visit several Web sites aimed at a specific ethnic group, such as the Latino Issues Forum (www.lif.org/) and Hispanic Online (www.hispaniconline.com/), or the Asian American Net

(www.asianamerican.net) and Asia-Nation: The Landscape of Asian America (www.asian-nation.org). Using a classification and division approach, write a report on the topics that seem to be important to this group.

4. WRITING ABOUT READING. Throughout her article, the author uses the word *Latino* to refer to the people under discussion. What does that term mean? How does it differ, if it does, from *Hispanic* (para. 2)? Lantigua also uses the words *Chicana, Colombian, Nuyorican, Dominican,* and *Tejana.* Write an essay about the use of ethnic language in "The Latino Show." Define the terms and explain why the author uses them as she does.

GAINING WORD POWER

In paragraph 4, Lantigua uses the word *monolingual*, which is formed by adding a familiar **prefix** to the word *lingual*. The prefix *mono-* means one, single, or alone; and *lingual* refers to languages. So *monolingual* means "speaking or using only one language." We use this prefix often, as in *monotone* (one tone of voice), *monopoly* (a commercial activity controlled by one company), and *monosyllable* (a word with just one syllable). Can you think of other terms that use this prefix? See if you can figure out the meaning of the following words: monologue, monochromatic, monogamy, monogram, monomania, monorail, monotheism. Then use a dictionary to check your definitions.

EDITING SKILLS: USING APOSTROPHES

Using apostrophes makes most writers at least a bit nervous. To get a grip on this slippery punctuation mark, think about these basic rules:

1. Use an apostrophe to indicate that two words have been pushed together to form a contraction. Put the apostrophe where you leave the letters out.

   would not = wouldn't   is not = isn't
   you are = you're   he is = he's
   they will = they'll   we have = we've

2. Use an apostrophe plus *s* with singular nouns to show possession.
   the heat of the sun = the sun's heat
   the rent for one year = one year's rent
   the wig belonging to Judy = Judy's wig
   cards from UNICEF = UNICEF's cards

3. Use an apostrophe after the *s* with plurals to make them possessive.

> papers from three students = three students' papers
> alibis of four criminals = four criminals' alibis

If the plural does not already end in *s*, add an *s* after the apostrophe.

> games for children = children's games
> poetry by men = men's poetry

For more information about apostrophes, see Chapter 7, pp. 203–04.

EXERCISE

In the Lantigua essay, there are seventeen separate words that use apostrophes. Copy the seventeen words exactly. Don't count repeats. Next to each one, write whether the apostrophe makes the word a contraction or a possessive. What does the apostrophe in the title *That '70s Show* indicate?

Now return to your classification essay, and make sure that you have used apostrophes correctly.

✪ WEB SITE

www.laprensa-sandiego.org/archieve/april09-04/study.htm

Report of a study entitled "Looking for Latino Regulars on Prime-Time Television: The Fall 2003 Season," conducted by UCLA's Chicano Studies Research Center.

STUDENT ESSAY USING DIVISION AND CLASSIFICATION

Contemplating Homicide at the Mall

Bobby Lincoln

Bobby Lincoln grew up in southwestern Illinois, in a town just across the river from St. Louis, Missouri. He enrolled in Eastern Illinois University as an education major and wrote this paper as a special assignment for his sophomore-year English class.

I think I started to dislike shopping when I started having to pay for   1
all of the things I bought and, consequently, had to start paying attention to every little detail. All of a sudden, shopping wasn't just a question of whether or not I liked something or wanted it; it now became a question of whether or not I *needed* it, and if so, how much? I had to consider the quality of the merchandise, the store's reputation, the limits of my bank account, and so on. But nothing has proved more of a challenge and an annoyance to my shopping life than the salespeople. Oh, they're everywhere, and they're more treacherous than ever. Like the flu, they have evolved into many strains in an attempt to wear down our defenses. In an effort to understand their intentions, you need to be aware of the different tactics they employ to make your shopping experience a walk in the park—a dark, scary, annoying park that tries to steal your money.

First you have the Chatty Cathy variety, who may or may not have   2
gulped down four cups of coffee before starting her shift—but most likely did. Consider my last visit to Build-A-Bear, the children's store that gives kids the opportunity to choose, stuff, dress, and name their own teddy bear (or a variety of animals). No sooner did my nephew and I walk in the door than Ms. Chat—perky, bubbly, and way too excited to be awake that early on her summer vacation—met us head on. "Hi, and welcome to Build-A-Bear," she said with a force that amazed me, because I didn't think anyone could smile ear-to-ear and still talk. "We have a new stuffed animal, a golden retriever, and it's *so cute,* and have you been here before, because if you haven't then I'll tell you what to do, because it's really *fun* and easy but mostly just fun and if you have any questions at all you just let me know and I'll help you with whatever you need, and—." We had already walked away. Cathy got the point.

The caffeine buzzers contrast with their opposite, the Mighty Uninter-   3
ested. These folks mainly show up at work to do as little as possible to earn their hourly wages. I had the privilege of working with several when I was a cashier for a local discount retail store. (Lesson learned: never, *ever* work at a

discount retail store.) One sticks out in particular. His name was Darryl, and it's a wonder he's still alive without having someone to eat and breathe for him; that's how unwilling he was to do anything. There were several nights when he would crouch like a Hobbit on the lowest shelf of his counter, completely hiding from any looming customer who might want to—*gasp!*—pay for some merchandise. On nights when he wasn't discovered by a manager, he'd spend an hour or two in this position. And when they did find him out, he acted like *he* was the injured party.

Then, of course, you have the ones who are downright rude: the   4
Snobs. My most obvious run-in with a Snob came in a small jewelry store in Paris, France (and in no way am I trying to suggest the French are rude; this is mere coincidence). It was the end of a backpacking trip through Europe, and I wanted to buy something nice and inexpensive for my sister. I did my best to speak the three or four French words I knew, in hopes the saleslady would cut me off and let me speak English. Apparently, however, she didn't speak English, so I had to resort to sign language, using gestures not unlike the ones that a trained gorilla would use when he wants to eat a banana or play peek-a-boo. On top of this embarrassment, I kept mixing French with the other languages I had been speaking during my trip, so *Oui* became *Sí* and *Merci* was *Danke*. And Madame Snob just stood there, watching my desperate attempts to make myself understood, not offering one bit of help. I finally gave up and waited until I got back home to buy my sister's gift.

As I said, these salespeople are everywhere, and they come in all   5
forms. They are frequently evil, but they can be stopped. If they're rude to you, smile sweetly, belch loudly, and walk away. If they seem uninterested, dangle the promise of extra commission in front of their noses and watch them spring to life. But perhaps most importantly, down a few double espressos of your own before you enter the store. Being a little ahead of their game might make all the difference.

CONSIDERING CONTENT AND METHOD

1. How does the author feel about the people he's describing? How serious is he?
2. The author uses just one example for each type. Is that enough? Are the examples sufficiently developed to fulfill their purpose?
3. Does the author have a serious point to make? If so, what is it?
4. Lincoln makes use of comparisons in his descriptions. Point out some that you think are effective.
5. What do you think of the conclusion? How successful is it?

CHAPTER 7

Strategies for Examining Two Subjects:
Comparison and *Contrast*

FOR DISCUSSION AND WRITING

Examine closely the two men portrayed in this famous advertisement for Apple computers. How are they different? In what ways are they similar?

Write a brief paper in which you compare and contrast the values and lifestyles suggested by the two figures in the ad. Consider age, body type, clothes, hairstyle, stance, facial expression, and so forth. What point is the designer of the ad making about the differences between the two people?

Every day we use **comparison-and-contrast** thinking to make decisions in our personal lives. Should I wear the pink shirt or the teal? Should I take my lunch to work or eat out? Will it be Taco Bell or McDonald's? Should I write a check or use my credit card? Often the factors influencing an everyday decision are weighed so quickly in our minds that we may not be aware of having examined both sides. But when faced with a major decision, we think longer and may even make a list of pros and cons: "Reasons for Getting a New Car" on the left side of the sheet; "Reasons for Keeping Old Blue" on the right side. Intelligent decision making helps keep our lives from lapsing into chaos. Comparing and contrasting serve as useful tools in the struggle.

THE POINT OF COMPARISON AND CONTRAST

Technically, we *compare* things that are similar and *contrast* things that are different. But in order to contrast things, we have to compare them. And a comparison will often point out the differences of items being compared. You can see how fuzzy the distinction gets, so don't worry about it.

Using Comparisons to Explain

Using comparisons is a dandy writing strategy for explaining something your readers don't know much about by comparing it to something they do know about. For instance, geologists like to explain the levels in the earth's crust by comparing them to the layers in an onion. Or if you want to explain something complicated, like the way our eyes work, you could compare the human eye to a camera, which is simpler and more easily understood.

Using Comparisons to Persuade

Comparisons can be an effective technique in persuasive writing to help clarify and convince. People who believe that illegal drugs should be decriminalized often compare the current drug-related gang warfare to the alcohol-related crime wave during Prohibition in the 1930s. When alcohol was made legal again, the gangsters were out of business and the violence subsided. The same thing would happen today, the argument goes, if drugs were legalized. Such a comparison, called an **analogy**, can be quite convincing if you can think of one that is sensible and clearly parallel.

Using Contrast to Decide

You can set up a contrast to help clarify differences—if, for instance, you are faced with a choice between products or people or pets or proposals (or whatever). You might want to make this investigation for your own benefit or to convince someone else that one thing is preferable to another. Say, your boss asks you to find out which photocopying machine would be the best buy for the office. Because the machines are all fairly similar, your report would focus on the differences in order to determine which one would give the best results for the least money. Or if you are trying to determine whether to borrow money or get a part-time job to help pay next year's tuition, you should consider carefully the advantages and disadvantages of each choice.

THE PRINCIPLES OF COMPARISON AND CONTRAST

Since the purpose of comparing and contrasting is to show similarities or differences, good organization is crucial to success. There are two standard ways of composing this kind of writing: the **block-by-block pattern** and the **point-by-point pattern**. These patterns can, of course, be expanded to include consideration of more than two elements.

Using the Block-by-Block Plan

Particularly useful for responding to comparison-or-contrast essay examination topics is this simple method of organization:

1. State your purpose.
2. Present key features of the first part of your comparison.
3. Make a transition.
4. Present corresponding features of the second part of your comparison.
5. Draw your conclusions.

This simple plan serves perfectly for showing how something has changed or developed: your earliest views about AIDS compared with the way you think now; Madonna's first album compared with her latest one; Picasso's early work compared with his later paintings; hair styles ten years ago compared with hair styles today. You will see how effectively this plan works when you read the first two essays in this chapter.

Similarities and Differences

A variation on the block-by-block plan is to cluster the points of comparison and contrast according to similarities and differences. Consider, for instance, the proverbial apples and oranges comparison. An advertising executive for the apple industry might organize a fact sheet promoting apples by first clustering the similarities between apples and oranges (their nutritional value and availability, for example) and then emphasizing their differences (more varied uses for apples and their lower cost). The purpose, to sell apples, is best served by posing the comparison but emphasizing the favorable contrasts.

Using the Point-by-Point Plan

When you have time to carefully organize your ideas, you may want to present the material in a way that highlights individual differences. In other words, you choose the points of comparison that best illustrate the similarities or differences and then organize the material to contrast those features.

Each major section of the comparison covers one point in terms of both (or all) the things being compared or contrasted. For example, a nutritionist might organize the fact sheet on apples and oranges by drawing conclusions one section at a time about the relative nutritional value, availability, and use, covering both apples and oranges under each of these points. For consistency, either apples or oranges would be discussed first in each section, like this:

APPLES VERSUS ORANGES

1. Relative cost
   a. Orange prices remain fairly constant throughout the year.
   b. Apples are least expensive during the fall harvest season.

2. Nutritional value
   a. Oranges contain lots of vitamins A and C and have 62 calories.
   b. Apples offer fiber and have 81 calories.

3. Availability
   a. Oranges are generally available year round.
   b. Apples are best during the fall.

4. Use
   a. Oranges can be used as snacks, salads, main dishes, and desserts.
   b. Apples can be used as snacks, salads, main dishes, and desserts.

You could use exactly the same material in writing a block-style essay as you would with this point-by-point pattern. The differences lie in the way you arrange your material.

THE PITFALLS OF COMPARISON AND CONTRAST

If you are using a block pattern, be sure to follow the same order in making your comparison. If you are writing about the differences between waterbeds and airbeds, you could start by explaining the main features of the waterbed—something like this:

1. fill it with a hose
2. adjusting for comfort tricky
3. needs a heater
4. heavy when full of water
5. reasonable in cost

Then, after switching to your discussion of airbeds, take up the same features in the same order:

1. inflate it with a button
2. adjusting for comfort easy
3. no need for a heater
4. light when full of air
5. expensive to buy

Keep the same order in your point-by-point organization, too. After grouping all the preceding information under headings something like these:

1. comfort
2. convenience
3. cost

be careful to discuss first waterbeds, then airbeds; waterbeds, then airbeds; waterbeds, then airbeds—in presenting the material in each category. As you read Mark Twain's "Two Views of the Mississippi," notice that in his second viewing, he describes the same details in the same order as he did in his first viewing.

Avoid Using Too Many Transitional Words

True, comparison-and-contrast writing involves making lots of **transitions**, but you won't necessarily need to signal each one with a transitional word. In the block pattern, you will need an obvious transition to let your readers know that you're going to shift to the second item or idea. You'll write a sentence such as, "Airbeds, *on the other hand*, are an excellent buy for several reasons" or "*On the contrary*, waterbeds can sometimes prove troublesome to maintain."

But when you follow the point-by-point pattern, you will probably not want to signal every shift back and forth with a transitional term. (Did you notice that the term *but* in the previous sentence provided a transition between paragraphs?) With the point-by-point method of organization, you will be making contrasts under each point. If you try to signal each one, your prose may get clunky. Once you have established the shifts back and forth, let your readers be guided by the pattern—and make sure you stick to it.

Avoid Repetition in Concluding

In a brief comparison or contrast essay, you need not summarize all your points at the end. Your readers can remember what you've said. Instead, draw a meaningful conclusion about the material. Maybe you'll want to assert that two apparently different religions are basically the same. Or you might stress that the differences are so crucial that conflict will always exist. If you are comparing products, come out in favor of one over the other—or else declare that neither amounts to a hill of beans—or perhaps invite your readers to judge for themselves. Just be sure to make a point of some sort at the end.

WHAT TO LOOK FOR IN COMPARISON AND CONTRAST

As you study the essays in this chapter, pay particular attention to the organization and the *continuity* (what makes it flow).

1. Look for a pattern (or maybe a combination of patterns) that each writer uses in presenting the material. Decide whether you think the method of organization is effective or whether there might be a better way.
2. Underline the transitional terms (such as *on the other hand, but, still, yet, on the contrary, nevertheless, however, contrary to, conversely, consequently, then, in other words, therefore, hence, thus, granted that, after all*). Notice what sort of meaningful links are provided between paragraphs when no purely transitional terms appear.
3. Look at the introductions and conclusions to see what strategies are used to set up the comparison or contrast at the beginning and to reinforce the writer's point at the end.

PREPARING TO READ

Do you think it's possible for two people to look at the same thing and see it quite differently? Consider how a loving owner might view an overweight, spindly legged dog and how a neighbor might view the same animal. Can you think of other examples?

••

Two Views of the Mississippi

••

MARK TWAIN

Before becoming Mark Twain, America's most beloved humorist, Samuel Clemens (1830–1910) was a riverboat pilot, a journalist, and an unsuccessful gold miner. He said late in his life that his days on the river were the happiest he ever spent. In Life on the Mississippi *he explains in detail how he became a pilot—how he learned to "read" the river. In the following slightly edited passage, Twain tells of one drawback to that otherwise rewarding experience.*

TERMS TO RECOGNIZE

trifling *(para. 1)*	small, a tiny detail
acquisition *(para. 1)*	something gained or acquired
solitary *(para. 2)*	all alone
conspicuous *(para. 2)*	obvious
opal *(para. 2)*	a gemstone showing many shades of pink, blue, lavender, and gold
radiating *(para. 2)*	spreading
somber *(para. 2)*	dark
unobstructed *(para. 2)*	not hidden or blocked from view
rapture *(para. 3)*	joy, delight
wrought *(para. 3)*	brought about, caused
bluff reef *(para. 3)*	steep ridge of sand just beneath the surface of the water
shoaling *(para. 3)*	building up mud and sand
compassing *(para. 4)*	guiding (as with a compass)

Now when I had mastered the language of this water, and had come   1
to know every trifling feature that bordered the great river as familiarly as I

knew the letters of the alphabet, I had made a valuable acquisition. But I had lost something, too. I had lost something which could never be restored to me while I lived. All the grace, the beauty, the poetry had gone out of the majestic river!

I still keep in mind a certain wonderful sunset which I witnessed when steamboating was new to me. A broad expanse of the river was turned to blood; in the middle distance the red hue brightened into gold, through which a solitary log came floating black and conspicuous; in one place a long, slanting mark lay sparkling upon the water; in another the surface was broken by boiling, tumbling rings, that were as many-tinted as an opal; where the ruddy flush was faintest was a smooth spot that was covered with graceful circles and radiating lines, ever so delicately traced; the shore on our left was densely wooded, and the somber shadow that fell from this forest was broken in one place by a long, ruffled trail that shone like silver; and high above the forest wall a clean-stemmed dead tree waved a single leafy bough that glowed like a flame in the unobstructed splendor that was flowing in the sun. There were graceful curves, reflected images, woody heights, soft distances; and over the whole scene, far and near, the dissolving lights drifted steadily, enriching it every passing moment with new marvels of coloring.

I stood like one bewitched. I drank it in, in a speechless rapture. The world was new to me, and I had never seen anything like this at home. But as I have said, a day came when I began to cease from noting the glories and charms which the moon and sun and the twilight wrought upon the river's face; another day came when I ceased altogether to note them. Then, if that sunset scene had been repeated, I should have looked upon it without rapture, and should have commented upon it, inwardly, after this fashion: "This sun means that we are going to have wind to-morrow; that floating log means that the river is rising, small thanks to it; that slanting mark on the water refers to a bluff reef which is going to kill somebody's steamboat one of these nights, if it keeps on stretching out like that; those tumbling 'boils' show a dissolving bar and a changing channel there; the lines and circles in the slick water over yonder are a warning that that troublesome place is shoaling up dangerously; that silver streak in the shadow of the forest is the 'break' from a new snag, and he has located himself in the very best place he could have found to fish for steamboats; that tall dead tree, with a single living branch, is not going to last long, and then how is a body ever going to get through this blind place at night without the friendly old landmark?"

No, the romance and beauty were all gone from the river. All the value any feature of it had for me now was the amount of usefulness it could furnish toward compassing the safe piloting of a steamboat.

RESPONDING TO READING

Do you agree with Twain that gaining knowledge takes away the appreciation of beauty? Have you ever had the opposite experience, when learning increased your appreciation of a work of art?

CONSIDERING CONTENT

1. What two modes of writing does Twain mainly use in this selection?
2. In the opening sentence, what does he mean by the "language" of the river?
3. What did he lose by learning to be a riverboat pilot? What did he gain?
4. What contrast does he present in paragraphs 2 and 3?
5. At the beginning of his description in the second paragraph, he says, "A broad expanse of the river was turned to blood. . . . " What does that mean? Do you know what that figure of speech is called?
6. Can you find a thesis statement? If so, where?

CONSIDERING METHOD

1. Point out two **similes** (comparisons using *like* or *as*) in paragraph 2.
2. The second sentence in paragraph 2 is extremely long. Reread this complicated sentence and carefully decide where you would put in periods to create several shorter sentences.
3. What major transitions does Twain use—first in setting up the contrast, then in shifting from the before to the after?
4. In paragraph 3, Twain personifies the river—that is, he gives it human characteristics. Point out three examples of this technique of **personification**. Why do you think he used this figure of speech?
5. Does the contrast follow a point-by-point or a block pattern of organization? Make a brief outline of the way the comparison is arranged.

WRITING STEP BY STEP

Many times we feel nostalgic (warm and sentimental) about the past—about favorite former recording groups, TV programs, friends, cars, houses, articles of clothing, and so forth. Get together with several friends or classmates and talk about what you liked best in "the good old days." Take notes when meaningful memories from your past come to mind.

Choose something long gone that you still feel a fondness for—something now replaced by something newer, but not necessarily better. Then, using a block pattern, write an essay contrasting your lost prize with today's version.

A. Begin by letting your readers know that you have a fine, new whatever—fancy bicycle, designer jeans, sports car, neighborhood bakery, favorite restaurant, TV series, or rock group—but that the new version can't measure up to the one you enjoyed before.

B. Then, describe your former favorite. Use plenty of precise descriptive details, as Mark Twain does in his second paragraph. Show your reader what makes you feel the way you do about this treasure from the past.

C. Next, make a transition similar to Twain's: "But as I have said, . . . " Or write your own: "Then, after old Shep died, I bought an unbelievably dumb purebred Russian wolfhound" or "Finally, I sent my faithful Ford to the junkyard and spent a fortune on a classic MG that gives me nothing but trouble."

D. Now describe your replacement, focusing on its shortcomings—the many ways in which it doesn't measure up to the one you loved previously. Follow the same order here in presenting the new failings that you followed in describing the old virtues. (Notice that Twain uses exactly the same order in telling the two ways he saw the river. In his third paragraph, he begins with the sunset, then mentions the log, then the slanting mark on the water, then the "tumbling 'boils,'" then the lines and circles, then the streak in the shadow, and finally the dead tree—just as he did in his second paragraph.)

E. In your final paragraph, express again your regret at having to make do with this unsatisfactory replacement and your longing to have the old something back.

OTHER WRITING IDEAS

1. Write an essay following the preceding step-by-step instructions, but choose instead a thing that you replaced with something new that you think is a great deal better.

2. USING THE INTERNET. Use a search engine such as Google to locate information about piloting a steamboat today. What technological advances have made the job much easier and safer? Write an essay explaining how riverboat piloting today differs from piloting in Twain's day.

3. COLLABORATIVE WRITING. People of different ages sometimes see things differently. Write about an attitude (toward work, religion, education, sports, television, the law, or something else) that you think is different for people who are older or younger than you. Consult with your peers as well as people from the other generation to find out what their understanding of this difference is. Incorporate any useful ideas into your essay.

4. WRITING ABOUT READING. Do you agree with Twain that gaining knowledge can take some of the "romance" out of life? Have you ever had a similar experience—perhaps learning something that robbed you of a childish illusion or discovering something that caused you to question your former understanding of an event? Explain in writing how the change occurred.

GAINING WORD POWER

Twain says the sunset put him in a state of "speechless rapture." The **suffix** -*less* means "without," "lacking," or "not able to." So, speechless means "without speech" or "unable to speak."

For the following list of words, write out brief definitions that show what the **root** word means with the suffix added. If you don't know the meaning of the root word, look it up in your trusty dictionary.

1. clueless	4. dauntless
2. ruthless	5. meaningless
3. mirthless	6. peerless

Now, use each word in a sentence that conveys the meaning—something beyond "I am clueless" or "She is clueless" or "Clyde is clueless."

EDITING SKILLS: QUOTATION MARKS INSIDE QUOTATIONS

Once in a while, when you have enclosed conversation or quoted material in quotation marks, you may need quotation marks around a word or phrase within the passage. You can't use regular quotation marks inside quotation marks because your reader would never be able to tell what ended where. So inside regular double quotation marks, you use single quotation marks around any words that also need quotation marks.

Notice that in his third paragraph, Twain puts a passage in quotation marks because, as he describes his second way of looking at the river, he is giving us a "conversation" with himself. Within that pretended speech, the word "boils" also needs quotation marks because it has an unusual meaning (as did the word "conversation" in the previous sentence). So, he puts "boils" in single quotation marks because it is already inside double marks. Here is another example:

Mr. Blackwell observed, "Baggy clothes are definitely 'in' this season."

On your keyboard, you may have an opening single quotation mark. Check the keys beside the numbers at the top. The closing mark is one you use all the time: the apostrophe. It can also serve as the left-hand quotation mark if you don't have a special key for an opening mark.

Here are some other uses of quotation marks, including some instances where single marks are used inside double ones:

1. To enclose words used as words:

   It's all right to begin a sentence with "and" as long as you don't do it too often.

   (You can use italics or underlining to indicate words used as words, if you prefer.)

2. To enclose titles of short works—short stories, poems, essays, chapters of books, or song titles:

   Edgar Allan Poe's story "The Pit and the Pendulum"

   Robert Frost's poem "The Road Not Taken"

   Richard Selzer's essay "The Discus Thrower"

   Bob Dylan's song "Mr. Tambourine Man"

   But underline or put in italics the titles of longer, separately published works:

   Alice Walker's novel <u>The Color Purple</u>

   Arthur Miller's play <u>Death of a Salesman</u>

   Steven Spielberg's movie *Jurassic Park*

   Georges Bizet's opera *Carmen*

3. To enclose quoted material within a quotation:

   "What did your instructor do when you didn't turn in your term paper?"

   "I went into her office with my paper in my hand, and she said, 'I hope you just got out of the hospital; otherwise, you just failed the course.'"

EXERCISE

In the following sentences, insert regular quotation marks and single quotation marks where needed. You may use italics in some cases if you prefer.

1. Proofread carefully to be sure you have not confused its and it's.
2. Reggie said to me, You be there on time or I'm leaving without you, Squirt.
3. Then I said to Reggie, You call me Squirt again and I'm not going anywhere with you ever again!
4. Serena wrote an analysis of Sandra Cisneros's short story Woman Hollering Creek.

5. I liked this poem, Kesha observed, but when Frost says The woods are lovely, dark, and deep, what does deep mean?

Now go through your writing for this class (your essays and your journal entries), and see whether you've been using quotation marks correctly. Then make up a sentence of your own using single quotation marks inside regular quotation marks.

WEB SITE

www.greatriver.com/
The Mississippi River Home Page provides information about riverboats today, as well as in the late nineteenth century when Twain was piloting.

PREPARING TO READ

Are you the kind of person who gets fidgety if the socks aren't tidily arranged by color in your drawer? Or are you a casual type who seldom manages to get the socks from the laundry basket into the drawer? Have you tried to change, or do you not feel any need to?

••

Neat People vs. Sloppy People

••

SUZANNE BRITT

Suzanne Britt is a freelance journalist who teaches English at Meredith College in Raleigh, North Carolina. She has written for the New York Times, *the* Baltimore Sun, *and* Newsday. *In her collection of witty essays* Skinny People Are Dull and Crunchy like Carrots *(1982), Britt clearly favors fat folks. In the following essay, which comes from her book* Show and Tell *(1983), she sides solidly with slobs, demonstrating that taking an unusual stand—even a not very reasonable stand—can be an effective strategy for humorous writing.*

TERMS TO RECOGNIZE

vs. *(title)*	abbreviation of *versus*, meaning in contrast with or against
rectitude *(para. 2)*	uprightness, correctness
metier *(para. 3)*	a person's area of strength or expertise
excavation *(para. 5)*	digging out, uncovering and removing
meticulously *(para. 5)*	giving great attention to details
scrupulously *(para. 5)*	carefully doing the right thing
cavalier *(para. 6)*	free and easy
vicious *(para. 9)*	hateful, spiteful
salvaging *(para. 9)*	saving from destruction, rescuing
swath *(para. 12)*	a long strip
organic *(para. 12)*	having to do with living things

I've finally figured out the difference between neat people and sloppy   1
people. The distinction is, as always, moral. Neat people are lazier and meaner than sloppy people.

Sloppy people, you see, are not really sloppy. Their sloppiness is merely the unfortunate consequence of their extreme moral rectitude. Sloppy people carry in their mind's eye a heavenly vision, a precise plan, that is so stupendous, so perfect, it can't be achieved in this world or the next. 2

Sloppy people live in Never-Never-Land. Someday is their metier. Someday they are planning to alphabetize all their books and set up home catalogues. Someday they will go through their wardrobes and mark certain items for tentative mending and certain items for passing on to relatives of similar shape and size. Someday sloppy people will make family scrapbooks into which they will put newspaper clippings, postcards, locks of hair, and the dried corsage from their senior prom. Someday they will file everything on the surface of their desks, including the cash receipts from coffee purchases at the snack shop. Someday they will sit down and read all the back issues of *The New Yorker*. 3

For all these noble reasons and more, sloppy people never get neat. They aim too high and wide. They save everything, planning someday to file, order, and straighten out the world. But while these ambitious plans take clearer and clearer shape in their heads, the books spill from the shelves onto the floor, the clothes pile up in the hamper and closet, the family mementos accumulate in every drawer, the surface of the desk is buried under mounds of paper, and the unread magazines threaten to reach the ceiling. 4

Sloppy people can't bear to part with anything. They give loving attention to every detail. When sloppy people say they're going to tackle the surface of the desk, they really mean it. Not a paper will go unturned; not a rubber band will go unboxed. Four hours or two weeks into the excavation, the desk looks exactly the same, primarily because the sloppy person is meticulously creating new piles of papers with new headings and scrupulously stopping to read all the old book catalogues before he throws them away. A neat person would just bulldoze the desk. 5

Neat people are bums and clods at heart. They have cavalier attitudes toward possessions, including family heirlooms. Everything is just another dust-catcher to them. If anything collects dust, it's got to go and that's that. Neat people will toy with the idea of throwing the children out of the house just to cut down the clutter. 6

Neat people don't care about process. They like results. What they want to do is get the whole thing over with so they can sit down and watch the rasslin' on TV. Neat people operate on two unvarying principles: Never handle any item twice, and throw everything away. 7

The only thing messy in a neat person's house is the trash can. The minute something comes to a neat person's hand, he will look at it, try to decide if it has immediate use and, finding none, throw it in the trash. 8

Neat people are especially vicious with mail. They never go through   9
their mail unless they are standing directly over a trash can. If the trash
can is beside the mailbox, even better. All ads, catalogues, pleas for char-
itable contributions, church bulletins, and money-saving coupons go
straight into the trash can without being opened. All letters from home,
postcards from Europe, bills and paychecks are opened, immediately
responded to, then dropped in the trash can. Neat people keep their
receipts only for tax purposes. That's it. No sentimental salvaging of
birthday cards or the last letter a dying relative ever wrote. Into the trash
it goes.

Neat people place neatness above everything, even economics. They   10
are incredibly wasteful. Neat people throw away several toys every time they
walk through the den. I knew a neat person once who threw away a perfectly good dish drainer because it had mold on it. The drainer was too
much trouble to wash. And neat people sell their furniture when they move.
They will sell a La-Z-Boy recliner while you are reclining in it.

Neat people are no good to borrow from. Neat people buy everything   11
in expensive little single portions. They get their flour and sugar in two-
pound bags. They wouldn't consider clipping a coupon, saving a leftover,
reusing plastic non-dairy whipped cream containers, or rinsing off tin foil
and draping it over the unmoldy dish drainer. You can never borrow a neat
person's newspaper to see what's playing at the movies. Neat people have
the paper all wadded up and in the trash by 7:05 A.M.

Neat people cut a clean swath through the organic as well as the   12
inorganic world. People, animals, and things are all one to them. They are
so insensitive. After they've finished with the pantry, the medicine cabinet,
and the attic, they will throw out the red geranium (too many leaves), sell
the dog (too many fleas), and send the children off to boarding school (too
many scuff marks on the hardwood floors).

RESPONDING TO READING

Do you think that Britt is right in preferring sloppy people? In your journal, make a list of some advantages of being neat; then make a list of some disadvantages of being sloppy.

CONSIDERING CONTENT

1. In the first paragraph, what is the moral difference that Britt finds
   between neat and sloppy people? Is this the difference you would
   give? Is she serious about this moral difference? How can you tell?
2. Does the essay have a thesis statement? If so, where does it appear?

3. What is "Never-Never Land," mentioned at the beginning of paragraph 3? Do you know where the term comes from?
4. What kinds of things does Britt say messy people are always planning to do? Point out her exact details.
5. What faults does she find with neat people? Again, point out details from every paragraph.
6. Is she being fair? If not, can you explain why not?

CONSIDERING METHOD

1. How does Britt let you know in her opening paragraphs that she isn't entirely serious?
2. Which pattern of organization does she use in presenting her contrast?
3. Can you find a transitional sentence that leads smoothly into the second part of the contrast?
4. Point out several words that Britt uses for humorous exaggeration. Point out several humorous examples.
5. You probably noticed that this essay has no **conclusion**. Would it be more effective if it had one, do you think? Try writing a brief concluding sentence and see whether it adds or detracts.

Combining Strategies

Britt employs a number of writing strategies in developing her essay. Her organization is a block-by-block comparison/contrast, and the entire piece involves definition—neat people and sloppy people. She also employs lots of examples, illustrations, explanations, and descriptions. Although the writing is humorous, its tongue-in-cheek purpose is persuasion. Reexamine the essay and identify an example of each of these strategies.

WRITING STEP BY STEP

Get together with a few friends or classmates to discuss various kinds of people who can be classified into types the way Britt does with neat versus sloppy (such as *plump vs. thin, fun-loving vs. serious, perky vs. droopy*, or *exercise nuts vs. couch potatoes*). In this brainstorming session, jot down any details that might be useful to include in an essay comparing the two types you choose. You can make your contrast either humorous or serious. If you decide to be humorous, you will probably also decide to defend the less positive group—praising fat folks instead of thin people, for instance. Or you may decide to make fun of both sides by contrasting two negative types, such as *eggheads vs. airheads*.

A. Begin with a two- or three-sentence introduction letting your readers know that you'll be contrasting two types of people and favoring one group (as Britt puts it, "Neat people are lazier and meaner than sloppy people").

B. Organize your contrast in a block pattern, first discussing the important characteristics of one type, then the same or similar characteristics of the other type.

C. Be sure to include plenty of examples that will show your readers the behavior you're explaining. Take another look at Britt's essay, and notice the kinds of details she uses—how many of them and how specific: not just *a corsage* but *the dried corsage from their senior prom*, not just *a recliner* but a *La-Z-Boy recliner*, not just *the geranium* but *the red geranium*.

D. In the body of your essay, begin every paragraph (as Britt does) with the name of your type—*plump people*, for instance. Vary this system of deliberate repetition once or twice by adding a transition, like the one Britt adds at the start of her fourth paragraph: "*For all these noble reasons and more*, sloppy people never get neat." (Leave out the *noble* part unless you're being funny.) Consider transitions like these:

Besides all these features, plump people . . .
In addition to these troubles, plump people . . .
Furthermore, plump people . . .
As a matter of fact, plump people . . .

E. When you finish discussing your first type, include a transitional sentence. Britt shifts smoothly from praising sloppy people to criticizing neat ones with this sentence: "A neat person would just bulldoze the desk" (end of para. 5).

   If you can't come up with a similar sentence that supplies a bridge from one type to the next, it's just fine to begin the second half of the contrast with a transitional term like one of these:

Thin people, *on the other hand*, . . .
Contrary to popular belief, thin people . . .
Thin people, *however*, . . .
By contrast, thin people . . .

F. If you can think of some insight concerning your contrast, offer it as a conclusion. But don't simply tack on something obvious. That's worse than no conclusion at all. Be sure to end your last paragraph with an impressive sentence—either a short, forceful one or a nicely balanced one, like Britt's. Work on that final sentence. Make it one that leaves your readers feeling satisfied.

OTHER WRITING IDEAS

1. Using a block-by-block pattern, contrast two types of players in a sport or game such as basketball, tennis, poker, chess, or a video game. In your conclusion explain what you think causes the differences between the two types.

2. USING THE INTERNET. Britt humorously presents neat people as being overly particular, but excessively neat people sometimes can have serious problems. Visit the Web site of the Obsessive Compulsive Foundation (www.ocfoundation.org/) and read about this psychological disorder. Write an essay contrasting an obsessively neat person with someone who is just normally neat. You could use Adrian Monk, the obsessively neat detective on the popular TV series *Monk*, as a prime example; if you're not a *Monk* watcher, substitute someone you know who exhibits obsessive/compulsive traits. You might also compare the obsessive form of another trait—such as punctuality, caution, or perfectionism—with its normal form.

3. COLLABORATIVE WRITING. Get together with friends or classmates, and discuss major life changes that you and they have experienced. Talk about what your lives were like before and after the changes occurred. Consider situations such as life before marriage and life after; life in your folks' home and life in the dorm or your own apartment; life at your previous job and life at your new one. Then write an essay about one of your life changes, telling first what your life was like before, then how things were after. Focus on one factor of your experience that changed greatly, like the amount of freedom or the amount of responsibility you had.

4. WRITING ABOUT READING. Starting with the lists you made in responding to Britt's essay, write one of your own organized like hers (but probably with a more serious tone) showing how neatness makes life easier and sloppiness leads to problems. Include plenty of details and examples to show the advantages of being tidy and the folly of being perpetually scattered.

GAINING WORD POWER

In her last paragraph Britt writes of the "*organic* as well as the *inorganic* world." You know from the Terms to Recognize that *organic* means "having to do with living things." So what does the same word mean when you add the

prefix *in-*? That prefix commonly means "no," "not," or "without." Thus, in her sentence *inorganic* means "not organic"—having to do with things that are *not* living.

This prefix is quite common, partly because it has several different meanings. Besides making a word negative, *in-* often means "in," "into," "within," or "toward," as in a baseball *infield*, an *inboard* motor, or to *instill* values.

Knowing these meanings of this prefix can help you make sense of new words. For each of the following terms, write out the meaning of the prefix *in-*, followed by the meaning of the **root** word, as in this example using *indefinite*:

in- = not   *definite* = certain, precise, clear

Get help from your dictionary if you need it.

inhale	inhuman	insomnia
injustice	inland	inability
inroad	invisible	indigestion
indirect	inlay	insane

EDITING SKILLS: USING APOSTROPHES

Apostrophes probably cause more problems than other marks of punctuation. Even experienced writers feel shaky about using them. If you study the following rules about using apostrophes, you should be able to use them more confidently.

1. *Use an apostrophe to indicate that a noun is possessive.* Possessive nouns usually indicate ownership, as in *Miguel's hat* or *the lawyer's briefcase.* But sometimes the ownership is only loosely suggested, as in *the rope's length* or *a week's wages.* If you are not sure whether a noun is possessive, try turning it into an *of* phrase: *the length of the rope, the wages of a week.*
   a. If the noun does not end in *s*, add *'s*.
      Rita climbed into the driver's seat.
      The women's lounge is being redecorated.
   b. If the noun is singular and ends in *s*, add *'s*.
      The boss's car is still in the parking lot.
      Have you met Lois's sister?
   c. If the noun is plural and ends in *s*, add only an apostrophe.
      The workers' lockers have been moved.
      A good doctor always listens to patients' complaints.

2. *Use an apostrophe with contractions.* Contractions are two-word combinations formed by omitting certain letters. The apostrophe goes where the letters are left out, not where the two words are joined.

does not = doesn't	he is or he has = he's
would not = wouldn't	let us = let's
you are = you're	I am = I'm

3. *Do not use an apostrophe to form the plural of a noun.* The letter *s* gets pressed into service in a number of ways; its most common use is to show that a noun is plural (more than one of whatever the noun names). No apostrophe is needed with a simple plural:

Two *members* of the starting team are suspended for the next three *games* for repeated curfew *violations*.

EXERCISE

1. Examine this sentence from paragraph 11 in Suzanne Britt's essay: "You can never borrow a neat person's newspaper to see what's playing at the movies." Two words in this sentence end in *'s*; one is possessive and one is a contraction. Do you see the difference? Explain how you can tell.
2. Find two other possessive nouns in Britt's essay, and explain what they mean by turning each into an *of* phrase.
3. Find two other contractions that end in *'s* in Britt's essay. What do these contractions stand for?
4. Find six other contractions in Britt's essay, and explain their meaning.
5. Find several examples of plural nouns that end in *s* (without an apostrophe).

Now go back over the essay you have just written, and check your use of apostrophes. Have you left an apostrophe out of a possessive? Have you put an unneeded apostrophe in a plural noun? Have you misplaced any apostrophes in contractions?

For more information about apostrophes, see Chapter 6, pages 180–81.

🖱 WEB SITE

http://owl.english.purdue.edu/owl/resource/621/01
You can print out the Online Writing Lab's handout on using apostrophes and consult it when writing and editing your papers.

PREPARING TO READ

Have you ever noticed that girls and boys play differently? Think about preschool, playground, and athletic activities. Why do you think those differences occur?

••

A Whole New Ballgame

••

BRENDAN O'SHAUGHNESSY

A former teacher and coach at St. Ignatius College Prep in Chicago, Brendan O'Shaughnessy now lives with his family in Indianapolis, where he is the city hall reporter for the Indianapolis Star. *He has also written freelance for the* Chicago Tribune, *which is where the article reprinted below appeared on December 1, 2002.*

TERMS TO RECOGNIZE

baiting *(para. 2)*	teasing, needling
insinuation *(para. 2)*	an implied meaning or reference
incredulous *(para. 4)*	unbelieving, doubting, skeptical
gaffe *(para. 4)*	a social blunder or mistake
demeanor *(para. 10)*	outward behavior
intimidated *(para. 11)*	made timid or fearful

The first day of freshman basketball tryouts, I learned that coaching girls is different. I was demonstrating the correct way to set a cross screen. I positioned my legs shoulder-width apart and crossed my hands—fists clenched—over my groin to protect myself from the injury that all men fear. I paused, confused, understanding from the girls' bewildered looks that something was wrong. The other coach, a 15-year veteran of coaching girls, recognized my rookie mistake and bailed me out. He raised his arms and covered his chest, and I knew that I had entered alien territory. 1

I had coached boys basketball for six years before circumstances in the athletic department forced me to switch to "the other side." I looked forward to the challenge in the same way that I had anticipated the move from teaching at an all-boys' school to a coed institution five years before. At the very least, I figured, I would be more likely to get cookies at Christmas 2 and a gift at the awards banquet. Baiting a feminist friend, I told her that I was excited about the change because I could be more relaxed, less intense, and besides, I wouldn't get any technicals. I just assumed girls didn't take their basketball as seriously as boys. The insinuation hit its mark. She scolded me, saying that girls were just as eager to win and play well as boys. She also suggested I read Madeleine Blais's *In These Girls, Hope Is a Muscle*, a book about a girls team's basketball season.

From the book and from my teaching experience, I began the season   3
with certain expectations about coaching girls. I would need to be more encouraging, less critical. Most boys need a little tearing down before they can be rebuilt on a more solid fundamentals base. Boys want to be Allen Iverson and inherently assume they know more than their old-school coach, who watched "Hoosiers" one too many times. Girls, whose experience of playground games and watching the all-stars is often limited, do not start with as many bad habits. I expected they would be more coachable. They wouldn't need their inflated athletic egos broken down, but rather built from the ground up.

Smugly thinking I was prepared, I got a rude awakening with my   4
screen-setting gaffe that first day. Imagine my incredulous stare when a girl trying out, in an attempt to explain why she had thrown up and had to sit out of wind sprints, told me she hadn't run since gym class—the year before. I was also surprised—and relieved—that we did not have to cut, since only 20 girls stuck out the trials for the two teams. With boys, two or three times as many students usually came out for the teams as could be taken.

I immediately noted differences in the early practices. Girls' attention   5
to directions was far superior to the boys, most of whom found it physically impossible not to be distracted by any movement anywhere in the gym. Whereas the boys generally either went deadpan or shot me the evil "how dare you" death stare when I corrected their play, the girls often sincerely apologized for any mistake. My stereotypically gawky center, when told not to leave her feet on defense, said, "I know. I'm sorry. I'm terrible." Embarrassed, I tripped out a halting reassurance. I tried to build up her confidence by calling her "the rebound machine," but she just thought I was goofy.

Strangest of all, they actually wanted to talk to me and the other   6
coach, something teenage boys found equivalent to having their nose hairs, if they had any, individually plucked out in front of an audience of teenage girls. The girls came running up before practice to tell us about their classes, about who said what at lunch, about who had spilled perfume on her uniform. Uncomfortable after years of boys slinking away into corners, I usually responded, "Stretch out."

Before the first game, I realized that some of their silliness was simply   7
due to their age, not their sex. In the pregame huddle, the other coach said
we needed to play hard or go home with a big L. One of the girls asked if
everyone would have to take the "L" home instead of the bus if we lost. During the game, one player attempted to high-five a referee after making a
shot. But it was more than their tender age. While I was giving a post-game
speech, one player interrupted and said, "Those are the coolest sweatpants.
They zip all the way down." When my grandfather died, the whole team
signed a condolence card with individual attempts to comfort me. Another
time, returning from a late game, when the bus broke down on the highway
in 15-degree weather, one player cut the tension with, "Coach, want a
chocolate-chip cookie? I made them."

I began to observe that the team split into two groups: the hard, aggres-   8
sive players and the softer, nice players. One side had girls who would steal a
ball from their teammates in order to shoot. The other side had girls who apologized to their defenders if they scored. Some would crash the boards and
clear out space with vicious elbows, and others would avoid any chance of
injury or even breaking a sweat. The aggressive group rolled their eyes at the
limp-wristed run of one girl they called "the dancer" or "Basketball Barbie."
The timid girls rolled their eyes and called our best shooter a "ball hog."

After six wins and a growing gulf between the cliques, we experienced   9
our first loss. Actually, we got blown out by 35 points. We could barely get the
ball down the court. A coach learns all he needs to know about his team by
how they react to a loss. My team began to motivate each other in practice.
They started to pull for each other. Best of all, the gap between the groups of
player types began to slowly close. In time, we were a single unit again.

And I was swept up in the intensity of their effort. I don't know   10
exactly when it began, but it was cemented when I was called for a technical
foul in a Christmas tournament game. Whereas boys' freshman coaches
tend to be overly passionate, like myself, sporting buzz cuts and angry
demeanors, girls' coaches usually were more welcoming. One informed us
that her name was Poppy, offered our team bagels and Gatorade, and said,
"We're all about fun here." It was all I could do to refrain from saying,
"We're all about kicking your butt."

Fast forward to the conference championship game, where we faced   11
the same team that had blown us out by 35 earlier in the season. Since
then, this powerhouse had won every game, none by fewer than 20 points.
Not intimidated this time, our girls played them even for a quarter. When
the opponent went on a second-quarter run, I impolitely objected to an
over-the-back foul and was hit with another technical. Shocked, I realized

that I had been given more technicals in a single season of coaching girls than I ever had as a boys' coach. My feminist friend would be proud. The team responded. The collective jaw of the bench dropped to the hardwood when "Basketball Barbie" hit a shot, slapped the floor and yelled, "C'mon, girls, let's play some defense." I couldn't have been more pleased if it had been my own daughter.

No, it didn't lead to a win, but we never gave up either, clawing to a   12
nine-point loss and the bittersweet distinction of holding that team to their narrowest margin of victory all season. Even in defeat, the girls had come a long way in their separate challenges. Some had overcome a natural timidity by learning to play aggressively, and others had learned to trust their team. My lesson? New depths to the same game I've always loved.

RESPONDING TO READING

Have you watched both girls and boys play basketball ? Did you observe any differences between the teams in the way they played? Do you think, as O'Shaughnessy does, that the girls are just as dedicated to winning as the boys?

CONSIDERING CONTENT

1. What are the rewards O'Shaughnessy anticipates or initially expects as a result of switching from coaching boys to coaching girls?
2. In paragraph 2, what are *technicals*? Why did he think he wouldn't get any technicals coaching girls?
3. What expectations did he have about how he would need to coach girls differently than boys? What differences does he actually find?
4. In paragraphs 4, 5, and 6, he says that in early practices he notes differences between the girls' and boys' behavior. What are some of those differences?
5. The girls refer to one of their teammates with a "limp-wristed run" as "Basketball Barbie." What sort of player do you envision from that name?
6. How does being called for a technical foul let the coach know his team is now "a unit" and "cemented"? Why would his feminist friend be proud that he received more technicals coaching girls than boys?

CONSIDERING METHOD

1. How does O'Shaughnessy capture your interest in his opening paragraph?
2. His essay is organized using a point-by-point contrast. Why do you think he chose this pattern rather than using the simple block-by-block method?

3. What other patterns of development can you identify in the essay?
4. Why do you think he mentions his feminist friend near the beginning and again near the end?
5. What does his use of basketball jargon (*cross screen, wind sprints, blown out, over-the-back foul*) tell you about his intended audience?
6. What is the author's thesis? Is it stated or implied?

WRITING STEP BY STEP

Think of a situation, place, object, or person *then* and *now*. Choose something that has changed a lot: wedding receptions years ago and today, your desk before and after cleaning, your sluggish first computer and your smart new computer, your childhood tennis shoes and your new athletic shoes, your granny then and now.

Write a comparison focusing mainly on the *now*, but mentioning the *then* occasionally to show the contrast. If you can get your friends to help, brainstorm with them to think of good points you can use in drawing the comparison. You need qualities that fit both *then* and *now*, but think of a lot more details about the *now*.

A. Begin by giving the subject of your comparison in a sentence or two. Don't state it directly but imply it: "I had no idea that wedding receptions were not always elaborate productions until my mom told me about her wedding thirty years ago," or "I was slow to appreciate the benefits of my new computer because it took so much effort to learn to use it. My old computer was easy by comparison."

B. As you discuss the *now*, remind your readers, whenever you take up a new point, how it was *then*. Use transitional words when you need them: *by comparison, on the other hand, on the contrary, but, still, after all, like, nevertheless, contrary to, however, granted that.*

C. In your last paragraph, tell how you feel about the change. Would you rather have the *then* instead of the *now*—or do you find the *now* a great improvement?

D. If you're stuck for an ending, try concluding with a question and then answering it: "If I had known then how much easier my computer would make writing, would I have complained so loudly? Maybe not," or "If I could go back to planning a reception that cost less than $10,000, would I? You bet I would!"

OTHER WRITING IDEAS

1. Think of two possible views on one of these aspects of life: the value of work, the role of family, or the importance of sports. Write a paper contrasting two people who represent the two views.

2. COLLABORATIVE WRITING. In a small group discuss gender stereotypes—the way society expects women and men to behave. From the notes you take, choose three or four categories—such as manner of speaking, walking, dressing, and showing emotion; or typical careers, leisure activities, and taste in movies. Organize your essay using the point-by-point method, first doing the women's role, then the men's (or the reverse, but be consistent from section to section). At the end, draw a conclusion about how society treats people who do not conform to these roles and expectations.

3. USING THE INTERNET. Visit the Gender Equity in Sports site at http:bailiwick.lib.uiowa.edu/ge/GEREDESIGN.html, click on the "About Title IX" link, and read the material. Then, with this information in mind, speculate in writing about the role Title IX may have played in bringing about the changes that O'Shaughnessy observed.

4. WRITING ABOUT READING. Consider how our society's expectations for girls are reflected in O'Shaughnessy's article. Does it also reveal society's expectations for boys? Discuss the ways in which the author shows how gender roles in organized sports have changed and whether you see these changes as positive or negative.

GAINING WORD POWER

Decide whether the italicized words in the following list are used correctly or not. Then, write *yes* or *no* beside each sentence. After you finish, look back at the Terms to Recognize definitions to check your work.

_____1. Billy Bob's *demeanor* made him appear lazy and disinterested.

_____2. Secretly he studied hard and made *incredulous* improvement.

_____3. Then a jealous classmate *intimidated* that he had cheated.

_____4. I thought that such an *insinuation* was outrageous and spiteful.

_____5. So, I bought him a double latte *gaffe* as a reward for his success.

EDITING SKILLS: CHOOSING *ITS* OR *IT'S*

Look at this sentence from O'Shaughnessy's article:

The insinuation hit its mark.

Why does he use *its* and not *it's* in that sentence?
    Now look at the uses of *it's* and *its* in the following sentences:

It's been a hard day's night.

It's raining on my parade.

This knife has lost *its* edge.

That horse just won *its* last race.

Notice that in the first two sentences, the words *it has* or *it is* can be substituted for *it's*. Not so in the next two sentences. Those two uses of *its*—without the apostrophe—are possessive, as in "Each piece has *its* own place in the puzzle."

You can use the substitution test to see whether you have used the right form. If you have written *it's*, you should be able to read the sentence with *it is* or *it has* instead. That substitution won't work with the possessive *its*, which carries a sense of ownership or belonging.

The plan failed because of *its* flaws.

I like that sitcom in spite of *its* dysfunctional characters.

Many writers are tempted to put an apostrophe in the possessive *its* because so many other possessives require apostrophes: the *plan's* flaws, the *sitcom's* characters. No wonder it's confusing. Try putting the possessive *its* on a mental list with the other possessives—*his, hers, ours, theirs*—which also have no apostrophes. This mental grouping may help you choose the correct form.

EXERCISE

Fill in the blanks in the following sentences with *its* or *it's*. Be prepared to explain your choices.

1. Your proposal has much in _____ favor, but _____ unlikely that the committee will vote for it.
2. _____ an old car, but _____ paint job is new.
3. The dog bit _____ own tail; _____ not an exceptionally smart dog.
4. _____ important that a company give _____ employees job security.
5. _____ a whole new ballgame.

WEB SITE

www.womenssportsfoundation.org/cgi–bin/iowa/issues/index.html

This page from the Women's Sports Foundation highlights current issues in gender equity and suggests topics for action.

PREPARING TO READ

Before looking at the following essay, consider whether you think children are born smart or whether they get smart by studying hard in school. Jot down your thoughts in your journal.

••

The Trouble with Talent: Are We Born Smart or Do We Get Smart?

••

KATHY SEAL

A California-based freelance journalist, Kathy Seal frequently writes about children and education in such popular magazines as Parents *and* Family Circle. *In the essay we reprint here, first published in* Lear's *magazine in July 1993, she examines an attitude that may help to explain why math scores of American children have fallen far behind those of children in Japan.*

TERMS TO RECOGNIZE

rote *(para. 4)*	routine, mechanical repetition
efficacy *(para. 12)*	ability to bring about an effect
rampant *(para. 12)*	widespread, out of control
per se *(para. 16)*	in and of itself
mammoth *(para. 19)*	huge
conviction *(para. 19)*	firmly held belief

Jim Stigler was in an awkward position. Fascinated by the fact that Asian students routinely do better than American kids at elementary math, the UCLA psychologist wanted to test whether persistence might be the key factor. So he designed and administered an experiment in which he gave the same insolvable math problem to separate small groups of Japanese and American children. 1

Sure enough, most American kids attacked the problem, struggled briefly—then gave up. The Japanese kids, however, worked on and on and on. Eventually, Stigler stopped the experiment when it began to feel 2 inhumane: If the Japanese kids were uninterrupted, they seemed willing to plow on indefinitely.

"The Japanese kids assumed that if they kept working, they'd eventually   3
get it," Stigler recalls. "The Americans thought 'Either you get it or you don't.'"

Stigler's work, detailed in his 1992 book *The Learning Gap*, shatters   4
our stereotypical notion that Asian education relies on rote and drill. In
fact, Japanese and Chinese elementary schoolteachers believe that their
chief task is to stimulate thinking. They tell their students that anyone who
thinks long enough about a problem can move toward its solution.

Stigler concludes that the Asian belief in hard work as the key to suc-   5
cess is one reason why Asians outperform us academically. Americans are
persuaded that success in school requires inborn talent. "If you believe that
achievement is mostly caused by ability," Stigler says, "at some fundamental
level you don't believe in education. You believe education is sorting kids,
and that kids in some categories can't learn. The Japanese believe *everybody*
can master the curriculum if you give them the time."

Stigler and his coauthor, Harold W. Stevenson of the University of   6
Michigan, are among a growing number of educational psychologists who
argue that the American fixation on innate ability causes us to waste the
potential of many of our children. He says that this national focus on the
importance of natural talent is producing kids who give up easily and artful
dodgers who would rather look smart than actually learn something.

Cross-cultural achievement tests show how wide the gap is: In a series   7
of studies spanning a ten-year period, Stigler and Stevenson compared
math-test scores at more than 75 elementary schools in Sendai, Japan;
T'aipei, Taiwan; Beijing, China; Minneapolis; and Chicago. In each study,
the scores of fifth graders in the best-performing American school were
lower than the scores of their counterparts in the worst-performing Asian
school. In other studies, Stigler and Stevenson found significant gaps in
reading tests as well.

Respect for hard work pervades Asian culture. Many folk tales make   8
the point that diligence can achieve any goal—for example, the poet Li Po's
story of the woman who grinds a piece of iron into a needle, and Mao Tse-
tung's recounting of an old man who removes a mountain with just a hoe.
The accent on academic effort in Asian countries demonstrates how expectations for children are both higher and more democratic there than in
America. "If learning is gradual and proceeds step by step," says Stigler,
"anyone can gain knowledge."

To illustrate this emphasis, Stigler videotaped a Japanese teacher at   9
work. The first image on screen is that of a young woman standing in front

of a class of fifth graders. She bows quickly. "Today," she says, "we will be studying triangles." The teacher reminds the children that they already know how to find the area of a rectangle. Then she distributes a quantity of large paper triangles—some equilateral, others right or isosceles—and asks the class to think about "the best way to find the area of a triangle." For the next 14 1/2 minutes, 44 children cut, paste, fold, draw, and talk to each other. Eventually nine kids come to the blackboard and take turns explaining how they have arranged the triangles into shapes for which they can find the areas. Finally, the teacher helps the children to see that all nine solutions boil down to the same formula: $a = (b \times h) \div 2$ (the area equals the product of the base multiplied by the height, divided by two).

Stigler says that the snaillike pace of the lesson—52 minutes from   10
start to finish—allows the brighter students enough time to understand the concept in depth, as they think through nine different ways to find the areas of the three kinds of triangles. Meanwhile, slower students—even learning-disabled students—benefit from hearing one concept explained in many different ways. Thus children of varied abilities have the same learning opportunity; and the result is that a large number of Japanese children advance relatively far in math.

Americans, on the other hand, group children by ability throughout their   11
school careers. Assigning students to curricular tracks according to ability is common, but it happens even in schools where formal tracking is not practiced.

So kids always know who the teacher thinks is "very smart, sorta smart,   12
and kinda dumb," says social psychologist Jeff Howard, president of the Efficacy Institute, a nonprofit consulting firm in Lexington, Massachusetts, that specializes in education issues. "The idea of genetic intellectual inferiority is rampant in [American] society, especially as applied to African-American kids."

A consequence is that many kids face lower expectations and a   13
watered-down curriculum. "A student who is bright is expected just to 'get it,'" Stigler says. "Duller kids are assumed to lack the necessary ability for ever learning certain material."

Our national mania for positive self-esteem too often leads us to puff 14
up kids' confidence, and we may forget to tell them that genius is 98 percent perspiration. In fact, our reverence for innate intelligence has gone so far that many Americans believe people who work hard in school must lack ability. "Our idealization of a gifted person is someone so smart they don't have to try," says Sandra Graham of UCLA's Graduate School of Education.

Columbia University psychologist Carol Dweck has conducted a   15
fascinating series of studies over the past decade documenting the dangers of believing that geniuses are born rather than made. In one study,

Dweck and UCLA researcher Valanne Henderson asked 229 seventh graders whether people are "born smart" or "get smart" by working hard. Then they compared the students' sixth and seventh grade achievement scores. The scores of kids with the get-smart beliefs stayed high or improved, and those of the kids subscribing to the born-smart assumption stayed low or declined. Surprisingly, even kids who believed in working hard but who had low confidence in their abilities did very well. And the kids whose scores dropped the most were the born-smart believers with high confidence.

Dweck's conclusion: "If we want our kids to succeed, we should 16 emphasize effort and steer away from praising or blaming intelligence per se."

Psychologist Ellen Leggett, a former student of Dweck's at Harvard, 17 has found that bright girls are more likely than boys to believe that people are born smart. That finding could help to explain why many American girls stop taking high school math and science before boys do.

Seeing intelligence as an inborn trait also turns children into quitters, 18 says Dweck. "Kids who believe you're born smart or not are always worried about their intelligence, so they're afraid to take risks," Dweck explains. "But kids who think you can get smart aren't threatened by a difficult task or by failures, and find it kind of exciting to figure out what went wrong and to keep at it." Or, in Jeff Howard's words, "If I know I'm too stupid to learn, why should I bang my head against the wall trying to learn?"

Getting Americans to give up their worship of natural ability and to 19 replace it with the Asian belief in effort seems a mammoth undertaking. But Dweck maintains that it's possible to train kids to believe in hard work. The key to bringing kids around, says Dweck, is for the adults close to them to talk and act upon a conviction that effort is what counts.

The Efficacy Institute is working on exactly that. The institute's work 20 is based on theories that Howard developed as a doctoral candidate at Harvard, as he investigated why black students weren't performing in school as well as whites and Asians. Using the slogan "Think you can; work hard; get smart," the institute conducts a seminar for teachers that weans them from the born-smart belief system.

"We tell teachers to talk to kids with the presumption that they can 21 all get As in their tests," explains project specialist Kim Taylor. Most kids respond immediately to their teachers' changed expectations, Howard says. As proof, he cites achievement-test scores of 137 third grade students from six Detroit public schools who were enrolled in the Efficacy Institute program during 1989 and 1990. The students' scores rose 2.4 grade levels (from 2.8 to 5.2) in one year, compared with a control group of peers whose scores only went up by less than half a grade level.

Institute trainers now work in approximately 55 school districts, from 22 Baltimore to St. Louis to Sacramento. In five cities, they're working to train every teacher and administrator in the school district.

While current efforts for change are modest, no less a force than the 23 Clinton administration is weaving this new thinking into its education agenda. During a talk this past spring to the California Teachers Association, U.S. Secretary of Education Richard Riley pledged to work on setting national standards in education. "These standards," he says, "must be for all of our young people, regardless of their economic background. We must convince people that children aren't born smart. They get smart."

....

RESPONDING TO READING

Did reading the essay change your mind about kids being born smart or getting smart through hard work? In your journal explain how you think Americans' attitudes on the subject could be changed, especially if the government or the National Education Association decided to spend money on the effort.

CONSIDERING CONTENT

1. According to researchers, what happened when groups of American kids and groups of Japanese kids were given insolvable math problems to work on?
2. How do most Americans think Asian students are taught? According to researchers quoted by Seal, is this impression true?
3. How did the Japanese instructor teach about triangles in the example given in paragraph 9? What are the advantages of this method of teaching?
4. What is the typical American attitude about learning—that kids are born smart or that they get smart by working hard? What is the Japanese attitude?
5. Do you know what Seal means by "our national mania for positive self-esteem" (para. 14)? What problems do researchers think it causes?
6. How is the Efficacy Institute trying to change the American attitude and instead "train kids to believe in hard work" (para. 19)?

CONSIDERING METHOD

1. How does Seal's opening sentence help get you interested in her material?
2. Find two specific examples that help readers understand why the Japanese kids beat the American kids on achievement tests. How helpful are these examples?

3. What other method of providing evidence and explaining ideas does the author use in the second part of her article about Americans' attitudes?

4. Seal employs the block organization for her contrast. Find the sentence in which she makes the transition from explaining how Japanese kids learn to considering how American kids learn. What transitional term does she use?

5. The essay has a brief concluding section following the contrast of the two educational systems. What is the purpose of these final paragraphs (19–22)?

6. The essay concludes with a direct quotation (para. 23). What makes this ending effective?

WRITING STEP BY STEP

Think of an issue on which you and your parents—or you and your spouse—strongly disagree. With your parents, for instance, you might differ in your attitudes toward premarital sex; or they might disapprove of your taste in music, clothing, or hairstyles. With your spouse, you might disagree about household chores, child care, financial matters, or vacation plans. Choose an issue that you feel confident you are right about, but be sure that you are also quite familiar with the evidence for the opposing point of view.

A. Begin your essay by presenting the problem, as Kathy Seal does in her introduction when she states "the fact that Asian students routinely do better than American kids at elementary math" (para. 1). You can start by admitting that you have this heated disagreement in your immediate family about whatever it is.

B. Next explain how other members of your family view this matter, just as Seal explains how Japanese schoolchildren are taught math (paras. 2–10). Try to include brief specific examples as Seal does in paragraphs 8 and 9. And be fair. Give as much space to presenting this opposing view as you will give to your own viewpoint in the second part of the essay.

C. Write a transitional sentence similar to the one that Seal uses at the start of paragraph 11: "Americans, on the other hand, group children by ability throughout their school careers."

D. Now, present your side of the issue. Offer plenty of specific examples. The evidence that Seal uses in analyzing the attitudes of Americans about how children learn are mainly quotations from researchers, but these quotations are full of specifics—problems, beliefs, research studies, testing results.

E. If possible, include a final section similar to Seal's paragraphs 19–22 in which she tells what the Efficacy Institute is doing to encourage American kids to work harder in school. Try to think of a way of resolving the problem you described in your essay. It's possible that focusing on the opposing viewpoint (as you did in the first part of your essay) may reveal a middle ground. Look for a compromise. If you find a solution that stops short of involving the law and justice system, present it here.

F. If you can think of no way of resolving the problem, conclude by admitting that you and your family will simply have to agree to disagree. But consider the final quotation in Seal's essay. Modeling the deliberate repetition of a word, try to end with two forceful sentences similar to these: "We must convince people that children aren't born smart. They get smart" (para. 23).

OTHER WRITING IDEAS

1. Using a block pattern of organization, write a comparison for your classmates of two sports. Focus your attention on which one is more complicated to play or more fun to watch, and use your comparison to explain why you think so.

2. USING THE INTERNET. Write an essay, using your own experience as well as those of people you know, to contrast the pros and cons of family vacations. Use an Internet search engine to visit the sites of typical vacation destinations (the Grand Canyon, Las Vegas, Disneyland, and so forth) to gather additional ideas. In your brainstorming, consider the preferences of both the parents and the children, but write from the viewpoint of one or the other.

3. COLLABORATIVE WRITING. Seal thinks Americans should "give up their worship of natural ability" and "replace it with the Asian belief in effort." She quotes psychologist Carol Dweck's assertion "that it's possible to train kids to believe in hard work" (para. 19). Do you believe that hard work is what's required in learning ? Get together with a group of classmates and discuss whether this is an entirely useful idea. What advantages did Seal include in her essay? What additional advantages or distinct disadvantages were generated in your brainstorming session? Write an essay contrasting the two viewpoints and conclude by recommending one side or the other.

4. WRITING ABOUT READING. Seal provides an interesting illustration of the way a Japanese teacher presents a concept in math instruction (para. 9). Write an essay contrasting that technique with the way you

were taught some concept (like in math, grammar, or spelling) in grade school or high school. Conclude by stating which method you think is better and why.

GAINING WORD POWER

In paragraph 10, Kathy Seal uses the interesting word *snaillike* to describe the slow pace of the Japanese teacher's math instruction. The term *-like* is a **combining form** meaning "resembling or characteristic of." By adding *-like* to other words (many of them names for animals), you can produce useful new descriptive terms. You could write, for instance, of a child's shell-like ear, and your readers would be able to picture the delicate curve of the ear. Notice that you hyphenate *shell-like*, when there are three *l*s together, but not *snaillike*, when there are only two.

1. Add *-like* to the end of each word listed below.

   war   child   bird   barn   ostrich
   bell   lady   cat   flower   cow

2. Then write a definition that includes the characteristic conveyed by that new word: *slow as a snail, curved like a shell.*
3. Finally, write a sentence for each new word that makes use of the descriptive characteristic: The *snaillike* traffic on the freeway resulted from an accident.

EDITING SKILLS: USING DASHES

The dash is a handy mark of punctuation that will give emphasis to whatever follows it—as long as you don't use it too often. Notice how the dash works in this sentence from Seal's essay:

> Sure enough, most American kids attacked the problem, struggled briefly— and then gave up.

Seal could have used a comma after *briefly*, but she chose the dash because readers pay more attention to what follows a dash than to what follows a comma. Using the dash is unusual, unexpected—thus emphatic.

You can also use a pair of dashes to set off a few words in the middle of a sentence if you want to emphasize them, as Seal does here:

> Meanwhile, slower students—even learning-disabled students—benefit from hearing one concept explained in many different ways.

Commas would be quite correct there but dashes give emphasis to the words set off.

There's another handy use for the dash—to avoid comma clutter. Look at this sentence from Seal's essay:

> Then she distributes a quantity of large paper triangles—some equilateral, others right or isosceles—and asks the class to think about "the best way to find the area of a triangle."

Again, commas would be correct before and after that phrase, but when the group of words set off contains one or more commas, putting dashes around it makes the whole sentence easier to read.

Finally, you can use a dash instead of a colon to introduce an example, as Seal does here:

> Many folk tales make the point that diligence can achieve any goal—for example, the poet Li Po's story of . . . and Mao Tse-tung's recounting of. . . .

When typing, use two hyphens to form a dash (—), but if you are writing on a word processor, you may find that it has a separate key for the dash. In either case, do not put a space before or after the dash. And remember not to use dashes too often, or they will lose their good effect.

EXERCISE

Put in a dash or replace a comma with a dash whenever you think it would improve the sentence.

1. My friend Yolanda said she just turned twenty-nine for the third time.
2. It's time I started saving for a Florida vacation, for a cruise to the Bahamas, for a new Lexus, for my retirement.
3. All kinds of spices, even pepper, garlic, and onion, give Eddie indigestion.
4. Madonna's costume, what there was of it, shocked even broad-minded me.
5. Marvin had only one chance and a slim one at that.

Now examine the sentences in the essay you just wrote. Can you improve any of them by inserting dashes? Try to revise at least two of your sentences using dashes.

WEB SITE

www.efficacy.org/

To find further information about ways in which "virtually all children can get smart," visit this Web site for the Efficacy Institute.

STUDENT ESSAY USING COMPARISON AND CONTRAST

Watching from All Sides

Lynn Cooper

When her children had reached school age, Lynn Cooper returned to Illinois State University to finish her degree in speech and theater education. She acted in several plays in high school and in community theater, experiences that led her to choose her major and to write this essay.

New styles of plays and productions in contemporary theater have forced designers and architects to experiment with the orientation of the audience to the stage. One of the most prominent examples of these designs is the arena stage. Also called theater in the round, this kind of staging can be quite intimate because it puts the audience in raised seats on all sides with the players performing in the round space in the middle. In contrast, the traditional theater is usually larger and seats the whole audience in front of the acting area, looking into a boxlike set through a frame or *proscenium arch*. Any theatergoer can easily see the differences between these two arrangements. The necessary differences in scenic design, lighting design, and acting techniques may not be as apparent, but they are crucial to the performance and its reception.

For the scenic designer, arena staging offers challenges not present in a proscenium set. In order to keep the view clear all around, the setting in which the action takes place must be indicated without the aid of the large, high vertical scenic backdrops that are employed on the traditional stage. These often represent a relevant background like a starry sky, an apartment's back wall, or a cityscape. Without the usual *flats* or artificial walls to paint and decorate, designers for a show done in the round must find other ways to convey the nature and mood of the setting. The designer for an arena production focuses instead on smaller details, such as set furniture and handheld props, which the closer audience will be able to see much more clearly. But because the audience is seated all around, these set pieces must look presentable from all views. A kitchen counter on a traditional stage can have an unfinished back, but a kitchen counter in the round has to be realistic from all sides. This requirement means more construction and finishing time for arena sets.

Lighting must also be designed differently for these two types of presentation. In an arena stage, lighting should look more natural because it can and must be focused on the stage from all directions. But since the play must also be seen from all sides, lighting problems are in some ways compounded. For example, in a proscenium setting, the lighting designer need not worry about lights shining in the spectators' eyes, a common problem when staging in the round. Arena lighting must also strictly define the

1

2

3

playing area in a pool of light, whereas the proscenium playing space is usually established by the flats and backdrops. Also, actors in the arena must be adequately lit from all four sides, unlike actors in a proscenium frame who usually don't need to be lit from the back and sides.

    The actors, too, must alter their techniques to suit the circumstances.   4
The most conspicuous difference is that acting on a proscenium stage requires a less natural style of movement. For one thing, actors have to direct their performances downstage—that is, toward the audience out in front of them—and avoid facing upstage or turning too much to the sides. Also, in order to be seen and heard by the people in the balcony and the back rows, actors on a proscenium stage need to project their voices and exaggerate their facial expressions and gestures. By contrast, the actors in theater in the round are always facing away from some audience members, so the artificial need to display all actions toward one direction disappears, but the necessity of being expressive from the back emerges. Moreover, this more realistic movement, combined with the comparative intimacy of theater in the round, demands more truth and subtlety in all elements of the performance. This style also requires greater attention from the actors, most of whom find concentration easier in the familiar proscenium theater, where the audience is farther away. Nevertheless, in spite of, or perhaps because of, these greater demands on their skills, some actors enjoy doing arena plays even more than acting on regular stages.

    Clearly, the differences between proscenium and arena staging are   5
important in producing plays. The modern theater in the round is one in a long progression of possible methods of theatrical presentation, each of which has created new production problems as well as dramatic advantages. These variations in staging alter the audience's relationship to both the play and its performance and can change how the theatergoer responds to and understands the production.

CONSIDERING CONTENT AND METHOD

1. What purpose and audience did Lynn have in mind when writing this essay? How does the last sentence of the essay help to answer this question?
2. Do a quick outline of the major points in this essay. Which method of comparison and contrast has Lynn used to achieve her purpose? Is it a good choice?
3. Are the transitional phrases in this essay helpful and well placed? Identify several examples and explain their value to the essay.
4. Has Lynn used adequate illustration to support and clarify her points about each type of staging? Which examples work best?
5. Are the theater terms in the essay adequately defined? Explain.

Strategies for Explaining How Things Work: *Process* and *Directions*

"Here you go, right on page 13 of the manual: 'Never stop walking while the treadmill is on.'"

FOR DISCUSSION AND WRITING

Cartoons are often funny because we recognize ourselves, or people we know, acting in slightly exaggerated ways in familiar situations. Do you know people like the two characters in this cartoon? Have you found yourself in a similar situation? Write a brief response to John

McPherson's cartoon. Focus on what makes it humorous and what pointers it might provide for writing and reading actual instructions.

Listen to our rural relatives explaining how to get to the family reunion: "Just follow the hard road down to where the Snivelys' cow barn used to stand before the fire; then turn off on the gravel track and go a piece until you get to the top of the second big rise after the creek. Look for Rabbithash's old pickup." All eighty-six aunts, uncles, and cousins find these directions perfectly clear, but anyone from farther away than Clay City is going to have some difficulty getting there before the potato salad goes funny.

THE POINT OF WRITING ABOUT PROCESS AND DIRECTIONS

When you want to include second-cousins-once-removed and even complete strangers in your audience, you will try to write out directions that don't rely on so much in-group information (such as where the Snivelys' barn *used* to be). Communicating directions so that almost anyone can understand them is a difficult task, as you know if you have ever tried to do it. Explaining a process is quite similar: after you've performed a certain task over and over, it's hard to explain to someone else exactly how it's done. Do you remember how hard it was to shift the manual transmission while turning the corner when you first learned to drive? Could you easily explain it to a sixteen-year-old? And when a child asks, "Where does the rain come from?" wouldn't most people rather come up with a cute story than really grapple with the workings of nature?

But sometimes, frequently on the job, you must come up with an orderly, step-by-step explanation of how something is done or how it works. The explanation may be just part of a larger report or essay; for example, proposing a solution to the company's mail problems must include an account of how the current mail system works. This chapter includes models of several types of **process writing**.

THE PRINCIPLES OF PROCESS AND DIRECTIONS

The basic organizing principle behind process and direction writing involves time. You are usually concerned with a series of events, and these events may not float through your mind in the same order they should appear in your written work. Your readers will be frustrated and confused by flashbacks or detours to supply information that you should have covered earlier. Therefore, the scratch outline takes on great importance in this type of writing effort. A blank piece of unlined paper or a new document in your word processing program will help you to get started. On this page, you will list the steps or stages of the process as you first think of them—only be sure to space the items widely apart. In the spaces you can add points you forgot the first time through: these can be major steps ("Collect the dog shampoo and old towels before you attempt to collect the dog"), substeps ("Pile up more old towels than you think you will possibly need"), or warnings ("Don't speak to your beast in a tone of panicky sweetness; he'll know you're up to something"). Once you consider your notes complete, read through them while visualizing the process to pinpoint anything you have forgotten.

"How to Wash Your Dog" doesn't represent the only angle you can take on process writing, although it is a useful one. In "Shopping Can Be a Challenge," Carol Fleischman uses an extended example to outline the strategies and pitfalls of being a shopper who also happens to be blind. Garrison Keillor's directions on "How to Write a Personal Letter" combine practical and emotional features of the process—not only showing us how to do it but also persuading us that it is worth doing. Emily Nelson's "Making Fake Flakes" reveals a trick of movie-making magic by tracing the prop department's creation of potato-flake "snow" in a variety of settings. In your future writing projects, all these techniques for explaining a process and giving directions will be useful.

THE PITFALLS OF PROCESS AND DIRECTIONS

The problems you encounter in process writing usually have their roots in understanding your audience. For instance, several years ago when we first joined the Internet, we were assured that the printed directions we received were quite complete. They began, "Once you are connected to the CCSO Terminal, follow these steps to log on." Once we were *what*? To *what*? Obviously, the directions were written for people much more "connected" than we are. You have no doubt had similar experiences; hundreds of cartoons around Christmas time portray frantic parents trying to follow "easy" assembly instructions for their children's toys.

Reviewing Your Process

When you revise your process writing, think about the people who will be reading it. Ask yourself these questions:

1. Have I chosen the best starting point? Think about how much your audience already knows before you decide where to begin describing the process. Don't assume your readers have background knowledge that they may not have. And remember that your audience may need to be persuaded to learn what you wish to teach.
2. Have I provided enough definitions of terms? See Chapter 5 for help in writing definitions and deciding when they are needed.

3. Have I been specific enough in the details? "Dig a trench" is more specific than "Dig a hole," but how deep should the trench be? How wide? How long?

Addressing Your Audience

Another decision you will need to face in your process writing concerns not only who your audience is but also how you intend to speak to them. In this book, we address you, our readers, as "you." This straightforward, informal voice is desirable in much writing. Sometimes, you can keep the informality yet leave the "you" out, using imperative sentences (or commands) such as "Gather the towels before catching the dog," or "Dig a trench two feet wide." You may also choose to describe a third person performing or observing the process: "The experienced video game player works quickly," or "The first feature a palm reader examines is the life line, running from between the thumb and first finger in a curve down to the wrist." However you decide to deal with addressing your audience, you should be careful not to mix these approaches accidentally.

WHAT TO LOOK FOR IN PROCESS AND DIRECTIONS

The readings in this chapter differ greatly in their treatment of topics, even though they have process and directions in common. As you read, consider these questions:

1. What are the differences among the introductions? Can you account for these differences by looking at the purpose of each author?
2. How does each author signal where a new step, stage, or part begins?
3. How does each author address the readers? Is this way of addressing readers suitable?
4. Are there any points at which you would like further details or explanation? Where, what, and why?
5. What strategies other than process and directions appear within these readings—for example, narration, description, or comparison and contrast?

PREPARING TO READ

How do you respond when you encounter people with disabilities? Have
you had any specific experiences that led to significant or even slight
changes in your attitudes or behaviors in these situations?

••

Shopping Can Be a Challenge

••

CAROL FLEISCHMAN

Carol Fleischman, who lives in Niagara Falls, New York, is a regular contributor to the Buffalo News. *Her articles cover a wide range of everyday events, from yard sales to wedding showers, but her recurring theme is life as a blind person, especially the joys and challenges of working with assistance dogs. "Shopping Can Be a Challenge" first appeared in 1998 and won the International Association of Assistance Dog Partners "Best Article of the Year Award."*

TERMS TO RECOGNIZE

ritual *(para. 1)*	set form or order of events
beeline *(para. 2)*	straight path, direct route
booming *(para. 5)*	deep, resonant sound
in earshot *(para. 6)*	within hearing distance
chastised *(para. 14)*	strongly criticized, scolded
preoccupied *(para. 23)*	busy, distracted
reminiscent *(para. 24)*	similar to, reminding one of
foiled *(para 24)*	prevented, stopped

Have you ever tried to buy a dress when you can't see? I have,   1
because I'm blind. At one time, I would shop with friends. This ritual ended
after the time I happily brought home a dress a friend had helped me
choose, and my husband, Don, offered a surprising observation: "The fit is
great, but do you like all those huge fish?" The dress went back. Now I rely
on Don and my guide dog, Misty, as my shopping partners.

We enter the store and make a beeline for the dress department. Don   2
usually sees two or three salespeople scatter. The aisles empty as if a
bomber had come on the scene. Then I realize I'm holding the "live wire."
But I'm not judgmental—once I, too, was uneasy around large dogs.

Although Misty is better behaved than most children, I know a 65-pound German shepherd is imposing.

On one recent shopping trip, a brave saleswoman finally approached   3
us. "Can I help you?" she said to my husband.

"Yes, I'm looking for a dress," I replied. (After all, I'm the one who   4
will be wearing it.) "Maybe something in red or white."

"RED OR WHITE," she said, speaking very slowly and loudly even   5
though my hearing is fine. I managed not to fall as Misty jumped back on
my feet, frightened by the woman's booming voice.

Don was distracted too. I heard him rustling through hangers on a   6
nearby rack. I called his name softly to get his attention, and another man
answered my call. Bad luck. What were the chances of two Dons being in
earshot?

"This is great!" Don said, holding up a treasure. I swept my hand   7
over the dress to examine it. It had a neckline that plunged to the hemline.
"Hmmm," I said. I walk three miles daily with Misty and stay current with
fashion, but I'm positive this costume would look best on one of the Spice
Girls. Finally, I chose three dresses to try on.

Another shopper distracted Misty, even though the harness sign   8
reads: "Please do not pet. I'm working." She said, "Your dog reminds me of
my Max, who I recently put to sleep," so I was sympathetic. We discussed
her loss for 15 minutes. Some therapists don't spend that much time with
grieving clients.

Don was back. He told me the route to travel to the dressing room. I   9
commanded Misty: right, left, right, and straight ahead. We wove our way
past several small voices.

"Mom, why is that dog in the store?"   10

"Mom, is that a dog or a wolf?"   11

And my personal favorite: "But that lady's eyes are open."   12

I trust parents to explain: "The lady is giving her guide dog com-   13
mands. Her dog is a helping dog. They're partners." I questioned whether
this positive message had been communicated, though, when I heard an
adult say: "Oh, there's one of those blind dogs."

Other people, though well-intentioned, can interfere with my effective   14
use of Misty. Guide dogs are highly trained and very dependable but occasionally make potentially dangerous mistakes. On my way through the
aisles, Misty bumped me into a pointed rack, requiring my quick action. I
used a firm tone to correct her, and she dived to the ground like a dying
actress. Witnessing this performance, another shopper chastised me for
being cruel. I was shocked. Misty's pride was hurt, but I needed to point out

the error in order to avoid future mistakes. If I did not discipline her, what would prevent Misty from walking me off the curb into traffic?

Composing myself, I was delighted by the saleswoman's suggestion: 15 "Can I take you to your dressing room?" I was less delighted when she grabbed me and pushed me ahead while Misty trailed us on a leash. I wriggled out of the woman's hold. Gently pushing her ahead, I lightly held her elbow in sighted-guide technique (called so because the person who sees goes first).

"This is better. Please put my hand on the door knob. I'll take it from 16 here," I said.

In the room, Misty plopped down and sighed with boredom. I sighed 17 with relief that she was still with me. On one shopping trip, I was so preoccupied with trying on clothes that Misty sneaked out beneath the dressing room's doors. I heard her tags jingling as she left but was half-dressed and couldn't retrieve her. Fortunately, Don was outside the door and snagged her leash.

I modeled the dresses for Don and, feeling numb, bought all three. As 18 we left the store, Misty's magnetism, reminiscent of the Pied Piper's, attracted a toddler who draped himself over her. She remained calm, as he tried to ride her. The boy's fun was soon foiled by his frantic mother. When we returned to our car, I gave Misty a treat and lots of praise. A good day's work deserves a good day's pay for both of us.

"Shop till you drop" or "retail therapy" could never be my motto. To 19 me, "charge" means going into battle.

RESPONDING TO READING

Does shopping ever feel like a battle to you? Do any of your reasons for feeling that way overlap with Fleischman's? Can you come up with other imaginative comparisons for the shopping experience?

CONSIDERING CONTENT

1. Why did Fleischman stop shopping with her friends? What makes her husband and dog better shopping partners?
2. List the mistakes made by the people Fleischman encounters as she shops? Now make a list of proper etiquette for interacting with a person who is blind.
3. What reasons does Fleishman offer for sighted people's troublesome behaviors? Can you provide other reasons?
4. Why does Fleishman say she is "feeling numb" in paragraph 18? What other emotions does she experience during this shopping trip?

CONSIDERING METHOD

1. Identify the stages of Fleischman's typical shopping trip. Why does she choose not to use a more direct, step-by-step format for her process essay?
2. Describe Fleischman's tone. Does it change over the course of the essay?
3. How does Fleischman offer proof in paragraph 7 that she stays "current with fashion"?
4. In the second paragraph, Fleischman writes "The aisles empty as if a bomber had come on the scene." Find other words and phrases that continue this battle comparison.

Combining Strategies

Fleischman uses an extended example, narration, and description to provide a clear understanding of her shopping process and to achieve a persuasive purpose. What are the advantages of her approach? What other strategies might be used with this topic if one were writing for a different audience, such as trainers of assistance dogs?

WRITING STEP BY STEP

You probably have your own shopping style. Write an essay called "Shopping Can Be _____," filling in the blank with the word that best captures your feelings about this everyday activity. You will be following the form of "Shopping Can Be a Challenge."

A. Start by asking a question that will catch most readers' interests.
B. Develop your introduction with an illustration of a past shopping experience that shaped your current technique or attitude.
C. Use an extended example of a typical shopping expedition to organize your essay. Be sure to provide concrete support—names, dialogue, description of people and places.
D. Select one of the comparisons you came up with in your Responding to Reading response and use it to help convey your tone and purpose throughout the essay. For example, you might compare shopping to a treasure hunt, which would suggest an entertaining, exciting experience. Also revise your phrasing—nouns, adjectives, adverbs, and verbs—to

further communicate your attitude. For example, if your image as a shopper is "The Great Hunter," here is a revision you might make:

> First draft: The hunt was almost over, but I managed to buy some discount socks at the last minute.
>
> Revision: The hunt was almost over, but I managed to snare some small game (discount socks) at the last minute.

OTHER WRITING IDEAS

1. Choose an activity that you do, and explain to your readers how they would benefit from doing it too.

2. COLLABORATIVE WRITING. Meet with your classmates to discuss other challenges that people with disabilities experience in their everyday activities. Talk about a range of disabilities and then construct a list of problems commonly encountered by people with these different types of disabilities. Consider things like conducting a conversation or performing simple actions. Write an essay based on the results of your group brainstorming and personal experiences.

3. USING THE INTERNET. Interacting with the blind is also an issue in the workplace. Visit Internet sites offering advice on this topic, and then write a process essay on meeting and interacting with the blind in a work environment.

4. WRITING ABOUT READING. Fleischman's dog Misty died a few years after Fleischman wrote this article. She wrote of its devastating effects in another article in April 2001. Using a newspaper database such as Lexis-Nexis, find this article, and use it with "Shopping Can Be a Challenge" to outline Fleischman's guidelines for working with an assistance dog.

GAINING WORD POWER

In paragraph 8, Fleischman writes about a dog who was "*recently* put to sleep." In paragraph 3, we read the phrase "one *recent* shopping trip." Both words share the meaning of new or not long ago. *Recent* is an adjective, describing the noun *trip*. *Recently* is the adverb form of the same word; adverbs describe words other than nouns, in this case the verb *put*. Most adverbs are made by adding –*ly* to adjectives; for example, *happily* comes from *happy* (para. 1), *usually* comes from *usual* (para. 2), and *finally* comes from *final* (para. 3).

This reading includes ten other adverbs that end in –*ly*. Find at least five of them. Then write their adjective form, checking with the dictionary for spelling if necessary. Then express the shared meaning between the two forms, again using the dictionary. Here's an example to get you started:

Adverb: slowly

Adjective: slow

Shared meaning: at a low speed, not moving quickly

EDITING SKILLS: USING PARENTHESES

When you want to include an idea that is interesting but not crucial to your discussion, put it in parentheses. Here's an example from Fleischman's third and fourth paragraphs:

> On one recent shopping trip, a brave saleswoman finally approached us. "Can I help you?" she said to my husband.
> "Yes, I'm looking for a dress," I replied. (After all, I'm the one who will be wearing it.)

The interaction is captured in the dialogue (speech or conversation recorded in writing), but in the final parenthetical sentence, Fleischman comments on the dialogue, and the parentheses tell the reader that the remark is reinforcement for the implied (but unspoken) point she is making. This example shows the use of parentheses to highlight a mocking tone.

Parentheses are also used in these ways:

1. To enclose brief definitions within a sentence (like the examples in the previous paragraph):

   > I tightly held her elbow in a sight-guide technique (called so because the person who sees goes first).

   > Writers use transitions to improve *continuity* (the flow of their ideas).

   Notice that the period goes after the parenthesis at the end unless the whole statement begins and ends within the parentheses.
2. To enclose examples and brief explanations (like the one in item 1 and this one you are presently reading).
3. To enclose dates within a sentence:

   > John Stuart Mill (1806–1873) favored women's equality with men.

EXERCISE

Find five examples of parentheses in this chapter, and explain which of the uses discussed applies to each example.

Then look at the essay you just completed. Is there any material that should be enclosed in parentheses? Consider adding a definition, a date, a comment, or a brief explanation with parentheses that would add to the reader's understanding of your ideas.

WEB SITES

www.support–dogs.org.uk
The Web site Support Dogs Online offers advice on a variety of uses for assistance dogs, from alerting people with epilepsy about an upcoming seizure to performing everyday tasks, such as turning on lights and opening doors.

PREPARING TO READ

How do you feel when you receive a letter? Does anyone regularly write to you? To whom do you write, and why? Do you keep letters and read them again later?

···

How to Write a Personal Letter

···

GARRISON KEILLOR

Garrison Keillor is a famous radio program host. His show, A Prairie Home Companion, *reaches over 4 million listeners a week and is especially popular because of Keillor's spoken essays about the Minnesota town of Lake Wobegon, a make-believe place where "all the men are strong, all the women are good-looking, and all the children are above average." Listeners are delighted by the charming quirkiness of Lake Wobegon citizens and their everyday lives. In the essay reprinted here from* We Are Still Married *(1989), Keillor's neighborly style comes through as he gives advice and support to letter writers.*

TERMS TO RECOGNIZE

wahoo *(para. 2)*	probably a type of *yahoo*, which is a coarse, crude person
anonymity *(para. 4)*	namelessness, being unknown
obligatory *(para. 6)*	required by custom or etiquette
sensate *(para. 6)*	filled with feelings
sensuous *(para. 8)*	pleasing to the senses
salutation *(para. 10)*	the greeting that opens a letter
declarative *(para. 10)*	making a statement
episode *(para. 13)*	an incident or event, a unit of a longer story
urinary tract *(para. 13)*	the system relating to the kidneys and bladder and their functions
means *(para. 14)*	mode or process

We shy persons need to write a letter now and then, or else we'll dry up and blow away. It's true. And I speak as one who loves to reach for the phone, dial the number, and talk. The telephone is to shyness what Hawaii is to February; it's a way out of the woods. And yet: a letter is better.

Such a sweet gift—a piece of handmade writing, in an envelope that is 2 not a bill, sitting in our friend's path when she trudges home from a long day spent among wahoos and savages, a day our words will help repair. They don't need to be immortal, just sincere. She can read them twice and again tomorrow: *You're someone I care about, Corinne, and think of often, and every time I do, you make me smile.*

We need to write; otherwise nobody will know who we are. They will 3 have only a vague impression of us as A Nice Person, because, frankly, we don't shine at conversation, we lack the confidence to thrust our faces forward and say, "Hi, I'm Heather Hooten; let me tell you about my week." Mostly we say "Uh-huh" and "Oh really." People smile and look over our shoulder, looking for someone else to meet.

So a shy person sits down and writes a letter. To be known by 4 another person—to meet and talk freely on the page—to be close despite distance. To escape from anonymity and be our own sweet selves and express the music of our souls.

Same thing that moves a giant rock star to sing his heart out in front 5 of 123,000 people moves us to take ballpoint in hand and write a few lines to our dear Aunt Eleanor. *We want to be known.* We want her to know that we have fallen in love, that we quit our job, that we're moving to New York, and we want to say a few things that might not get said in casual conversation: *Thank you for what you've meant to me. I am very happy right now.*

The first step in writing letters is to get over the guilt of *not* writing. 6 You don't "owe" anybody a letter. Letters are a gift. The burning shame you feel when you see unanswered mail makes it harder to pick up a pen and makes for a cheerless letter when you finally do. *I feel bad about not writing, but I've been so busy*, etc. Skip this. Few letters are obligatory, and they are *Thanks for the wonderful gift* and *I am terribly sorry to hear about George's death* and *Yes, you're welcome to stay with us next month.* Write these promptly if you want to keep your friends. Don't worry about the others, except love letters, of course. When your true love writes *Dear Light of My Life, Joy of My Heart, O Lovely Pulsating Core of My Sensate Life*, some response is called for.

Some of the best letters are tossed off in a burst of inspiration, so 7 keep your writing stuff in one place where you can sit down for a few minutes and—*Dear Roy, I am in the middle of an essay but thought I'd drop you a line. Hi to your sweetie too*—dash off a note to a pal. Envelopes, stamps, address book, everything in a drawer so you can write fast when the pen is hot.

A blank white 8" × 11" sheet can look as big as Montana if the pen's 8 not so hot—try a smaller page and write boldly. Get a pen that makes a sensuous line, get a comfortable typewriter, a friendly word processor—whichever feels easy to the hand.

Sit for a few minutes with the blank sheet of paper in front of you, 9 and meditate on the person you will write to, let your friend come to mind until you can almost see her or him in the room with you. Remember the last time you saw each other and how your friend looked and what you said and what perhaps was unsaid between you, and when your friend becomes real to you, start to write.

Write the salutation—*Dear* You—and take a deep breath and plunge 10 in. A simple declarative sentence will do, followed by another and another. Tell us what you're doing and tell it like you were talking to us. Don't think about grammar, don't think about style, don't try to write dramatically, just give us your news. Where did you go, who did you see, what did they say, what do you think?

If you don't know where to begin, start with the present: *I'm sitting at* 11 *the kitchen table on a rainy Saturday morning. Everyone is gone and the house is quiet.* Let your simple description of the present moment lead to something else; let the letter drift gently along.

The toughest letter to crank out is one that is meant to impress, as 12 we all know from writing job applications; if it's hard work to slip off a letter to a friend, maybe you're trying too hard to be terrific. A letter is only a report to someone who already likes you for reasons other than your brilliance. Take it easy.

Don't worry about form. It's not a term paper. When you come to 13 the end of one episode, just start a new paragraph. You can go from a few lines about the sad state of pro football to the fight with your mother to your fond memories of Mexico to your cat's urinary-tract infection to a few thoughts on personal indebtedness and on to the kitchen sink and what's in it. The more you write, the easier it gets, and when you have a True True Friend to write to, a *compadre*, a soul sibling, then it's like driving a car; you just press on the gas.

Don't tear up the page and start over when you write a bad line—try 14 to write your way out of it. Make mistakes and plunge on. Let the letter cook along and let yourself be bold. Outrage, confusion, love—whatever is in your mind, let it find a way to the page. Writing is a means of discovery, always, and when you come to the end and write *Yours ever* or *Hugs and Kisses*, you'll know something you didn't when you wrote *Dear Pal*.

Probably your friend will put your letter away, and it'll be read again 15 a few years from now—and it will improve with age. And forty years from now, your friend's grandkids will dig it out of the attic and read it, a sweet and precious relic of the ancient Eighties that gives them a sudden clear glimpse of you and her and the world we old-timers knew. You will have then created an object of art. Your simple lines about where you went, who you saw, what they said, will speak to those children, and they will feel in their hearts the humanity of our times.

You can't pick up a phone and call the future and tell them about our 16 times. You have to pick up a piece of paper.

RESPONDING TO READING

After reading Keillor's essay, are you encouraged to try writing a letter to a friend? Why or why not? Answer these questions in your journal.

CONSIDERING CONTENT

1. Why are letters preferable to face-to-face communication for shy people? What other reasons might make letters preferable to conversation, according to Keillor?
2. What are some differences between Keillor's advice and other writing instructions or rules you have heard? Why do you think these differences exist?
3. Did you ever have to write a letter or essay "meant to impress" (para. 12)? What was the experience like? How did you feel about the writing you produced?
4. Note two or three spots where Keillor deals with the emotions a letter writer might have. Why is it important to give advice about these?
5. What does Keillor mean by "an object of art" in paragraph 15? What has changed the ordinary letter into art? Do you think this claim makes sense or exaggerates?
6. What about using e-mail or blogs or text messages? Does Keillor's essay have any relevance to these electronic forms of communication? Do you think he would see them as similar to or different from postal letters?

CONSIDERING METHOD

1. Make a brief list of Keillor's pieces of advice. What is the reasoning behind the order he uses?

2. Who is the "we" Keillor refers to in the essay? Who is the "you"? What kinds of people might think the essay does not apply to them?

3. Does this writing strike you as formal or informal? Point out words and phrases that influenced your decision. Why do you think Keillor made this choice about the level of formality?

4. What are the lines and phrases printed in italics? Can you identify their purpose?

WRITING STEP BY STEP

In the reading, Keillor advocates writing a letter, even when a phone call is possible. Write an essay in which you promote doing something in the old-fashioned way even though new ways are available. For possible inspiration, think about writing by hand rather than on a word processor, baking bread, sewing clothes, building furniture, doing math without a calculator, reading a novel rather than watching the movie, conducting a courtship, or raising children.

A. In the beginning of your essay, suggest one or two reasons the old way might be better than the new way.

B. Use "I," "we," and "you" to refer to yourself, yourself and your readers, and your readers.

C. Use everyday language and familiar examples to get your points across to a wide audience.

D. Explain why some people feel hesitant about doing things the old way.

E. Suggest ways that the reader can overcome this reluctance. Look at paragraphs 6 through 13 for examples of how Keillor does this.

F. Include, if relevant, some "don'ts" to help your reader avoid problems, as Keillor does in paragraphs 10, 12, and 13.

G. In your closing, reinforce your main point by looking at the positive effect(s) the actions you promote could have. You might look into the future, as Keillor does.

OTHER WRITING IDEAS

1. Try writing a letter to a friend, using Keillor's advice if you want. At the same time, take notes about how you go about performing the task. Record the thoughts and feelings that you experience along the way as well as the techniques you use. Write an essay describing the experience of writing the letter. Use direct quotations from the letter in italics to illustrate your points.

2. COLLABORATIVE WRITING. The reading emphasizes writing letters as an outlet for shy people. Another form of communication, public speaking, brings out the shy side of almost everyone. Meet with a small group of your classmates to discuss your emotional responses to public speaking. Include solutions you have come up with for handling these feelings. Write an essay modeled on Keillor's in which you give emotional and practical advice to a person who reluctantly must make a speech or give a presentation.

3. USING THE INTERNET. Find out what "speed dating" is and how it works. Then write an essay describing the process for an audience of your peers.

4. WRITING ABOUT READING. Keillor asserts that "writing is a means of discovery" (para. 14). What does this mean? Write an essay about a piece of writing you once did (or tried to do) that led you to an unexpected discovery. The discovery could be about yourself, the writing process, the subject matter, school, the intended audience, or a combination of things.

GAINING WORD POWER

Add to the following fragments, making them into reasonable sentences. Be sure that your additions show your understanding of the terms from the reading.

1. President Weber began his after-dinner speech with an obligatory
   _____.

2. To protect her anonymity, the writer _____.

3. Preparing _____ is more sensuous than _____.

4. Henry sat down and wrote this salutation: _____.

5. An office memo usually begins with a plain declarative statement, such as "_____."

EDITING SKILLS: USING SHORT SENTENCES FOR EMPHASIS

Experienced writers vary their sentences, both in structure and length. If you look at Garrison Keillor's sentences, you will see that most of them are at least ten words long and many are over twenty. But sometimes he throws in a very short sentence for effect:

The toughest letter to crank out is one that is meant to impress, as we all know from writing job applications [21 words]; if it's hard work to slip off a letter to a friend, maybe you're trying too hard to be terrific [20 words].

A letter is only a report to someone who already likes you for reasons other than your brilliance [18 words]. Take it easy [3 words].

Keillor also uses two short sentences to open paragraph 13—"Don't worry about form. It's not a term paper"—and a six-word sentence to end the first paragraph. These sentences express important points; they grab our attention by being noticeably different from the longer sentences around them.

EXERCISE

Look through Keillor's essay to find at least five more sentences that contain fewer than eight words. Note where he places them, and describe their effect.

Examine the sentences in your own essay. Can you find a place to use a short sentence for emphasis? Try to begin or end a paragraph with a short statement. Also take a look at your conclusion; that's another good place to sum up the main point in a short sentence. If you can't think of a new sentence, try shortening one that you've already written.

WEB SITE

http://prairiehome.publicradio.org/features/

Take a look at this link on the Prairie Home Companion Web site. Do you see connections between the way Keillor approaches letter writing and his radio show's content and style?

PREPARING TO READ

How important are special effects to your enjoyment of movies and TV? When you watch TV sitcoms and dramas, do you notice when something seems wrong or fake or out of place?

••

Making Fake Flakes

••

EMILY NELSON

Emily Nelson is a staff reporter for the Wall Street Journal. *Her reports are often feature articles drawn from recent business and entertainment news. "Making Fake Flakes" first appeared in the* Journal *in June 2003.*

TERMS TO RECOGNIZE

riddled *(para. 1)*	punctured with numerous holes
props *(para. 2)*	articles or objects used by actors
sloshing *(para. 2)*	splashing, floundering
formula *(para. 3)*	a set model or prescription
alien *(para. 4)*	outsider, a being from outer space
lavish *(para. 4)*	abundant, extravagant, grand
acrylic *(para. 5)*	synthetic plastic
dubbing *(para. 6)*	inserting, substituting for the original
mussed *(para. 8)*	made messy, disordered
pulverizes *(para. 11)*	crushes, breaks into pieces

A special-effects whiz in Hollywood, Howard Jensen can create fireball explosions and make cars look riddled with bullets. But his current job—to create falling snow for TV shows such as "Boston Public"—is one of the hardest, he says. So he turned to potato flakes. 1

Turn on the TV, and that gentle, romantic snow falling is, quite likely, the same stuff sold at the supermarket for making mashed potatoes. Props crews can easily load the potato flakes into rolling drums on cranes that sprinkle down flakes. Industrial fans, called "Ritters" in the industry after 2 their inventor, keep the flakes aloft. From afar, the effect looks just like ide-alized snow. Up close, however, potato flakes look like . . . potato flakes. They don't melt when they land on a person or on the ground. And they have a way of turning into potatoes. The cast of "ER" once found itself sloshing through mashed potatoes when it rained during filming.

Snow, it turns out, is a big production worry for TV studios these days. For years, much of TV was set indoors in the same style that made Archie Bunker's living room so familiar in "All in the Family." Today, viewers raised on big-budget movies expect greater realism and seasonal, outdoor shots in TV productions, a formula that's worked well for NBC's "Law and Order." Many sitcoms, including "Malcom in the Middle," regularly use out-side scenes. Moreover, networks are asking shows to change seasons with the calendar, which gives viewers a sense they're watching in real time.   3

But while TV studios can create talking animals and alien neighbors, snow can be trickier. Unlike rain, snow doesn't make any noise. For a good thunderstorm, technicians simply mix in lightning and raindrop sounds on a soundtrack. Even a frosty puff of breath is hard to reproduce without expensive digital manipulation. And unlike lavish movies that travel to win-try locales and use elaborate post-production digital effects, budgets in television are often tight. Production schedules are so short that most dra-matic shows must crank out an episode every eight days, leaving little money or time to add in special effects.   4

Depending on a script's demands—blizzard or flurries?—TV crews mix in a variety of materials. Besides potato flakes, firefighters' foam, acrylic flakes, soap and starch products, slivers of plastic (which can sting actors in high winds), polyester blankets (best for roofs and backdrops), and real ice are popular.   5

Snow scenes on TV call for unusual shortcuts. Characters on a sit-com standing in the snow, for example, rarely talk. That's because the snow-blowing machine makes a racket—usually replaced with background music alone, to save the expense of dubbing in dialogue. When the plot on "Dawson's Creek" called for the cast to go on a ski trip, the outdoor shots were close-ups, allowing the crew to cover just a small area with fake snow—in this case a white foam used by fire departments.   6

"We've attempted many ways, and I can't say any of them look too convincing," says Paul Stupin, the show's executive producer, who says small TV screens are more forgiving than movie screens. "Dawson's Creek," set in Massachusetts, also takes meteorological license, filming in North Carolina where it rarely snows. On "Friends" recently, the cast admired a snowfall by looking out the window—a cheap shorthand that requires   7 attaching a tumbler above the window frame, which sprinkles white plastic flakes. Producers hoped viewers didn't notice that in the same scene, Chandler walks in without so much as a flake on his coat.

Jonathan Prince, executive producer and writer for NBC drama "American Dreams," wanted snow so badly for a recent shoot that he changed the plot of an episode to afford it. For a romantic but fake snowfall on star Meg Pryor's first kiss, Mr. Prince had Meg and her family arrive late to church, thereby avoiding the need to hire congregation extras. In search of the perfect setting for a snowball fight, Mr. Prince ordered in truckloads of crushed ice. On the day before filming, as the cast played with the ice on the Los Angeles lot, Mr. Prince watched, in horror, as hair and make-up got mussed and, even worse, it looked like they were throwing white rocks.

"Real snowballs don't explode in powdery fluff the way we wish they do," Mr. Prince says regretfully. "They only do that on television." So the props crew brought in potato flakes. "We were throwing mashed potatoes at each other," he says. "There are no runny noses. It's perfect TV."

Sometimes TV shows in colder climates manage to write snow out of the script to avoid finding or making it, as when writers for "Everwood," a new TV drama set in Colorado, added an unusually warm breeze that the town celebrates with a festival in one episode. They reversed the weather in two other episodes, writing in a blizzard that keeps everyone housebound and keeps the cameras inside. A show where the cast never gets outside is called "a bottle episode."

Another problem with real ice is that it's expensive. Potato flakes cost about $90 per 50-pound box; last year, a winter episode of "Ally McBeal" required five boxes. North Hollywood Ice Co., charges $130 per ton of ice, usually with a 10-ton minimum, plus tax and $35 an hour each for five operators. Sold in large blocks, the ice is fed through a noisy snow blower that chips it, pulverizes it, and blows it out airborne through a hose. This is good for laying snow on the ground but not falling snow. Crushed ice doesn't float—it falls with a thud or melts. Potato flakes or plastic versions fall more realistically. "We still haven't figured out a way to get it lofting down and pretty," says Fred Rymond, manager at North Hollywood, which hauled 30 tons of ice, in blocks weighing 300 to 400 pounds each, to a set for a recent blizzard on "Boston Public."

Idahoan Foods sells its potato flakes in major supermarket chains such as Albertson's and Safeway, but it also ships the same stuff in 800-pound shipments to special-effects companies, says Ruth Shriver, a sales coordinator at the Lewisville, Idaho, potato processor. When Ms. Shriver spotted snow falling while watching "The West Wing" recently, she said, "Is that potato flakes? It could be my stuff."

RESPONDING TO READING

Will having learned how artificial snow is made change your experience of watching TV? Will it take away from the romantic mood the director is often aiming for in outdoor winter scenes, for example?

CONSIDERING CONTENT

1. What are the most common materials used to create fake snow on TV?
2. Why do TV characters who are simply standing in snow stay silent? What other pitfalls do the special effects people run into when using artificial snow and how do they solve each problem?
3. What do time and cost have to do with the decisions TV studios make about their use of special effects?
4. What's a "Ritter"? What other production terms are introduced and defined in the essay?

CONSIDERING METHOD

1. Why does Nelson begin her introduction with images of "fireball explosions" and cars "riddled with bullets"?
2. How many different snow-making techniques are described in the essay? Can you identify a plan for how Nelson ordered her examples?
3. Find examples of Nelson's use of humor in "Making Fake Flakes." Why did she choose this tone for a process essay?
4. Why does Nelson use so many different TV shows to illustrate her points? Would a single extended example work?
5. Why does Nelson include the brief account of Ruth Shriver's experience at the end of the essay?

WRITING STEP BY STEP

Choose a topic and a process similar to the ones in "Making Fake Flakes." Your topic should be something everyone is familiar with, like snow on TV; however, the details of the process itself should offer readers a few surprises or new insights, like how difficult it is to create that snow using potato flakes and ice. You might, for example, reveal some behind-the-scenes secret about a job you have performed (dipping perfect softserve ice cream cones, frying perfect fries, quieting uncontrollable children) or a hobby you have perfected (staying upright while windsurfing, keeping up your stamina on a cross-country bike race, sewing a designer knock-off at half the price).

   A. Direct your writing to a general audience. Assume that the majority of your readers would not be familiar with the details of the process, that most of them, for example, have never worked at a fast-food restaurant or sewn their own clothes.

B. Begin by calling your readers' attention to the difference between what they think they know about your process and the point you wish to make about it. Nelson, for example, wishes to counter the idea that complex special effects are more difficult to achieve than simple ones.

C. Because your purpose is to inform, not instruct, organize your essay as Nelson does, providing the what, when, how, and why of your process by providing several successful examples and a few failed ones.

D. Develop your essay with specific details and colorful, concrete language to keep your reader's interest and attention. Nelson, for example, describes cars "riddled with bullets," and amuses her readers with images of the cast of *ER* "sloshing through mashed potatoes when it rained during filming."

E. If possible, conclude your essay with an amusing incident or reference, as Nelson does.

OTHER WRITING IDEAS

1. Write an essay in which you use process to explain a problem and then suggest a solution. For example, show how being overweight is a problem and then offer guidelines for losing weight. Other topics are smoking, excessive alcohol consumption, lack of work experience, poor study habits, and chronic lateness.

2. COLLABORATIVE WRITING. Identify and explain the stages of an emotional process, such as falling in love (or falling out of love). Work with a group of your classmates to come up with emotional processes and ideas about the different stages before you write your individual essay.

3. USING THE INTERNET. Look on the Internet, using a search engine such as Google or Yahoo, to find a complicated set of instructions, like those for programming a cell phone. Study them until you figure them out. Then write a new set of instructions that a beginner would find easy to follow.

4. WRITING ABOUT READING. "Making Fake Flakes" is about creating illusions, making what's not real seem real. Have you ever tried to create an illusion, to make people believe in something that wasn't true? For example, did you ever convince your parents you were ready to take on adult responsibilities, when, in fact, you weren't quite sure yourself that you were ready? Select such an experience and explain how you achieved your goal of creating an illusion.

GAINING WORD POWER

romantic	seasonal	frosty
wintry	dramatic	powdery

The preceding words are all used as *adjectives* in the reading. That is, they describe or modify other words (nouns) to make their meaning more specific and vivid. Look back through the reading to find the adjective-plus-noun combinations. We have done the first example for you.

romantic _____snow_____   wintry _____

seasonal _____   dramatic _____

frosty _____   powdery _____

The adjective *romantic* obviously comes from the noun *romance*. Using your dictionary, find the nouns that are related to these other four adjectives:

adj.:industrial   noun:_____

adj.:expensive   noun:_____

adj.:digital   noun:_____

adj.:meteorological   noun:_____

Now list one other related word, its meaning, and its part of speech for the four adjectives. Use your dictionary for help. For example, *expensive* is related to the verb *expend*, which means "to lay out." Both have to do with spending. Choose one set of three related words and try using them in three sentences of your own.

EDITING SKILLS: PUNCTUATING QUOTATIONS

Quotations from experts and from your reading will often enhance your writing. However, most people find the punctuation of quotations tricky. This exercise will help you put the periods, commas, and quotations marks in the right places. (For advice on using single quotation marks inside regular double quotations marks, see pages 194–96.)

EXERCISE

Copy the following passages *exactly*:

"We've attempted many ways," says Paul Stupin, the show's executive producer, "and I can't say any of them look too convincing."

"Real snowballs don't explode in powdery fluff the way we wish they do," Mr. Prince says regretfully. "They only do that on television." So the props crew brought in potato flakes. "We were throwing mashed potatoes at each other," he says. "There are no runny noses. It's perfect TV."

When Ms. Shriver spotted snow falling while watching "The West Wing" recently, she said, "Is that potato flakes? It could be my stuff."

Notice that you can put the tag line (the part that tells who is being quoted) before the quotation, after the quotation, or in the middle of the quotation. Exchange your copies with a classmate and check each other's writing for exact, accurate placement of all the punctuation. Then look at your process essay to make sure you have punctuated quotations correctly.

WEB SITE

http://entertainment.howstuffworks.com/lightsaber.htm
At this HowStuffWorks.Com site, the complex real-time and digital processes for creating the *Stars Wars* light sabers are concisely and clearly explained. Links on the site take you to explanations of other special effects techniques, as well.

Change Agent: How Baker Pulled Off the "Werewolf" Metamorphosis

. . . .

STEVE DALY

Steve Daly is a staff writer for Entertainment Weekly. *For the special 2007 Oscar guide, he wrote this account of how Rick Baker made a human actor into a werewolf onscreen. Baker won the first Academy Award for makeup in 1982, for his work on* American Werewolf, *and he is now known as a film prosthetics genius. Daly's description benefits from a combination of written words and photographs. Without the photos, it would be difficult for the reader to understand the amazing process described in the words.*

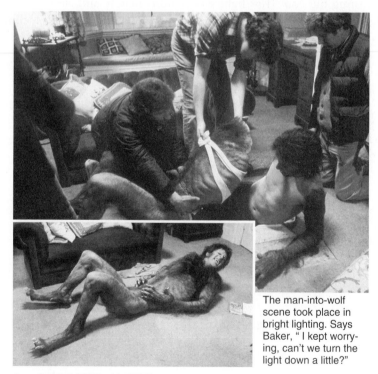

The man-into-wolf scene took place in bright lighting. Says Baker, " I kept worrying, can't we turn the light down a little?"

Source: © 1981 Bob Willoughby MPTV.net

Writer-director John Landis told Rick Baker the big metamorphosis scene in *American Werewolf* "should be painful." So it was, on screen and on set. Star David Naughton endured more than a week's filming encased in fur-covered latex pieces glued to his body. "We tortured him," says Baker. For full-figure shots designed to sell the idea of the wolf's expanded torso (complete with pronounced rib cage and extremely narrow hips), the crew cut a hole in a raised floor (top photo), laid a breast piece over Naughton, then ran metal rods up through two separate animatronic legs, puppeteering them from below to complete the illusion that it was all one were-man. Separate fake hands and feet were rigged for other close-ups to expand via cables and pistons, and a dummy "change-o-head," which involved 10 months' work to get a single shot lasting a few seconds, showed the werewolf's snout growing. Says Baker, "We never had time to test a lot of the transformation stages. We did the makeup on the day, and shot it."

FOR DISCUSSION AND WRITING

Many processes are best explained with a combination of words and graphics. For instance, directions for cooking and sports techniques often depend on graphics for clarity. Looking around at home, at your workplace, and at school, make a list of examples where written text and graphics are combined to explain a process or give directions. Choose one example and explain what the graphics contribute beyond the words.

OTHER WRITING IDEAS

1. Write some basic instructions for using a machine, such as a microwave oven, a photocopier, a cell phone, a washing machine. Write for readers who don't know how to work the machine. Include one or more graphics (such as a diagram or chart) to help explain how the process works.
2. Using a diagram or drawing, explain some sports activity that you know well, such as how to hit a forehand in tennis, how to throw a curve ball or a spiral pass, how to bowl a strike, how to execute a swan dive.

Source: J. Sackerman Das Fotoarchiv

3. What exactly is the "goth look"? What steps do you think the peo-
    ple in this photo took to create the appearance they wanted?.

WEB SITE
www.themakeupgallery.info

The Makeup Gallery features nearly 5,000 images of actresses in character and
prosthetic makeup from literally hundreds of movies and TV shows. The trans-
formations from actress into character are illustrated with before and after
shots and, wherever possible, with behind-the-scenes shots of the makeup
process. Who do you think visits this site and why?

STUDENT ESSAY USING PROCESS AND DIRECTIONS

A Graceful Stride

Ann Moroney

Ann Moroney wrote this essay in her first-semester English class at Eastern Illinois University. She attended a large high school in the western suburbs of Chicago and came to Eastern Illinois to major in journalism and information sciences.

A common misconception about hurdle races is that the runner "jumps" over the hurdle. This observation is completely false. A hurdle runner does just that—runs. The hurdler takes long steps, or strides, over the hurdle and sprints on to the next one. As simple as this process may sound, running hurdles is complicated. For one thing, the hurdle itself is thirty-three inches high, which comes to about the hip. "Stepping" over something this high is really quite difficult, as I found out my freshman year in high school. I also had to master a number of other skills to run hurdles efficiently.

The first problem to tackle when it comes to running hurdles is the fear. At every one of my races, I sat in my blocks looking at the line of hurdles in front of me with fear in my heart. No matter how good I became or how long I'd been running, I always felt *fear*: fear that I'd trip over the hurdle and fall on the track, fear that I'd knock the hurdle over in front of everybody, and fear that I'd actually get over the first hurdle with no problem and become a hurdler for four years. Throughout my experience, I found only one way to get over the fear: stop thinking and start running.

The main thing to concentrate on is form. Form is the way the runner carries himself or herself over the hurdles. The better the form is, the faster the run will be. Form includes many elements. The runner must coordinate legs, arms, torso, and eyes into a fluid sprint through ten hurdles on 100 meters of track.

The lead leg, the one to go over the hurdle first, should be slightly bent, but more or less straight in front of the body. The toe should be pointing toward the sky and the heel should line up with the middle of the hurdle. (As my former track coach Ms. Tolefree always said, "Heel to the Gill," referring to the brand name printed directly in the middle of the hurdle.) Just as the body comes over the hurdle, the lead leg should snap down to the ground. The goal is to bring the leg down as close to the back of the hurdle as possible without actually hitting it. The sooner the feet are on the ground, the faster the runner can continue running.

The runner must also concentrate on the trail leg—the one that   5
comes second over the hurdle. The knee should be bent with the leg at the
side, the thigh parallel to the hurdle. (Imagine sitting on the ground with
one leg bent at the side, mimicking a frog.) As the lead leg snaps down, the
trail leg will be following over the hurdle. The hip will rotate so the leg is
once again perpendicular to the ground. The knee should snap up to the
chest as close as possible, as this will help the runner stretch out the stride.
(As Ms. Tolefree was fond of saying, "Your knee is like the scope on a rifle. It
directs where your stride will go. If your knee is high, your stride will be long.
If it's low, your stride will be short.") After clearing the hurdle, the runner
must continue striding through the rest of the hurdles.

Another important part of form is arms; they not only keep balance,   6
but they also keep the form tight. The arm opposite the lead leg is the lead
arm. It should be reaching out in front of the body toward the toe of the
lead leg. The other arm, the one opposite the trail leg, is the trail arm. It
should come back in a biceps-flexing fashion and stay at the side until the
body is clear of the hurdle. It's usually a good idea to keep the hands open;
a closed fist takes up energy and tenses the muscles in the rest of the body.

The final elements of form have to do with small, yet significant,   7
mechanics. Air time is a major factor when running hurdles. The goal is to
remain in the air for as little time as possible; the faster the feet return to
the track, the faster the runner can continue running. So the body should be
as low to the hurdle as possible without hitting it. Also, the torso should
lean slightly forward—but not be bent, because taking the time to straighten
up will slow the runner down. A slight lean forward will get the runner over
the hurdle and on to the next one. The final point involves the eyes. Hur-
dlers should not look at the hurdle they are about to step over. Looking further down the track instead of directly in front of them keeps runners
running.

Running hurdles takes time, practice, and commitment. During the   8
split second it takes to clear a hurdle, the runner must take into account a
wide variety of movements to run the race successfully. A good, hard practice schedule is the only way to acquire a productive hurdling technique.
And developing a graceful stride is not as easy as it looks.

CONSIDERING CONTENT AND METHOD

1. Why does the author begin with a misconception? Is that a good way to begin?
2. What information did you find new and interesting? Was there anything you didn't understand? Did this essay increase your appreciation of hurdling?
3. Were you surprised that this essay was written by a female student? Why or why not?
4. Where does the author include personal comments? Do these comments add or detract from the explanations?
5. What do you think of the comments from the coach, Ms. Tolefree? Why are they included?

Strategies for Analyzing Why Things Happen: *Cause* and *Effect*

:–)   F2T   :–D   PAW   :'(

FOR DISCUSSION AND WRITING

Do you understand these symbols and abbreviations? Do you use this kind of shorthand in e-mails, instant messages, or text messages? Why or why not? Does your age have anything to do with your answer? Write briefly about the reasons why people might choose to use these methods of communication. For example, what range of purposes do you believe e-mail or text messages serve? And what effects can these message forms have on the relationship between its users?

Human beings are naturally curious. We all want to know why. Why does the car keep stalling? Why are some people better at math than others? Why does a leaf change color? Why did Prince William and Kate Middleton break up? This common human impulse to understand why things happen provides a powerful motive for reading and writing.

THE POINT OF CAUSE-AND-EFFECT WRITING

We study **causes** and their **effects** in order to understand events and solve problems. If we can find out why the car keeps stalling, we can fix it. If we can figure out why some people are good at math, maybe we can help those who aren't. If we know why a leaf changes color, we'll have a greater appreciation for nature and its processes. If we know why the Prince and girlfriend split, we might get on *Oprah*. A lot of the writing done in college courses requires cause–and–effect thinking; students are frequently asked to explain things like the origins of the Russian Revolution, the roots of prejudice, the causes of volcanic eruptions, the effects of hunger on learning, the reasons for Hamlet's delay. The good news about this kind of writing is that it feeds off the natural curiosity of both reader and writer. Inquiring minds want to know why, and you get to tell them.

When you develop an essay by analyzing causes, you are explaining to your readers *why* something happened. If you go on to explore the effects, you are analyzing *what* happened—the consequences. For example, if your topic is divorce and you write "Why Teenage Marriages Fail," that's primarily a cause paper. But if you write "What Divorce Does to Young Children," that's primarily an effect paper. You will probably stick to one purpose in a single essay, but you might take up both causes and effects if you have the time and the assignment allows you to.

THE PRINCIPLES OF CAUSE-AND-EFFECT WRITING

Analyzing cause-effect relationships is one of the primary methods of reasoning. It requires careful thinking and planning.

Types of Causes and Effects

When you think about causes and effects, you need to realize that they can be *immediate* or *remote*. The immediate causes are usually the obvious ones; they occur just before a result appears. An immediate cause for breaking up with your boyfriend might be that he didn't call you last night to tell you he'd be two hours late. But you also know there are deeper, more important reasons for the breakup, for example, his habit of forgetting to call and his general lack of concern for your feelings. These are the remote causes, the ones further removed from the effect they produce. They are also called *underlying causes* because they are often more difficult to see.

Effects can also be immediate or remote. The immediate effect of failing to get gas is that your car stops running. But the remote effects can stretch out for quite a while: you block traffic and cause an accident; you're late for class and miss an important lecture; you do poorly on the next exam and get a lower grade in the class; your car insurance goes up because of the accident; you have to change majors because you don't have the required grade point average to be admitted into advanced courses. Remote effects are also called *long-term effects*.

Patterns of Cause and Effect

1. If you want to focus on causes, begin by describing a condition or problem or result (such as breaking up with your boyfriend), and then fully

explain the causes or reasons (for the breakup). With this approach, you may be able to use **chronological order** (according to time) if you can trace the causes from the earliest to the most recent. More likely, though, your organization will fall into some **logical order** that reflects the relative importance of the causes: from the least significant to the most critical or from personal reasons to more general ones.

2. If you want to focus on effects, start with some condition or event and explain the consequences. For example, you might begin by describing the breakup with your girlfriend and then go on to show how it affected you. Again, you can present the effects chronologically: at first you were depressed; then you began to spend more time with your friends; you also had more to time to study, so your grades improved; finally, you began to date again and found a much better girlfriend. Or you can arrange the effects according to importance: from a fairly obvious result to the most subtle, from effects on yourself to effects on other people.

3. Since causes and effects are closely related, you might find that tracing a chain or sequence of events, including both causes and effects, is the best way to approach your topic. In a causal chain the first cause produces an effect, which becomes the cause of the next effect, and so on. In the example about running out of gas, there were two chains. First, running out gas caused a blocked intersection, which led to an accident, which resulted (some time later) in higher insurance costs. Also, running out of gas caused you to be late for class and miss an important lecture, which contributed to a lower grade, which affected your grade point average, which prevented you from getting into the advanced program, which caused you to change majors. If you decide to describe a chain of causes and effects, be sure to outline it carefully.

THE PITFALLS OF CAUSE-AND-EFFECT WRITING

An explanation of causes and effects won't be successful if your readers find your thinking fuzzy or flawed. Here are some ways to avoid the most common faults of cause-effect reasoning:

1. Don't mix causes and effects. When talking informally about why things happen, you may shuttle back and forth between causes and their effects. But in writing, you need to follow a clear pattern: focus on causes, focus on effects, or describe an orderly chain of causes and effects.

2. Don't settle for obvious causes and immediate effects. Your explanations will be much more convincing if you look for underlying causes and long-term effects. As Jade Snow Wong shows in her essay in this chapter, her

date with a fellow student provided an opportunity to stand up to her parents, but it was not the cause of her rebellion. The "real" causes ran much deeper. It is, of course, possible to go too far back in searching for causes. You'll need to exercise some judgment in deciding which reasons are still valid and relevant.

3. Don't oversimplify. Most conditions and events are complex, involving multiple causes and numerous effects. In a short essay, you may have to concentrate on the primary reasons, but be sure to let your readers know that's what you are doing.

4. Don't omit any key links in a chain of causes and effects. You don't have to spell out every single step in a sequence of events, but be certain that your readers will be able to follow and make all the right connections themselves.

5. Don't worry about absolute proof. In explaining causes and effects, you can't always prove conclusively why something happened. But offer as much evidence as you can to help the reader see the connections that you see. You always need to support your causes and effects with specific details—examples drawn from personal experience, statistics, and statements by experts. You may want to conduct interviews and collect your own information or visit the library to find material on your topic.

WHAT TO LOOK FOR IN CAUSE-AND-EFFECT WRITING

As you read the selections in this chapter, ask yourself these questions:

1. Does the writer focus on causes or effects, or does the essay consider both? Make a list of the causes and the effects as you read.
2. Look for the point, or purpose, of the author's explanation of causes and effects.
3. Decide what kind of causes or effects the author presents—immediate, remote, or both. Does the writer follow a chain of causal relationships?
4. Does the author have a particular audience in mind? How can you tell?
5. What is the tone of the essay? Does the author sound serious, humorous, angry, irritated, sad, regretful, or something else? How does that tone relate to the author's purpose and audience?
6. Notice what writing strategies the author uses to develop the explanations. Take note of examples, descriptions, narratives, comparisons, definitions, and so on.

PREPARING TO READ

What kind of relationship do you have with your computer or PDA? Do you ever feel that it controls you instead of you controlling it? Give a few examples of times when you have felt this way and describe your responses to the experience.

··

The Boss in the Machine

··

Ellen Ullman

Ellen Ullman not only writes programs for computers but reflects as well on how computers affect the people who create and use them. She is a frequent guest columnist for online magazines such as Salon.com. *In 1997 Ullman published a memoir,* Close to the Machine: Technophilia and Its Discontents, *in which she used autobiography and anecdotes to bring to life her experiences as a commonplace programmer with an uncommon gift for reflection and observation. "The Boss in the Machine" first appeared in the* New York Times *in 2005 as an op-ed commentary.*

TERMS TO RECOGNIZE

icons *(para. 1)*	computer graphic symbols
coding *(para. 1)*	creating computer programming
Interface *(para. 2)*	the place where any two elements of a computer system meet
ogling *(para. 3)*	staring intensely, impertinently
dazzle *(para. 4)*	amazing display
glittering *(para. 4)*	sparkling, showy
fogy *(para.4)*	old-fashioned person
nanosecond *(para. 6)*	one billionth of a second
idles *(para. 7)*	rests, sits unused
throughput *(para. 9)*	the measure of how quickly a certain amount of data is delivered to a computer terminal or system
unfazed *(para. 9)*	unaffected

"There are unused icons on your desktop": this message sometimes appears in a balloon on the lower right-hand corner of my computer screen. I can't imagine why I should be alerted to this fact. The condition of my personal workspace is my own business, as I see it. But no matter what I might be doing at the moment—writing, reading, coding, thinking or (God forbid) simply letting my thoughts trail off where they may—the designers of the Windows XP operating system seem to think I should stop right now and clean up my desk.

That is why I was surprised to read that Microsoft researchers now   2
feel confident that they can figure out when it's all right to interrupt me. According to the project director for something called the Attentional User Interface, the researchers believe they "can detect when users are available for communication, or when the user is in a state of flow."

Nothing could frighten me more. Microsoft is the company whose   3
software once offered an ogling, talking paper clip (called "Clippit") to "help" me with my writing. Its software puts a little cartoon dog on its search dialogue screen, pops up regularly to tell me it's time to download yet another operating-system patch, and feels compelled to inform me—right now—that my desk needs tidying up.

Not that Microsoft is the only culprit; distraction is built into the   4
fabric of today's electronic world. Icons on the PC toolbar flash; ads on Web pages shimmer and dazzle; software companies send e-mail messages to say your software is out of date; word processors interrupt to correct your spelling; Web pages refuse to show themselves until you update a plug-in; lights on laptops blink at you every time the hard drive whirs into motion (which, I'm here to tell you, happens a lot more often than you would ever care to know). The screens of TV cable news programs make three-ring circuses seem calm. You can't even enjoy the 10th rerun of your favorite *Law and Order* episode without a glittering promo fluttering at the corner of the screen. Yet only an old fogy would admit to being overloaded. The ability to "multitask," to switch rapidly among many competing focuses of attention, has become the hallmark of a successful citizen of the 21st century.

It's scary to think that it took less than 50 years for what once was a   5
deep, internal machine concept—multitasking—to work its way outward and change the course of human social life. Introduced in the 1960's, multitasking is an engineering strategy for making computers more efficient. Human beings are the slowest elements in a system.

Between one keystroke and the next, for example, whole seconds   6
might pass, an eternity in the time horizon of chips (which now operate in nanoseconds). So while waiting on the doddering human, the chip switches its attention to some other task, something that can get done in the relatively huge interval between bursts of human input.

Notice that it's supposed to be the chip, not the human, that goes off   7
to do something else while the keyboard idles. But internal engineering principles have a way of becoming external; software designers unconsciously
adopt the values of the machine they're working on. After years of working
in an environment where efficiency is a god and idleness in any component
is intolerable, a programmer comes to think it's logical to keep humans as
busy as possible.

And soon we, the users, give in to the idea that rapidly switching the   8
focus of our attention is not just normal but advisable. So we drive and eat
and talk on the cellphone, check e-mail in the middle of conversations, stop
writing a paragraph to check its spelling, get used to ads that dazzle us
while we try to read Web pages or watch TV. Everything in our machines
encourages us to be like them: busy, attention-hopping.

Multitasking, throughput, efficiency: these are excellent machine con-   9
cepts, useful in the design of computer systems. But are they principles that
nurture human thought and imagination? Not that long ago, we didn't
think so. I am reminded of the scene in the 1976 movie "The Man Who Fell
to Earth" in which David Bowie, playing an alien, sits watching a bank of
television sets, each tuned to a different channel. The screens flash, the
sound blares—the sensory overload is almost unbearable. Yet he watches
unfazed. It is the surest sign that he is not human.

This may come as a shock to some engineering designers, but there   10
really are people in the world who would rather rub two thoughts together
than be efficient. Among such oddballs I would count many Silicon Valley
dreamers and truly creative programmers I have known, the sort of people
whose desks (and sometimes lives) tend to be messy.

I have a suggestion for Microsoft—no fancy programming required.   11
Just let us users hang out a "Do Not Disturb" sign. Then leave us alone.
We're dreaming.

RESPONDING TO READING

Has Ullman changed your view of computers? How might reading this article change your computer habits?

CONSIDERING CONTENT

1. Reread paragraphs 1 and 2, and then explain what Ullman means
   when she says at the start of the next paragraph, "Nothing could
   frighten me more."

2. What is multitasking? When and in what setting did it begin? How has its use changed since then?

3. What have been the effects of multitasking on people's everyday lives? Can you think of examples in your life? When someone claims that they are a good multitasker, what do you think they mean?

4. Explain Ullman's reasons for being concerned about the increasing influence of what she calls "machine concepts" (para. 9). Do you share her views?

5. Explain Ullman's point when she says near the end of the essay, "This may come as a shock to some engineering designers, but there really are people in the world who would rather rub two thoughts together than be efficient" (para. 10).

CONSIDERING METHOD

1. Which pattern of cause and effect writing did Ullman decide to use? What might have been the reasons for her choice?

2. How effectively does Ullman use examples to help prove her points? Begin by looking at paragraphs 4 and 9.

3. Does the fact that Ullman is a computer programmer have an effect on your response to her essay? Explain.

4. How would you describe the author's attitude toward computers and multitasking? Find words and phrases from throughout the essay that convey this attitude. Is this an effective way to approach the topic?

5. Locate places in the essay where Ullman has used either dashes or parentheses to interrupt the flow of her sentence. Explain the effects of these punctuation decisions.

WRITING STEP BY STEP

Write an essay about some form of modern technology (computers, cell phones, satellite television, iPods, the Internet, PDAs, for example) that you see as being a problem because of its negative effects on the people who use it.

A. Begin by brainstorming all the negative effects that you have observed or that you have heard others discuss.

B. Select those effects that seem most important or persuasive, and then brainstorm again to generate examples to illustrate and support your points. If necessary, talk with classmates or friends to find additional examples.

C. Start the essay with a strong example of the problem you wish to explore. Choose something your readers will be familiar with or perhaps provide a personal experience that illustrates your point. In either case, pick something that will allow you to convey the tone of your feelings about the topic.

D. Next provide a clear statement that explains the essential problem.

E. Order your effects according to some system of importance (for example, obvious to subtle, effects on a few people to effects on most people, temporary effects to long-term effects). Discuss each effect in a separate paragraph, and, as Ullman did, provide plenty of examples to illustrate each.

F. Remember to provide any background information that will help your readers better understand your topic and purpose.

G. Use Ullman as a model for concluding with a suggested change.

OTHER WRITING IDEAS

1. WRITING ABOUT READING. Consider how the computer programmers who have built multitasking into current computing practices might respond to Ullman's essay. Create a list of the possible positive effects of the pop-up notices and other "help" tools that she hates, for example. Write an essay based on this view of the topic.

2. USING THE INTERNET. Visit http://archive.salon.com/21st/feature/1997/10/09interview.html to read an interview with Ellen Ullman in which she explores additional topics related to technology and society. Select one of her topics—the use of technology to monitor employees, for example—and write an essay that examines the possible positive and/or negative effects.

3. COLLABORATIVE WRITING. Get together with a small group of classmates to talk about how computers impact the lives of students. Brainstorm a list of all the ways you use computers, and then make a list of the effects these practices have on your success or challenges as students. Write a cause-and-effect essay based on the results of your discussion.

GAINING WORD POWER

Look at this sentence from Ellen Ullman's article:

This may come as a shock *to* some engineering designers, but there really are people in the world who would rather rub *two* thoughts together than be efficient.

Why did Ullman use *to* at the start of the sentence but *two* later in the sentence? Words like *to* and *two*, which are pronounced the same but have different meanings and different spellings, are called **homophones**. There are a lot of these sound-alike words in English, and they cause problems for some writers. You can't just learn how to spell these words; you have to match the spelling with the meaning. And your computer's spell-checker won't help you choose the right one. Keeping a list of the ones that give you trouble will increase your awareness and save you time when you edit.

Each of the following words from Ullman's essay has a common homophone. Identify the homophone, and then write sentences that show the differences in meaning.

1. There (para. 1, 10)
2. I (para. 1, 2, 4, 9, 10, 11)
3. no (para. 1, 11)
4. read (para. 2, 8)
5. for (para. 2, 5, 6, 11)
6. right (para. 1, 2, 3)
7. seem (para. 1, 4)
8. scene (para. 9)
9. principles (para. 10)
10. In paragraph 11 Ullman uses the word *than*, and in paragraph 12 she uses *then*. What's the difference between *than* and *then*? Although they're not pronounced exactly the same, their sounds are similar enough to cause confusion in writing. Compose sentences that show the differences in meaning.

EDITING SKILLS: USING COMMAS

Writers put a comma after a word or group of words that comes in front of the main part of the sentence. That main part is called the **independent clause** because it can stand alone as a sentence. Look at these examples from Ullman's essay (italics added):

> *According to the project director for something called the Attentional User Interface,* the researchers believe they "can detect when users are available for communication, or when the user is in a state of flow."

> *After years of working in an environment where efficiency is a god and idleness in any component is intolerable,* a programmer comes to think it's logical to keep humans as busy as possible.

The italicized groups of words that come before the commas are called **dependent elements**: they cannot stand alone as sentences and are not really necessary to the meaning of the sentences.

Writers also put commas before and after dependent elements when they come in the middle of an independent sentence. Here are some examples from Ullman's essay (italics added):

The ability to "multitask," *to switch rapidly among many competing focuses of attention,* has become the hallmark of a successful citizen of the 21st century.

And soon we, *the users,* give in to the idea that rapidly switching the focus of our attention is not just normal but advisable.

These dependent elements are called **interrupters**: they break up the flow of the sentence and are not really necessary to the meaning of the sentence.

EXERCISE

In Ullman's essay, find another example of words or groups of words that are separated from the independent clause by commas. Then find an example of an interrupter set off by commas.

Now copy the following sentences, putting in commas where needed:

1. The rabbit nevertheless does shed fur.
2. Like most people Ralph does not know the name of his congressional representative.
3. Speaking of travel would you like to go to Seattle next week?
4. Jazz some people believe is America's greatest contribution to the arts.
5. The result as we have seen is not a pretty one.
6. The patient said the nurse is acting strangely.

Finally, check the essay you have just written to be sure you have used commas to separate dependent elements from the rest of the sentence.

WEB SITE

www.time.com/time/magazine/article/0,9171,1174696,00.html
Visit this *Time* magazine Web site to read about an anthropologist's study of modern families and multitasking. Does the article reinforce or challenge Ullman's views?

PREPARING TO READ

Do you enjoy horror movies? Why do you like to watch them? How do you react when you view them? If you don't enjoy horror movies, can you explain why they do not appeal to you?

Why We Crave Horror Movies

STEPHEN KING

You know Stephen King as the master of terror, the author of a string of best-selling horror novels. And you have probably seen some of the movies made from his novels: Carrie, Misery, Christine, Pet Sematary, *and* Firestarter *(among others). In the following essay, King offers an entertaining explanation of why people like being scared out of their wits.*

TERMS TO RECOGNIZE

grimaces *(para. 1)*	twisted facial expressions
hysterical *(para. 1)*	emotionally uncontrolled
province *(para. 3)*	proper area or sphere
depleted *(para. 3)*	used up, drained, worn out
innately *(para. 4)*	naturally, essentially
reactionary *(para. 4)*	wanting to return to an earlier time
menaced *(para. 6)*	threatened, endangered
voyeur *(para. 6)*	a peeping Tom, someone who enjoys watching something private or forbidden
penchant *(para. 7)*	a strong fondness or inclination
psychic *(para. 7)*	mental, psychological
status quo *(para. 9)*	existing condition or state of affairs
sanctions *(para. 10)*	expressions of disapproval, punishments
anarchistic *(para. 11)*	disorderly, ignoring the rules
morbidity *(para. 12)*	an interest in gruesome and horrible things
subterranean *(para. 12)*	underground

I think we're all mentally ill; those of us outside the asylums only hide 1
it a little better—and maybe not all that much better, after all. We've all known people who talk to themselves, people who sometimes squinch their faces into horrible grimaces when they believe no one is watching, people

who have some hysterical fear—of snakes, the dark, the tight place, the long drop . . . and, of course, those final worms and grubs that are waiting so patiently underground.

When we pay our four or five bucks and seat ourselves at tenth-row center in a theater showing a horror movie, we are daring the nightmare.   2

Why? Some of the reasons are simple and obvious. To show that we can, that we are not afraid, that we can ride this roller coaster. Which is not to say that a really good horror movie may not surprise a scream out of us at some point, the way we may scream when the roller coaster twists through a complete 360 or plows through a lake at the bottom of the drop. And horror movies, like roller coasters, have always been the special province of the young; by the time one turns 40 or 50, one's appetite for double twists or 360-degree loops may be considerably depleted.   3

We also go to re-establish our feelings of essential normality; the horror movie is innately conservative, even reactionary. Freda Jackson as the horrible melting woman in *Die, Monster, Die!* confirms for us that no matter how far we may be removed from the beauty of a Robert Redford or a Diana Ross, we are still light-years from true ugliness.   4

And we go to have fun.   5

Ah, but this is where the ground starts to slope away, isn't it? Because this is a very peculiar sort of fun, indeed. The fun comes from seeing others menaced—sometimes killed. One critic has suggested that if pro football has become the voyeur's version of combat, then the horror film has become the modern version of the public lynching.   6

It is true that the mythic, "fairy-tale" horror film intends to take away the shades of gray. . . . It urges us to put away our more civilized and adult penchant for analysis and to become children again, seeing things in pure blacks and whites. It may be that horror movies provide psychic relief on this level because this invitation to lapse into simplicity, irrationality and even outright madness is extended so rarely. We are told we may allow our emotions a free rein . . . or no rein at all.   7

If we are all insane, then sanity becomes a matter of degree. If your insanity leads you to carve up women like Jack the Ripper or the Cleveland Torso Murderer, we clap you away in the funny farm (but neither of those two amateur-night surgeons was ever caught, heh-heh-heh); if, on the other hand, your insanity leads you only to talk to yourself when you're under stress or to pick your nose on your morning bus, then you are left alone to go about your business . . . though it is doubtful that you will ever be invited to the best parties.   8

The potential lyncher is in almost all of us (excluding saints, past and present; but then, most saints have been crazy in their own ways), and every   9 now and then, he has to be let loose to scream and roll around in the grass. Our emotions and our fears form their own body, and we recognize that it demands its own exercise to maintain proper muscle tone. Certain of these emotional muscles are accepted—even exalted—in civilized society; they are, of course, the emotions that tend to maintain the status quo of civilization itself. Love, friendship, loyalty, kindness—these are all the emotions that we applaud, emotions that have been immortalized in the couplets of Hallmark cards and in the verses (I don't dare call it poetry) of Leonard Nimoy.

When we exhibit these emotions, society showers us with positive   10
reinforcement; we learn this even before we get out of diapers. When, as children, we hug our rotten little puke of a sister and give her a kiss, all the aunts and uncles smile and twit and cry, "Isn't he the sweetest little thing?" Such coveted treats as chocolate-covered graham crackers often follow. But if we deliberately slam the rotten little puke of a sister's fingers in the door, sanctions follow—angry remonstrance from parents, aunts and uncles; instead of a chocolate-covered graham cracker, a spanking.

But anticivilization emotions don't go away, and they demand peri-   11
odic exercise. We have such "sick" jokes as, "What's the difference between a truckload of bowling balls and a truckload of dead babies?" (You can't unload a truckload of bowling balls with a pitchfork . . . a joke, by the way, that I heard originally from a ten-year-old.) Such a joke may surprise a laugh or a grin out of us even as we recoil, a possibility that confirms the thesis: If we share a brotherhood of man, then we also share an insanity of man. None of which is intended as a defense of either the sick joke or insanity but merely as an explanation of why the best horror films, like the best fairy tales, manage to be reactionary, anarchistic, and revolutionary all at the same time.

The mythic horror movie, like the sick joke, has a dirty job to do. It   12
deliberately appeals to all that is worst in us. It is morbidity unchained, our most base instincts let free, our nastiest fantasies realized . . . and it all happens, fittingly enough, in the dark. For those reasons, good liberals often shy away from horror films. For myself, I like to see the most aggressive of them—*Dawn of the Dead*, for instance—as lifting a trap door in the civilized forebrain and throwing a basket of raw meat to the hungry alligators swimming around in that subterranean river beneath.

Why bother? Because it keeps them from getting out, man. It keeps   13
them down there and me up here. It was Lennon and McCartney who said that all you need is love, and I would agree with that.

As long as you keep the gators fed.   14

RESPONDING TO READING

Do you agree with King that we are all mentally ill and that our "anticivilization emotions don't go away"? Respond to these ideas in your journal.

CONSIDERING CONTENT

1. What does King mean when he says that we are all mentally ill? What is the nature of the "insanity" that we share?
2. What are the obvious reasons for enjoying horror movies? What are some of the not-so-obvious reasons?
3. King refers to our "anticivilization emotions" that occasionally need exercise. What are these emotions? Why do they need to be exercised?
4. Do you think Stephen King is biased in his defense of horror movies? Do you think you would respond differently to this essay if it were written by someone you had never heard of?

CONSIDERING METHOD

1. King begins with a startling statement about insanity. What is the effect and point of this opening?
2. How does he maintain the insanity theme throughout the essay? Do you think this is an effective strategy?
3. At what point in the essay does King reveal that he will be dealing with causes?
4. Does King deal with immediate causes or long-term causes or both? In what order does he arrange the causes he discusses?
5. Identify comments or passages that you think are humorous. What does the humor contribute to this essay?
6. What is the function of the two one-sentence paragraphs (paras. 5 and 14)?

Combining Strategies

King uses several *comparisons* to explain and support his defense of horror movies. What points does King make by comparing horror movies to the following?

a. riding a roller coaster
b. public lynching
c. mythic fairy tales
d. sick jokes.

Do you think these are good comparisons?

WRITING STEP BY STEP

Think of another form of entertainment that people seem to crave, and write an essay explaining why. You might write about soap operas, MTV, video games, action movies, reality TV, sports programs, jogging (or other exercise activities), bodybuilding, shopping, online chat rooms, or the like.

A. Begin with a startling statement, as Stephen King does.

B. Give background about the subject by explaining your opening statement.

C. Discuss the obvious or immediate causes first. Identify at least three reasons and explain them.

D. Then examine the long-term or underlying causes. Show how these causes produce the craving that you are writing about.

E. Be sure to name specific programs or games.

F. Use figurative language and analogies to help explain the causes. Even include a little humor the way King does, if you want to.

G. Write a conclusion in which you comment on the behavior you have analyzed. Make your comment an outgrowth of your discussion of underlying causes.

OTHER WRITING IDEAS

1. Write an essay about the effects of watching too much TV. Use your own observations and experiences to support your conclusions.

2. COLLABORATIVE WRITING. Working with a group of classmates, interview a variety of people to find out why they like a certain type of entertainment (TV hospital shows, arcade games, stock car races, line dancing, rock concerts, ballet, situation comedies, or the like). Ask them to give you specific reasons. Then write a group report explaining why this form of entertainment is popular. Use several direct quotations from the interviews to support your explanations.

3. USING THE INTERNET. Find out what researchers say about the effects of television violence on children. Be sure to locate sites that offer more than one point of view. Then write an essay for parents, informing them of these effects and suggesting what they can do to counter them.

4. WRITING ABOUT READING. Check out King's ideas about the cravings for horror movies by watching one and analyzing your reactions to it. Did the movie "re-establish [your] feelings of essential normality"? In what ways did it provide "psychic relief" or satisfy your "anti-civilization emotions"? How did you feel before watching the movie? How did you feel afterwards?

GAINING WORD POWER

What does it mean to do "a complete 360"? (King uses the expression in para. 3.) You may know that 360 refers to the number of degrees in a circle and that the phrase means to go all the way around to where you started, to travel in a complete circle. One way of expressing the opposite idea is to say you did "an about-face," which is a military command for pivoting around to face in the opposite direction.

Both of these phrases—"a complete 360" and "an about-face"—are figurative expressions; they're supposed to put a picture in our minds by referring to an object (like a circle) or an action (like a military maneuver). Figurative language requires interpretation; we have to figure out the references and imagine the picture that the writer wants to put in our minds. Here are some more figurative phrases that Stephen King uses in his essay. Explain what they mean and tell what you see in your mind's eye. If you're not sure of what King means, ask other people for their interpretations.

1. "those final worms and grubs that are waiting so patiently underground"
2. "tenth-row center"
3. "shades of gray"
4. "clap you away in the funny farm"
5. "the couplets of Hallmark cards"
6. "before we get out of diapers"
7. "lifting a trap door in the civilized forebrain and throwing a basket of raw meat to the hungry alligators swimming around in that subterranean river beneath"

EDITING SKILLS: CHECKING PRONOUN REFERENCE

Whenever you use pronouns (words such as *he, she, it, his, her, their*, etc., that stand in for nouns), you must be sure that each has a clear antecedent (the noun that the pronoun stands for). If the antecedents aren't clear, your readers can get lost. Look at this sentence from Stephen King's essay:

> We've all known people *who* talk to *themselves*, people *who* sometimes squinch *their* faces into horrible grimaces when *they* believe no one is watching. . . .

The pronouns *themselves, who, their,* and *they* all clearly refer to the antecedent *people*.

Several pronouns are especially troublesome when they appear without specific antecedents: *this*, *which*, and *these*. King uses these words eleven times. Sometimes he places them right before the nouns they refer to—"this roller coaster," "this level," "this invitation," "these emotions"—so there is no misunderstanding about what they mean. But in other instances, he uses *this*, *these*, and *which* as free-standing pronouns. Find these other uses (in paras. 3, 6, 9, 10, and 11), and see if you can name the thing or idea to which these pronouns refer. Do you think King has used these pronouns clearly?

EXERCISE

The following sentences are vague because they contain pronouns without clear antecedents. Rewrite each sentence to make it clear.

Example: Clyde made Gary do his homework.

Revisions: Gary did his homework because Clyde made him. Gary did Clyde's homework because Clyde made him.

1. Hampton aced the history test because he made it so easy.
2. Carlo is working on the railroad in Tennessee, which depresses him.
3. Kesha dropped out of school after they took away fall break.
4. Our cat chased the ground squirrel until he got tired.
5. Although Juan's mother is a chemist, Juan hates it.
6. Rosa tried to support herself by painting and acting. This was a mistake.
7. Mel blamed his failure on his choice of occupation, which was unfortunate.
8. Washington wore a sombrero and sequined gloves to the prom. This was a big hit.

Now look at the essay you have just written. Pay particular attention to your use of pronouns. Make sure each has a clear antecedent.

⚓ WEB SITE

www.stephenking.com/

Find out more about Stephen King's views on horror stories and other aspects of writing at the official online resource for news and information about King and his works.

PREPARING TO READ

Did your parents ever forbid you to do something that you went ahead and did anyway? What happened? How did you feel about it later?

●●

Fifth Chinese Daughter

●●

JADE SNOW WONG

Jade Snow Wong grew up in San Francisco, the daughter of immigrant parents who brought with them from China an ancient and rigid set of family traditions. The following excerpt from Wong's autobiography, Fifth Chinese Daughter, *recounts the inevitable conflict between traditional parents and a young woman who is beginning to discover a different world beyond her home and neighborhood.*

TERMS TO RECOGNIZE

oblige *(para. 2)*	accommodate, please
adamant *(para. 3)*	unyielding, inflexible
edict *(para. 3)*	command, rule
incurred *(para. 4)*	acquired, taken on
nepotism *(para. 7)*	favoritism shown to relatives
incredulous *(para. 12)*	unwilling to admit or accept what is heard; unbelieving
unfilial *(para. 12)*	disrespectful to parents
revered *(para. 12)*	honored, respected
innuendos *(para. 14)*	sly suggestions, indirect hints
devastated *(para. 15)*	crushed, overwhelmed
perplexed *(para. 16)*	puzzled, confused

By the time I was graduating from high school, my parents had done   1
their best to produce an intelligent, obedient daughter, who would know more than the average Chinatown girl and should do better than average at a conventional job, her earnings brought home in repayment for their years of child support. Then, they hoped, she would marry a nice Chinese boy and make him a good wife, as well as an above-average mother for his children. Chinese custom used to decree that families should "introduce" chosen partners to each other's children. The groom's family should pay handsomely to the bride's family for rearing a well-bred daughter. They should also pay all

bills for a glorious wedding banquet for several hundred guests. Their daughter belonged to the groom's family and must henceforth seek permission from all persons in his home before returning to her parents for a visit.

But having been set upon a new path, I did not oblige my parents   2
with the expected conventional ending. At fifteen, I had moved away from home to work for room and board and a salary of twenty dollars per month. Having found that I could subsist independently, I thought it regrettable to terminate my education. Upon graduating from high school at the age of sixteen, I asked my parents to assist me in college expenses. I pleaded with my father, for his years of encouraging me to be above mediocrity in both Chinese and American studies had made me wish for some undefined but brighter future.

My father was briefly adamant. He must conserve his resources for   3
my oldest brother's medical training. Though I desired to continue on an above-average course, his material means were insufficient to support that ambition. He added that if I had the talent, I could provide for my own college education. When he had spoken, no discussion was expected. After this edict, no daughter questioned.

But this matter involved my whole future—it was not simply asking for   4
permission to go to a night church meeting (forbidden also). Though for years I had accepted the authority of the one I honored most, his decision that night embittered me as nothing ever had. My oldest brother had so many privileges, had incurred unusual expenses for luxuries which were taken for granted as his birthright, yet these were part of a system I had accepted. Now I suddenly wondered at my father's interpretation of the Christian code: was it intended to discriminate against a girl after all, or was it simply convenient for my father's economics and cultural prejudice? Did a daughter have any right to expect more than a fate of obedience, according to the old Chinese standard? As long as I could remember, I had been told that a female followed three men during her lifetime: as a girl, her father; as a wife, her husband; as an old woman, her son.

My indignation mounted against that tradition and I decided then   5
that my past could not determine my future. I knew that more education would prepare me for a different expectation than my other female schoolmates, few of whom were to complete a college degree. I, too, had my father's unshakable faith in the justice of God, and I shared his unconcern with popular opinion.

So I decided to enter junior college, now San Francisco's City College,   6
because the fees were lowest. I lived at home and supported myself with an after-school job which required long hours of housework and cooking but

paid me twenty dollars per month, of which I saved as much as possible. The thrills derived from reading and learning, in ways ranging from chemistry experiments to English compositions, from considering new ideas of sociology to the logic of Latin, convinced me that I had made a correct choice. I was kept in a state of perpetual mental excitement by new Western subjects and concepts and did not mind long hours of work and study. I also made new friends, which led to another painful incident with my parents, who had heretofore discouraged even girlhood friendships.

The college subject which had the most jolted me was sociology. The   7
instructor fired my mind with his interpretation of family relationships. As he explained to our class, it used to be an economic asset for American farming families to be large, since children were useful to perform agricultural chores. But this situation no longer applied and children should be regarded as individuals with their own rights. Unquestioning obedience should be replaced with parental understanding. So at sixteen, discontented as I was with my parents' apparent indifference to me, those words of my sociology professor gave voice to my sentiments. How old-fashioned was the dead-end attitude of my parents! How ignorant they were of modern thought and progress! The family unit had been China's strength for centuries, but it had also been her weakness, for corruption, nepotism, and greed were all justified in the name of the family's welfare. My new ideas festered; I longed to release them.

One afternoon on a Saturday, which was normally occupied with my   8
housework job, I was unexpectedly released by my employer, who was departing for a country weekend. It was a rare joy to have free time and I wanted to enjoy myself for a change. There had been a Chinese-American boy who shared some classes with me. Sometimes we had found each other walking to the same 8:00 A.M. class. He was not a special boyfriend, but I had enjoyed talking to him and had confided in him some of my problems. Impulsively, I telephoned him. I knew I must be breaking rules, and I felt shy and scared. At the same time, I was excited at this newly found forwardness, with nothing more purposeful than to suggest another walk together.

He understood my awkwardness and shared my anticipation. He asked   9
me to "dress up" for my first movie date. My clothes were limited but I changed to look more graceful in silk stockings and found a bright ribbon for my long black hair. Daddy watched, catching my mood, observing the dashing preparations. He asked me where I was going without his permission and with whom.

I refused to answer him. I thought of my rights! I thought he surely   10
would not try to understand. Thereupon Daddy thundered his displeasure and forbade my departure.

I found a new courage as I heard my voice announce calmly that I   11
was no longer a child, and if I could work my way through college, I would
choose my own friends. It was my right as a person.

My mother had heard the commotion and joined my father to face me;   12
both appeared shocked and incredulous. Daddy at once demanded the
source of this unfilial, non-Chinese theory. And when I quoted my college professor, reminding him that he had always felt teachers should be revered, my
father denounced that professor as a foreigner who was disregarding the
superiority of our Chinese culture, with its sound family strength. My father
did not spare me; I was condemned as an ingrate for echoing dishonorable
opinions which should only be temporary whims, yet nonetheless inexcusable.

The scene was not yet over. I completed my proclamation to my   13
father, who had never allowed me to learn how to dance, by adding that I
was attending a movie, unchaperoned, with a boy I met at college.

My startled father was sure that my reputation would be subject to   14
whispered innuendos. I must be bent on disgracing the family name; I was
ruining my future, for surely I would yield to temptation. My mother under-
scored him by saying that I hadn't any notion of the problems endured by
parents of a young girl.

I would not give in. I reminded them that they and I were not in   15
China, that I wasn't going out with just anybody but someone I trusted!
Daddy gave a roar that no man could be trusted, but I devastated them in
declaring that I wished the freedom to find my own answers.

Both parents were thoroughly angered, scolded me for being shame-   16
less, and predicted that I would some day tell them I was wrong. But I dimly
perceived that they were conceding defeat and were perplexed at this breakdown of their training. I was too old to beat and too bold to intimidate.

RESPONDING TO READING

Has college affected you in the same way that it affected Jade Snow Wong?
Write in your journal about the effects college has had on you; compare your
reactions to Wong's.

CONSIDERING CONTENT

1. What did you learn about Wong's parents and their traditional beliefs
   in the first paragraph?
2. What caused Wong to rebel against her parents? What situations and
   experiences contributed to her quest for independence?

3. Why was Wong sure that more education would prepare her for a different future from her classmates? Did it?

4. Why did the sociology course affect Wong so strongly? What did she learn in that course that changed her views and fed her rebellion?

5. What action did Wong take to demonstrate her independence? Why did she choose this particular way of disobeying her parents? Do her actions seem risky and rebellious to you?

6. In what ways was Wong a lot like her father? Which of his beliefs and attitudes actually contributed to his daughter's rebellion?

CONSIDERING METHOD

1. Why is the first paragraph important? How does the information in this paragraph prepare you for Wong's actions?

2. What does Wong accomplish by mentioning her oldest brother? What is she trying to show?

3. What is the function of the questions in paragraph 4? Why does Wong express these ideas in questions instead of in statements? (See page 326 for an explanation of rhetorical questions.)

4. How much time passes in this selection? How does Wong indicate the passage of time? Where does she move back in time? Why does she do so?

5. Paragraph 8 opens with these words: "One afternoon on a Saturday . . ." What do these words signal? What mode of writing begins at this point?

6. Wong doesn't use direct quotations or quoted conversation. How does she report what she said to her parents and what they said to her? What is the effect of this indirect presentation?

7. How would you describe the tone of this selection? Does Wong sound angry, sad, upset, calm, confident, relieved, happy, or what?

WRITING STEP BY STEP

As we grow older, we sometimes change our minds about our parents. We begin to see things more from their point of view. Think of a piece of advice, a household rule, or a parental opinion that you used to hate but now understand. If you don't want to write about your parents, think of another adult, such as a teacher or a coach, who set down rules or gave advice that you once rejected but now think appropriate. Write an essay in which you explain what caused you to change your mind.

A. Begin with a statement of your general point. You might say something like "I used to think my parents' advice was outdated and pointless, but a lot of it makes sense to me today" or "Now that I'm coaching pee-wee soccer, I follow some of the same rules I used to hate when I was a player."

B. Explain the particular rule, opinion, advice, or guideline you used to resist. Re-create specific incidents and arguments you used to have that illustrate your earlier response.

C. Analyze your change in attitude. Cite specific reasons or causes, and explain them.

D. If there was a key incident or turning point in your thinking, focus on that event and describe it in detail.

E. Conclude by revealing how you feel about this change in thinking. Does it mean that you've grown up or that you've sold out?

OTHER WRITING IDEAS

1. Write an essay about why adolescents leave home. Or write an essay about the effects of their leaving home.

2. COLLABORATIVE WRITING. Explain why some jobs or professions seem to be done mainly by women (like child care, housework, nursing, elementary school teaching). As you plan your paper, talk to some women who do these jobs or who are preparing to enter one of these professions, and ask their opinions. Also talk to some men, and ask them how they would feel about teaching grade school, being a nurse, cleaning houses, or taking care of children for a living.

3. USING THE INTERNET. Talk to someone who comes from a cultural background different from yours. If you can, spend some time with this person's friends and family. Also locate Internet sites that will give you information about this cultural group. Then, with your classmates as audience, write an essay explaining what you learned about this culture and how it affected your attitudes toward these people.

4. WRITING ABOUT READING. In the last paragraph, Wong writes that she "dimly perceived" that her parents "were conceding defeat and were perplexed at this breakdown of their training" (para. 16). What were they conceding and why were they perplexed? Write an essay that answers these questions. Include personal experiences that might help to explain or support your conclusions.

GAINING WORD POWER

Come up with definitions of your own for the italicized words in the following sentences. Use the clues from the surrounding words and sentences to help you. Then check your definition against a dictionary definition.

1. "Chinese custom used to *decree* that families should 'introduce' chosen partners to each other's children." (para. 1)
2. "Having found that I could *subsist* independently, I thought it regrettable to *terminate* my education." (para. 2)
3. "I pleaded with my father, for his years of encouraging me to be above *mediocrity* in both Chinese and American studies had made me wish for some undefined but brighter future." (para. 2)
4. "My *indignation* mounted against that tradition and I decided then that my past could not determine my future." (para. 5)
5. "I was kept in a state of *perpetual* mental excitement by new Western subjects and concepts and did not mind long hours of work and study." (para. 6)
6. "My new ideas *festered*; I longed to release them." (para. 7)
7. "He was not a special boyfriend, but I had enjoyed talking to him and had *confided* in him some of my problems. *Impulsively*, I telephoned him. I knew I must be breaking rules, and I felt shy and scared." (para. 8)
8. "I was too old to beat and too bold to *intimidate*." (para. 16)

EDITING SKILLS: USING PARALLEL STRUCTURE

Look at these last two sentences from paragraph 3 in Wong's essay:

When he had spoken, no discussion was expected.

After his edict, no daughter questioned.

When you look at the sentences in this format, with one on top of the other, you can see how they match up in size and form. This correspondence is called **parallelism**, or parallel structure. Parallel structure often occurs within a sentence, as the following sentences from Wong's essay show. (The parallel parts are italicized for you.)

As long as I could remember, I had been told that a female followed three men during her lifetime: *as a girl, her father; as a wife, her husband; as an old woman, her son.*

I was *too old to beat* and *too bold to intimidate.*

Writers use parallel structure to catch the reader's attention and, as Wong does, to compare or contrast important points. Parallel structures also add emphasis and variety to a sentence or paragraph.

EXERCISE

Copy two of the sentences previously quoted; write two or three sentences of your own that imitate Wong's use of parallel structure. Then examine the following sentences, and write your own sentences that imitate the parallel structures.

1. "This freedom, like all freedoms, has its dangers and its responsibilities."
   —James Baldwin

   Imitation: This new attendance policy, like all school policies, has its supporters and its critics.

2. "We must stop talking about the American dream and start listening to the dreams of Americans."
   —Reubin Askew

   Imitation: We must stop asking silly questions and start questioning silly policies.

Look over your own essay and revise two or three sentences, using parallel structure. Read the new sentences aloud. If they sound clear and effective, keep them in your essay.

🌐 WEB SITE

http://sun3.lib.uci.edu/~dtsang/aas2.htm
This is the Web site for Asian American Studies Resources: an extensive collection of sites for studying Asian cultures, complied by Daniel Tsang, the Asian American Studies Bibliographer for the library at the University of California at Irvine.

PREPARING TO READ

Do you eat fast food? How much and how often? Do you think it's healthy?

● ●

Supersize Me

● ●

GREG CRITSER

Educated at Occidental College and UCLA, Greg Critser lives in Pasadena, California. He is a regular contributor to USA Today, *the* Los Angeles Times, *and* Harper's Magazine. *In 1999, his articles on obesity won a James Beard nomination for best feature writing, and he is frequently interviewed by PBS and other news media on the subject of food politics. The following selection comes from the second chapter of his book* Fat Land: How Americans Became the Fattest People in the World *(2003).*

TERMS TO RECOGNIZE

contentious *(para. 4)*	quarrelsome, heated
truculent *(para. 9)*	fierce, hostile, aggressively self-assertive
entrepreneurism *(para. 10)*	the practice of taking business risks
primal *(para. 10)*	primary, first in importance
maligned *(para. 14)*	criticized, attacked, smeared
table d'hôte *(para. 15)*	a complete meal offered at a fixed price
à la carte *(para. 15)*	a menu or list that prices each item separately
immutable *(para. 21)*	unchangeable, permanent
maw *(para. 23)*	the mouth or jaws of a hungry animal

David Wallerstein, a director of the McDonald's Corporation, hated   1
the fifth deadly sin because it kept people from buying more hamburgers. Wallerstein had first waged war on the injunction against gluttony as a young executive in the theater business. At the staid Balaban Theaters chain in the early 1960s, Wallerstein had realized that the movie business was really a margin business; it wasn't the sale of low-markup movie tickets that generated profits but rather the sale of high-markup snacks like popcorn and Coke. To sell more of such items, he had, by the mid-1960s, tried about every trick in the conventional retailer's book: two-for-one specials, combo deals, matinee specials, etc. But at the end of any given day, as he tallied up his receipts, Wallerstein inevitably came up with about the same amount of profit.

Thinking about it one night, he had a realization: People did not   2
want to buy two boxes of popcorn *no matter what*. They didn't want to be
seen eating two boxes of popcorn. It looked piggish. So Wallerstein flipped
the equation around: Perhaps he could get more people to spend just a little more on popcorn if he made the boxes bigger and increased the price
only a little. The popcorn cost a pittance anyway, and he'd already paid for
the salt and the seasoning and the counter help and the popping machine.
So he put up signs advertising jumbo-size popcorn. The results after the first
week were astounding. Not only were individual sales of popcorn increasing;
with them rose individual sales of that other high-profit item, Coca-Cola.

Later, at McDonald's in the mid-1970s, Wallerstein faced a similar   3
problem: With consumers watching their pennies, restaurant customers were
coming to the Golden Arches less and less frequently. Worse, when they did,
they were "cherry-picking," buying only, say, a small Coke and a burger, or,
worse, just a burger, which yielded razor-thin profit margins. How could he
get people back to buying more fries? His popcorn experience certainly suggested one solution—sell them a jumbo-size bag of the crispy treats.

Yet try as he may, Wallerstein could not convince Ray Kroc, McDon-   4
ald's founder, to sign on to the idea. As recounted in interviews with his
associates and in John F. Love's 1985 book, *McDonald's: Behind the Arches*,
the exchange between the two men could be quite contentious on the issue.
"If people want more fries," Kroc would say, "they can buy two bags."

"But Ray," Wallerstein would say, "they don't want to eat two bags—   5
they don't want to look like a glutton."

To convince Kroc, Wallerstein decided to do his own survey of cus-   6
tomer behavior, and began observing various Chicago-area McDonald's.
Sitting in one store after another, sipping his drink and watching hundreds
of Chicagoans chomp their way through their little bag of fries, Wallerstein
could see: People *wanted* more fries.

"How do you know that?" Kroc asked the next morning when Waller-   7
stein presented his findings.

"Because they're eating the entire bagful, Ray," Wallerstein said.   8
"They even scrape and pinch around at the bottom of the bag for more and
eat the salt!"

Kroc gave in. Within months receipts were up, customer counts were   9
up, and franchisees—the often truculent heart and soul of the McDonald's
success—were happier than ever.

Many franchisees wanted to take the concept even further, offering   10
large-size versions of other menu items. At this sudden burst of entrepre-
neurism, however, McDonald's mid-level managers hesitated. Many of them

viewed large-sizing as a form of "discounting," with all the negative connotations such a word evoked. In a business where "wholesome" and "dependable" were the primary PR watchwords, large-sizing could become a major image problem. Who knew what the franchisees, with their primal desires and shortcutting ways, would do next? No, large-sizing was something to be controlled tightly from Chicago, if it were to be considered at all.

Yet as McDonald's headquarters would soon find out, large-sizing   11
was a new kind of marketing magic—a magic that could not so easily be put back into those crinkly little-size bags.

Max Cooper, a Birmingham franchisee, was not unfamiliar with market-   12
ing and magic; for most of his adult life he had been paid to conjure sales from little more than hot air and smoke. Brash, blunt-spoken, and witty, Cooper had acquired his talents while working as an old-fashioned public relations agent—the kind, as he liked to say, who "got you into the newspaper columns instead of trying to keep you out." In the 1950s with his partner, Al Golin, he had formed what later became Golin Harris, one of the world's more influential public relations firms. In the mid-1960s, first as a consultant and later as an executive, he had helped create many of McDonald's most successful early campaigns. He had been the prime mover in the launch of Ronald McDonald.

By the 1970s Cooper, tired of "selling for someone else," bought a cou-   13
ple of McDonald's franchises in Birmingham, moved his split-off ad agency there, and set up shop as an independent businessman. As he began expanding, he noticed what many other McDonald's operators were noticing: declining customer counts. Sitting around a table and kibitzing with a few like-minded associates one day in 1975, "we started talking about how we could build sales—how we could do it and be profitable," Cooper recalled in a recent interview. "And we realized we could do one of three things. We could cut costs, but there's a limit to that. We could cut prices, but that too has its limits. Then we could raise sales profitably—sales, after all, could be limitless when you think about it. We realized we could do that by taking the high-profit drink and fry and then packaging it with the low-profit burger. We realized that if you could get them to buy three items for what they perceived as less, you could substantially drive up the number of walk-ins. Sales would follow."

But trying to sell that to corporate headquarters was next to impossi-   14
ble. "We were maligned! Oh, were we maligned," he recalls. "A 99-cent any-thing was heresy to them. They would come and say 'You're just cutting prices! What are we gonna look like to everybody else?' "

"No no no," Cooper would shoot back. "You have to think of the   15
analogy to a fine French restaurant. You always pay less for a *table d'hôte* meal than you pay for *à la carte*, don't you?"

"Yes, but —"   16

"Well, this is a *table d'hôte,* dammit! You're getting more people to the   17
table spending as much as they would before—and coming more often!"

Finally headquarters relented, although by now it hardly mattered.   18
Cooper had by then begun his own rogue campaign. He was selling what
the industry would later call "value meals"—the origin of what we now call
supersizing. Using local radio, he advertised a "Big Mac and Company," a
"Fish, Fry, Drink and Pie," a "4th of July Value Combo." Sales, Cooper says,
"went through the roof. Just like I told them they would."

Though it is difficult to gauge the exact impact of supersizing upon   19
the appetite of the average consumer, there are clues about it in the now
growing field of satiety—the science of understanding human satisfaction. A
2001 study by nutritional researchers at Penn State University, for example,
sought to find out whether the presence of larger portions *in themselves*
induced people to eat more. Men and women volunteers, all reporting the
same level of hunger, were served lunch on four separate occasions. In each
session, the size of the main entree was increased, from 500 to 625 to 700
and finally to 1000 grams. After four weeks, the pattern became clear: As
portions increased, all participants ate increasingly larger amounts, despite
their stable hunger levels. As the scholars wrote: "Subjects consumed
approximately 30 percent more energy when served the largest as opposed
to the smallest portion." They had documented that satiety is not satiety.
Human hunger could be expanded by merely offering more and bigger
options.

Certainly the best nutritional data suggest so as well. Between 1970   20
and 1994, the USDA reports, the amount of food available in the American
food supply increased 15 percent—from 3300 to 3800 calories or by about
500 calories per person per day. During about the same period (1977–
1995), average individual caloric intake increased by almost 200 calories,
from 1876 calories a day to 2043 calories a day. One could argue which
came first, the appetite or the bigger burger, but the calories—they were on
the plate and in our mouths.

By the end of the century, supersizing—the ultimate expression of the   21
value meal revolution—reigned. As of 1996, some 25 percent of the $97 billion
spent on fast food came from items promoted on the basis of either larger size
or extra portions. A serving of McDonald's french fries had ballooned from
200 calories (1960) to 320 calories (late 1970s) to 450 calories (mid-1990s)
to 540 calories (late 1990s) to the present 610 calories. In fact, everything on
the menu had exploded in size. What was once a 590-calorie McDonald's

meal was now . . . 1550 calories. By 1999, heavy users—people who eat fast food more than twenty times a month—accounted for $66 billion of the $110 billion spent on fast food. Twenty times a month is now McDonald's marketing goal for every fast-food eater. The average Joe or Jane thought nothing of buying Little Caesar's pizza "by the foot," of supersizing that lunchtime burger or supersupersizing an afternoon snack. Kids had come to see bigger everything—bigger sodas, bigger snacks, bigger candy, and even bigger doughnuts—as the norm; there was no such thing as a fixed, immutable size for anything, because anything could be made a lot bigger for just a tad more.

There was more to all of this than just eating more. Bigness: The con- 22 cept seemed to fuel the marketing of just about everything, from cars (SUVs) to homes (mini-manses) to clothes (super-baggy) and then back again to food (as in the Del Taco Macho Meal, which weighed four pounds). The social scientists and the marketing gurus were going crazy trying to keep up with the trend. "Bigness is addictive because it is about power," commented Inna Zall, a teen marketing consultant, in a page-one story in *USA Today*. While few teenage boys can actually finish a 64-ounce Double Gulp, she added, "it's empowering to hold one in your hand."

The pioneers of supersize had achieved David Wallerstein's dream. 23 They had banished the shame of gluttony and opened the maw of the American eater wider than even they had ever imagined.

RESPONDING TO READING

After reading this selection, do you think you'll try to change your eating habits? Why or why not?

CONSIDERING CONTENT

1. What did David Wallerstein figure out about moviegoers and the amount of popcorn they bought? What did he do about it?
2. Why did McDonald's managers resist the idea of offering large-size versions of menu items?
3. What scheme did Max Cooper come up with to raise sales at McDonald's?
4. What did the 2001 Penn State study reveal about the effect of portion size on eating behavior?
5. What link between supersizing and caloric intake does Critser make? Does this conclusion seem valid and reasonable?
6. According to Critser, how has the concept of "bigness" spread beyond the fast food market? Do you agree that "Bigness is addictive because it is about power"?

CONSIDERING METHOD

1. What is Critser's point of view? Who are his intended readers, and what message does he want to convey to them?
2. Explain the **analogy** between "value meals" and the menu in a fine French restaurant (paras. 14–18). Does this seem like a valid comparison?
3. Who are the two sources for the first part of the article (paras. 1–18)? Why does Critser rely on these people for the information in this part?
4. Look at the statistics in paragraphs 19, 20, and 21. What point do they support in each paragraph? What are their sources?
5. What effects does the closing paragraph achieve?

WRITING STEP BY STEP

Greg Critser examines the problem of increased obesity in Americans and uncovers a surprising cause: the supersizing of fast foods. In this writing assignment you will have a similar goal.

Think of a problem or condition that you know something about, and look beneath the surface to discover both the *immediate* and the *remote* (or underlying) causes. One place to start is on your campus: the lack of a day-care center, a parking crisis, the widespread occurrence of cheating or plagiarism, trouble getting the courses needed to graduate, the ineffectiveness of student government, or the difficulty in obtaining funds for a new student group. You could also write about a family problem, if you think it would interest your readers.

A. Brainstorming is a productive way to discover the best topic for this assignment. Don't stop at the first problem that comes to mind, but remember that you must know the topic well enough to explore it in some depth. Also review past issues of your campus newspaper or chat with classmates, teachers, and friends to identify possibilities.

B. Once you've decided what to write about, make a list of all the causes that you and others have thought of so far, even the ones you don't necessarily see as important or correct.

C. Cluster these causes on your list. Put immediate or easily observable causes in one group, indirect or less easily seen ones in another. Next, cluster around the indirect causes, trying to identify where those causes might originate. Critser's examination led him to super-sizing and then to value meals, which led him to the connection between portion size and consumption, and finally to the possible link between increased calories and the growing popularity of fast food.

D. You will need to select the most important causes for the problem to allow you space to explain each one fully. Consider which points are least familiar, even surprising, to your readers and most likely to influence their thinking on the problem. A new perspective can sometimes move those with set ideas to reconsider their views.

E. A sketch outline of your chain of causes will let you know how well prepared you are to begin your draft. If the chain reveals a need for more examples or explanations, return to brainstorming and further conversations with people who know about the problem.

F. Before you begin the draft, review Critser's organization. He takes a chronological approach, starting with the first step in the process of increasing serving sizes. He could have started with the final effects—increased calories and obesity—and worked his way back to the primary causes. Your readers' familiarity with the problem and their attitudes toward it should help you decide where to start and how to organize your points.

G. In your conclusion, consider using Critser's technique of summing up his main message and driving the point home. Or you could try putting the next step in the hands of your readers by suggesting what they can do with the information and insights you have given them.

OTHER WRITING IDEAS

1. Brainstorm a list of causes for some problem you are facing, such as paying your bills, getting all your work done, dealing with a difficult friend or teacher, sticking to your diet. Organize the list into immediate and long-term causes. Write an essay analyzing the causes of your problem and concluding with your solution.

2. COLLABORATIVE WRITING. Conduct an informal survey among your friends and relatives about their favorite junk food: What do they like about it? When do they eat it? How often? Using this information, do some freewriting about why you think people love this kind of food. Then gather your thoughts, and write an essay about the popularity of junk food.

3. USING THE INTERNET. Do an online search for information about the Slow Food Movement. Then, for a introductory class in health studies or your school newspaper, write an article about the origins and goals of this movement. Be sure to give credit to the sources of your information.

4. WRITING ABOUT READING. In the last five paragraphs of his essay, Critser examines the links between supersizing and increased food consumption in America. Review those paragraphs and write an

evaluation of them. What claims does Critser make? How persuasive are his evidence and conclusions?

GAINING WORD POWER

Explain as thoroughly as you can what the following phrases mean in Critser's essay.

1. the fifth deadly sin (para. 1)
2. high-markup snacks (para.1)
3. cost a pittance (para. 2)
4. mid-level managers (para. 10)
5. hot air and smoke (para. 12)
6. the prime mover (para. 12)
7. kibitzing with like-minded associates (para. 13)
8. went through the roof (para. 18)

EDITING SKILLS: ELIMINATING WORDINESS

A good writer would never write only short, simple sentences, but a good clean sentence is better than a wordy, cluttered one. Look at these spare sentences from Critser's article:

It looked piggish.
People wanted more fries.
Kroc gave in.

A less skillful writer might have used a lot more words to say the same thing, like this:

It would make them appear to be gluttonous and piggish to people who might be watching.

The general public desired to consume additional french-fried potatoes.

Finally, after much hemming and hawing, Kroc relented and yielded in the end to Wallerstein's opinion.

There's nothing actually wrong with those sentences except what English teachers call *verbiage* and everybody else calls **wordiness.** Be careful not to say the same thing twice ("gluttonous and piggish," "relented and yielded," and "finally" and "in the end"). And avoid these common expressions:

Wordy	**Concise**
tall in height	tall
past history	history
blue in color	blue
advance forward	advance
expensive in price	expensive
consensus of opinion	consensus
continue to remain	remain
join together	join
few in number	few
positive benefits	benefits
at this point in time	at this time

EXERCISE

If you have trouble saying things succinctly, practice by streamlining the following wordy sentences. Keep the same meaning but eliminate the extra words. Here's an example:

The masculine-gendered style used online in ListServe communications is, at this point in time, characterized by an adversarial attitude.

(Revised) The male style used in communications on ListServe is adversarial.

1. It is my desire to be called Ishmael.
2. In my opinion there are many diverse elements about this problem that one probably ought to at least think about before arriving at an opinion on the matter.
3. The obnoxious children were seldom corrected or reprimanded because their baffled and adoring parents thought their objectionable behavior was normal and acceptable.
4. There came a time when, based on what I had been reading, I arrived at the feeling that the food we buy at the supermarkets to eat is sometimes, perhaps often, bad for us.
5. By and large, a stitch sewed or basted as soon as a rip is discovered may well save nine times the amount of sewing necessary if the job is put off even for a relatively short time.

Now go through your final draft one more time looking only for verbal clutter. Then, in the words of Mark Twain, "When in doubt, leave it out."

WEB SITES

www.newstarget.com/fast_food.html
This site provides articles, features, and online resources covering the health consequences of fast food consumption.

www.fatcalories.com
Find information here about fast foods that can help reduce the risk of obesity, diabetes, high blood pressure, and heart disease.

STUDENT ESSAY ANALYZING CAUSES

Almost a Winner

Brian L. Carter

Brian Carter was raised in Portland, Oregon. After high school, he worked at casinos in Reno, Nevada, where he became interested in statistics and human folly, leading him to a psychology major. He wrote this essay when he returned to community college.

One of my first jobs, after turning twenty-one, was carrying slot-machine change for customers in a major casino in Reno. I wore a thick canvas apron loaded with about ten pounds of rolled quarters, nickels, and dimes. My simple task was to seek out slot customers in need of coins, and plenty were. On some shifts I never stopped moving. It was a physically demanding job, but mentally it was a snooze. So I amused myself by observing the behavior of the slot players. I decided that most were irrational at best, and insane at worst. What rational person purchases $20 worth of nickels to play a slot machine that has a maximum jackpot of $7.50? Why would someone play a machine and refuse to leave, even to go to the bathroom? Something was going on here. In no other human activity do people act like this. What is it about slot machines that gives them the power to produce such potentially destructive effects? 1

The question was answered when I took a basic psychology class. I learned about B. F. Skinner, a psychologist who conducted experiments on the behavior of animals and humans. In a series of famous experiments, he showed that pigeons could quickly learn to peck a bar to get a pellet of food for each peck. If it took three bar pecks to produce a food pellet, the pigeons would keep pressing even faster. When rewards (like food) come at a constant rate, such as every three or five responses (pecks), this is called a fixed schedule. Skinner then made the reward occur on a variable, random schedule: a food pellet might drop on the 17th peck or the 10th peck, or even twice in a row. This produced even more energetic bar pecking compared to fixed schedules. Skinner also used a random schedule and then stopped dropping food pellets altogether, just to see how long the pigeons would continue to bar peck. He was astonished to see them peck for hours with no reward. Then, when it seemed like the pigeons were going to give up, dropping just one food pellet would cause them to begin bar pecking again, for hours. 2

I realized slot machines operated on much the same principle. Their rewards were certainly random, one could go several plays without winning anything, but an occasional reward would cause the player to keep going 3 long into the night. Now, the behavior of slot players made sense to me. I began to see them as trapped pigeons in one of Skinner's laboratory experiments, conditioned to think they would receive another reward soon if they just kept playing.

But things were to get worse for these slot pigeons. The introduction   4
of the computerized slot machine, which directly controlled the outcome of every spin of the wheels, was about to go beyond the work of Skinner. By law, a slot machine is only required to show, accurately, which combination of wheel symbols pays which amounts—-for example, three cherries in a row pays $3, or four Cadillacs in a row pays $500. There is no law that says slot machines must display how likely it is for each winning row of symbols to show up. The odds are the ratio of no-pay tries to payoff tries, and these are heavily in favor of the casino.

Yet, the computer slot-machine companies introduced a scheme that   5
would hook slot players more than ever before. All slot reel combinations either pay off or don't pay off. But the slot manufacturers came up with the idea to include far more "near misses" in their nonpay combinations. In this setup a slot player would see two Cadillacs on the pay line but a third Cadillac just missing the line. Because slot machines display three lines on each try, the tempting third Cadillac would appear just above or just below the actual line, and these near misses would occur more often than they would by chance. The payouts of the machine would be the same mathematically as before. A near miss pays as much as a wide miss—that is, nothing. But this rigged system gave the illusion that the slot player was always getting close to the jackpot. Not only wins, but near-wins also acted as random rewards. Put this little trick on top of the psychological influences already operating on the slot player, and you can see why the casinos should be offering free diapers to slot players.

Luckily for the slot players, the Nevada Gaming Control Board   6
banned this practice. The board ruled that slot machine reels *must* operate at random and cannot be fixed to show a higher than random rate of near misses. This ruling reinstated the status quo and returned slot players to mere pigeons, pumping money into a device that will surely bankrupt them if they play it long enough. The casinos didn't protest the gaming board's ruling. They still have the most powerful means of getting money from their customers: the psychology of reinforcement scheduling.

CONSIDERING CONTENT AND METHOD

1. Does the introduction encourage you to read on? If so, what caught your interest?
2. What is the difference between a fixed and a variable schedule of

rewards? Name something in your life that has a fixed schedule of rewards, and something that has a variable schedule. Does the difference make you behave differently in these settings?

3. What causes slots players to keep playing even though they usually lose?

4. What effect did computerization have on the sequencing of slot machine symbols? Why was computerization necessary for this effect?

5. Explain the effect of near misses on slot machine players. Have you noticed any similar effects of near misses in other areas of life?

Strategies for Influencing Others:
Argument and *Persuasion*

IMAGES AND IDEAS

Source: The Advertising Archive

FOR DISCUSSION AND WRITING

What point does this poster make? Does it make its point by appealing to your reasoning or to your emotions? Create your own parody of a well-known advertisement. A parody imitates a serious work but exaggerates or adds details that poke fun at the original. Write a paragraph or two explaining what advertisement you are parodying, what changes you plan to make, and what point your parody makes.

You already know when to use persuasion: when you hope to get your readers to agree with you and maybe, as a result, to take some kind of action—like giving you a refund or picketing city hall. And on essay tests and in classroom assignments you are often asked to take a stand or support a conclusion.

All the writing strategies that you studied in previous chapters can be used to persuade your readers or to argue a point. You can use comparison/contrast to demonstrate the superiority of whole wheat over white bread, or cause–effect analysis to convince your readers that rap music reinforces violent attitudes toward women, or definition to show that computer nerds are more interesting than most people think. In this chapter, you will use all the strategies for organizing your thoughts and ideas as you learn how to influence readers' opinions about controversial or unfamiliar issues.

THE POINT OF ARGUMENT AND PERSUASION

Your purpose in this type of writing is to encourage the readers to accept your point of view, solution, plan, or complaint as their own. Traditionally, the word **persuasion** refers to attempts to sway the readers' emotions, while the word **argument** refers to tactics that address the readers' logic. Most convincing writing today mixes the two types of appeal. A personal testimony from a paraplegic accident victim pleading with readers to use their seat belts persuades through emotional identification. A list of statistics concerning injury rates before and after seat belt laws went into effect argues the point through rationality. A combination of the two tactics would probably be quite effective. In everyday language, *persuasion* means influence over the audience, whether emotional or rational.

THE PRINCIPLES OF ARGUMENT AND PERSUASION

Presenting a conventional persuasive essay involves five tasks:

1. State the **issue** your essay will address, and put it in a context: Why is it controversial or problematic? Why do people care about it? Why do people disagree about it?
2. State your main point or thesis. What point of view, solution, or stance do you wish the readers to adopt? This is your **claim**.
3. Provide well-developed **evidence** on your own side of the issue. You can develop your point through facts, statistics, examples, expert testimony, and logical reasoning (cause and effect, analogy), just to name a few strategies. This is the longest part of a conventional argument, and each piece of evidence will probably take a paragraph or more to develop.
4. Respond to opposing viewpoints. This is called the **refutation** section. Especially when arguments against your own are widely known, you need to acknowledge them and counter them, or your essay will have obvious holes in it. You might minimize their importance,

demonstrate that they are not logical or factual, or offer alternative ways of thinking about them.

5. Close by reminding your reader of your main point and the strength of your evidence. Many persuasive essays include a call to action, encouraging readers to do something in support of your cause.

Writers often alter this conventional plan, especially tasks 3 and 4. There are several typical arrangements you can use to fit your topic, audience, purpose, and the nature of your evidence:

The Counterargument. You can anticipate what people on the other side of the issue would say and organize your argument as a point-by-point refutation. This approach works well for tackling controversial topics and for clearing up common misconceptions. In this chapter, for example, "Misunderstood Medicine" argues for mandatory administration of the HPV vaccine by countering the main objections to such a proposal.

The Pro and Con Argument. Another way to present an argument is to look at the pros and cons of an issue. These may also be called advantages and disadvantages or strengths and weaknesses. This approach is commonly used when you are trying to make a difficult decision or settle a dispute amicably.

The Problem-Solution Argument. You can use this approach when you want to argue directly for a change in a policy or system. You need to identify the problem, demonstrate that it's relevant or serious, explain why current methods aren't working, propose a solution, and show how it will work. Sometimes you can merely call people's attention to a problem without offering a solution, but most of the time you will want to recommend a course of action to reduce or eliminate the problem. In this chapter, "When Life Imitates Video" presents a lengthy indictment of violent video games and ends with the author's call for a solution.

THE ELEMENTS OF GOOD ARGUMENT

Claims, evidence, and refutation are the basic building blocks of argument. You must understand them in order to write persuasively and effectively.

Claims

The "engine" that propels any argument is its claim. Claims fall into three categories:

1. *Claims of fact* assert that something is true: "Women currently do not receive equal pay for equal work."

2. *Claims of value* support or deny the worth or merit of something: "Getting a college education is more important than playing sports."

3. *Claims of policy* state that certain conditions, courses of action, or practices should be adopted: "A six-month maternity leave policy ought to be required by law."

For any argument to be effective, it must begin with a claim that's significant, reasonable, and supportable by evidence.

Evidence

Some of the most frequently used kinds of evidence are these:

- *Personal observation or experience:* "I came the closest to achieving a decent fit between income and expenses only when I worked seven days a week." This is the least widely accepted form of evidence because it comes from a narrow band of experience and may not be representative. But it can be very persuasive in communicating the human significance of an issue.
- *Facts:* "Rents usually have to be less than 30 percent of one's income to be considered 'affordable.'" Facts are noncontroversial pieces of information that can be confirmed through observation or by generally accepted sources; they are persuasive to the extent that they relate to the statement they support.
- *Relevant examples:* "One waitress shares a room in a boarding house for $250 a week; another lives with her mother; the night cook pays $170 a week for a one-person trailer; the hostess lives in a van parked behind a shopping center at night." Examples are most persuasive when they are objective and clearly relevant.
- *Testimony:* "Maggie Spade of the Economic Policy Institute explains that the low-income housing crisis exists partly because it is not reflected in the official poverty rate, which is based on the cost of food, not shelter." Testimony should come from sources that the readers will accept as credible; it carries its greatest weight when the meaning of the facts or data is not self-evident and some judgment or interpretation is required to reach a conclusion.
- *Data:* "Almost 60 percent of poor renters, amounting to a total of 4.4 million households, spend more than half of their income on shelter." This is probably the most readily accepted form of evidence because of its apparent objectivity and scope.

To be persuasive, all evidence in support of a claim must meet certain standards:

1. It must be reasonably up to date.
2. It must be sufficient in scope.
3. It must be relevant to the claim.

Thus, you wouldn't use 1995 unemployment data in support of a 2005 policy decision (recentness). Neither would you rely on unemployment data from only one month to formulate a long-term unemployment policy (scope). Nor would you use employment data from Canada to comment on the American unemployment picture, unless your argument involved an overall comparison of the two countries' economies (relevance).

Refutation

Arguments always assume that other points of view are possible; otherwise, there would be no reason to argue. You may feel so strongly about an issue that you want to attack those who disagree with you and ridicule their opinions, but that strategy can backfire, especially if you're trying to influence readers who are undecided. Your case will be strengthened if you treat opposing views with respect and understanding.

This acknowledgment of and response to the opposing views is called *refutation*. There is no best place in an argument to refute the opposition. Sometimes you will want to bring up opposing arguments early and deal with them right away. Another approach is to anticipate objections as you develop your own case point by point. Wherever you decide to include your refutation, your goal is to point out problems with the opponents' reasoning and evidence. You can refute opposing arguments by showing that they are unsound, unfair, or flawed in their logic. Frequently, you will present contrasting evidence to reveal the weakness of your opponents' views and to reinforce your own position.

When an opposing argument is so compelling that it cannot be easily countered, you should concede its strength. This approach will establish that you are knowledgeable and fair-minded. You can sometimes accept the opponents' line of thought up to a certain point—but no further. Or you can show that their strong point addresses only *one* part of a complex problem.

A SAMPLE ANNOTATED ARGUMENT

The following essay about the controversy surrounding the HPV vaccine was written by a student at Eastern Illinois University. The writer makes a claim of policy: that the vaccine should be given to all recommended patients. She then presents the major objections to this policy and refutes the opposing arguments. The marginal notes identify key features and strategies in building an argument.

Misunderstood Medicine

Stephanie Pescitelli

Claims of fact |　Last year, the Food and Drug Administration (FDA) approved a vaccine that is 100 percent effective in preventing a virus that will infect 6 million people in the United States this year. This virus is responsible for 70 percent of the cases of the second most deadly cancer in women; it is also directly related to six other types of cancer and associated with warty growths on the vocal cords of children. It may seem obvious that this medical

Claim of policy (thesis) | miracle should be given to all recommended patients to prevent the pain and cost of cancer and disease, but several sociological and psychological factors are blocking widespread administration in the United States. Currently, only the state of Texas has a plan to make this vaccine compulsory. Why is there resistance to receiving this vaccine's benefits?

Claim of fact |　The virus is the human papillomavirus (HPV). The vaccine is Gardasil, which is administered in three doses and, according to the American Cancer Society (ACS), will prevent infection of four out of 100 sexually transmitted HPV strains. Two of these strains are responsible for 70 percent of all cervical cancer cases, and the other two cause 90 percent of | Evidence (data)

Claim of policy | genital warts. The vaccine is currently available to the public, but its health-preserving potential can be maximized only if immunization is made mandatory for girls ages 11–12, as recommended by the Advisory Committee on Immunization Practices. | Evidence (expert testimony)

　Gardasil, however, is different from most other vaccines: the virus it prevents is spread through

First major objection

sexual activity. Some parents of preteens argue that administering a vaccine intended to prevent a sexually transmitted disease (STD) will undermine their rights to discuss the sensitive issues of sex with their daughters at a later time. In an article in the *Washington Post*, the associate executive director of the Christian Medical and Dental Associations, Gene Rudd, argues for these parental rights: "There are those who would say, 'We can provide a better, healthier alternative than the vaccine, and that is to teach abstinence.'" Religious and family organizations have also claimed that eliminating fear of contracting this virus will encourage promiscuity in young women. In Texas, as an acknowledgment of these concerns, parents opposed to having their daughters receive the HPV vaccine for personal and religious reasons can opt out and make their children exempt.

Refutation of first objection

However, preserving a loved one's brief innocence is no excuse for failing to protect her from a potentially harmful virus, and possibly even life-threatening cancer. While remaining abstinent is the best way to avoid infection, the American Cancer Society reports that 7% of males and females become sexually active before age 13, 24% of females are active by age 15, 40% by age 16, and 70% by age 18. These statistics, combined with the fact that four out of five sexually active females will contract HPV during their lifetime, make clear why early administration is imperative. Furthermore, the ACS report states that there is no evidence that the vaccine encourages recipients to engage in sexual activity as a result of a lifted fear of STDs.

Evidence (data)

Evidence (expert opinion)

Second major objection

Other people argue that the HPV vaccine should not be required of sixth graders because it was only recently approved, and its long-term safety and efficiency have not been established. Parents of three girls in Texas have sued Governor Perry, claiming that he has overstepped his authority with his mandate. Their attorney, Kenneth Chaiken, is

Evidence (example)

quoted in the *Austin Chronicle*, declaring that "The school-age girls of Texas are not guinea pigs who may be subjected to medical procedures at the apparent whim of Texas' governor."

Refutation of second objection | While it is true that a vaccine intended to prevent one health problem should not introduce another, Gardasil's safety and efficiency *have* been tested and proven, according to the FDA and a panel of twenty-one scientists on a board for the ACS. The only issue in question is whether or not the vaccine will require booster shots down the road, and there is no way to tell how long it will take to determine this possibility. Waiting for the data will unnecessarily expose millions of people to HPV. | Concession

Evidence (expert testimony)

Conclusion: summary of refutation | The health and well-being of American citizens should not be placed in the hands of those who rely on biased rumors and media hype. Rather, this and all other health policy decisions should be based on medical science and the judgment of health professionals. *The Journal of Family Practice* projects that if the rest of the United States followed Texas's suit, 200,000 cases of HPV infection could be prevented, as well as 3300 cases of cervical cancer. Failure to implement this vaccine will do an injustice to both current and future victims of cervical cancer across this nation. How can we deny our daughters, sisters, mothers, and ourselves the safety from such a fate? | Evidence (expert testimony, data)

THE PITFALLS OF ARGUMENT AND PERSUASION

If you follow the preceding suggestions, you should be able to write a convincing essay. But there are some risks to be aware of in this kind of writing.

Taking on Too Much

Narrowing your topic is always a good idea, but it's especially important in argumentation. You won't be able to write a sensible essay on "What's Wrong with the American Economy." Select a more manageable problem, such as unemployment or unbridled greed. Even those problems are probably too broad to cover in a short essay. Always consider moving the issue closer to home. For example, if someone in your family has been unemployed, you are probably equipped to write about the psychological effects of unemployment on the individual. If you have found yourself in terrifying and unnecessary credit card debt, you can probably write persuasively about uncontrolled consumerism. In these cases, you have credibility to discuss the issue. Credibility is an important part of your appeal, and you will notice that each author in this chapter establishes the right to claim knowledge about his or her subject, either explicitly or implicitly.

Mistaking the Audience

The readers you most want to reach with a controversial essay are the ones in the middle—those who are undecided and might be swayed by your ideas. People with extreme opinions on either side are likely to be unmovable. Even with persuadable audiences, you must expect some resistance. Be sure your tone does not bolster this resistance by being insulting or condescending. The voice of sweet reason and a "we're in this together" attitude invite your readers to agree with you.

Logical Fallacies

Flaws in reasoning can undermine your cause and harm your credibility. Be sure that you are not guilty of these common logical fallacies:

1. *Overgeneralization.* Recently, a national survey found that the number of unmarried women among highly educated people was much larger than among the less educated. Articles on the alarming shortage of men willing to marry educated females abounded, and solutions to the difficulty were proposed. Actually, most of the single, educated females had chosen their unmarried status. The problem was the false generalization that all unmarried women *wanted* husbands and were seeking them. The shortage of marriage-minded men was not proven.

2. *Either-or thinking.* Be sure that you don't present only two alternatives when more exist. For example, some writers in education want us to believe that either we set national standards for mathematical achievement, or our children will continue to fall behind other countries' children in math skills. The fallacy is that national standards are not the only route to high math achievement: smaller classes, better teaching conditions, early intervention policies, and parent involvement are just a few ideas left out of the either-or reasoning. (In fact, the existence of national standards is not correlated with math achievement internationally.)

3. *False analogy.* Analogy is a compelling form of argument, but you must take care that the two cases you compare are really similar. If you argue that your college should imitate a successful general education program used at another university, you must be sure that the two institutions have similar students, faculty, goals, and organizational structures. Otherwise, adopting a plan that works for someone else could be disastrous. Recently, a U.S. congressman claimed that foreign dignitaries, while in our country, should say the Pledge of Allegiance because, similarly, we show respect at the Olympics when other countries' national anthems are played. The analogy falls apart when you consider what the Pledge of Allegiance actually *says*.

4. *Faulty claims about causation.* Remember that two things that occur closely in time or one after the other are not necessarily causally related. In our cities, ice cream sales and murder rates both increase in the summer; can we say that eating ice cream causes aggression? No, probably it's the heat that encourages both. We say "children who are hugged are more likely to be nice," and "children who are beaten are more likely to be unpleasant." But the causes and effects could be the other way around. Maybe nice children are hugged *because* they're nice, and unpleasant children get beaten *because* they're unpleasant.

WHAT TO LOOK FOR IN ARGUMENT AND PERSUASION

Here are some questions to ask yourself as you study the selections in this chapter.

1. What issue is being addressed? What stance or point of view am I being asked to adopt?
2. What claim or claims does the author make? What kind of claims are they? Are they significant and reasonable?
3. Does the author explain the issue clearly and completely? Are there any holes or gaps in the author's thinking?
4. What evidence does the author use to support the claims? Is this evidence sufficient, relevant, and up to date?
5. Does the writer refute possible objections? How effective is this refutation? Has the author ignored any important objections?
6. Is the conclusion satisfactory? Has the author persuaded me?

DEBATE: DO SAME-SEX COUPLES MAKE GOOD PARENTS?

The growing acceptance of homosexuals in traditional social roles—public office, marriage, adoption, military service—remains problematic and unsettling for many Americans. Some politicians and religious leaders are especially concerned about homosexuals having children. They feel that same-sex households lack the appropriate gender role models, endorse unconventional sexuality as a valid option, and expose children to possible ridicule and rejection by their peers.

Yet, despite this opposition, families headed by gay men and lesbians now number in the tens of thousands, according to the San Diego-based Family Pride Coalition. The majority of homosexual parents are raising children from earlier heterosexual marriages. But for same-sex couples who want their own children, there are more resources than ever: Internet sites that offer information about sperm donors and surrogate mothers; children's books that feature same-sex parents; adoption agencies that accept gay men and lesbians as parents; and networks that provide social support and legal advice. Even some clergy members are indirectly blessing these families by baptizing their children.

The following articles touch on many of the issues in this debate, which is really part of the larger debate on the changing shape and redefinition of the American family.

PREPARING TO READ

Were you or was anyone you know raised by a same-sex couple? If so, how does that family situation affect relationships with peers? If you don't know anyone like this, how do you imagine you would feel if you found out that a friend's parents were homosexual? Do you think that knowledge would alter your feelings for your friend or his or her parents?

• •

Two Mommies Is One Too Many

• •

JAMES C. DOBSON

James Dobson is the founder and chairman of Focus on the Family, a Christian nonprofit organization that describes itself as "dedicated to nurturing and defending families worldwide." A licensed psychologist in California, Dobson has written a number of books that set forth his social and religious views, including Dare to Discipline *(1982),* Bringing Up Boys *(2003), and* Marriage Under Fire *(2004). The following article appeared in the December 18, 2006, issue of* Time *magazine.*

TERMS TO RECOGNIZE

social conservatives *(para. 1)*	those who believe in traditional values and institutions, and generally regard change as suspect
implicit *(para. 1)*	suggested, unspoken, understood
phenomenon *(para. 3)*	something that happens or exists in society and nature
emulate *(para. 3)*	copy, do something the way someone else does
intuitively *(para. 5)*	based on a feeling rather than knowledge or facts
purview *(para. 6)*	accepted range or scope of someone's job, role, or activity
legacy *(para. 7)*	result or carryover from a previous time or event

A number of social conservatives, myself included, have recently been asked to respond to the news that Mary Cheney, the Vice President's daughter, is pregnant with a child she intends to raise with her lesbian partner. Implicit in this issue is an effort to get us to criticize the Bush Administration or the Cheney family. But the concern here has nothing to do with politics. It is about what kind of family environment is best for the health and development of children, and, by extension, the nation at large.   1

With all due respect to Cheney and her partner, Heather Poe, the majority of more than 30 years of social-science evidence indicates that children do best on every measure of well-being when raised by their married mother and father. That is not to say Cheney and Poe will not love their child. But love alone is not enough to guarantee healthy growth and development. The two most loving women in the world cannot provide a daddy for a little boy—any more than the two most loving men can be complete role models for a little girl.   2

The voices that argue otherwise tell us more about our politically correct culture than they do about what children really need. The fact remains that gender matters—perhaps nowhere more than in regard to child rearing. The unique value of fathers has been explained by Dr. Kyle Pruett of Yale Medical School in his book *Fatherneed: Why Father Care Is as Essential as Mother Care for Your Child.* Pruett says dads are critically important simply because   3 "fathers do not mother." *Psychology Today* explained in 1996 that "fatherhood turns out to be a complex and unique phenomenon with huge consequences for the emotional and intellectual growth of children." A father, as a male parent, makes unique contributions to the task of parenting that a mother cannot emulate, and vice versa.

According to educational psychologist Carol Gilligan, mothers tend to stress sympathy, grace, and care to their children, while fathers accent justice, fairness, and duty. Moms give a child a sense of hopefulness; dads provide a sense of right and wrong and its consequences. Other researchers have determined that boys are not born with an understanding of "maleness." They have to learn it, ideally from their fathers. 4

But set aside the scientific findings for a minute. Isn't there something in our hearts that tells us, intuitively, that children need a mother and a father? Admittedly, that ideal is not always possible. Divorce, death, abandonment and unwed pregnancy have resulted in an ever-growing number of single-parent families in this culture. We admire the millions of men and women who have risen to the challenge of parenting alone and are meeting their difficult responsibilities with courage and determination. Still, most of them, if asked, would say that raising children is a two-person job best accomplished by a mother and father. 5

In raising these issues, Focus on the Family does not desire to harm or insult women such as Cheney and Poe. Rather, our conviction is that birth and adoption are the purview of married heterosexual couples. Traditional marriage is God's design for the family and is rooted in biblical truth. When that divine plan is implemented, children have the best opportunity to thrive. That's why public policy as it relates to families must be based not solely on the desires of adults but rather on the needs of children and what is best for society at large. 6

This is a lesson we should have learned from no-fault divorce. Because adults wanted to dissolve difficult marriages with fewer strings attached, reformers made it easier in the late 1960s to dissolve nuclear families. Though there are exceptions, the legacy of no-fault divorce is countless shattered lives within three generations, adversely affecting children's behavior, academic performance, and mental and physical health. No-fault divorce reflected our selfish determination to do what was convenient for adults, and it has been, on balance, a disaster. 7

We should not enter into yet another untested and far-reaching social experiment, this one driven by the desires of same-sex couples to bear and raise children. The traditional family, supported by more than 5,000 years of human experience, is still the foundation on which the well-being of future generations depends. 8

Mom's the Word

JEFF PEARLMAN

Jeff Pearlman is a staff correspondent for Newsday, *a daily newspaper that primarily serves Long Island and the New York City borough of Queens. Best known for his work on sports, Pearlman has written two successful books about baseball:* The Bad Guys Won, *an account of the 1986 New York Mets, and* Love Me, Hate Me *(2006), an unauthorized biography of Barry Bonds. The following article appeared in the April 10, 2005, edition of* Newsday.

TERMS TO RECOGNIZE

closer *(para. 3)*	a baseball pitcher brought in late in the game to protect a lead and close out the game
Grapefruit League *(para. 4)*	teams that train and play pre-season exhibition games in Florida
longevity *(para. 10)*	long life, staying power
stigma *(para. 13)*	mark of shame or disapproval
hapless *(para. 18)*	unlucky
frustrated *(paras.* 24, 26)	annoyed, impatient, discouraged
relented *(para. 25)*	gave in
brigade *(para. 37)*	a large group

SARASOTA, Fla.—Within the four walls of the major league club-house, the concept of homosexuality fits about as comfortably as a pair of mittens on a porcupine. For the most part, men who love men and women who love women are not gays or lesbians, but "queers" and "dykes." Trip over a mitt and you're a "faggot." As for ideas of civil unions and gay marriage—forget about it. "Baseball is very set in its ways," Cincinnati Reds outfielder Jacob Cruz said. "Always has been." 1

Within these confines, there is a man who seems to hover above it all. He is a 25-year-old right-handed relief pitcher with the Reds, a quiet Long Island kid with blazing brown eyes and a blazing 95-mph fastball. He is as open as he needs to be, not afraid to tell the truth about his family, but aware that its implications might not sit perfectly with the 40 or so other young men who surrounded him recently in the Reds' spring training club-house. "I'm a blue-state guy in a red-state sport," Joe Valentine said. "But that won't stop me from being proud of who I am." 2

Who is Joe Valentine? He is a 1997 graduate of Deer Park High   3
School. He is a former All-American at Jefferson Davis Community College
in Alabama. He is a happily married North Babylon resident who wants to
start a family. He is a potential future closer for the Reds.

One more thing. Consider the following dialogue, which took place   4
on a lazy spring training morning between a pitcher fighting to make the
club and a baseball writer wrapping up another run-of-the-mill Grapefruit
League interview.

"Joe, can I give your parents a call?"   5

"Sure."   6

"OK, what are their names?"   7

"Deb and Doreen."   8

That's right: Joe Valentine is the son of two gay women. He tells you   9
this without an iota of emphasis, almost as if he were explaining the
mechanics of a slider or giving directions to the nearest 7-Eleven. There is no
additional explanation, no awkward pause for effect. Nothing. "It's no different than having a mother and father," he said. "These are the two women
who raised me, and they are wonderful people. It's just not a big deal to
me. Why should it be?"

In an enlightened world, it shouldn't. But major league baseball is to   10
enlightenment what Pauly Shore is to career longevity. It took until 1959 for
every team to have at least one black player. There never has been a female
umpire. And in the history of the league, no active player has ever come out
of the closet to express his homosexuality.

"I've got nothing against those people," Washington Nationals relief   11
pitcher T.J. Tucker said recently. "But I don't get why anyone would want to
be like that." Moments after Tucker's comment, a Nationals front office
employee approached a reporter and asked him not to bring the subject of
homosexuality into the clubhouse. "Makes the players uncomfortable," the
employee said.

Years ago, then-Giants second baseman Jeff Kent was changing out   12
of his uniform when he glanced at the nearby reporters and cracked, "There
are no queers here, are there?" The comment barely raised an eyebrow.

Valentine is aware of the stigma. That is why his family asked that this   13
story not be published until Valentine secured a spot on the major league
roster. "We've almost never been treated badly," said Deb Valentine, Joe's
birth mother. "But we live in the real world, and you don't 100 percent
know how people will react." Here's the startling thing: Thus far in Joe
Valentine's life, few have reacted.

Born in Las Vegas on Christmas Eve 1979, Joe is the biological son of   14
Deb Valentine and a man she prefers not to discuss, a man Joe does not
know. Deb declined to discuss the circumstances of the pregnancy, but
when she delivered Joe at Sunrise Hospital, the person by her side was
Doreen Price, her life partner since they first met in a bowling alley in 1975.

At the time, homosexuality was an unacceptable lifestyle in approxi-   15
mately 99 percent of America. Las Vegas was the 1 percent. "Vegas was
Vegas," Deb said. "Open-minded. Accepting. Embracing. Doreen was my
coach in the hospital, and nobody there raised an eyebrow. Vegas was 10
times more liberal than New York is even today. Being gay just wasn't a big
deal."

The couple operated a hair salon in Las Vegas, and in 1982 moved to   16
North Babylon, where they opened Hair Studio 231, which lasted four
years. When Joe was just 16 months old, Doreen was throwing him a baseball. At 2, he fielded his first grounder with his nose. "Blood all over,"
Doreen said. "But we wiped it off, and he was back looking for the
baseball."

At age 5, Joe signed up for Little League, and by 8 he was one of the   17
best athletes around. His gift was a strong right arm. His Little League
coach for two seasons? Doreen, who had played competitive softball. "Joe
could always throw," she said. "I mean, he had a real powerful arm. And he
kept working and working to get better. I think we knew he was a special
kind of baseball player."

Remarkably—and against all hardball logic—Valentine rarely pitched.   18
He was a catcher whose greatest joy came from nailing a hapless runner trying to swipe second. Young Joe loved everything about squatting behind the
plate. The power of calling a game. The dirt crumbling between his fingers.
The pop-pop-pop of rawhide meeting leather. The collisions at home.
"I wanted to be in the middle of the action," he said. "Not making random
appearances here and there."

By the time he arrived at Deer Park as a sophomore in 1994 (Joe   19
attended St. Anthony's in Huntington as a freshman), Valentine was one of
the better young ballplayers on Long Island. "He was exceptional," Deer
Park coach Carmine Argenziano said. "Even when we had pitchers who had
poor moves and couldn't hold anyone on, no one would run on Joe. He was
a weapon back there." In fact, Argenziano once said, "He used to throw it
back to our pitchers harder than they threw it to him. It was scary."

Meanwhile, Deb and Doreen attended every Deer Park game. People   20
in the stands assumed Deb was Joe's "mom" and Doreen his "aunt," and

none of the three would argue. "If it eases what people need to believe," Doreen said, "so be it."

Joe swears he never has been embarrassed by his family. It is all he 21 has ever known. But the unpredictability of facial expressions that greet "These are my mothers" is, well, awkward. Making things easier, the two women never held hands, kissed or hugged at the games. Partially to avoid controversy, but also because it's not who they are. "We went to watch baseball," Doreen said. "We're not trying to make statements."

By the end of his senior year, most of his teammates and their par- 22 ents knew Joe was the product of a gay relationship. Heck, the kids used to hang out at Joe's house. "One day I heard a teacher talking about Joe, and that he had two mothers," Argenziano said. "I was shocked, truly shocked. But you know what? I also didn't care. Those two women did a helluva job raising one fine man. A helluva job."

College recruiters began showing up during Valentine's senior season 23 in 1997. Not big time schools like Arizona State and Miami, but local colleges willing to overlook his so-so hitting ability.

After batting .370 as a senior and making his second All-County 24 team, Valentine played for the Bayside Yankees, a summer-league team that has produced more than 20 major league players. During Valentine's first summer with Bayside, coach Marc Cuseta often was frustrated by his catcher's refusal to take the mound. "You know how high school kids are," Cuseta said. "They wanna be the star, bat third and be in the lineup every day. Joe was no different."

But when it finally became clear to Valentine that his future as a 25 catcher was limited because of his hitting, he relented. In the summer of 1998, Bayside turned him into its closer, and after several weeks of just throwing mid-90s fastballs and hoping they sailed over the plate, Valentine picked up the slider that's now his major-league "out" pitch.

Valentine accepted a scholarship to Dowling College but grew frustrated 26 with the program and left during his first semester. Eventually, Cuseta called an old pal, Keith Griffin, the baseball coach at Jefferson Davis CC in Brewton, Ala., and told him about an under-the-radar pitcher with an infinite upside.

Joe Valentine was moving to the heart of the Bible Belt. With his gay 27 parents. They expected the worst. When Deb and Doreen followed Joe south and settled into an apartment in nearby Pensacola, Fla., they envisioned one hostile face after another. This was Alabama, after all, onetime home of church bombings and tree lynchings. Perhaps if they played it cool, nobody would notice. But inevitably, someone would get the picture, that Joe's "aunt" (wink-wink) wasn't his aunt. It didn't take long.

"I remember people finding out and thinking it was something to   28
joke about," Valentine said. "They'd say, 'Oh, so you must be gay, huh?'"

"What?" Valentine would reply.   29

"Well, you must be gay," one person said. "But how come you don't   30
act all foo-fooey? You're not elegant. You're just a regular guy."

"What the hell is 'foo-fooey?'" Valentine says now. "People can be so   31
incredibly narrow-minded. But I'm not someone who starts fights over this
stuff. I'm a patient guy."

Deb and Doreen attended every Jefferson Davis game that season,   32
becoming unofficial team mothers as their son compiled an 8–1 record and
was named to the NJCAA All-Region XXII team. They'd invite Joe's teammates out for lunch and dinner. Sometimes even cook. Gay? Straight? Most
of the players were just happy to be looked after.

"If you're a good boy, I don't care if you're from Mars," Griffin said.   33
"And Joe was as good a boy as I've ever had around. He's hardworking, he's very
competitive, and he's got a big heart. I'll tell you, very few seemed to care that
his parents were gay. They were wonderful people. And Joe—he's a man's man."

Valentine's decision to attend Jefferson Davis was a good one. In June   34
1999, he was selected by the Chicago White Sox in the 26th round of the
amateur draft.

Throughout his six-year, four-organization professional baseball   35
career, Joe Valentine rarely has volunteered information about his parents.
Again, it's not that he's embarrassed. But why risk starting trouble? Every so
often, however, when he's comfortable, Valentine lets his guard down.
Three years ago, while playing for the Double-A Birmingham Barons, Valentine roomed with Gary Majewski, a right-handed pitcher from Houston.
One night they were watching TV, shooting the breeze. "I don't remember
how we got on the subject," said Majewski, now with the Nationals. "He
just sort of told me. I was like, 'Um, OK.' Joe is a cool dude."

And Valentine can play. After bouncing from the White Sox to the   36
Tigers to the White Sox to the A's to the Reds, he made his big league debut
with Cincinnati in 2003. He pitched in 24 games last season, going 2–3 with
four saves and a 5.22 ERA. He initially struggled in spring training this year
but made the Reds out of camp. Valentine pitched the eighth inning of a
6–1 victory over the Mets on Thursday, striking out two, and pitched a
scoreless seventh against Houston last night, retiring Craig Biggio, Jeff Bag-
well, and Morgan Ensberg on grounders.

Deb and Doreen, who are retired and live in North Port, Fla., plan on   37
seeing Joe pitch as often as possible. And when they show up in the family

area after games, surrounded by the brigade of wives and husbands and kids, their son will, as always, proudly greet them with a hug. They are his loved ones. His moms.

"I don't see myself as an activist for gay rights, although I will speak up 38 if I need to," Valentine said. "I think people need to judge others for who they are. Not by any prejudiced ideas or thoughts. I'm a baseball player who was raised by two wonderful, loving mothers. How can anyone criticize that?"

RESPONDING TO READINGS

After reading these essays, have your opinions and feelings about same-sex parents changed in any way? Explain.

CONSIDERING CONTENT

1. What objections does James Dobson have to same-sex parenting?
2. Which of Dobson's views are refuted by the story of Joe Valentine's two moms?
3. What does Dobson mean when he refers to "our politically correct culture"? What point is he making with this reference?
4. What does Joe Valentine mean when he says "I'm a blue-state guy in a red-state sport"?
5. Why did Deb and Doreen not hold hands, kiss, or hug at the games they attended? Why does Valentine rarely volunteer information about his parents?
6. Dobson admits that a family that has both a mother and a father is an ideal that "is not always possible," and he says he admires the millions of single parents in the country (para. 5). Why, then, does he object to same-sex households that have two parents?

CONSIDERING METHOD

1. What support does Dobson offer for his claim that "children do best on every measure of well-being when raised by their married mother and father"?
2. What authorities does Dobson cite to bolster his argument? How effective are these citations?
3. What is "no-fault divorce" and what lesson does Dobson claim Americans should have learned from it? What do you think about comparing no-fault divorce to gay parenthood?
4. Why does Pearlman include quotations from Valentine's coaches (paras. 22, 33)? What point is Pearlman trying to make by quoting these opinions?

5. Why did Pearlman use the title "Mom's the Word"? What common expression does it echo? What's the relevance to the article?

6. Pearlman's argument consists of an extensive example. Dobson's argument consists of a series of claims with supporting details. Were these good choices given the authors' goals? Would the reverse strategy work as well for either author?

7. Reread the final paragraph in Dobson's article. How effective was it for you as a reader? Would it be convincing to someone opposing Dobson's overall point of view?

8. Why does Pearlman close with a quotation from Joe Valentine? Is it effective? How do you think Dobson would respond to Valentine's final question?

WRITING STEP BY STEP

Write an essay in which you argue either for or against same-sex parenting.

A. Before you start writing, make lists of reasons why you support and why you oppose homosexuals having children. Next to each reason, try to write a brief response or a counterargument. Decide the position you would like to argue.

B. Identify at least three major reasons to support your choice. These reasons will be your claims.

C. Start your essay by stating your position and giving a brief overview of your main claims.

D. Take up each of your claims one by one. Explain each reason in its own separate paragraph, and provide evidence to demonstrate the validity of that reason. If you want, you can use quotations from the essays you have just read, but be sure to give credit to the authors you are quoting.

E. Be sure to consider any objections to your claims that readers might have. Consult the notes you made for step A. If you're not sure what these objections would be, ask classmates, friends, family members, or instructors for their ideas. You might also find additional information on Internet sites such as those listed at the end of this chapter. Refute these objections by minimizing their importance, questioning their factuality, providing a contrary example, or offering a different point of view. You can include your refutations as part of the argument for each claim, or you can put them in a separate paragraph.

F. Close by summarizing your main ideas. Consider using a clincher sentence to drive home your major claim, as Dobson and Pearlman do.

OTHER WRITING IDEAS

1. COLLABORATIVE WRITING. Write the paper outlined in the step-by-step assignment, but argue for or against one of the following issues. Feel free to narrow these topics further if you find them too general.

   a. It should (should not) be harder than it is now to get a divorce.

   b. Having a working mother does (does not) harm a child's welfare.

   c. Free speech should (should not) be restricted on the Internet.

   d. Giving clean needles to intravenous drug users is (is not) the best way to decrease the spread of AIDS in America.

   e. Date rape is (is not) a serious problem on college campuses.

   f. The selling of human organs for transplant should (should not) be legalized.

   g. People should (should not) give money to panhandlers.

   h. Over-the-counter drugs should (should not) be regulated more closely.

   If these topics don't appeal to you, choose a controversial issue that you feel strongly about. Before you begin writing, get together with a group of classmates to brainstorm arguments for and against the topic you have chosen. If possible, interview people whose experience might provide firsthand insight into the topic.

2. USING THE INTERNET. Find out about same-sex marriage, civil unions, family partnerships, and gay adoptions in other countries. You can find information at www.religioustolerance.org/hom_mary.htm. Write a report that would be suitable for a class in sociology or cultural studies, summarizing your research.

3. WRITING ABOUT READINGS. Analyze the strategy that each author uses to present his ideas about same-sex parents. Which approach do you think is more effective? Be sure to cite specific details in explaining your conclusions. You can use your thoughts about question 6 in Considering Method as a starting point.

GAINING WORD POWER

The prefix *hetero-* means "other, opposite, or different," and the prefix *homo-* means "same." So heterosexual means "attracted to people of the opposite sex," and homosexual means "attracted to people of the same sex." Do you know other words that use these same prefixes? What is the difference between a heterogeneous society and a homogeneous one? What is a homonym and how is it different from a heteronym? Would you prefer a heterochromatic painting or a homochromatic one? Use a dictionary to help you answer these questions.

EDITING SKILLS: SUBJECT-VERB AGREEMENT

Look at the verbs in the following sentences:

The fact <u>remains</u> that gender <u>matters</u>.

Joe <u>swears</u> he has never been embarrassed by his family.

He <u>tells</u> you this without an iota of emphasis.

Fatherhood <u>turns</u> out to be a complex and unique phenomenon.

The verbs that we have underlined are in the present tense; they express actions that are happening at the present time or that happen all the time. We also use the present tense to state facts or general truths. You will notice that the verbs end in *s*. That's because the subject of each verb is singular (fact, gender, Joe, he, fatherhood). When the subject of a present-tense verb is *he, she,* or *it*—or a noun that could be replaced by *he, she,* or *it*—we put an *s* on the end of the verb.

This ending is an exception. Present-tense verbs with other subjects do not require the *s* ending:

> Moms <u>give</u> a child a sense of hopefulness; dads <u>provide</u> a sense of right and wrong and its consequences.
>
> We <u>admire</u> the millions of men and women who have risen to the challenge of parenting alone.
>
> I <u>think</u> people need to judge others for who they are.

Because we don't always put an ending on a present-tense verb, some people forget to add it. That causes an error in subject-verb agreement. And sometimes it is difficult to tell what the subject of a verb really is, as in this sentence:

> Gay parenting, like no-fault divorce and single mothers, <u>remains</u> unacceptable in come circles.

The subject of the verb <u>remains</u> is <u>parenting</u>, but the words in between might lead a writer to think that <u>no-fault divorce and single mothers</u> are the subjects—and to mistakenly leave the *s* ending off. Phrases that intervene between the subject and the main verb often mislead writers about what the verb needs to agree with. Now take a look at this example:

> Opponents of gay marriage often <u>argue</u> that same-sex households don't provide good role models for children.

Can you figure out why there is no *s* on the verb <u>argue</u>? That's because the subject is <u>opponents</u>, a word that does not mean *he, she,* or *it.* When trying to figure out the subject-verb agreement, you just have to forget about the words that come between <u>opponents</u> and <u>argue.</u>

EXERCISE

In each of the following sentences, underline the subject and then circle the verb that agrees with it. Example:

A <u>verb</u> in the present tense take/takes an s ending when its subject is *he, she,* or *it*—or a noun that means *he, she,* or *it.*

1. An anthropologist study/studies buildings, tools, and other artifacts of ancient cultures.
2. Anthropologists always look/looks for signs of social change.
3. A box of fruit arrive/arrives at the house every month.
4. An adult student who has children find/finds little time for partying.
5. Low scores on the Scholastic Aptitude Test discourage/discourages students from applying to some colleges.
6. It give/gives me great pleasure to introduce tonight's speaker.
7. The first baseman, along with most of his teammates, refuse/refuses to sign autographs after the game.
8. Bonsai trees require/requires careful pruning.
9. Many movies of the past year contain/contains scenes of violence.

Now check over the essay you have just written. Look at all the verbs, especially those in the present tense. Did you use the *s* ending on the appropriate verbs? Edit your writing carefully for subject-verb agreement.

WEB SITES

www.family.org/
More details about James Dobson's views and writings can be found on the Focus on the Family Web site.
www.colage.org/resources/facts.htm
The organization Children of Lesbians and Gays Everywhere (COLAGE) presents facts, figures, and research findings on children with gay parents.

DEBATE: IS MEDIA VIOLENCE HARMFUL TO CHILDREN AND ADOLESCENTS?

On April 20, 1999, when Eric Harris and Dylan Klebold walked into Columbine High School and went on a deadly shooting spree, they added a sense of urgency to the evolving debate over the effects of media violence, especially of violent video games. Parents, kids, teachers, psychologists, and others entered into an ongoing discussion of several key questions: Is there a direct connection between media violence and real violence? Is the use of violence in children's and adolescents' media new or simply taking on new forms? Are there ways to use media violence for positive purposes?

PREPARING TO READ

Do you play violent video games, watch violent films, or listen to music with violent lyrics? Why or why not? List what you believe are the positive and negative effects of participating in such virtual or indirect violence.

••

Violent Media Is Good for Kids

••

GERARD JONES

Gerard Jones is a popular and prolific author of comic books, graphic novels, and essays on media and culture. His most recent work, Men of Tomorrow: Geeks, Gangsters, and the Birth of the Comic Book *(2004), won the comic industry's prestigious Eisner Award. In an earlier book,* Killing Monsters: Why Children Need Fantasy, Superheroes, and Make-Believe Violence *(2002), Jones expanded on the argument he outlines in "Violent Media Is Good for Kids," first published in the magazine* Mother Jones *in 2000.*

TERMS TO RECOGNIZE

progressive *(para. 1)*	socially forward thinking
persona *(para. 1)*	an assumed role
bumptious *(para. 1)*	pushy, assertive
benevolence *(para. 3)*	goodwill, generosity
fervently *(para. 5)*	with emotional intensity
embolden *(para. 6)*	gain courage

resilient *(para. 8)*	able to recover easily
potency *(para. 8)*	ability to grow and change
incomprehensible *(para.* 10)	unknowable
protagonist *(para.* 10)	main character
tumultuous *(para. 13)*	wild, stormy

At 13 I was alone and afraid. Taught by my well-meaning, progres- 1
sive, English-teacher parents that violence was wrong, that rage was something to be overcome and cooperation was always better than conflict, I
suffocated my deepest fears and desires under a nice-boy persona. Placed in
a small, experimental school that was wrong for me, afraid to join my peers
in their bumptious rush into adolescent boyhood, I withdrew into passivity
and loneliness. My parents, not trusting the violent world of the late 1960s,
built a wall between me and the crudest elements of American pop culture.

Then the Incredible Hulk smashed through it. 2

One of my mother's students convinced her that Marvel Comics, despite 3
their apparent juvenility and violence, were in fact devoted to lofty messages of
pacifism and tolerance. My mother borrowed some, thinking they'd be good
for me. And so they were. But not because they preached lofty messages of
benevolence. They were good for me because they were juvenile. And violent.

The character who caught me, and freed me, was the Hulk: overgen- 4
dered and undersocialized, half-naked and half-witted, raging against a
frightened world that misunderstood and persecuted him. Suddenly I had a
fantasy self to carry my stifled rage and buried desire for power. I had a fantasy self who was a self: unafraid of his desires and the world's disapproval,
unhesitating and effective in action. "Puny boy follow Hulk!" roared my fantasy self, and I followed.

I followed him to new friends—other sensitive geeks chasing their own 5
inner brutes—and I followed him to the arrogant, self-exposing, self-
assertive, superheroic decision to become a writer. Eventually, I left him
behind, followed more sophisticated heroes, and finally my own lead along
a twisting path to a career and an identity. In my 30s, I found myself writing
action movies and comic books. I wrote some Hulk stories, and met the
geek-geniuses who created him. I saw my own creations turned into action
figures, cartoons, and computer games. I talked to the kids who read my
stories. Across generations, genders, and ethnicities I kept seeing the same
story: people pulling themselves out of emotional traps by immersing themselves in violent stories. People integrating the scariest, most fervently
denied fragments of their psyches into fuller senses of selfhood through fantasies of superhuman combat and destruction.

I have watched my son living the same story—transforming himself   6
into a bloodthirsty dinosaur to embolden himself for the plunge into
preschool, a Power Ranger to muscle through a social competition in
kindergarten. In the first grade, his friends started climbing a tree at school.
But he was afraid: of falling, of the centipedes crawling on the trunk, of
sharp branches, of his friends' derision. I took my cue from his own fantasies and read him old Tarzan comics, rich in combat and bright with
flashing knives. For two weeks he lived in them. Then he put them aside.
And he climbed the tree.

But all the while, especially in the wake of the recent burst of school   7
shootings, I heard pop psychologists insisting that violent stories are harmful to kids, heard teachers begging parents to keep their kids away from
"junk culture," heard a guilt-stricken friend with a son who loved Pokémon
lament, "I've turned into the bad mom who lets her kid eat sugary cereal
and watch cartoons!" That's when I started the research.

"Fear, greed, power-hunger, rage: these are aspects of our selves that   8
we try not to experience in our lives but often want, even need, to experience
vicariously through stories of others," writes Melanie Moore, Ph.D., a psychologist who works with urban teens. "Children need violent entertainment in order to explore the inescapable feelings that they've been taught to
deny, and to reintegrate those feelings into a more whole, more complex,
more resilient selfhood." Moore consults to public schools and local gov-
ernments, and is also raising a daughter. For the past three years she and I
have been studying the ways in which children use violent stories to meet
their emotional and developmental needs—and the ways in which adults
can help them use those stories healthily. With her help I developed Power
Play, a program for helping young people improve their self-knowledge and
sense of potency through heroic, combative storytelling.

We've found that every aspect of even the trashiest pop-culture story   9
can have its own developmental function. Pretending to have superhuman
powers helps children conquer the feelings of powerlessness that inevitably
come with being so young and small. The dual-identity concept at the heart of
many superhero stories helps kids negotiate the conflicts between the inner self
and the public self as they work through the early stages of socialization. Identification with a rebellious, even destructive, hero helps children learn to push
back against a modern culture that cultivates fear and teaches dependency.

At its most fundamental level, what we call "creative violence"—   10
head-bonking cartoons, bloody videogames, playground karate, toy
guns—gives children a tool to master their rage. Children will feel rage. Even

the sweetest and most civilized of them, even those whose parents read the better class of literary magazines, will feel rage. The world is uncontrollable and incomprehensible; mastering it is a terrifying, enraging task. Rage can be an energizing emotion, a shot of courage to push us to resist greater threats, take more control, than we ever thought we could. But rage is also the emotion our culture distrusts the most. Most of us are taught early on to fear our own. Through immersion in imaginary combat and identification with a violent protagonist, children engage the rage they've stifled, come to fear it less, and become more capable of utilizing it against life's challenges.

I knew one little girl who went around exploding with fantasies so violent 11 that other moms would draw her mother aside to whisper, "I think you should know something about Emily. . . . " Her parents were separating, and she was small, an only child, a tomboy at an age when her classmates were dividing sharply along gender lines. On the playground she acted out "Sailor Moon" fights, and in the classroom she wrote stories about people being stabbed with knives. The more adults tried to control her stories, the more she acted out the roles of her angry heroes: breaking rules, testing limits, roaring threats.

Then her mother and I started helping her tell her stories. She wrote 12 them, performed them, drew them like comics: sometimes bloody, sometimes tender, always blending the images of pop culture with her own most private fantasies. She came out of it just as fiery and strong, but more self-controlled and socially competent: a leader among her peers, the one student in her class who could truly pull boys and girls together.

I worked with an older girl, a middle-class "nice girl," who held her- 13 self together through a chaotic family situation and a tumultuous adolescence with gangsta rap. In the mythologized street violence of Ice T, the rage and strutting of his music and lyrics, she found a theater of the mind in which she could be powerful, ruthless, invulnerable. She avoided the heavy drug use that sank many of her peers, and flowered in college as a writer and political activist.

I'm not going to argue that violent entertainment is harmless. I think 14 it has helped inspire some people to real-life violence. I am going to argue that it's helped hundreds of people for every one it's hurt, and that it can help far more if we learn to use it well. I am going to argue that our fear of "youth violence" isn't well-founded on reality, and that the fear can do more harm than the reality. We act as though our highest priority is to prevent our children from growing up into murderous thugs—but modern kids are far more likely to grow up too passive, too distrustful of themselves, too easily manipulated.

We send the message to our children in a hundred ways that their [15] craving for imaginary gun battles and symbolic killings is wrong, or at least dangerous. Even when we don't call for censorship or forbid "Mortal Kombat," we moan to other parents within our kids' earshot about the "awful violence" in the entertainment they love. We tell our kids that it isn't nice to play-fight, or we steer them from some monstrous action figure to a pro-social doll. Even in the most progressive households, where we make such a point of letting children feel what they feel, we rush to substitute an enlightened discussion for the raw material of rageful fantasy. In the process, we risk confusing them about their natural aggression in the same way the Victorians confused their children about their sexuality. When we try to protect our children from their own feelings and fantasies, we shelter them not against violence but against power and selfhood.

When Life Imitates Video

••

JOHN LEO

Columnist John Leo has written for a wide variety of publications, including Time, *the* New York Times, Commonweal, *the* Village Voice, *and* U.S. News and World Report, *and has served as deputy commissioner for the New York City Environmental Protection Agency and advisor to the* Columbia Journalism Review. *His most recent writing includes a book on contemporary society,* Incorrect Thoughts *(2000), and regular contributions to* TownHall.com, *a conservative Web community that gathers talk show hosts, writers, and others into dialogue about politics and culture.*

TERMS TO RECOGNIZE

scenario *(para. 1)*	an imagined plot or sequence of events
cackled *(para. 1)*	laughed in a shrill, harsh manner
morbid *(para. 1)*	gloomy and unwholesome
arsenal *(para. 2)*	collection
maiming *(para. 3)*	crippling, disfiguring
maltreated *(para. 4)*	abused, badly treated
aversion *(para. 5)*	a strong feeling against, rejection of
primitive *(para. 5)*	simplistic, basic
empathy *(para. 6)*	identification with or understanding of another person's feelings or experience
sociopath *(para. 6)*	personality disorder associated with antisocial behavior

Was it real life or an acted-out video game? Marching through a   1
large building using various bombs and guns to pick off victims is a conventional video-game scenario. In the Colorado massacre, Dylan Klebold and Eric Harris used pistol-grip shotguns, as in some video-arcade games. The pools of blood, screams of agony, and pleas for mercy must have been familiar—they are featured in some of the newer and more realistic kill-for-kicks games. "With each kill," the *Los Angeles Times* reported, "the teens cackled and shouted as though playing one of the morbid video games they loved." And they ended their spree by shooting themselves in the head, the final act in the game *Postal*, and, in fact, the only way to end it.

Did the sensibilities created by the modern, video kill games play a role in the Littleton massacre? Apparently so. Note the cool and casual cruelty, the outlandish arsenal of weapons, the cheering and laughing while hunting down victims one by one. All of this seems to reflect the style and feel of the video killing games they played so often. 2

No, there isn't any direct connection between most murderous games and most murders. And yes, the primary responsibility for protecting children from dangerous games lies with their parents, many of whom like to blame the entertainment industry for their own failings. But there is a cultural problem here: We are now a society in which the chief form of play for millions of youngsters is making large numbers of people die. Hurting and maiming others is the central fun activity in video games played so addictively by the young. A widely cited survey of 900 fourth- through-eighth-grade students found that almost half of the children said their favorite electronic games involve violence. Can it be that all this constant training in make-believe killing has no social effects? 3

The conventional argument is that this is a harmless activity among children who know the difference between fantasy and reality. But the games are often played by unstable youngsters unsure about the difference. Many of these have been maltreated or rejected and left alone most of the time (a precondition for playing the games obsessively). Adolescent feelings of resentment, powerlessness, and revenge pour into the killing games. In these children, the games can become a dress rehearsal for the real thing. 4

Psychologist David Grossman of Arkansas State University, a retired Army officer, thinks "point and shoot" video games have the same effect as military strategies used to break down a soldier's aversion to killing. During World War II only 15 to 20 percent of all American soldiers fired their weapons in battle. Shooting games in which the target is a man-shaped outline, the Army found, made recruits more willing to "make killing a reflex action." Video games are much more powerful versions of the military's primitive discovery about overcoming the reluctance to shoot. Grossman says Michael Carneal, the schoolboy shooter in Paducah, Ky., showed the effects of video-game lessons in killing. Carneal coolly shot nine times, hitting eight people, five of them in the head or neck. Head shots pay a bonus in many video games. Now the Marine Corps is adapting a version of *Doom*, the hyperviolent game played by one of the Littleton killers, for its own training purposes. 5

More realistic touches in video games help blur the boundary between fantasy and reality—guns carefully modeled on real ones, accurate-looking wounds, screams, and other sound effects, even the 6 recoil of a heavy rifle. Some newer games seem intent on erasing children's empathy and concern for others. Once the intended victims of video slaughter were mostly gangsters or aliens. Now some games invite players to blow away ordinary people who have done nothing wrong— pedestrians, marching bands, an elderly woman with a walker. In these games, the shooter is not a hero, just a violent sociopath. One ad for a Sony game says: "Get in touch with your gun-toting, testosterone-pumping, cold-blooded murdering side."

These killings are supposed to be taken as harmless over-the-top jokes. But the bottom line is that the young are being invited to enjoy the killing of vulnerable people picked at random. This looks like the final lesson in a course to eliminate any lingering resistance to killing.

7

SWAT teams and cops now turn up as the intended victims of some video-game killings. This has the effect of exploiting resentments toward law enforcement and making real-life shooting of cops more likely. This sensibility turns up in the hit movie *Matrix*: world-saving hero Keanu Reeves, in a mandatory Goth-style, long black coat packed with countless heavy-duty guns, is forced to blow away huge numbers of uniformed law-enforcement people.

8

"We have to start worrying about what we are putting into the minds of our young," says Grossman. "Pilots train on flight simulators, drivers on driving simulators, and now we have our children on murder simulators." If we want to avoid more Littleton-style massacres, we will begin taking the social effects of the killing games more seriously.

9

RESPONDING TO READINGS

After reading these articles, would you change or add to the lists that you made in responding to the Preparing to Read prompt? How do you explain the changes you made? If you didn't make any changes, why didn't you?

CONSIDERING CONTENT

1. What did Jones learn about the value of violent media from his own and his son's childhood experiences with the Hulk and Tarzan? How might Leo interpret those experiences?
2. What are "point and shoot" video games? What effects does Leo fear from such games? Would Jones see the games as necessarily having the same effects?
3. What claims are made by each author about the relationship between aggression and human nature? How do their positions on this issue affect their attitudes toward violent media?

4. What does Jones mean by the term "creative violence"? Would Leo accept that violence can be creative?

5. Both authors discuss the part adults should play in children's use of and exposure to violent media. Outline the similarities and differences in the way the two authors view the role of adults.

CONSIDERING METHOD

1. Briefly outline each essay. Which organizational strategy best describes the development of each essay?

2. What types of evidence are used by Leo and Jones? Which forms of evidence did you find most persuasive? Which author seems to have the most authority on this topic? Explain your reasoning.

3. How effective are Jones and Leo in anticipating opposing arguments? Give one example of refutation from each essay to support your view. Tell why one of these examples is more effective than the other.

4. Both authors occasionally use very short sentences, even fragments, in their essays. Find an example in each essay and analyze why the author made the decision to use this type of sentence.

5. Describe the tone of each essay. *Tone* refers to the emotional quality of the writing—serious, light, friendly, angry, and so on. How did the tone affect your response to the argument?

6. Find what you believe is a flaw in the argument in a section of one of the two essays. Is the problem a logical fallacy? Explain.

WRITING STEP BY STEP

After reading these two essays, and reflecting on your own attitudes toward violent media, would you allow or even encourage teenagers to play violent video games, listen to music with violent lyrics, or watch violent films? Under what circumstances would such activities be permissible? Select one type of violent media and write an essay arguing your position.

A. Look back over your responses to Preparing to Read and expand any thoughts that would help you in exploring the position you plan to take and in preparing to refute the opposition's views.

B. List at least three major reasons to support your position. These will be your claims.

C. Review your options for arranging an argument (p. 294–95) and decide which bests suits your topic and position. Make a sketch or outline based on your claims. Think of what people on the other side of the issue would say. Be sure to include refutation at appropriate points in the argument, or group your refutations in one place.

D. Identify the types of evidence you have available or would need to gather to support your position. Consider, for example, using personal experience and research, as Jones does, or examples, as Leo does. You might interview other people to gather evidence and get suggestions for research sources.

E. Begin the essay with either a personal experience or anecdote, using Jones's or Leo's essay as your model.

F. Close by summarizing your main argument. You might end with a rhetorical question, as Jeff Pearlman does (p. 311); with a short emphatic sentence, as Anna Quindlen does (p. 350); or with a prediction about what the future holds, as James Dobson does (p. 305).

OTHER WRITING IDEAS

1. WRITING ABOUT READING. Select one of the two essays and write a letter to the author in which you disagree with his point of view. Be sure to cite specific points that you dispute, and explain the reasons for your difference of opinion. Pretend that you will really send your letter to the author. How might this reality affect the tone of your writing?

2. USING THE INTERNET. Spend some time on the Internet reading reviews of at least two video games with violent content, ones you have played or ones mentioned in the Jones and Leo essays (such as *Mortal Kombat, Postal,* or *Doom*). You can find professional reviews and players' responses at sites such as Amazon.com, for example. Make a list of the reasons people give for recommending or enjoying the games. Then make a list of any criticisms of the games that have to do with the negative effects on the players. Now write a pro-and-con essay on allowing teenagers to play video games. Evidence can include personal experience, information from the Jones and Leo articles, and evidence gained from your Internet research.

3. COLLABORATIVE WRITING. Parenting, especially making decisions about the lives of teenagers, is a complicated business. Get together with a group of your classmates and brainstorm a list of issues teens and their parents must negotiate: dating, driving, clothing style, neatness at home, post–high school plans. Either as a group or on your own, select one topic to explore further and to narrow to a specific question, for example, "At what age should a parent allow a teen to begin dating?" Write an essay using the "Writing Step by Step" guidelines.

GAINING WORD POWER

Make a list of loaded language (highly connotative language) used in each article. Gerard Jones, for example, describes one of the young women with whom he worked as having used Ice T's rap music to feel "powerful, ruthless, and invulnerable." But he then uses the phrase "flowered in college" to capture the positive effects of these feelings on her life. This is in stark contrast to the harshness and violence often associated with media violence. Which author uses the most emotionally charged words and phrases? What effect does this usage have on you as a reader? Select a few examples and rewrite them to achieve a different, perhaps more neutral, effect.

EDITING SKILLS: USING QUESTIONS

Notice how John Leo poses questions to open his arguments:

Was it real life or an acted-out video game?

Did the sensibilities created by the modern video games play a role in the Littleton massacre?

Can it be that all this constant training in make-believe killing has no social effects?

These are **rhetorical questions**; they don't require answers. In fact, authors intend to answer them for their readers. You can use rhetorical questions for various purposes: to provoke thought, to set a tone, to add emphasis to a point, to assert or deny a claim indirectly, or to establish the direction of a discussion. They will add variety to your writing, but like any special technique, they lose their effect when used too often.

EXERCISE

1. Gerard Jones chose not to use rhetorical questions as part of his argument. Look at the essay, especially paragraphs 8 through 15, and insert at least two rhetorical questions that would serve one or more of the five purposes outlined in the definition of the term above. Or rewrite one or two of Jones's sentences and turn them into effective rhetorical questions.

2. Look at one of the essays you have written for this course, and find a spot where you could have used a rhetorical question for one of the five purposes. Rewrite the surrounding sentences from your essay,

with the new rhetorical question included. Explain why you like the new version better, or why not.

☜ WEB SITE

www.media-awareness.ca/english/issues/violence/index.cfm
This Web page from the Canadian Media Awareness Network presents a comprehensive introduction to the issues related to media violence. The Research on the Effects of Media Violence link would be a good first step in finding sources for writing a documented essay.

PERSPECTIVES ON IMMIGRATION TO THE UNITED STATES

Since European explorers landed on America's shores, the United States has been a nation of immigrants, and tension between those who are already citizens and those who want to be citizens is nothing new. Do immigrants bring valuable diversity and a needed work force to the country, or do they threaten American values, take jobs from citizens, and create a drain on social services? An estimated 850,000 undocumented immigrants enter the country each year, mostly across the border with Mexico, making illegal immigration one of the most pressing political concerns of the day. The heated national and regional debates have focused on a number of issues: border security, social and educational programs for temporary workers, criminal penalties for existing illegals, tougher laws requiring employers to verify the status of their workers, guest worker plans, and an easier path for immigrants to become legal. These issues will not be easily resolved, especially since public opinion is deeply divided, as many polls indicate:

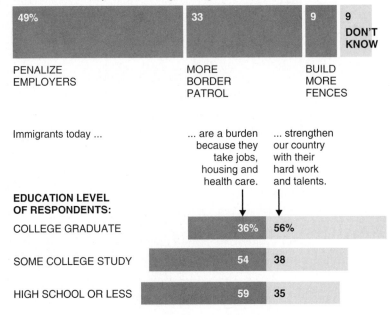

The readings in this section address many of the questions involved in the ongoing debate about immigrants in the United States. Also included are several visual texts that demonstrate how arguments can be made or enhanced graphically.

PREPARING TO READ

Before reading the following three essays on immigration, jot down a list of your own thoughts about the matter. What have you heard or read about it? What do your parents and friends think about it? Does immigration touch you personally—for example, were your parents or grandparents immigrants? Does your neighborhood include many immigrants? Print or write your thoughts and memories—they don't need to be organized or in complete sentences—on pages leaving wide blank margins.

••

We Don't Need "Guest Workers"

••

Robert J. Samuelson

In 1984, Robert Samuelson became a contributing editor at Newsweek *magazine, where he writes a biweekly column on business and economics. He began his career in 1969 as a business reporter for the* Washington Post, *and he still writes articles for that newspaper as well as for the* Los Angeles Times, *the* Boston Globe, *and other influential publications. He has won a number of journalism awards, including the Gerald Loeb Award for Best Commentary (1993 and 1986). Samuelson has also written two books:* The Good Life and Its Discontents: The American Dream in the Age of Enlightenment *(1997) and* Untruth: Why the Conventional Wisdom Is (Almost Always) Wrong *(2001). The following article appeared in the* Washington Post.

TERMS TO RECOGNIZE

assimilate *(para. 4)*	adapt, fit in, absorb into an established culture
Minutemen *(para. 4)*	self-appointed civilian groups formed to deter illegal crossings of U.S. borders, especially the border with Mexico
replenished *(para. 4)*	supplied, refilled
staunch *(para. 9)*	firm, steadfast, true
exploitation *(para. 10)*	being taken advantage of
incontestable *(para. 10)*	unquestioned, certain

March 22, 2006. Economist Philip Martin of the University of Califor- 1
nia likes to tell a story about the state's tomato industry. In the early 1960s,
growers relied on seasonal Mexican laborers, brought in under the government's "bracero" program. The Mexicans picked the tomatoes that were
then processed into ketchup and other products. In 1964 Congress killed
the program despite growers' warnings that its abolition would doom their
industry. What happened? Well, plant scientists developed oblong tomatoes that could be harvested by machine. Since then, California's tomato
output has risen fivefold.

It's a story worth remembering, because we're being warned again 2
that we need huge numbers of "guest workers"—meaning unskilled laborers
from Mexico and Central America—to relieve U.S. "labor shortages."
Indeed, the shortages will supposedly worsen as baby boomers retire. President Bush wants an open-ended program. Sens. Edward M. Kennedy
(D-Mass.) and John McCain (R-Ariz.) advocate initially admitting 400,000
guest workers annually. The Senate is considering these and other plans.

Gosh, they're all bad ideas. 3

Guest workers would mainly legalize today's vast inflows of illegal 4
immigrants, with the same consequence: We'd be importing poverty. This
isn't because these immigrants aren't hardworking; many are. Nor is it
because they don't assimilate; many do. But they generally don't go home,
assimilation is slow, and the ranks of the poor are constantly replenished.
Since 1980 the number of Hispanics with incomes below the government's
poverty line (about $19,300 in 2004 for a family of four) has risen 162 per-
cent. Over the same period, the number of non-Hispanic whites in poverty
rose 3 percent and the number of blacks, 9.5 percent. What we have now—
and would with guest workers—is a conscious policy of creating poverty in
the United States while relieving it in Mexico. By and large, this is a bad bar-
gain for the United States. It stresses local schools, hospitals, and housing;
it feeds social tensions (witness the Minutemen). To be sure, some Americans get cheap housecleaning or landscaping services. But if more mowed
their own lawns or did their own laundry, it wouldn't be a tragedy.

The most lunatic notion is that admitting more poor Latino workers 5
would ease the labor market strains of retiring baby boomers. The two aren't
close substitutes for each other. Among immigrant Mexican and Central American workers in 2004, only 7 percent had a college degree and nearly 60 percent
lacked a high school diploma, according to the Congressional Budget Office
(CBO). Among native-born U.S. workers, 32 percent had a college degree and
only 6 percent did not have a high school diploma. Far from softening the social
problems of an aging society, more poor immigrants might aggravate them by
pitting older retirees against younger Hispanics for limited government benefits.

It's a myth that the U.S. economy "needs" more poor immigrants. The 6
illegal immigrants already here represent only about 4.9 percent of the labor
force, the Pew Hispanic Center reports. In no major occupation are they a
majority. They're 36 percent of insulation workers, 28 percent of drywall
installers, and 20 percent of cooks. They're drawn here by wage differences,
not labor "shortages." In 2004, the median hourly wage in Mexico was $1.86,
compared with $9 for Mexicans working in the United States, said Rakesh
Kochhar of Pew. With high labor turnover in the jobs they take, most new illegal immigrants can get work by accepting wages slightly below prevailing levels.

Hardly anyone thinks that most illegal immigrants will leave. But 7
what would happen if new illegal immigration stopped and wasn't replaced
by guest workers? Well, some employers would raise wages to attract U.S.
workers. Facing greater labor costs, some industries would—like the tomato
growers in the 1960s—find ways to minimize those costs. As to the rest,
what's wrong with higher wages for the poorest workers? From 1994 to
2004, the wages of high school dropouts rose only 2.3 percent (after infla-
tion) compared with 11.9 percent for college graduates.

President Bush says his guest worker program would "match willing 8
foreign workers with willing American employers, when no Americans can
be found to fill the jobs." But at some higher wage, there would be willing
Americans. The number of native high school dropouts with jobs declined
by 1.3 million from 2000 to 2005, estimates Steven Camarota of the Center
for Immigration Studies, which favors less immigration. Some lost jobs to
immigrants. Unemployment remains high for some groups (9.3 percent for
African Americans, 12.7 percent for white teenagers).

Business organizations understandably support guest worker pro- 9
grams. They like cheap labor and ignore the social consequences. What's
more perplexing is why liberals, staunch opponents of poverty and inequality, support a program that worsens poverty and inequality. Poor immigrant
workers hurt the wages of unskilled Americans. The only question is how
much. Studies suggest a range "from negligible to an earnings reduction of
almost 10 percent," according to the CBO.

It's said that having guest workers is better than having poor illegal 10
immigrants. With legal status, they'd have rights and protections. They'd
have more peace of mind and face less exploitation by employers. This
would be convincing if its premise were incontestable: that we can't control
our southern border. But that's unproved. We've never tried a policy of real
barriers and strict enforcement against companies that hire illegal immigrants. Until that's shown to be ineffective, we shouldn't adopt guest
worker programs that don't solve serious social problems—but add to them.

Enforcement

The number of border patrol agents nation-wide rose 179 percent from 1992 to 2006.

But actions against businesses that employ illegal immigrants (here, warnings of impending fines) by 2004 had virtually stopped.

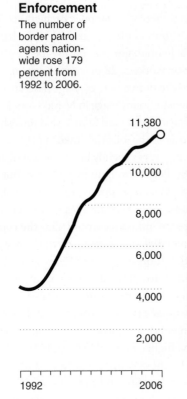

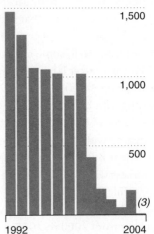

Next Step for Immigration

••

ARNOLD SCHWARZENEGGER

Born in Austria in 1947, Arnold Alois Schwarzenegger moved to the United States in 1968 and became a U.S. citizen in 1983, although he also retains his Austrian citizenship. Schwarzenegger first gained fame as a bodybuilder, winning the title of Mr. Universe five times. He began appearing in motion pictures in 1973 and became a major star primarily because of such hit films as Conan the Barbarian *(1982) and* The Terminator *(1984) and its sequels. In 1986 he married TV journalist Maria Shriver, niece of the late John F. Kennedy. Schwarzenegger was elected in 2003 to serve the remainder of Gray Davis's term as governor of California. He was re-elected in 2006 and was sworn in for his second term in January of 2007. The following article appeared in the* Los Angeles Times.

TERMS TO RECOGNIZE

comprehensive *(para. 3)*	all-inclusive, extensive, thorough
human trafficking *(para. 6)*	recruiting and transporting people for illicit purposes, like enforced labor or prostitution
amnesty *(para. 8)*	a pardon, forgiveness
anarchy *(para. 8)*	lawlessness, lack of order
rhetoric *(para. 11)*	high-blown language that says nothing

March 28, 2006. Thirty-eight years ago, I first arrived in America owning nothing but a dream. I had few friends, little money and knew even less English. But of this I was certain: Here was a land where I could go as far and as fast as my dreams and my desire would take me. Now, nearly 40 years later, my immigrant dream has come true. And thanks to my journey, I bring a unique perspective to the immigration discussion. I don't just talk about immigrants—I am an immigrant. [1]

A few days ago, huge crowds assembled in California and proclaimed: "*Aqui estamos.*" I say to each one of them: Yes, we are here. Now we must ask: Where do we go from here? [2]

As our nation begins a national debate on immigration, I propose that we lower our voices and lift our sights. We need a debate that attacks the issue without attacking individuals. And we need a comprehensive new law that respects immigrants and protects our nation. Frankly, the debate in Congress thus far has focused too much on politics and too little on principles. [3]

Ever since I first ran for office, I've talked about the importance of having a comprehensive immigration policy. Now the moment has arrived.

Our goal should be to create a policy that reflects our national 4 motto: *e pluribus unum*—Out of many, one. Here are the basic immigration principles that have always guided me and that I believe should guide Congress.

First, immigration is about our security. The first order of business for 5 the federal government is to secure our borders. And Washington simply must do a better job of it. We learned on 9/11 that not all those who cross our borders want to share in the American dream. A few want to replace it with a nightmare. If we don't know who is coming over our borders, we won't know what they might do. And in a post-Sept.11 world, that is a risk we cannot take. Congress must strengthen our borders.

That's why as governor of California, I have supported legislation to 6 end human trafficking and stop the issuance of driver's licenses to those who aren't legal residents. By bringing folks out of the shadows and into the light, we help immigrants, and we help America. Criminalizing immigrants for coming here is a slogan, not a solution. Instead, I urge Congress to get tough on those illegal immigrants who are a danger to society. If an illegal immigrant commits a serious crime, he must leave the country—one strike and you're out. No excuses, no delays.

Second, immigration is about our economy. The freest nation in the 7 world, and the freest economy in history, depend on a free flow of people. Immigrants are here to work and contribute. I support efforts to ensure that our businesses have the workers they need and that immigrants are treated with the respect they deserve. We should pass a commonsense temporary-worker program so that every person in our nation is documented.

We can embrace the immigrant without endorsing illegal immigration. 8 Granting citizenship to people who are here illegally is not just amnesty—it's anarchy. We are a country of immigrants, yes. But we are also a nation of laws. People who want to be citizens will want to do it the right way.

Finally, immigration is about our values. Too often the debate centers 9 on what immigrants owe us. Too seldom do we ask what we owe them. Above all, we owe it to our country and our immigrants to share our values. We should talk about our history, our institutions, and our beliefs. We should assimilate immigrants into the mainstream. We want immigrants to not just live in America but to live as Americans.

Marine Lance Cpl. O. J. Santa Maria is a fine example of this. He is 10 an immigrant who was living in Daly City, Calif., when he enlisted in the Marines. During the Iraq war, he was severely wounded. Because of his military service, he was granted citizenship. When the oath of citizenship was read to him, he stood up from his wheelchair in pain and in tears. "It's for the respect," he said later when asked why he stood. "I'm taking an oath to the Constitution of the United States of America." Lance Cpl. Santa Maria wanted to be an American, and we should be glad he became one. We are a better nation because of this immigrant Marine.

As a river gains strength and momentum from joining waters, so   11
America is blessed and enriched by new people and new energy. But we still need a new immigration law to properly channel the flow. And we need a comprehensive approach based in reality, not rhetoric.

This is the time for a permanent solution to our broken immigration   12
system. This is the chance to again become a country of immigrants and a nation of laws.

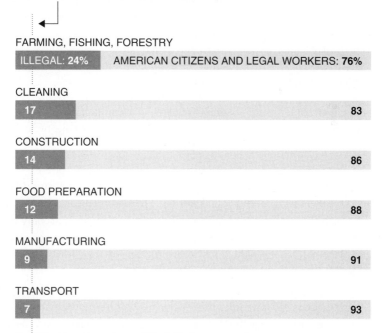

Where They Work

It is suggested that illegal workers do the jobs that others aren't willing to do. But it is estimated that legal workers hold most of the jobs even in occupations where illegals are highly concentrated (that is, beyond their **4.9% share** of the overall labor force).

FARMING, FISHING, FORESTRY

| ILLEGAL: 24% | AMERICAN CITIZENS AND LEGAL WORKERS: 76% |

CLEANING

17   83

CONSTRUCTION

14   86

FOOD PREPARATION

12   88

MANUFACTURING

9   91

TRANSPORT

7   93

Illegal immigrants make up **2%** of all other occupations.

We Are All Immigrants

••

ANNA QUINDLEN

Anna Quindlen was born in Philadelphia, Pennsylvania, of Irish-American and Italian-American descent. After graduating in 1974 from Barnard College in New York City, she began her journalism career as a reporter for the New York Post. *She then held several posts at the* New York Times. *Her regular column for the* Times, *"Public and Private," won the Pulitzer Prize for commentary in 1992. She currently writes a biweekly column for* Newsweek *magazine. Quindlen has also written four bestselling novels, four nonfiction books, and two children's books. The following column appeared in* Newsweek.

TERMS TO RECOGNIZE

polyglot *(para. 2)* — using several languages
glut *(para. 3)* — excess, surplus
demonize *(para. 3)* — represent as evil or diabolical
demagoguery *(para. 4)* — practice of appealing to emotions and prejudices
amped up *(para. 4)* — turned up, increased
lax *(para. 5)* — loose, not firm or strict
rhetoric *(para. 6)* — high-blown language that says nothing
sanctions *(para. 7)* — penalties
incensed *(para. 8)* — angered, infuriated
dago *(para. 9)* — demeaning slang for an Italian
xenophobic *(para. 10)* — unduly fearful or disapproving of foreigners and foreign cultures

May 15, 2006. On May Day a persistent rumble came from Market   1
Street in San Francisco, but it was not the oft-predicted earthquake, or at least not in the geologic sense. Thousands of people were marching down the thoroughfare, from the Embarcadero to city hall, holding signs. NO HUMAN BEING IS ILLEGAL. I AM A WORKER, NOT A CRIMINAL. TODAY I MARCH, TOMORROW I VOTE. I PAY TAXES.

The polyglot city by the bay is so familiar with the protest march that   2
longtime citizens say it handles the inconveniences better than any place else. Some of them remember the Vietnam War marches, the feminist rallies. The May Day demonstration bore some resemblance to both, which was not surprising. Immigration is the leading edge of a deep and wide sea change in the United States today, just as those issues were in their own time.

Of course, this is not a new issue. The Founding Fathers started out   3
with a glut of land and a deficit of warm bodies. But over its history America's more-established residents have always found ways to demonize the newcomers to the nation needed to fill it and till it. It was only human, the contempt for the different, the shock of the new.

Today, because so many immigrants have entered the country illegally   4
or are living here on visas that expired long ago, the demagoguery has been amped up full throttle. Although the conventional wisdom is that immigrants are civic freeloaders, the woman with a sign that said I PAY TAXES was reflecting the truth. Millions of undocumented immigrants pay income taxes using a special identification number the IRS provides. They pay into the Social Security system, too, even though they're not eligible to collect benefits. In fact, they may be helping to keep the system afloat, with $7 billion currently in a designated suspense file, much of which is believed to have come from undocumented workers.

A man carrying a sign saying I AM A WORKER, NOT A CRIMINAL   5
said he pays taxes, too, through his construction job. All three of his children were born in the United States. Although he said he had a hard time deciphering government forms—and don't we all?—he had applied for a green card and had been waiting for four years. In 2004 there was a backlog of more than 6 million unprocessed immigration petitions, a record high. So much for suggestions that immigrants are lax about regularizing their status. Clearly the laxity is at least partly federal.

It's true that immigrants use government services: schools, public hos-   6
pitals. It's also true that many pay their way through income and sales taxes. Despite the rhetoric, no one really knows whether they wind up being a loss or a gain for the economy. Certainly lots of them work. A state like Arizona, for instance, could not keep pace with the demand for new homes at reasonable cost without immigrant workers, many of them undocumented.

The counterargument is that that drives down the wages of American   7
citizens. It's galling to hear that argument from members of Congress, who have not raised the federal minimum wage for almost a decade. Most of those politicians blame the workers for their willingness to accept low wages. Don't hold your breath waiting for significant sanctions against those companies that shut their eyes to the immigration status of their employees—and that also make large political contributions.

Americans who are really incensed by millions of undocumented   8
immigrants can take action, just as those marching in the streets did. They can refuse to eat fruits and vegetables picked by those immigrants. They can

refuse to buy homes on which they worked. After all, if a migrant worker like Cesar Chavez could organize a national boycott of grapes, then opponents of immigration could surely organize something similar. But they won't. We like our cheap houses and our fresh fruit. And our government likes the bait-and-switch, taking taxes from workers whose existence it will not recognize. The borders are most porous in Washington, D.C.

Full disclosure: I'm the granddaughter of immigrants, and I know   9
how much of the melting pot is a myth. My grandparents always referred to my father as "an American boy," which meant he was not from Italy. It was not a compliment. They didn't melt; their daughter did, although one of the only times I ever saw her bitter was when she explained what the word "dago" meant.

There are big decisions to be made about the vast wave of undocu-   10
mented workers in this country, issues that go beyond slogans and placards. But there's no premium in discussing those issues in xenophobic half-truths, in talking about what undocumented immigrants cost the country without talking about what they contribute, in talking about them as illegals when they are nannies, waiters, roofers, and the parents of American citizens. One fact is indisputable: the essence of America is free enterprise and human rights. It's why people come here in the first place. WE ARE ALL IMMI-GRANTS, read signs on Market Street. Some of us just got here sooner.

RESPONDING TO READINGS

Review the page or pages you wrote for Preparing to Read. In the wide margins next to your points, write notes inspired by reading the essays by Samuelson, Schwarzenegger, and Quindlen and by examining the graphics in this section. These notes might record similarities, differences, elaborations on your reactions on your reactions, or changes in your thoughts and factual knowledge.

CONSIDERING CONTENT

1. Samuelson begins his essay with a story about the tomato industry. What is the point of this story? When does he refer to it later? Is this a topic either Schwarzenegger or Quindlen covers? Compare their views.

2. Why does Samuelson label our immigration system "a conscious policy of creating poverty"? Why is the word "conscious" important in that phrase? When you wrote your own thoughts before reading the essays, did you include considerations about poverty?

3. According to Samuelson, why will immigrant workers fail to make up for retiring baby boomers in the workforce?

4. Why did U. S. high school dropouts lose jobs to immigrants (para. 8), according to Samuelson? Was the idea of citizens losing jobs to noncitizens in your own thinking originally?

5. What concrete policy changes regarding immigration law would each writer endorse? That is, can you tell what each writer would *do* if he or she had the power to make the decisions?

6. What are Schwarzenegger's three main points? How do they compare to Samuelson's main points?

7. Was O. J. Santa Maria an illegal immigrant when he enlisted in the Marines and was wounded in battle? How do you know?

8. What was the reason for the protest Quindlen describes in her introduction? Who were the protesters?

9. Quindlen writes that historically, Americans have always demonized newcomers who were needed to build the country. Do you think this is true? Can you think of an example? Was this idea included in your pre- or post-reading notes?

10. In paragraph 5, Quindlen suggests that the federal government is partly to blame for the number of illegal immigrants in this country. Why does she think so?

11. What would Samuelson reply to Quindlen's paragraph 6?

12. What are the relevant credentials of each writer? Do their credentials affect how seriously you take their arguments?

CONSIDERING METHOD

1. In each piece, find at least one example of the author's use of very short sentences for emphasis. Did you notice any of these when you first read the essays? Why are these short sentences effective?

2. Compare the openings of the three pieces. Which opening caught your attention most? Why?

3. Look through the essays for examples of logical fallacies. Hint: The *either-or fallacy* and the *non sequitur* are particularly prominent in political argument.

4. In each essay, point out where you think the author's main point is most strongly expressed. Compare your choices with other students' to see whether you agree or disagree. Does each writer put the main point in the same place within his or her essay?

5. Which essay has the most facts and figures? Does this affect your acceptance of the author's points? Which essay has the least amount of concrete support? Does this affect your response to the author's point of view?

6. Review each essay to identify how each writer deals with the opposition—how he or she handles a refutation. Choose what you consider the strongest and the weakest refutation in the whole batch of essays. Explain your choices.

7. Schwarzenegger writes, "I propose that we lower our voices and lift our sights" (para. 3). This is an example of parallel structure used for memorable style and high impact. Find at least two other parallel structures in Schwarzenegger's writing. Can you find any in Samuelson's and Quindlen's writing?

WRITING STEP BY STEP

Research the immigration laws and practices in some other developed country, like Austria, Canada, Japan, or Sweden. You will be explaining these laws and arguing for lessons the United States can or cannot learn from them.

A. In your opening, explain how you have learned about the immigration policies of both the United States and the other country. Your purpose is to give yourself some credibility as a person worth listening to on these topics.

B. Summarize the U.S. policies on immigration in the next section. It might be helpful to review the notes you made in the Responding to Reading section.

C. Summarize the policies of the other developed country in your next section. Include some of the pros and cons of these policies as they are practiced in the other country.

D. In the next paragraph or two, specify the main differences between the two countries' approaches to immigration.

E. In the next part of your paper, begin by suggesting changes needed in the American system, and then answer the question, "Should the United States adopt any of the other country's approaches to immigration?" Choose two or three policies of the other country, and explain why they would be or would not be good for the United States. This section of your paper may take two to four paragraphs.

F. In a separate section, or integrated into your paragraphs for part E of this essay, be sure that you consider what people opposing your suggestions might say. Include refutations for these points.

G. Conclude with a paragraph about what we can learn from other countries' political systems.

OTHER WRITING IDEAS

1. Choose another national problem that you might read about in today's newspapers and magazines, such as the nation's health care, wage differentials between men and women, drug addiction, or pollution of water resources. As you did in the Step by Step essay, find out how another developed country views the situation and deals with it. Follow the Step by Step guidelines to write an essay about what approaches the United States could and could not adopt fruitfully.

2. COLLABORATIVE WRITING. Samuelson reports the 2004 poverty line at $19,300 for a family of four. Find out what the poverty line is now and what some of the definitions and issues surrounding it are today. Get together with other students to discuss the idea of the poverty line and what controversial questions it brings up. Choose one of these controversies and write a persuasive essay about it.

3. USING THE INTERNET. How many U. S. citizens today do not have high school diplomas? How many students enter high school and do not complete it? Are there geographical or other differences in the graduation rates across the nation? Are high school dropouts employed, and where? After completing Internet research using reputable Web sites to answer these questions, write an essay in which you inform your reader about the situation and propose some changes in policy that would help solve one or more of the problems involved in high school noncompletion.

4. Write a 750-word guest editorial for your hometown newspaper explaining what your community can do to ease the problems of illegal immigration in the United States. Be sure to let your readers know what steps they personally can take. The notes you made in the Responding to Readings section might come in handy for this writing task.

5. WRITING ABOUT READING. What points in the three selections are supported or confirmed by the graphs "Enforcement" and "Where They Work"? Do the graphs call into question the views expressed in the readings? What point does the cartoon "A Congressman Checks in Back Home" make? Which reading does it seem to support the most?

GAINING WORD POWER

Writers sometimes make references to familiar or significant people, places, objects, or events from history, the Bible, and literature. These references are called **allusions;** they help a writer to set the tone or heighten the meaning without going into a long explanation. Define the following references from the essays in this section. Use a dictionary or other reference works to help you.

1. Who are the Minutemen (Samuelson, para. 4), and why did they choose this name for their group?
2. What is the origin of the national motto, *e pluribus unum* (Schwarzenegger, para. 4)? When and why was it adopted as the motto of the United States?
3. What is "the American dream" (Schwarzenegger, para. 5)? Ask a number of people to see how they define this phrase. Can you find a definite, authoritative definition?
4. What is an embarcadero (Quindlen, para. 1)? How does the origin of the word relate to the topic of immigration?
5. Who were the Founding Fathers (Quindlen, para. 3)? Were there any Founding Mothers?
6. What is the "bait-and-switch" (Quindlen, para. 8) strategy? Where and when is it ordinarily used? How does Quindlen apply it to the immigration topic?

EDITING SKILLS: USING COLONS

Copy the following passages exactly.

Guest workers would mainly legalize today's vast inflows of illegal immigrants, with the same consequences: We'd be importing poverty.

This would be convincing if its premise were incontestable: that we can't control our southern border.

But of this I was certain: Here was a land where I could go as far and as fast as my dreams and my desire would take me.

I say to each one of them: Yes, we are here.

It's true that immigrants use government services: schools, public hospitals.

One fact is indisputable: the essence of America is free enterprise and human rights.

If you copied correctly, you put a colon (:) in each passage. Reread what you copied, and see whether you can come up with a rule about the use of the colon.

You probably noticed that the colon comes after a complete sentence. Go back and reread the first portion of each example. The colon then introduces something that specifies or expands on the sentence before the colon. The second part doesn't have to be a complete sentence, as you see in the last example. (It doesn't have to be a direct quotation, either.) If you think of the colon as a verbal equal sign (=), you get the main relationship it suggests between the two parts. Neglecting to put a full sentence before a colon, when you are introducing a list, is one of the most frequent mistakes in written English.

EXERCISE

Complete the following passages that include colons.

1. Sami has already bought her party supplies: _____.
2. Beau's next statement gave away his secret plans: _____.
3. The plans were not completely reasonable: _____.
4. _____: a paperback detective novel, a historical romance, and a Far Side cartoon.
5. _____: Austin cried only a little while.

Now edit the essay you just wrote, looking for places where you could have used a colon instead of a period or a semicolon. After consulting with your instructor, change the punctuation mark to a colon.

🌐 WEB SITES

www.dhs.gov/ximgtn/statistics/index.shtm
The Department of Homeland Security's Office of Immigration Statistics offers studies and publications on a variety of topics relating to the status of immigrants and the enforcement of immigration laws.
www.cis.org
The Center for Immigration Studies site provides independent, nonpartisan research and policy analysis of the economic, social, demographic, fiscal, and other impacts of immigration on the United States.
http://pewhispanic.org/
You will find reports, surveys, factsheets, and other materials "chronicling Latinos' diverse experiences in a changing America" on this site from the Pew Hispanic Center, a wing of the Pew Research Center for the People and the Press.

Combining Strategies: Further Readings

This chapter provides you with additional reading selections. Although some of these readings are developed by one controlling strategy, most of them illustrate combinations of various strategies. As you read, use the following questions to analyze how a writer combines strategies:

- What are the purpose and thesis of the essay? Who is the intended audience?
- Which strategy controls or dominates the essay?
- How does this strategy help readers to understand the essay's thesis and purpose?
- What other strategies appear in the essay?
- What do these strategies contribute to the readers' understanding of the essay's thesis and purpose?

Also keep in mind our suggestions for being an active reader: preview the selection, make predictions, pay attention to conventions, mark the text, use the dictionary, make inferences and associations, and summarize your reactions on paper. After reading the selection actively, you can then follow the process you've used in earlier chapters: reflect on the content, analyze the writer's techniques, and write something of your own that relates to the reading. When possible, discuss the readings and your written responses with your classmates.

Do We Fear the Right Things?

....

DAVID G. MYERS

David G. Myers is a professor of psychology at Michigan's Hope College, where he has repeatedly been voted "outstanding professor" by students. His writings have appeared in more than four dozen journals and magazines, from Science *to* Scientific American, *and in a dozen books. You can enjoy Myers's flair for instruction in his best-selling introduction-to-psychology textbook,* Psychology. *The essay we reprint here appeared in the* Observer, *the journal of the American Psychological Society. The marginal notes identify the major rhetorical strategies.*

"Freedom and fear are at war," President Bush has told us. The terrorists' goal, he says, is "not only to kill and maim and destroy" but to frighten us into inaction. Alas, the terrorists have made progress in their fear war by diverting our anxieties from big risks toward smaller risks. Flying is a case in point. 1

> Cause-effect: why we fear flying and how it affects our lives (¶s 1–13).

Even before the horror of September 11 and the ensuing crash at Rockaway Beach, forty-four percent of those willing to risk flying told Gallup they felt fearful. "Every time I get off a plane, I view it as a failed suicide attempt," movie director Barry Sonnenfeld has said. After five crashed airliners, and with threats of more terror to come, cancellations understandably left airlines, travel agencies, and holiday hotels flying into the red. 2

Indeed, the terrorists may still be killing us, in ways unnoticed. If we now fly twenty percent less and instead drive half those unflown miles, we will spend two percent more time in motor vehicles. This translates into eight hundred more people dying as passengers and pedestrians. So, in just the next year the terrorists may indirectly kill three times more people on our highways than died on those four fated planes. 3

> Comparison and contrast: flying risks vs. driving risks (¶s 3–6).

Ah, but won't we have spared some of those folks fiery plane crashes? Likely not many, especially 4 now with heightened security, hardened cockpit doors, more reactive passengers, and the likelihood that future terrorists will hit us where we're not looking. National Safety Council data reveal that in the last half of the 1990s Americans were, mile for mile, thirty-seven times more likely to die in a vehicle crash than on a commercial flight. When I fly to New York, the most dangerous part of my journey is the drive to the Grand Rapids airport. (My highway risk may be muted by my not drinking and driving, but I'm still vulnerable to others who do.)

Or consider this: From 1990 through 2000 there were 1.4 deaths per ten million passengers on U.S. scheduled airlines. Flying understandably feels dangerous. But we have actually been less likely to crash and die on any flight than, when coin tossing, to flip twenty-two heads in a row.

Will yesterday's safety statistics predict the future? Even if not, terrorists could take down fifty more planes with sixty passengers each and—if we kept flying—we'd still have been safer this year in planes than on the road. Flying may be scary, but driving the same distance should be many times scarier.

Definition: characteristics of fears, developed through comparison and contrast

Why do we fear the wrong things? Why do so many smokers (whose habit shortens their lives, on average, by about five years) fret before flying (which, averaged across people, shortens life by one day)? Why do we fear terrorism more than accidents, which kill nearly as many per week in just the United States as did terrorism with its 2,527 worldwide deaths in all of the 1990s? Why do we fear violent crime more than clogged arteries?

Classification and division: types of fear, developed with examples (¶s 8–11)

Psychological science has identified four influences on our intuitions about risk. First, we fear what our ancestral history has prepared us to fear. Human emotions were road tested in the Stone Age. Yesterday's risks prepare us to fear snakes, lizards, and spiders, although all three combined now kill only a dozen Americans a year. Flying may

5

6

7

8

be far safer than biking, but our biological past predisposes us to fear confinement and heights, and therefore flying.

Second, we fear what we cannot control. Skiing, by one estimate, poses one thousand times the health and injury risk of food preservatives. Yet many people gladly assume the risk of skiing, which they control, but avoid preservatives. Driving we control, flying we do not. "We are loathe to let others do unto us what we happily do to ourselves," noted risk analyst Chauncey Starr.

Third, we fear what's immediate. Teens are indifferent to smoking's toxicity because they live more for the present than the distant future. Much of the plane's threat is telescoped into the moments of takeoff and landing, while the dangers of driving are diffused across many moments to come, each trivially dangerous.

Fourth, we fear what's most readily available in memory. Horrific images of a DC-10 catapulting across the Sioux City runway, or the Concorde exploding in Paris, or of United Flight 175 slicing into the World Trade Center, form indelible memories. And availability in memory provides our intuitive rule-of-thumb for judging risks. Small wonder that most of us perceive accidents as more lethal than strokes, and homicide as more lethal than diabetes. (In actuality, the Grim Reaper snatches twice as many lives by stroke as by accident and four times as many by diabetes as by homicide.)

Vivid, memorable images dominate our fears. We can know that unprovoked great white shark attacks have claimed merely sixty-seven lives worldwide since 1876. Yet after watching *Jaws* and reading vivid accounts of last summer's Atlantic coastal shark attacks, we may feel chills when an underwater object brushes our leg. A thousand massively publicized anthrax victims would similarly rivet our attention more than yet another 20,000+ annual influenza fatalities, or than

9

10

11

Examples: 12
vivid, memo-
rable fears

another 30,000+ lives claimed by guns (via suicide, homicide, and accident).

Examples: overestimated and underestimated risks.

As publicized Powerball lottery winners cause us to overestimate the infinitesimal odds of lottery success, so vivid airline casualties cause us to overestimate the infinitesimal odds of a lethal airline ticket. We comprehend Maria Grasso's winning $197 million in a 1999 Powerball lottery. We don't comprehend the 328 million losing tickets enabling her jackpot. We comprehend the 266 passengers and crew on those four fated flights. We don't comprehend the vast numbers of accident-free flights—16 million consecutive fatality-free takeoffs and landings during one stretch of the 1990s. The result: We overvalue lottery tickets, overestimate flight risk, and underestimate the dangers of driving.   13

Argument: reasons to resist exaggerated fear (¶s 14–15)

The moral: It's perfectly normal to fear purposeful violence from those who hate us. But with our emotions now calming a bit, perhaps it's time to check our fears against facts. "It's time to get back to life," said terror-victim widow Lisa Beamer before boarding the same flight her husband had taken on September 11. To be prudent is to be mindful of the realities of how humans die. By so doing, we can take away the terrorists' most omnipresent weapon: exaggerated fear.   14

And when terrorists strike again, remember the odds. If, God forbid, anthrax or truck bombs kill a thousand Americans, we will all recoil in horror. Small comfort, perhaps, but the odds are 284,000 to one that you won't be among them.   15

CONSIDERING CONTENT AND METHOD

1. What are the four reasons why we fear the wrong things, according to Myers? Can you think of other examples to go along with each reason?
2. Make a list of the examples Myers uses in pursuing his point. Do you find the examples persuasive?

3. Why does this essay include so many numbers? For instance, look at paragraph five, which has five numbers in two sentences. What was your response to the statistics in the essay? Why do you think you responded the way you did? What was Myers expecting about his audience for this essay?

WEBSITE

www.davidmyers.org/Brix?pageID=65

You will find an annotated version of "Do We Fear the Right Things?" on this site.

Salvation

....

L ANGSTON H UGHES

Langston Hughes (1902–1967) wrote often about the experience of African Americans in the United States in his newspaper columns, poetry, plays, and essays. He was a war correspondent during the Spanish Civil War and traveled the world doing jobs like dock worker and restaurant waiter. Hughes was an outstanding figure in the 1920s arts movement called the Harlem Renaissance in New York City. In the autobiographical essay we reprint here, Hughes reminisces about social pressure.

I was saved from sin when I was going on thirteen. But not really saved.   1
It happened like this. There was a big revival at my Auntie Reed's church. Every night for weeks there had been much preaching, singing, praying, and shouting, and some very hardened sinners had been brought to Christ, and the membership of the church had grown by leaps and bounds. Then just before the revival ended, they held a special meeting for children, "to bring the young lambs to the fold." My aunt spoke of it for days ahead. That night I was escorted to the front row and placed on the mourners' bench with all the other young sinners, who had not yet been brought to Jesus.

My aunt told me that when you were saved you saw a light, and   2
something happened to you inside! And Jesus came into your life! And God was with you from then on! She said you could see and hear and feel Jesus in your soul. I believed her. I had heard a great many old people say the same thing and it seemed to me they ought to know. So I sat there calmly in the hot crowded church, waiting for Jesus to come to me.

The preacher preached a wonderful rhythmical sermon, all moans   3
and shouts and lonely cries and dire pictures of hell, and then he sang a song about the ninety and nine safe in the fold, but one little lamb was left in the cold. Then he said, "Won't you come? Won't you come to Jesus? Young lambs, won't you come?" And he held out his arms to all us young sinners there on the mourners' bench. And the little girls cried. And some of them jumped up and went to Jesus right away. But most of us just sat there.

A great many old people came and knelt around us and prayed, old   4
women with jet-black faces and braided hair, old men with work-gnarled hands. And the church sang a song about the lower lights are burning, some poor sinners to be saved. And the whole building rocked with prayer and song.

Still I kept waiting to see Jesus.   5

Finally all the young people had gone to the altar and were saved, but   6
one boy and me. He was a rounder's son named Westley. Westley and I
were surrounded by sisters and deacons praying. It was very hot in the
church, and getting late now. Finally Westley said to me in a whisper: "God-
damn! I'm tired o' sitting here. Let's get up and be saved." So he got up and
was saved.

Then I was left all alone on the mourners' bench. My aunt came and   7
knelt at my knees and cried, while prayers and songs swirled all around me
in the little church. The whole congregation prayed for me alone, in a
mighty wail of moans and voices. And I kept waiting serenely for Jesus, waiting, waiting—but he didn't come. I wanted to see him, but nothing happened to me. Nothing! I wanted something to happen to me, but nothing
happened.

I heard the songs and the minister saying: "Why don't you come? My   8
dear child, why don't you come to Jesus? Jesus is waiting for you. He wants
you. Why don't you come? Sister Reed, what is this child's name?"

"Langston," my aunt sobbed.   9

"Langston, why don't you come? Why don't you come and be saved?   10
Oh, Lamb of God! Why don't you come?"

Now it was really getting late. I began to be ashamed of myself, hold-   11
ing everything up so long. I began to wonder what God thought about
Westley, who certainly hadn't seen Jesus either, but who was now sitting
proudly on the platform, swinging his knickerbockered legs and grinning
down at me, surrounded by deacons and old women on their knees praying.
God had not struck Westley dead for taking his name in vain or for lying in
the temple. So I decided that maybe to save further trouble, I'd better lie,
too, and say that Jesus had come, and get up and be saved.

So I got up.   12

Suddenly the whole room broke into a sea of shouting, as they saw   13
me rise. Waves of rejoicing swept the place. Women leaped into the air. My
aunt threw her arms around me. The minister took me by the hand and led
me to the platform.

When things quieted down, in a hushed silence, punctuated by a few   14
ecstatic "Amens," all the new young lambs were blessed in the name of
God. Then joyous singing filled the room.

That night, for the last time in my life but one—for I was a big boy   15
twelve years old—I cried. I cried, in bed alone, and couldn't stop. I buried
my head under the quilts, but my aunt heard me. She woke up and told my
uncle I was crying because the Holy Ghost had come into my life, and

because I had seen Jesus. But I was really crying because I couldn't bear to tell her that I had lied, that I had deceived everybody in the church, and I hadn't seen Jesus, and that now I didn't believe there was a Jesus any more, since he didn't come to help me.

CONSIDERING CONTENT AND METHOD

1. How does the style of this narrative reflect the child's point of view? How does it reflect the grown author's point of view?
2. Review the opening of Chapter 3 on narration and description. Point out elements of narrative and descriptive strategies in "Salvation."
3. How does this essay follow a cause and effect strategy (Chapter 9)? In other words, what causes and effects are described or suggested in "Salvation"?
4. In reading this essay, do you get the idea that Hughes is criticizing religion? What else might he be criticizing?

⚡ WEBSITE

www.learner.org/catalog/extras/vvspot/Hughes.html
"Spotlight on Langston Hughes" from the Voices & Visions series contains a video clip plus links to information and commentary about Hughes and his work.

More Room

....

JUDITH ORTIZ COFER

Born in Puerto Rico, Judith Ortiz Cofer moved with her family to the United States in 1955 and settled in Paterson, New Jersey. Besides essays, she writes poetry and fiction. The following piece appeared in Silent Dancing: A Partial Remembrance of a Puerto Rican Childhood, *published in 1990.*

TERMS TO RECOGNIZE

geneology *(para. 2)*	family history
acrid *(para. 4)*	harsh, bitter
malingering *(para. 4)*	pretending to be ill
inviolate *(para. 5)*	pure, virginal (never entered)
obligatory *(para. 6)*	required
purgatives *(para. 6)*	medicines to cleanse the body
animosity *(para. 9)*	hostility, resentment
coup *(para. 9)*	brilliant, surprising tactic that overcomes an opponent
vortex *(para. 9)*	whirlpool
fecund *(para. 9)*	fruitful in offspring
acceded *(para. 10)*	gave in to, went along with
emanate *(para. 12)*	emit, give off

My grandmother's house is like a chambered nautilus; it has many   1
rooms, yet it is not a mansion. Its proportions are small and its design simple. It is a house that has grown organically, according to the needs of its inhabitants. To all of us in the family it is known as *la casa de Mamá.* It is the place of our origin; the stage for our memories and dreams of Island life.

I remember how in my childhood it sat on stilts; this was before it   2
had a downstairs—it rested on its perch like a great blue bird—not a flying sort of bird, more like a nesting hen, but with spread wings. Grandfather had built it soon after their marriage. He was a painter and housebuilder by trade—a poet and meditative man by nature. As each of their eight children were born, new rooms were added. After a few years, the paint didn't exactly match, nor the materials, so that there was a chronology to it, like

the rings of a tree, and Mamá could tell you the history of each room in her *casa,* and thus the geneology of the family along with it.

Her own room is the heart of the house. Though I have seen it   3
recently—and both woman and room have diminished in size, changed by the new perspective of my eyes, now capable of looking over countertops and tall beds—it is not this picture I carry in my memory of Mamá's *casa.* Instead, I see her room as a queen's chamber where a small woman loomed large, a throne room with a massive four-poster bed in its center, which stood taller than a child's head. It was on this bed, where her own children had been born, that the smallest grandchildren were allowed to take naps in the afternoons; here too was where Mamá secluded herself to dispense private advice to her daughters, sitting on the edge of the bed, looking down at whoever sat on the rocker where generations of babies had been sung to sleep. To me she looked like a wise empress right out of the fairy tales I was addicted to reading.

Though the room was dominated by the mahogany four-poster, it   4
also contained all of Mamá's symbols of power. On her dresser there were not cosmetics but jars filled with herbs: *yerba* we were all subjected to during childhood crises. She had a steaming cup for anyone who could not, or would not, get up to face life on any given day. If the acrid aftertaste of her cures for malingering did not get you out of bed, then it was time to call *el doctor.*

And there was the monstrous chifforobe she kept locked with a little   5
golden key she did not hide. This was a test of her dominion over us; though my cousins and I wanted a look inside that massive wardrobe more than anything, we never reached for that little key lying on top of her Bible on the dresser. This was also where she placed her earrings and rosary when she took them off at night. God's word was her security system. This chifforobe was the place where I imagined she kept jewels, satin slippers, and elegant silk, sequined gowns of heartbreaking fineness. I lusted after those imaginary costumes. I had heard that Mamá had been a great beauty in her youth, and the belle of many balls. My cousins had ideas as to what she kept in that wooden vault: its secret could be money (Mamá did not hand cash to strangers, banks were out of the question, so there were stories that her mattress was stuffed with dollar bills, and that she buried coins in jars in her garden under rose-bushes, or kept them in her inviolate chifforobe); there might be that legendary gun salvaged from the Spanish-American conflict over the Island. We went wild over suspected treasures that we made up simply because children have to fill locked trunks with something wonderful.

On the wall above the bed hung a heavy silver crucifix. Christ's ago-   6
nized head hung directly over Mamá's pillow. I avoided looking at this
weapon suspended over where her head would have lain; and on the rare
occasions when I was allowed to sleep on that bed, I scooted down to the
safe middle of the mattress, where her body's impression took me in like
mother's lap. Having taken care of the obligatory religious decoration with
the crucifix, Mamá covered the other walls with objects sent to her over the
years by her children in the States. *Los Nueva Yores* was represented by,
among other things, a postcard of Niagara Falls from her son Hernán, post-
marked, Buffalo, N.Y. In a conspicuous gold frame hung a large color photograph of her daughter Nena, her husband and their five children at the
entrance to Disneyland in California. From us she had gotten a black lace
fan. Father had brought it to her from a tour of duty with the Navy in
Europe. (On Sundays she would remove it from its hook on the wall to fan
herself at Sunday mass.) Each year more items were added as the family
grew and dispersed, and every object in the room had a story attached to it,
a *cuento,* which Mamá would bestow on anyone who received the privilege
of a day alone with her. It was almost worth pretending to be sick, though
the bitter herb purgatives of the body were a big price to pay for the spirit
revivals of her storytelling.

Except for the times when a sick grandchild warranted the privilege,   7
or when a heartbroken daughter came home in need of more than herbal
teas, Mamá slept alone on her large bed.

In the family there is a story about how this came to be.   8

When one of the daughters, my mother or one of her sisters, tells the   9
cuento of how Mamá came to own her nights, it is usually preceded by the
qualification that Papá's exile from his wife's room was not a result of ani-
mosity between the couple. But the act had been Mamá's famous bloodless
coup for her personal freedom. Papá was the benevolent dictator of her
body and her life who had had to be banished from her bed so that Mamá
could better serve her family. Before the telling, we had to agree that the old
man—whom we all recognize in the family as an *alma de Dios*, a saintly, soft-
spoken presence whose main pleasures in life, such as writing poetry and
reading the Spanish large-type editions of *Reader's Digest*, always took place
outside the vortex of Mamá's crowded realm—was not to blame. It was not
his fault, after all, that every year or so he planted a baby-seed in Mamá's
fertile body, keeping her from leading the active life she needed and desired.
He loved her and the babies. He would compose odes and lyrics to celebrate births and anniversaries, and hired musicians to accompany him in
singing them to his family and friends at extravagant pig-roasts he threw

yearly. Mamá and the oldest girls worked for days preparing the food. Papá sat for hours in his painter's shed, also his study and library, composing the songs. At these celebrations he was also known to give long speeches in praise of God, his fecund wife, and his beloved Island. As a middle child, my mother remembers these occasions as a time when the women sat in the kitchen and lamented their burdens while the men feasted out in the patio, their rum-thickened voices rising in song and praise of each other, *companeros* all.

It was after the birth of her eighth child, after she had lost three at birth or infancy, that Mamá made her decision. They say that Mamá had had a special way of letting her husband know that they were expecting, one that had begun when, at the beginning of their marriage, he had built her a house too confining for her taste. So, when she discovered her first pregnancy, she supposedly drew plans for another room, which he dutifully executed. Every time a child was due, she would demand, *More space, more space.* Papá acceded to her wishes, child after child, since he had learned early that Mamá's renowned temper was a thing that grew like a monster along with a new belly. In this way Mamá got the house that she wanted, but with each child she lost in health and energy. She had knowledge of her body and perceived that if she had any more children, her dreams and her plans would have to be permanently forgotten, because she would be a chronically ill woman, like Flora with her twelve children: asthma, no teeth, in bed more than on her feet.

And so after my youngest uncle was born, she asked Papá to build a large room at the back of the house. He did so in joyful anticipation. Mamá had asked him for special things this time: shelves on the walls, a private entrance. He thought that she meant this room to be a nursery where several children could sleep. He thought it was a wonderful idea. He painted it his favorite color—sky blue—and made large windows looking out over a green hill and the church spires beyond. But nothing happened. Mamá's belly did not grow, yet she seemed in a frenzy of activity over the house. Finally, an anxious Papá approached his wife to tell her that the new room was finished and ready to be occupied. And Mamá, they say, replied: "Good, it's for you."

And so it was that Mamá discovered the only means of birth control available to a Catholic woman of her time: sacrifice. She gave up the comfort of Papá's sexual love for something she deemed greater: the right to own and control her body, so that she might live to meet her grandchildren, me among them, so that she could give more of herself to the ones already there, so that she could be more than a channel for other lives, so that even

10

11

12

now that time has robbed her of the elasticity of her body and of her amazing reservoir of energy, she can still emanate the calm joy that can only be achieved by living according to the dictates of one's own heart.

CONSIDERING CONTENT AND METHOD

1. What do you think of Mamá's chosen method of birth control? Why do you think Papá agreed to it without resentment?
2. How are Mamá's bedroom walls decorated (para. 6)? What do these decorations tell you about her character? Why is the detail about the crucifix especially significant?
3. What is a "bloodless coup" (para. 9)? Explain how Mamá pulls hers off. Why is the nature of Papá's character important in understanding her success?
4. What is the function of the single short sentence punctuated as a paragraph (para. 8)? Why does Cofer divide the essay with a space break following that sentence?
5. How does the concluding paragraph clarify the meaning of the whole piece?

✪ WEB SITE

www.georgiaencyclopedia.org/nge/Article.jsp?id=h-488

The *New Georgia Encyclopedia* provides a biography of Judith Cofer along with links to several online articles and readings by her.

A Crime of Compassion

....

B ARBARA H UTTMANN

> *Barbara Huttmann has written two books about the rights of patients:* The Patient's Advocate *and* Code Blue: A Nurse's True-Life Story. *In the following essay, which originally appeared on the "My Turn" page of* Newsweek *magazine in 1983, Huttmann tells about her decision to let a suffering patient die.*

TERMS TO RECOGNIZE

resuscitated *(para. 3)*	revived, brought back to life
haggard *(para. 5)*	worn out
IV solutions *(para. 6)*	liquids given by injection (IV stands for intravenous—"in the vein")
irrigate *(para. 7)*	wash out, flush
lucid *(para. 10)*	aware, clear-minded
impotence *(para. 10)*	powerlessness
imperative *(para. 11)*	command, directive
riddled *(para. 13)*	pierced with numerous holes
pallor *(para. 15)*	paleness, lack of color

"Murderer," a man shouted. "God help patients who get *you* for a nurse." 1

"What gives you the right to play God?" another one asked. 2

It was the *Phil Donahue Show* where the guest is a fatted calf and the audience a 220-strong flock of vultures hungering to pick at the bones. I had told them about Mac, one of my favorite cancer patients. "We resuscitated him 52 times in just one month. I refused to resuscitate him again. I simply sat there and held his hand while he died." 3

There wasn't time to explain that Mac was a young, witty, macho cop who walked into the hospital with 32 pounds of attack equipment, looking as if he could single-handedly protect the whole city, if not the entire state. "Can't get rid of this cough," he said. Otherwise, he felt great. 4

Before the day was over, tests confirmed that he had lung cancer. And before the year was over, I loved him, his wife, Maura, and their three kids as if they were my own. All the nurses loved him. And we all battled his 5 disease for six months without ever giving death a second thought. Six months isn't such a long time in the whole scheme of things, but it was long enough to see him lose his youth, his wit, his macho, his hair, his bowel and bladder control, his sense of taste and smell, and his ability to do the slightest thing for himself. It was also long enough to watch Maura's transformation from a young woman into a haggard, beaten old lady.

When Mac had wasted away to a 60-pound skeleton kept alive by liquid food we poured down a tube, IV solutions we dripped into his veins, and oxygen we piped to a mask on his face, he begged us: "Mercy . . . for God's sake, please just let me go."   6

The first time he stopped breathing, the nurse pushed the button that calls a "code blue" throughout the hospital and sends a team rushing to resuscitate the patient. Each time he stopped breathing, sometimes two or three times in one day, the code team came again. The doctors and technicians worked their miracles and walked away. The nurses stayed to wipe the saliva that drooled from his mouth, irrigate the big craters of bedsores that covered his hips, suction the lung fluids that threatened to drown him, clean the feces that burned his skin like lye, pour the liquid food down the tube attached to his stomach, put pillows between his knees to ease the bone-on-bone pain, turn him every hour to keep the bedsores from getting worse, and change his gown and linen every two hours to keep him from being soaked in perspiration.   7

At night I went home and tried to scrub away the smell of decaying flesh that seemed woven into the fabric of my uniform. It was in my hair, the upholstery of my car—there was no washing it away. And every night I prayed that Mac would die, that his agonized eyes would never again plead with me to let him die.   8

Every morning I asked his doctor for a "no-code" order. Without that order, we had to resuscitate every patient who stopped breathing. His doctor was one of several who believe we must extend life as long as we have the means and knowledge to do it. To not do it is to be liable for negligence, at least in the eyes of many people, including some nurses. I thought about what it would be like to stand before a judge, accused of murder, if Mac stopped breathing and I didn't call a code.   9

And after the fifty-second code, when Mac was still lucid enough to beg for death again, and Maura was crumbled in my arms again, and when no amount of pain medication stilled his moaning and agony, I wondered about a spiritual judge. Was all this misery and suffering supposed to be building character or infusing us all with the sense of humility that comes from impotence?   10

Had we, the whole medical community, become so arrogant that we   11
believed in the illusion of salvation through science? Had we become so self-
righteous that we thought meddling in God's work was our duty, our moral
imperative and our legal obligation? Did we really believe that we had the
right to force "life" on a suffering man who had begged for the right to die?

Such questions haunted me more than ever early one morning when   12
Maura went home to change her clothes and I was bathing Mac. He had
been still for so long, I thought he at last had the blessed relief of coma.
Then he opened his eyes and moaned, "Pain . . . no more . . . Barbara . . .
do something . . . God, let me go."

The desperation in his eyes and voice riddled me with guilt. "I'll   13
stop," I told him as I injected the pain medication.

I sat on the bed and held Mac's hands in mine. He pressed his bony   14
fingers against my hand and muttered, "Thanks." Then there was one soft
sigh and I felt his hands go cold in mine. "Mac?" I whispered, as I waited for
his chest to rise and fall again.

A clutch of panic banded my chest, drew my finger to the code but-   15
ton, urged me to do something, anything . . . but sit there alone with
death. I kept one finger on the button, without pressing it, as a waxen pal-
lor slowly transformed his face from person to empty shell. Nothing I've
ever done in my 47 years has taken so much effort as it took *not* to press
that code button.

Eventually, when I was as sure as I could be that the code team would   16
fail to bring him back, I entered the legal twilight zone and pushed the button. The team tried. And while they were trying, Maura walked into the
room and shrieked, "No . . . don't let them do this to him . . . for God's
sake . . . please, no more."

Cradling her in my arms was like cradling myself, Mac, and all those   17
patients and nurses who had been in this place before, who do the best they
can in a death-denying society.

So a TV audience accused me of murder. Perhaps I am guilty. If a   18
doctor had written a no-code order, which is the only *legal* alternative,
would he have felt any less guilty? Until there is legislation making it a
criminal act to code a patient who has requested the right to die, we will
all of us risk the same fate as Mac. For whatever reason, we developed the
means to prolong life, and now we are forced to use it. We do not have the
right to die.

CONSIDERING CONTENT AND METHOD

1. Huttmann says that Mac's doctor believes "we must extend life as long as we have the means and knowledge to do it." Is that what you believe? What does Huttmann believe?

2. Huttmann was accused of "playing God" for letting Mac die. How does she turn the accusation around in paragraph 11? According to Huttmann, who is playing God?

3. How does Huttmann attempt to enlist sympathy for Mac's situation and for hers? Identify specific details that appeal to the readers' emotions.

4. Paragraph 11 is made up entirely of questions. Why does the author use this method of presenting these ideas?

5. Did Huttmann commit a crime? Explain your answer.

WEB SITE

www.chevychase.com/dr.death.html

For information about our society's most famous advocate of assisted suicide, read the unofficial home page of Dr. Jack Kevorkian, dubbed "Dr. Death."

Writing With Sources

Some writing projects will require you to go beyond personal knowledge and experience. At times, you may begin a paper and decide that you don't have enough information to cover the topic adequately or that you need additional support for your ideas. At other times, you may consult sources to explore a topic and decide how to approach it before you begin writing. You may also be assigned to write a research paper, one that will require the extensive use of sources.

USING SOURCES IN YOUR WRITING

Writers use sources to help them explain, develop, and strengthen their observations and opinions. That's what Brian Carter did with his essay "Almost a Winner" (see pages 290–91 in Chapter 9). Although Brian had worked out his own analysis of the causes for obsessive slot-machine playing, he wanted to find out what other people thought. So he went to the library to find material by experts who had published their findings on this form of gambling. After reading and taking notes from a number of books and articles, Brian revised his paper by incorporating facts and comments from several sources into his discussion. The revised, documented version of his essay appears on pages 382–84 at the end of this appendix.

The process for planning and developing an essay using sources will follow the same one described in Chapter 2 (pp. 15–22): to find ideas, devise a thesis, make a plan, compose a draft, improve the draft, target the readers, get feedback, and polish the final draft. You may not write a finished paper before looking at other sources, as Brian did, but you should begin with your own ideas. If you start with the sources themselves, you may end up presenting a summary of other writers' words and opinions instead of a discussion that clearly reflects your own thinking. The information you gather from sources should support your views, not replace them.

LOCATING SOURCES

Sources of information include books, magazine and newspaper articles, videos, interviews, government documents, Web sites, and online publications. Your college library is the best place to find these resources, and you will almost surely conduct your initial search for sources on a computer. Most college libraries offer workshops to help students locate materials, conduct computer searches, use online databases, and navigate the Internet. If these courses are not required, take one anyway—you could save yourself hours of aimless wandering. Your library's information desk will provide you with schedules for tours and research tutorials.

Using the Online Catalog

Most libraries today list their holdings in a computerized *public access catalog* (PAC) or an *online catalog* (OC). The PAC or OC terminal itself will tell you how to use it. The opening screen of the OC at the library Brian Carter used shows that he can search for books, journals and magazines, and other items owned by his library and by other libraries in the state. In electronic databases, you can usually search for sources by author, title, and publication year and also by subject, using *keywords*, or *descriptors*, to describe the source's contents. Subject searches work best when the keywords conform to a database's directory of terms. For your library's catalog, the directory is the *Library of Congress Subject Headings (LCSH)*, which is usually available in printed form in the library's reference room. Remember that computers are unforgiving about spelling and typing errors. When your results are not what you expected, check the accuracy of the search terms you used.

To begin his search of the OC, Brian typed in the LCSH heading "slot machines" and selected "subject" in the "search by" menu. The results showed that his library did not have any books on this specific topic, but when he extended his search to include other libraries in his state's system, he found 11 possible entries. Because he lacked sufficient time to get these books through interlibrary loan, Brian used a more general subject heading instead. When he entered "gambling," he discovered 18 entries, most of which contained sublistings for related subtopics. He saw which books were available and where they were located in the library. Although he now had some material to begin his review of the topic, Brian felt he also needed to find out what was available in periodicals.

Using Indexes and Databases

Even though you might find valuable material in books to use in documenting your ideas and critical judgments, your paper will not be well researched unless you also find periodical articles relevant to your topic. Periodicals include newspapers, popular magazines, and scholarly journals. Because they are published frequently, periodicals often contain the most recent information on a topic. Popular magazines include articles of interest to the general public and are written in everyday, nontechnical language. Magazine articles mention the sources within the articles and seldom include bibliographies or footnotes. By contrast, scholarly journals are written by and for academics or expert researchers and require formal citations in bibliographies or footnotes. Journals rarely contain advertising, eye-catching artistic touches, or slick covers. Each journal is devoted to a specific academic subject, often a very narrow one.

Periodical sources can now be accessed electronically through online databases and text archives that your library subscribes to. The library homepage that Brian was using allowed him to move from the online catalog to a list of more than a hundred searchable indexes, bibliographies, and other electronic reference tools. The reference librarian recommended that Brian look first at two computerized indexes to find publication information on articles about slot machines—*Academic Search Premier* and *Expanded Academic Index ASAP*— because they cover periodicals in psychology and sociology. Other databases, such as *Article 1st* and *Wilson Select Plus*, deal with a wider range of more general subjects. Brief descriptions of the databases are often found on the library's homepage.

When Brian typed "slot machines" in the "find" box of the search screen of Academic Search Premier, he got 215 hits. The display also prompted him to narrow his results by subject and gave him several words and phrases to add to his search term. Brian entered the phrase "near miss," which reduced the list considerably. He could view these entries one at a time or print out the entire list. Each citation included the article title and the name, volume, date, and page number of the periodical; it also supplied the call number for any publications in his library. Many of the entries contained a brief summary of the article's content, and two included the full text of the article for him to read or print. He could also send this information to his home computer by e-mail.

Brian browsed through these findings and printed the citations for several articles that looked promising. Because the library did not own a number of the periodicals, the librarian suggested requesting copies of the articles through interlibrary loan, but that would take several days. Another option was to consult a full-text database, such as *JSTOR (Journal Storage Project)* or *ProjectMUSE*, to see if the articles were available there. Brian discovered a useful-sounding article in *JSTOR* and printed it out.

These are some of the electronic tools that Brian used to search for possible sources. Your library may subscribe to many of the same indexes and databases, but you need to find out what's available and how to use them. Most of these are subscription services, but they are often available, without a fee, on computers at academic and public libraries. Your library may also allow you to access these resources from your home or other location through a proxy service that verifies your status as a registered library user.

Using the Internet

Online databases and text archives are stored on computers all over the world and are accessible over the Internet—through your library network, a local Internet provider, or a commercial service. The most popular tool for search-ing the Internet is the World Wide Web, a complex system for organizing and viewing information. The primary attraction of the Web is that its documents are linked to other pages by a technique called *hypertext*, which provides paths to additional material on other pages and at other Web sites. The Web is also searchable. Several different search engines—such as Netscape, Firefox, Google, Teoma, Yahoo!, Ask.com, and Microsoft Explorer—catalog Web sites in direc-tories and allow you to conduct keyword searches.

You can also join electronic communities called *newsgroups*, through which members exchange information about a common interest or affil-iation by posting questions and answers to online sites. Or you can become a member of an Internet discussion group, frequently called a *listserv*, whose subscribers use e-mail to converse on a particular subject. Ask your instructor about using listservs and newsgroups as sources for your writ-ing assignments.

If you need additional information about using the Web and the Internet, you might check out the Internet Detective (http://www.vts.intute.ac.uk/detective/), a free online tutorial designed to help you develop the skills and critical thinking required for Internet research. You can also visit one of these useful reference sites:

The Librarians' Index to the Internet	http://lii.org/search/file/netsearch
Searching the World Wide Web	http://owl.english.purdue.edu/internet/search/index.html
Finding Information on the Internet	http://www.lib.berkeley.edu/TeachingLib/Guides/Internet/FindInfo.html

EVALUATING SOURCES

With all the material available in print or on the Internet, the challenge isn't finding sources, but deciding how reliable they are. Just because an article or book appears in print or online doesn't mean that its opinions are credible or that its information is accurate.

Recognizing Bias

One of the most important goals of evaluating a source is to identify any bias in its treatment of a topic. The fact is that most writing is not neutral or objective and doesn't try to be. Authors and publications have political, social, economic, generational, and religious points of view that influence their presentation and determine what information they include—and exclude— especially when they deal with controversial subjects. These viewpoints alone do not make the sources unusable or untrustworthy, but you need to be aware of such potential biases and take them into account when deciding what to use and how to use it. For example, if you were to research the topic of home schooling, you might come across a periodical called *Growing without Schooling*. With a little investigation you would find that this publication is written by and for home schoolers. You might find a lot of valuable material in such a source, depending on your purpose and audience; but if you wanted something about the criticisms of home schooling, you would have to go to other sources.

Judging Online Sources

You should of course be concerned about the credibility of any source you use in your writing. You can generally rely on scholarly books and journal articles because they have been reviewed and edited, their authors are often recognized authorities, and their claims are documented. Popular books and periodicals aren't as reliable and sometimes have political biases, but the content has probably been reviewed and edited by publishers, editors, and librarians. Books are also reviewed after publication by specialists in the field, and magazines and journals frequently include letters to the editor from readers who question or support the articles' findings or conclusions.

Materials from the Internet are a different story. Anyone can create and post information and opinions on a Web site or in a newsgroup, and most postings are rarely reviewed for accuracy and completeness. When you use information from an electronic source, you want to be confident that it is reliable and that it comes from someone with the appropriate authority. Here are some guidelines for evaluating online materials:

- *Look for credentials.* What do you know about the people supplying the information? What's the basis of their expertise? Is the source also available in an established, conventional printed form?
- *Track down affiliations.* Who sponsors the online site? Is it a reputable group that you can easily identify? Is the information influenced by

commercial or political sponsorship? Does the site include links to other reputable resources?

- *Analyze motives.* What purpose does the site serve? Many online postings are trying to buy or sell something; others are promoting a favorite cause. These may not be good sources for research.
- *Consider currency and stability.* Is the material updated regularly? Is there an archive for older information?
- *Confirm your information.* Can you find other sources to verify what you've found online? Ideally, you want to have several different kinds of sources to achieve a credible balance of research material.

For more details about evaluating online sources, you can visit one of these sites:

Evaluating Web Sites, a comprehensive and instructive guide to judging information resources for reliability and accuracy, at http://www.lesley .edu/library/guides/research/evaluating_web.html.

LibrarySmart, an online guide to "smart information"; created and maintained by the Washington State Library, at http://www.librarysmart .com/working/home.asp

WORKING WITH SOURCES

Once you have located the books and articles you want to read and assimilate, you can begin reading, taking notes, and synthesizing the material.

Taking Notes

Many writers use note cards for keeping track of the facts and opinions they find. If you decide to use cards, work out some system for recording information. Here are some suggestions:

1. Fill out a bibliography card every time you consult a new source, and record all the details necessary for citing this source in your paper, including where to find the source again. Then put the author's last name, an abbreviated title, and the page number or numbers on all the note cards you use for this source.
2. Write only one idea or point on each card. This allows you to shuffle the cards as you figure out the precise organization of your paper.
3. Put subject headings on the cards—one or two words in the upper-right-hand corner to tell you what each note is about.

4. Summarize the ideas in your own words. If you think you might want to quote directly from the source, copy the author's exact words and enclose them in quotation marks.

Computers now come with a note card program, or you can purchase software for a note card system. You can use the computer note cards just as you would use index cards: title each card by topic, and then type your notes onto the card provided by the computer.

Using the Printout/Photocopy Option

If the time you can spend in the library is limited, you might want to print out an online article or photocopy portions of books in order to have these materials available to study at your convenience. In fact, you might find it easier to take notes from a printout than from a computer screen. You can underline or highlight key ideas, even color-coding these highlighted passages to fit different subtopics in your paper. You can also write comments or cross-references to other sources in the margins. It's still a good idea to put the information from printouts and photocopies on note cards. This procedure forces you to summarize the material in your own words and makes it much easier to organize your ideas and sort the separate items into categories.

Summarizing, Paraphrasing, and Quoting

In most of your notes, you will be summarizing or paraphrasing your source materials, rather than quoting the author's exact words. In a **summary** you condense the main point of an argument or passage in your own words. A summary is useful when you want to capture the gist of an idea without including the background or supporting details. Compare this long sentence from an article about professional football with the summary that follows it.

ORIGINAL

In an effort to keep everyone buying tickets and watching television as far as possible into this elongated sixteen-game season, the NFL juggled its schedule so that strong teams faced the toughest tests and weaker members were able to kindle local hopes while playing fellow stragglers. [46 words]

SUMMARY

To keep fans interested through the long season, the NFL scheduled teams against others of similar strength. [17 words]

In a **paraphrase** you restate comments and ideas from a source, using approximately the same number of words as the original. Although written in your own words and style, a good paraphrase will reflect the author's point more clearly than a summary does. Here's a paraphrase of the passage about the NFL schedule:

> To keep fans coming to games and watching them on television throughout the long season, the NFL rigged the schedule so that the strong teams played each other and the weaker teams kept local fans interested by playing other weak teams. [41 words]

You will also find comments and observations that are so well expressed that you want to use the original wording rather than summarize or paraphrase it. Be sure to record the exact words of the original quotation within quotation marks, as well as the number of the page on which it appears.

Devising a Working Outline

As you are reading and taking notes, you should also be thinking about the organization of your points and ideas. Chances are the best arrangement won't emerge until you have consulted several sources. But as you collect more and more notes, leaf through your cards or printouts occasionally to see if you can arrange them into three or four main categories to form the major points in your discussion. The sooner you can get a plan worked out, the more efficient your efforts become. You can see exactly what you are looking for and avoid wasting time on sources that would prove irrelevant or unnecessary.

WRITING A FIRST DRAFT

If you have an earlier version of your paper, as Brian Carter did, then you are ready to look at your notes to see where the source material fits and how it affects what you have already written. If you don't have a preliminary draft, now is the time to collect your notes, your bibliography cards, your photocopied pages, your prewriting, your working outline, and anything else you need for composing a first draft. The actual drafting of the paper is a lot like writing a draft for any other paper (as described on pp. 19–22 in Chapter 2). But this time you will incorporate the material from note cards into your text and give credit to the original sources for any information and ideas you gathered from them.

Organizing Your Notes

The first thing to do is to read through your note cards. Then, using the headings that you put on the cards, group the ones with similar ideas together in stacks. If you photocopied most or all of your sources, write headings on the first page of each photocopy and sort the articles that way. Next, consult your working outline, and arrange the stacks in the order that the headings appear there. As you write, the necessary information will be in front of you, ready to be incorporated into the draft of your paper.

If your stacks of cards or photocopies don't follow the outline but lie there in a confused, overlapping mess, all is not lost. You can still bring order out of chaos. Here are a few methods:

1. *Tinker with your outline.* It may seem like a step backward, but now that you have new information from your sources, the whole topic may look different. Look at the main headings and change any that don't seem to fit; add others that you have good material for but overlooked when you made the working outline.
2. *Put your note cards or photocopies into different groupings.* This process may suggest an organizing strategy that you wouldn't think of any other way.
3. *Set your notes aside and begin writing*—even if you begin in the middle of a thought. Force yourself, as in freewriting, to keep going, even if your paper seems repetitive, disorganized, and sketchy. Eventually, the writing will begin to take shape, giving you an idea about where to start your first draft.
4. *Explain your ideas to a friend who agrees to ask questions along the way.* Tape-record your discussion, and see whether it suggests a sensible order of exposition.

Using Quotations and Paraphrases

You want to be selective when using the words and ideas of others in your writing. Your main goal is to present *your* thinking or advance *your* arguments, not simply to paste together other people's thoughts and words. You need to work them into your analysis and explain how they support your points. Take a look at this example from a paper about drive-in movie theaters:

Why were these movie theaters so successful in the 1950s and 60s? As journalist Neal Karlen observes, "We had gone from Andy Hardy's front porch to the back seat of Dad's Chevy. In the fifties, nearly everybody had a car. No generation had ever had such opportunities to be alone together"

(45–46). Drive-ins also provided cheap entertainment for large families. Mom and Dad had the front seat with a big tub of popcorn; we kids curled up with sleeping bags in the back. It was a treat to see a triple feature and stay out really late.

As you can see, the student writer answers her question about the popularity of drive-ins with a direct quotation from a source. She pursues the point further by adding a couple of relevant observations taken from her own childhood experiences.

Integrating Sources

Whether you are quoting directly or simply paraphrasing someone else's ideas and observations, you should always give credit in the text of your paper to the person from whom you are borrowing—this process is called *documentation*. The MLA documentation style requires you to cite all sources *within* the paper. These in-text citations contain three important parts:

1. an introduction of the source, telling your reader that material from some authority is coming up, who or what the source is, and what the person's credentials are, if you know them.
2. the material from the source, quoted or paraphrased.
3. the parenthetical documentation, which tells your reader that your use of the source is over and gives the page number for the source of that particular material.

The example above from the paper about drive-in movies illustrates the three parts of a typical in-text citation. More details about in-text citations are given in the explanation of the MLA documentation style later in this appendix (pp. 388–89).

Using Attributions

If you want your paper to read smoothly, pay particular attention to the way you introduce quotations and paraphrases. You need a ready supply of introductory phrases to slide the source material in gracefully—phrases like "As Sutherland points out," "Professor Weber notes," and "According to Dr. Carter." The first time you mention a source you should also consider providing brief background information to establish the source as relevant or important. These attributions help your readers to evaluate the source and to separate the source material from your remarks about it. Here's an example:

Professor Gerald Early, director of the African and Afro-American Studies Program at Washington University in St. Louis, thinks that "Kwanzaa's success depends on exacerbating, consciously or unconsciously, black people's sense of alienation from Christmas" (4).

Some writers make no attempt to work in direct quotations or provide complete citations of their sources in their first draft because pausing to do so interrupts the flow of their writing. They just jot down the name of the person who provided the information or idea; they go back later to provide attributions, fill in page numbers, and integrate exact quotations.

AVOIDING PLAGIARISM

The failure to give proper credit to your sources is called **plagiarism.** It usually involves carelessly—or, far worse, deliberately—presenting the words or ideas of another writer as your own. You can avoid this dishonesty by using a moderate amount of care in taking notes. Put quotations marks around any passages, even brief phrases, that you copy word for word. Circle the quotation marks in red or highlight the quoted material in some way, as a reminder to give credit to the source.

You must also avoid the original wording if you decide to **paraphrase** your sources, rather than quoting directly. Changing a few words or rearranging the phrases is not enough: such close paraphrasing is still considered plagiarism. The following examples may help you to see the difference between plagiarism and paraphrasing. The original passage comes from page 18 in the book *The Language Instinct* by Steven Pinker.

ORIGINAL PASSAGE

Language is not a cultural artifact that we learn the way we learn to tell time or how the federal government works. Instead, it is a distinct piece of the biological makeup of our brains. Language is a complex, specialized skill, which develops in the child spontaneously, without conscious effort or formal instruction.

PLAGIARISM

Humans do not learn language the way we learn to tell time or how the federal government works. Language is a part of the biological makeup of our brains, a complex skill that a child develops spontaneously, without conscious effort or formal instruction (Pinker 18).

PLAGIARISM

Humans do not learn language in the way we learn to count or understand how a computer works. Language is a part of our physical makeup, a complex, specialized skill that develops automatically, without conscious effort or formal instruction (Pinker 18).

ACCEPTABLE PARAPHRASE

Linguist Steven Pinker claims that human beings do not learn language in the way that we learn to count or how to use a computer. Language is a discrete part of our brain's structure; it's a sophisticated skill that children learn automatically without direct instruction (18).

COMBINED PARAPHRASE AND DIRECT QUOTATION

According to linguist Steven Pinker, humans do not learn language in the way we learn to count or understand how a computer works. Language is a discrete part of our brain's structure, "a complex, specialized skill" that develops automatically, "without conscious effort or formal instruction" (18).

DIRECT QUOTATION

"Language is not a cultural artifact that we learn the way we learn to tell time or how the federal government works," says linguist Steven Pinker. "Instead, it is a distinct piece of the biological makeup of our brains" (18).

Crediting Your Sources

The most obvious reason for acknowledging your sources is to avoid plagiarism. But there are less tangible, more important reasons for providing the details about your sources. Documentation will build your credibility, establish the background of your writing, enable your readers to follow up on your work, and give recognition to the people whose ideas and information you have used.

The conventions of writing with sources require that you document ideas and information that originate in someone else's work. All of the following materials should be accompanied by a reference to the original:

- direct quotations
- paraphrases and summaries
- facts that are debatable or not widely known

- statistics, graphs, charts, diagrams, figures, and other kinds of "hard evidence"
- opinions, claims, or assertions of others, particularly when controversial or questionable

You don't need to document what is called "general knowledge"—that is, information that could be found in a variety of sources, particularly in an encyclopedia or dictionary—although you should use your own wording to convey these points. And you don't need to document your own thoughts, observations, and personal experiences. Sometimes, however, it is difficult to determine what falls into these last two categories. How do you know where your sources end and your own thinking begins? Which facts and ideas can you claim as your own and which ones came from your sources? One way to decide is to ask yourself, "Did I really know this information before I began looking at sources?"

Citing Sources Informally

A detailed, academic approach to citing sources is not always appropriate for some kinds of writing. Journalists, for example, routinely work source details into the text of an article, as seen in these examples from "The Trouble with Talent" by Kathy Seal (pp. 212–16):

> In fact, our reverence for innate intelligence has gone so far that many Americans believe people who work hard in school must lack ability. "Our idealization of a gifted person is someone so smart they don't have to try," says Sarah Graham of UCLA's Graduate School of Education.

> Columbia University psychologist Carol Dweck has conducted a fascinating series of studies over the past decade documenting the dangers of believing that geniuses are born rather than made.

> During a talk this past spring to the California Teachers Association, U. S. Secretary of Education Richard Riley pledged to work on setting national standards in education.

These references don't include the detailed, parenthetical citations that the MLA requires for academic papers, and the article doesn't include footnotes or a list of works cited. The author clearly knows the value of identifying her sources of information, but she also recognizes that a formal documentation style would not be appropriate for her audience and purpose. Several readings in this book contain informal citations. For your own writing, check with your instructor to see if citing sources informally is acceptable.

DOCUMENTING YOUR SOURCES: MLA STYLE

The documentation style of the Modern Language Association (MLA)—used in English, foreign languages, and some other humanities—requires that source citations be given in the text of the paper rather than in footnotes or endnotes. This in-text style of documentation involves parenthetical references.

Throughout this section, titles of books and periodicals are italicized. Your instructor may prefer that you underline these titles instead of italicizing them.

In-Text Citations

A. You will usually introduce the cited material, whether quoted or paraphrased, by mentioning the name of the author in your lead-in and then later giving the page number (or numbers) in parentheses. Put the parenthetical reference near the cited material, but preserve the flow of your writing by placing the citation where a pause would naturally occur, preferably at the end of the sentence, as in this example:

> Edmund Wilson tells us that the author of *Uncle Tom's Cabin* felt "the book had been written by God" (5).

B. Your readers can identify this source by consulting your Works Cited at the end of your paper. The entry for the source cited above would appear like this one:

> Wilson, Edmund. *Patriotic Gore: Studies in the Literature of the American Civil War.* New York: Oxford UP, 1966.

C. If you do not mention the author in your lead-in, include his or her last name in parentheses along with the page number, without an intervening comma, like this:

> One of the great all-time best-sellers, *Uncle Tom's Cabin* sold over 300,000 copies in America and more than 2 million copies world wide (Wilson 3).

D. If you are using a source written or edited by more than three people, use only the name of the first person listed, followed by "et al."
(meaning "and others"), in your lead-in.

> Blair et al. observe that the fine arts were almost ignored by colonial
> writers (21).

Since *et* means "and," it isn't an abbreviation and therefore doesn't
need a period.

E. If you refer to one of two or more works by the same author that are
used in your paper., put a comma after the author's last name and
include a shortened title in the parenthetical reference.

> (Gould, *Mismeasure* 138).

Preparing the List of Works Cited

On a separate page at the end of the paper, alphabetize your Works Cited list
for all sources mentioned in your paper. Format the list according to these
rules:

- Center Works Cited at the top of the page without underlining or bold face.
- Arrange your sources in alphabetical order by the last name of the author.
  If the author is not given in the source, alphabetize the source by the first
  main word in the title (excluding *A, An,* or *The).*
- Unless otherwise instructed by your teacher, double-space the entire
  list, both within and between entries.
- Use hanging indentation: put the first line of each entry flush with the
  left margin, and indent any subsequent lines in the entry one-half inch.
- In both titles and subtitles, capitalize the first and last words and all other
  words *except* articles (*a, an, the*), prepositions, coordinating conjunctions,
  and the *to* in infinitives.
- Omit any use of the words *page, pages, line,* and *lines.* Do not even include
  abbreviations for these terms. Use numbers alone.

> Kinsley, Michael. "Continental Divide." *Time* 7 Jul. 1997: 89–91.

- Shorten publishers' names: for example, use Prentice instead of Prentice
  Hall or Norton instead of W. W. Norton and Co. or Oxford UP instead
  of Oxford University Press or U of Illinois P instead of University of Illinois Press. See sample entries in the next section.

- For books, include the city of publication, usually given on the title page of the work cited. If you find two or more cities, use only the first.
- Abbreviate months as shown in the sample entries.

Works Cited List: Sample Entries

The following models will help you write Works Cited entries for most of the sources you will use. If you use a source not illustrated in these examples, consult the more extensive list of sample entries found in the *MLA Handbook for Writers of Research Papers*, 6th ed., or ask your instructor for guidance.

Books

Book by One Author. Begin with the author's last name, followed by a comma and the full first name. Provide the full title of the book, including the subtitle. It should be italicized or underlined and capitalized. Follow with the city of publication and a shortened version of the publisher's name. End with the year of publication.

> Chused, Richard H. *Private Acts in Public Places: A Social History of Divorce.* Philadelphia: U of Pennsylvania P, 1994.

Book by Two or Three Authors. List the first author (following the order on the title page of the book) in the same way as for a single-author book. List subsequent authors, first name first, separating the individuals' names with commas.

> Anderson, Terry, and Donald Leal. *Free Market Environmentalism.* Boulder: Westview, 1991.
> McCrum, William, William Cran, and Robert MacNeil. *The Story of English.* New York: Viking, 1986.

Book by More than Three Authors. List the first author in the same way as for a single-author book, followed by a comma and the abbreviation *et al.* ("and others").

> Medhurst, Martin J., et al. *Cold War Rhetoric: Strategy, Metaphor, and Ideology.* New York: Greenwood, 1990.

Revised Edition.

Combs, Cindy C. *Terrorism in the Twenty-First Century.* 3rd ed. Upper Saddle River: Prentice, 2003.

Edited Book or Anthology.

Wald, Catherine, ed. *The Resilient Writer: Tales of Rejection and Triumph from 23 Top Authors.* New York: Persea, 2005.

Selection within an Anthology.

Lamm, Nomy. "Fishnets, Feather Boas, and Fat." *Body Outlaws: Rewriting the Rules of Beauty and Body Image.* Ed. Ophira Edut. Emeryville: Seal P, 2003. 78–87.

Chapter or Section of a Book.

Vowell, Sarah. "Rosa Parks, *C'est Moi.*" *The Partly Cloudy Patriot.* New York: Simon, 2002. 119–24.

Two or More Sources by the Same Author. Use the author's name for only the first entry. For subsequent entries, use three hyphens followed by a period. List the entries in alphabetical order by title.

Gould, Stephen Jay. *The Mismeasure of Man.* New York: Norton, 1981.

---. *The Panda's Thumb: More Reflections in Natural History.* New York: Norton, 1980.

Journals, Magazines, and Newspapers

Article from a Journal with Continuous Pagination Throughout the Whole Volume. In some journals the page numbers in one issue pick up where the previous issue left off. After the journal title, give the volume number, followed by the year in parentheses, a colon, and the inclusive page numbers.

English, Robert D. "Sources, Methods, and Competing Perspectives on the End of the Cold War." *Diplomatic History* 21 (1997): 283–94.

Article from a Journal That Paginates Each Issue Separately. Put a period after the volume number and add the issue number.

> Holtug, Nils. "Altering Humans: The Case For and Against Human Gene Therapy." *Cambridge Quarterly of Healthcare Ethics* 6.2 (1997): 157–60.

Article from a Monthly or Bimonthly Magazine. If an article begins in one place, such as pages 56 to 59, and is continued elsewhere, such as on pages 64 to 68 and 72 to 73, just write 56+ for the page numbers (do not write 56–72).

> Russo, Tom. "Lights, Camera, Data!" *Popular Mechanics* Jan. 2007: 56+

Article from a Weekly or Biweekly Magazine. Place the number of the date before the month, followed by the year.

> Coghlan, Andy. "Warring Parents Harm Children as Much as Divorce." *New Scientist* 15 Jun. 1991: 24–28.

Article in a Newspaper. If the newspaper lists an edition, add a comma after the date and specify the edition.

> Weiner, Jon. "Vendetta: The Government's Secret War Against John Lennon." *Chicago Tribune* 5 Aug. 1984, final ed.: C1+.

Letter to the Editor.

> Kessler, Ralph. "Orwell Defended." Letter. *New York Times Book Review* 15 Dec. 1985: 26.

Editorial.

> "From Good News to Bad." Editorial. *Washington Post* 16 Jul. 1984: 10.

Electronic Sources

If you get material from a full-text database or online source, you need to indicate that you read it in electronic form. You will probably use a service to which your library subscribes. Many of the items you access have also appeared in print. Give the print information first, and complete the citation by giving the name of the database (italicized), the name of the online service (such as InfoTrac or EBSCO), the library you used, and the date of access. If you know the Uniform Resource Locator (URL) of the service's homepage, give it, in angle brackets, immediately after the date of access; or you may simply end with the date of access.

Article from a Searchable Database.

Uhler, Walter C. "Gorbachev's Revolution." *The Nation* 31 Dec. 2001: 40–45. *Academic Search Premier.* EBSCO. Eastern Illinois U Lib. 3 April 2002 <http://www.epnet.com>.

Carey, Benedict. "Déjà Vu: If It All Seems Familiar, There May Be a Rea son." *New York Times* 14 Sept. 2004: F1+. LexisNexis. Eastern Illinois U Lib. 28 Mar. 2005.

You might also consult journals, magazines, and newspapers that are available independently on the Internet. For these sources, cite the author, title, and publication data as usual; then give the number of pages, paragraphs, or other sections of the electronic version, if provided on the site—followed by the date of access and URL in angle brackets.

Article from an Online Magazine.

Yeoman, Barry. "Into the Closet: Can Therapy Make Gay People Straight?" *Salon.com* 22 May 2000. 14 Oct. 2000 <http://www.salon.com/ health/feature/2000/05/22/exgay/html>.

Review from an Online Newspaper.

Ebert, Roger. Review of *Real Women Have Curves*, dir. Patricia Cardoso. *Chicago Sun-Times Online* 25 Oct. 2002. 2 Feb. 2003 <http://www .suntimes.com/ebert/ebert_reviews/2002/10/102510.html>.

Article from an Online Reference Book or Encyclopedia.

Daniel, Ralph Thomas. "The History of Western Music." *Britannica Online: Macropaedia.* 1995. Online Encyclopedia Britannica. 14 June 1998 <http://www.eb.com:180/cgi-bin/g:DocF=macro/5004/45/ O.html>.

Article or Page from a Web Site.

"Key Facts about Avian Influenza (Bird Flu) and Avian Influenza A (H5N1) Virus." *Centers for Disease Control and Prevention.* 30 June 2006. 12 March 2007 <http://www.cid.gov/flu/avia/gen-info/ facts.htm>.

SAMPLE STUDENT ESSAY WITH SOURCES

People, Pigeons, and Payoffs

Brian L. Carter

In 2003 gambling casinos in the United States had three times more   1
attendees than all Major League Baseball franchises combined, according
to Professor Jeffrey Nealon (465). Most casino customers play slot
machines, even though they would win more playing other games. As journalist Martin Merzer points out, the house advantage is far larger for slots,
giving casinos at least 70 percent of their revenue from machines rather
than from table games (1A). An observer in a casino might easily decide
that most slots players are irrational at best, and insane at worst. Why do
Americans shove $1 billion or more into slot machines every day (Merzer
1A)? What rational person purchases $20 worth of nickels to play a slot
machine that has a maximum jackpot of $7.50? Why would someone play
a machine and refuse to leave, even to go to the bathroom? What is it
about slot machines that gives them the power to produce such potentially
destructive effects?

The question is answered in any basic psychology class. B. F. Skinner,   2
a psychologist who conducted experiments on the behavior of animals
and humans, understood the dynamics of reinforcement. In a series of
famous experiments, he showed that pigeons could quickly learn to peck
a bar to get a pellet of food for each peck. If it took three bar pecks to
produce a food pellet, the pigeons would keep pressing even faster. When
reinforcements (like food) come at a constant rate, such as every three or
five responses (pecks), this is called a fixed schedule. Skinner then made
the reward occur on a variable, random schedule: a food pellet might
drop on the 17th peck or the 10th peck, or even twice in a row. This produced even more energetic bar pecking compared to fixed schedules.
Skinner also used a random schedule and then stopped dropping food
pellets altogether, just to see how long the pigeons would continue to bar
peck. He was astonished to see them peck for hours with no reward.
Then, when it seemed like the pigeons were going to give up, dropping
just one food pellet would cause them to begin bar pecking again, for
hours (Domjan 163–74).

Slot machines operate on much the same principle. Their rewards are   3
certainly random; a customer can go several plays without winning anything, but an occasional reinforcement will cause the player to keep going
long into the night. One can see slot players as trapped pigeons in one of

Skinner's laboratory experiments, conditioned to think they will receive another reward soon if they just keep playing.

The introduction of the computerized slot machine, which directly controlled the outcome of every spin of the wheels, further extended the psychological effects of reinforcement. By law, a slot machine is only required to show, accurately, which combination of wheel symbols pays which amounts—for example, three cherries in a row pays $3, or four Cadillacs in a row pays $500. There is no law that says slot machines must display how likely it is for each winning row of symbols to show up. The odds are the ratio of no-pay tries to payoff tries, and these are astronomical.

Yet, the computer slot-machine companies introduced a scheme that would hook slot players more than ever before. All slot reel combinations either pay off or don't pay off. But with computerization, the slot manufacturers came up with the idea to include far more "near misses" in their nonpay combinations (Parke & Griffiths 407). In this setup a slot player would see two Cadillacs on the pay line but a third Cadillac just missing the line. Because slot machines display three lines on each try, the tempting third Cadillac would appear just above or just below the actual pay line, and these near misses would occur more often than they would by chance. The payouts of the machine would be the same mathematically as before. A near miss pays as much as a wide miss—that is, nothing. But this rigged system gave the illusion that the slot player was always getting close to the jackpot. Not only wins, but near-wins also acted as random rewards. Back in 1953 Skinner himself perceived the addictive effects of "almost winning the jackpot" (397). As addiction researchers Jonathan Parke and Mark Griffiths explain, "The player is not constantly losing but constantly nearly winning" (408). Put this little trick on top of the psychological influences already operating on slot players, and one can see why the casinos make sure customers get drinks and snacks without leaving their machines.

Luckily for the slot players, the Nevada Gaming Control Board banned the seductive near-miss practice in 1989 (Rose 1). The board ruled that slot machine reels *must* operate at random and cannot be fixed to show a higher than random rate of near misses. This ruling reinstated the status quo and returned slot players to mere pigeons, pumping money into a device that will surely bankrupt them if they play it long enough. The casinos didn't protest the gaming board's ruling. They still have the most powerful means of getting money from their customers: the psychology of reinforcement scheduling.

Works Cited

Domjan, Michael. *Domjan and Burkhard's The Principles of Learning and Behavior.* 2nd ed. Pacific Grove: Brooke/Cole, 1993.

Merzer, Martin. "Slots Spin Big Dreams, Casino Profits." *Miami Herald* 6 March 2005: 1A.

Nealon, Jeffrey T. "Take Me Out to the Slot Machines: Reflections on Gambling and Contemporary American Culture." *South Atlantic Quarterly* 105 (2006): 465–474. *JSTOR.* U of Houston Lib. 8 March 2007.

Parke, Jonathan, and Mark Griffiths. "Gambling Addiction and the Evolution of the 'Near Miss.'" *Addiction Research and Theory* 12 (2004): 407–411. *Academic Search Premier.* EBSCO. U of Houston Lib. 7 March 2007.

Rose, I. Nelson. "Nevada Draws the Line at Near-Miss Slots." *Gambling and the Law: Monthly Format* 1989. 7 March 2007 <http://www.gamblingandthelaw.com/columns/13.htm>.

Skinner, B. F. *Science and Human Behavior.* New York: Free Press, 1953.

Credits

385

Index